Teaching Reading
to Children
with Special Needs

Teaching Reading to Children with Special Needs

John F. Savage
Jean F. Mooney

Boston College

Allyn and Bacon, Inc.
Boston   London   Sydney

Library of Congress Cataloging in Publication Data

Savage, John F
  Teaching reading to children with special needs.

  Includes bibliographies and index.
  1. Handicapped children—Education—Reading.
I. Mooney, Jean F., joint author. II. Title.
LC4028.5.S28   371.9′044   78–13524

ISBN 0–205–06147–8
ISBN 0–205–06130–3

To Mary Jane
and
to Bob

Contents

Preface   *xi*

Glossary of Basic Terms   *1*

1   *Reading: An Overview*   *11*

Toward a Definition of Reading   13   Reading: Different
Approaches   14   Reading: Four Processes   19   Reading:
Basic Skills   23   Reading: The Affective Dimension   32
Conclusion   34

2   *Learning Problems*   *41*

The More Subtle Handicaps   43   Special Education and
Mainstreaming   45   The Concept of Discrepancy   48   Sources
of Problems   50   Types of Learning Problems   52
Prescriptive Teaching   56   Approaches to Remediation   61
Conclusion   64

3   *Assessment*   *3*

Evaluation   73   Diagnosis   76   The Teacher as Part of the
Diagnostic Process   88   Conclusion   105

4   *Problems in Auditory Learning*   *113*

Disorders of Hearing   115   Disorders of Auditory
Perception   121   Assessment of Problems in Auditory
Perception   127   Teaching to Strengths in
Reading   129   Working on Auditory
Skills   130   Conclusion   139

5   *Problems in Visual Learnings*   *143*

The Low-Vision Child: Impairments in the Sensory
System   145   Problems in Visual Perception   150
Teaching to Strengths   157   Working on Visual
Skills   158   Conclusion   167

6   *Language Disorders*   *171*

Language Development   173   Language Disorders   179
Approaches to Reading   186   Problems in Expressive
Language   196   Conclusion   201

7   *The Slow Learner*   *207*

The Relationship Between Reading and Intelligence   211
Teaching Reading to the Slow Learner   213   Reading
Expectancy   237   Conclusion   241

8   *Problems in Attitude and Behavior:*
The Emotional Dimension   *247*

Attitude and Behavior   250   Working with Parents and
Others   271   Conclusion   273

9   *Organizing and Managing Reading Instruction for the*
Special-Needs Child in the Regular Classroom   *279*

Organization   281   Management   292   Conclusion   308

10   *Help!*   *313*

Organization of Special Education Services   315   Special
Services   317   State and National Resources   321
Professional Organizations   322   Teacher Centers   324
Conclusion   324

11   *The Teacher on the Team*   *327*

Finding a "Champion"   333

Appendix A: Case Study (Individual Assessment and Instructional Plan) for Lori   337

Appendix B: Finding and Helping the Special-Needs Child in the Regular Classroom   363

Appendix C: "Information, Please": Where to Go for Information on Reading and Handicapped Learners   373

Appendix D: A Consumer's Guide to Interpreting the ITPA   377

Name Index   381

Subject Index   387

Preface

Reading is the number one curriculum concern in schools. It is the central focus of instruction in the primary grades and it retains the lion's share of teaching time in upper elementary and middle school classrooms. More research has been done on reading than on any other curriculum topic. More money is spent annually on reading materials than on materials for any other subject area. More articles have been written, more conferences held, and more concern expressed about the improvement of reading instruction than about any other aspect of the school's instructional program.

Yet despite all the time, effort, and money invested to improve reading instruction in schools, the results have been far from spectacular. Concern about reading and reading failure remains a dominant issue in school and society. Among those children who experience the most problems in learning to read are children with special needs: children with sensory and perceptual deficits; the so called "dyslexic" or learning disabled child; children with language disorders; the slow learner; and the "emotionally disturbed child." These are the children who, in the past, were often segregated into special classes.

The time of widespread educational segregation is over. There is a national trend—spurred by legislation at both the national and state levels—to move children with special learning problems into the mainstream of education, to integrate children with special learning needs into the regular classroom. Schools are now faced with the responsibility of providing reading instruction for *all* children, those who learn with ease as well as those who don't. Schools have always been faced with this responsibility, of course, but the trend of educating more special children in regular class settings has forced educators to look at reading instruction for children with special needs in a new light.

Teaching Reading to Children with Special Needs will help teachers better understand some of the unique problems that children have in learning how to read and to suggest means whereby reading instruction can be adapted to meet the special learning needs of children. It aims to provide a rationale for the selection of reading approaches and materials that accomodate various types of handicapping conditions. While some practical teaching suggestions are woven in at appropriate places in many of the chapters, exhaustive lists of teaching activities are not included. The text is not a teaching "cookbook." Rather, it attempts to help teachers understand some of the learning problems that children have, to provide a basis for the selection of the most appropriate strategies from the wide variety that may be chosen.

The Organization

Teaching Reading to Children with Special Needs consists of eleven closely interrelated chapters. The first three chapters provide a foundation. Chapter 1 deals with the general topic of reading, with specific attention to the components of the reading act, approaches to beginning reading instruction, basic skills that are taught as part of reading, and the affective dimensions of learning to read. The second chapter provides a definition and overview of various learning problems. Although children get into difficulty for many and varied reasons, the major concentration is on the kinds of educational problems children may present instead of on causal factors. Learning problems are viewed from a generic base and include a variety of mildly handicapping conditions. The third chapter is devoted to assessment, the formal and informal procedures and devices that are most often used to determine the learning needs of children and to provide instructional leads by which these learning needs can be met.

The next five chapters deal with more specific problems the children have in learning how to read. Chapters 4 and 5 deal with problems that children have in processing information through their auditory and visual channels respectively. Chapter 6 concerns children with language disorders, deficits in receptive and expressive language that make learning to read more difficult. Chapter 7 focuses on the slow learner, the child whose cognitive deficit makes him/her a candidate for corrective and remedial instruction, as well as those children who may have been conventionally classified as "mentally retarded." Chapter 8 treats the topic of attitude and behavior problems related to reading.

Each of these five chapters on different learning problem areas treats the topic according to a gradation of behavior, looking at problems that range from mild to serious in each area. The problems presented are real, the kind that teachers can expect to encounter in any normal classroom. Despite the trend to integrate children with special learning needs into the regular classroom, the needs of very seriously handicapped learners are still reserved for special educational settings.

The final three chapters deal with "support systems" related to reading instruction for special needs children in regular classrooms. Chapter 9 is concerned with organizational and management matters involved in classroom reading instruction. Chapter 10, simply entitled "HELP!", examines what resource services are available to the classroom teacher and suggests ways in which the teacher can use these extra (and often expert) hands in meeting the special learning needs of children. The final chapter is a brief account of the role of the classroom teacher as a member of a multidisciplinary team in providing reading instruction for special needs children.

The four appendices are intended to extend further useful information to classroom teachers. Appendix A is a model individual assessment and individualized educational program (IEP) for a child with special needs. Appendix B consists of summary charts of observable behavior, classroom accomodations, remedial strategies, and reading techniques that can be used for children with learning problems in the classroom. Appendix C lists sources of additional information useful for planning and implementing reading instruction for special needs children. Appendix D is a consumer's guide to interpreting the ITPA.

The Audience

Teaching Reading to Children with Special Needs was written principally for the classroom teacher, the person whose job it is to teach reading to twenty-five or so children on a day-to-day basis. Although not primarily intended for resource teachers, remedial reading teachers, learning disabilities tutors, or special class teachers, much of the content presented will be extremely useful for these learning specialists as well, since their job also involves providing reading instruction for children with special learning needs.

Because it focuses for the most part on beginning reading skills, the book is particularly appropriate for those who toil in the elementary vineyards. However, because the reading instructional needs of special students are so basic in the middle school, junior high school, and high school years, much of the material will be appropriate for teachers who work at these levels as well.

The book is designed to serve a number of functions. It can be used as a text for an introductory reading or learning disabilities course at the preservice level. Because it contains a great deal of material directly applicable to their work in classrooms, the book will also be a useful source of information to up-date the knowledge and skills of those teachers in graduate or inservice programs. It may also provide a useful resource and reference for administrators whose responsibility it is to plan, coordinate, supervise, or otherwise oversee reading instruction in schools.

Acknowledgements

Enormous thanks are due to the many friends and colleagues who read parts of this manuscript as it was being developed and who provided technical professional advice, critical comments, helpful suggestions, and encouraging reactions.

Especially helpful was Dr. John Junkala who reviewed the chapters on learning problems, auditory learning, and the final chapters on the teacher's role. Dr. Anthony Bashir provided input to the chapter on auditory learning and language disorders. Mrs. Wilma Hull and Dr. Ouida Fay Morris brought their special expertise to bear on the chapter on visual learning problems. Dr. Katherin Best provided initial input to the chapter on the slow learner and Dr. Lillian Buckley was particularly helpful in her review of the chapter on organizing a classroom reading program. Dr. Alec Peck gave great guidance in the chapter on problems of attitude and behavior. Mrs. Beth Davis critically reviewed the section on Informal Reading Inventories, and Dr. Mary-Ellen Meegan did the same for the section on bibliotherapy. Ms. Susan Hayes, Dr. John Junkala, Dr. Francis Kelly, and Ms. Marguerite Farnsworth contributed to the preparation of the case study presented in Appendix A.

Each of these people contributed his or her time and expertise in helping make this book what it is.

Ms. Suzanne Schoenthaler, Ms. Susan Young, and Ms. Linda Latham did an exceptional job in attending to the many fine details of manuscript preparation.

Thanks are also due to Mr. Jack Malnati, our photographer, and to the staff and children of the Brophy School in Framingham, Mass. (Mr. Anthony Sannicandro, principal) and the Woodland School in Weston, Mass. (Mr. Jerry Kellett, principal) where many of the photographs were taken.

Finally, and most lovingly, deep appreciation is due to our families, who gave up much time with their parents while this book was being written.

*Teaching Reading
to Children
with Special Needs*

Glossary of Basic Terms

In most texts, the glossary is included at the end of the book. However, in the spirit of sound reading instruction—which suggests that vocabulary be presented prior to reading—the glossary is presented here at the beginning.

This glossary includes brief definitions of technical and semitechnical terms that are used throughout the text. Becoming acquainted with the terms prior to reading will facilitate the reading process. Undoubtedly, many of these terms will already be familiar to most readers. Nevertheless, they are included to provide a frame of reference for the context in which the terms are used. In other words, these are the definitions accepted and used by the authors in the chapters that follow.

Ability grouping.   The process of organizing large groups of children into smaller groups for instruction on the basis of their general reading ability or level of achievement.

Accommodation.   A process of adapting a learning environment and curriculum to meet the needs of students with learning and/or behavior problems.

Achievement test.   A measuring instrument used to assess the amount or level of learning that a person has acquired.

Acoustic trauma.   Damage to the auditory nerve endings caused by repeated exposure to loud noise.

Acuity.   Sharpness in the reception of auditory (hearing) or visual (seeing) information.

Affective learning.   That aspect of learning which relates to a person's emotional reaction (feelings, attitudes, values, interests, appreciation) to an experience.

Albinism.   An hereditary disease involving the loss of pigment in the iris of the eye as well as in hair and skin; associated with poor vision and sensitivity to light.

Amplification.   The process of increasing the loudness of sounds through the use of a hearing aid.

Analytic phonics.   An approach to phonics instruction in which letter-sound relationships are taught by analyzing known words into component phonetic elements.

Ancillary services.   Special assistance programs, i.e., counseling, speech therapy, remedial reading.

Anomia.   See **Dysnomia**

Aphasia.   A deficit in symbolic functioning whereby an individual can not understand and/or use spoken language.

Apraxia.   See **Dyspraxia**

Astigmatism.   An eye condition that results in blurred vision.

Audiometer.   An instrument used for testing and measuring auditory acuity.

Auditory discrimination.   The ability to recognize likenesses and differences in sounds; for example, the difference between a high-pitched and low-pitched musical sound and/or the difference between the vowel sounds in the words *pin* and *pan*.

Auditory figure-ground.   The ability to focus attention on an auditory stimulus in the face of competing stimuli; for example, the ability to attend to the teacher's directions while other sounds are going on in the environment.

Auditory memory.   The ability to recall auditory information.

Auditory perception.   The ability to differentiate, organize, and interpret information received through the ear.

Basal Reading Series.   A sequentially graded series of instructional materials (readers, workbooks, teachers' editions, etc.) written specifically as vehicles for the development of children's basic reading skills.

Behavior modification.   A highly structured and systematic program for shaping social and academic behavior of pupils by organizing the stimuli and events in the environment so that appropriate reinforcement is provided contingent upon the learner's behavior.

Bibliotherapy.   The dynamic interaction between a reader and a piece of literature, through which the reader satisfies emotional needs or finds solutions to personal-social problems by identifying with story characters or situations.

Blend.   A sequence of two or three letters that represent closely related but separate sounds in words; for example, *bl*end, *cr*ew, *str*um. Also called *Clusters*.

Cataract. A condition involving the clouding of the lens of the eye.

Cloze procedure. The systematic deletion of words from a printed passage for the purpose of determining the reader's ability to supply the deleted words; a technique used in developing and testing reading comprehension and in determining the readability level of written materials.

Conductive hearing loss. Loss of hearing due to a problem in the outer or middle ear. Results in an almost equal reduction of sounds at all frequencies.

Configuration. The general shape, appearance, or distinguishing characteristics of a word; sometimes used as an aid in recognizing words.

Congenital. Present at birth.

Consonant clusters. See **Blend**.

Context clues. Clues found in surrounding text that aid the reader in determining the pronunciation and meaning of unknown words; the ability to use these clues in reading.

Contract. A joint agreement between a pupil and a teacher to achieve an objective or accomplish a series of tasks.

Controlled reader. An electronic device that projects lines of print at predetermined rates of speed and is used to help children develop a range of visual skills related to reading.

Criterion-referenced test. An evaluative instrument based on performance objectives and designed to judge a person's ability to reach a stated level of performance (criterion) on a specific task.

Critical-creative reading comprehension. The process of applying higher mental functioning to what one has read; i.e., judging the validity or accuracy of printed information, relating what one has read to experience, thinking of alternative endings to stories, etc.

Cross-age tutoring. Having older pupils (often those with reading problems) help younger children in appropriate reading-related tasks.

Decoding. The process (in reading) of translating printed symbols into their representative spoken sounds.

Diagnostic test. A measuring device used to determine causes of learning problems and/or areas of specific strengths and weaknesses.

Dialect. A specific form of spoken language used in a particular geographic region or by a particular social group; differs from the standard form of language in sound features, vocabulary, and grammatical forms.

Differential diagnosis. The process of discerning the nature of a learning or behavior problem; i.e., distinguishing a receptive from an expressive language problem.

Digraph. A combination of two letters that represent a single phoneme; for example, *ch*um, *th*aw, *sh*ip (consonant digraphs) or s*ea*t, r*ai*n, b*oa*t (vowel digraphs).

Diphthong. A vowel letter combination that represents closely related (or blended) sounds; for example, *ou*t, b*oi*l.

Dyslexia. A severe reading problem considered to be the result of brain dysfunction.

Dysnomia. A problem in recalling words for spontaneous use; also called anomia.

Dyspraxia. Difficulty recalling the patterns for performing motor movements; can be verbal (e.g., articulating words) or nonverbal (e.g., tying shoes); also called apraxia.

Electroencephalogram (EEG) A device used to identify abnormal conditions in the brain through the measurement of electrical energy generated in various areas of the cortex.

Encephalopathy. A disease or abnormal condition in the brain.

Etiological diagnosis. The process of determining root causes of learning problems; i.e., what caused the child to get into difficulty in the first place; often has medical implications.

Farsightedness. Difficulty seeing clearly at near point (doing close work).

Febrile diseases. Usually refers to diseases of childhood (measles, mumps, etc.) involving a high temperature.

Gestalt learning. The process of attending to the totality of the material to be learned without consideration of the individual parts.

Glaucoma. Increased pressure due to an accumulation of fluid in the eyeball; when untreated, causes permanent loss of vision.

Grapheme. A symbol used to represent sound features (phonemes) in written language.

High-interest, low-vocabulary materials. Reading materials on topics appropriate to older pupils' interest written at a lower-grade reading level.

Individualized Educational Program (IEP). A written account of educational objectives, strategies, curriculum modifications, and classroom accommodations for a child with learning and/or behavior problems; required by P.L. 94–142.

Individualized reading.   A classroom organizational approach to reading that is based on self-selection and self-pacing in reading material and in which individual help is provided by the teacher on a planned basis.

Inferential reading comprehension.   The process of deriving meaning or information not directly stated in printed materials; i.e., "reading between the lines."

Informal Reading Inventory (IRI).   An informal instrument consisting of sequentially graded reading selections, used to assess a reader's independent, instructional, and frustration reading level, and to indicate areas of instructional need.

Intelligence Quotient (IQ).   An index of the relative or estimated mental capacity of an individual.

Inversion.   Producing a symbol (i.e., letter or numeral) upside down—e.g., p for b.

IQ test.   An instrument designed to measure or estimate a person's cognitive functioning and/or learning ability.

Kinesthetic.   An awareness of the movement in muscles, tendons, and joints.

Language experience approach.   An approach to reading instruction in which the learner dictates stories or accounts of personal experience. This oral dictation is transcribed, and the written materials provide the vehicle for reading and follow-up skill development.

Linguistic approach.   A basic approach to reading that emphasizes mastery of sound-symbol relationships at the initial stages and that controls both sounds and symbols in beginning reading materials.

Literal reading comprehension.   The process of deriving meaning or understanding information directly presented in print.

Long-term memory.   The ability to retrieve information that has been stored for a period of time.

Look-say approach.   A meaning-emphasis approach to beginning reading that stresses word recognition and context as the primary reading skill in the initial stages of instruction. Also called the Sight Method.

Mainstreaming.   The process of integrating children with special needs into a regular educational setting for all or part of the school day.

Management system.   A commercially prepared program with criterion-referenced tests designed to monitor and report pupils' progress in reading skills.

Mental age.   ·A score designed to indicate a person's relative level of intellectual ability; a figure arrived at by multiplying an individual's IQ score by his/her chronological age and dividing the product by 100.

Miscue.   An oral response to printed text that does not conform to what is written, but involves the substitution of a similar or equivalent form; a deviation from the exact text that does not interfere with the reader's comprehension.

Morpheme.   A simple, basic, meaning-bearing unit of language. For example, *unhappiness* has three morphemes: *un-* (meaning not), *happy,* and *-ness* (meaning condition of).

Morphemic analysis.   See **Structural analysis**

Motivation.   The stimulus or condition that provokes or sustains behavior and/or interest in an activity.

Multidisciplinary evaluation.   The process of assessing a child's learning and/or behavior problems through the collaboration of professionals from various appropriate and related fields.

Muscle imbalance.   An eye condition in which one or both eyes are not straight but deviate to one side; results in double vision.

Nearsightedness.   Difficulty seeing clearly at a distance.

Norm-referenced test.   An evaluative instrument in which a person's performance is judged in comparison with the average performance of others in a large reference group at similar age or educational levels.

Nystagmus.   An eye condition involving rapid and involuntary movement of the eyes.

Otitis media.   An infection in the middle ear due to an upper respiratory infection (e.g., a head cold).

Paraprofessional.   A person trained to assist licensed practitioners in management and instructional activities.

Phoneme.   A basic, minimal, indivisible unit of sound. For example, *pin* has three phonemes, /p/, /i/, and /n/.

Phoneme-grapheme correspondence.   The relationship between basic spoken sounds and the written symbols used to represent these sounds.

Phonetic analysis.   The process of analyzing words according to letter-sound relationships and syllables.

Phonetic approach.   A basic decoding approach to reading that emphasizes mastery of sound-symbol relationships as the major initial step in instruction.

Phonics.   The direct study of sound-symbol relationships for the purpose of learning to read and spell.

Phonogram.   A common word part used in teaching word patterns; for example, *op* in *hop*, *top*, etc.

Phonology.   The study of the sounds of a language.

Prescriptive teaching.   Involves the designation and educational strategies of specific behavioral objectives for a student, based on an individual assessment of his/her needs as a learner.

Programmed reading.   Reading materials that conform to principles of programmed learning, in which material is broken into small "frames," is presented sequentially to the learner, and a direct active response is demanded.

Psycholinguistics.   The study of the relationship between psychological and linguistic behavior. In reading, psycholinguistics takes into account both the nature of the language and the characteristics of the learner.

Reading comprehension.   The process of acquiring or deriving meaning and understanding from printed language; involves cognitive functioning related to what one reads. See also **Literal reading comprehension; Inferential reading comprehension.**

Reading expectancy.   The estimated level of a child's reading potential, or the level s/he may be expected to achieve in reading; most often determined on the basis of a person's mental capacity.

Reading readiness.   The condition or state of development which, when reached, allows the child to successfully begin the process of learning to read without undue difficulty; preparedness to undertake a reading activity at any level of instruction.

Reading specialist.   An educator, usually with special training and certification, who supervises reading instruction, coordinates schoolwide reading programs, and/or provides remedial reading instruction in schools.

Reading-study skills.   A constellation of skills involving the efficient use of reading for information (alphabetization, skimming, scanning, using reference materials, etc.)

Reinforcement.   A direct response to a pupil's academic or social behavior.

Remediation.   An educational process designed to improve deficient skills in specific area(s).

Reversal.   Producing a symbol (i.e., letter or numeral) backwards—e.g., b for d.

Self-concept.   A person's view of self, reflecting his/her good and bad points; a generalized image of self in relation to others.

Semantics.   The study of meanings of words.

Sensorineural hearing loss.   Loss of hearing due to damage to the auditory nerve; usually affects high-frequency more than low-frequency sounds.

Short-term memory.   Immediate recall of information following its presentation.

Sight method.   See **Look-say approach**

Sight word.   A whole word that a reader can recognize in pronunciation and meaning without the aid of word-analysis techniques.

Skills grouping.   The process of organizing large groups of children into smaller groups for instruction on the basis of the specific skills being taught rather than of the pupils' ability levels.

Slow learner.   A person with below-average intellectual or learning ability, one who learns more slowly and understands less clearly than most other people of the same chronological age.

Snellen Chart.   A visual screening device that uses letters of different sizes to be read by a subject at a distance of twenty feet; used to measure far-point vision, but does not detect other visual defects that can affect reading.

Structural analysis.   The process of arriving at the pronunciation and meaning of unknown words by identifying the morphemes or structural units (roots, prefixes, and suffixes) of the words. Also called morphemic analysis.

Symbolization.   The process of representing experiences in their absence; in language, words for objects, places, ideas, etc.

Syntax.   The rules by which words are put together to form sentences.

Synthetic phonics.   An approach to phonics instruction that moves from learning letter-sound relationships to blending (or synthesizing) these separate sounds into words.

T and A.   The surgical procedure for removing the tonsils and adenoids.

Tachistoscope.   A device that quickly flashes symbols, words, or phrases for practice in instant recognition of same.

Tactile perception.   The ability to differentiate and interpret information received through touch.

Task analysis.   A systematic procedure for taking a task apart to determine what is required for the successful completion of the task; e.g., specifying what processing demands and/or subskills are required for the completion of a task.

Taxonomy.   An orderly classification scheme for systematically identifying, ordering, and organizing items within a subject field.

Telegraphic speech.   A child's systematic deletion of certain grammatic structures in which meaning is preserved; for example, "Car big" for "Daddy's car is big."

Therapeutic diagnosis.   The process of determining how current factors influence a child's learning progress or problems.

Trade books.   Books written for general use, information, and/or pleasure; not part of a series of graded instructional textbooks.

Visual discrimination.   The ability to recognize likenesses and differences in visual shapes; for example, the difference between a square and a triangle and/or the difference between the letters *b* and *d*.

Visual figure-ground.   The ability to focus on a visual stimulus in the face of competing visual stimuli; for example, the ability to focus on one word in a printed passage.

Visual memory.   The ability to recall visual images.

Visual perception.   The ability to differentiate, organize, and interpret information received through the eye.

Word analysis.   The process of analyzing unknown words encountered in print.

Word banks.   Collections of word cards or lists of words that children "build up" for use in a variety of reading-related activities.

Word calling.   The ability to decode a word without knowledge of its meaning.

Word recognition.   The process of identifying the pronunciation and meaning of words encountered in print.

1

Reading:
An Overview

Preview

Reading can be defined or viewed in a number of different ways—primarily as a process of getting meaning from print, as a decoding activity, or as a psycholinguistic operation. From these different views come different approaches or "methods" of beginning reading instruction. No matter how one defines reading, the act itself involves the reader's sensations, perceptions, cognition, and language. Learning to read involves mastering a constellation of skills along with the development of attitudes and values related to reading. The processes, skills, and affective dimensions of reading are essentially the same for children with special needs as they are for "normal" children.

What happens when we read? What is going on at this very moment as you read the words on the page in front of you?

Reading involves an interaction between a reader and a piece of written material. At the very basic level, the interaction starts with the reader seeing black lines surrounded by white space. These lines register on the retina of the eye and are transmitted to the brain. The reader recognizes these symbols— individually and in combination—and attaches significance to them. The words create an image or an idea in the reader's mind. Now the true process of interaction begins. Upon assimilating the message that the printed material is intended to convey, the reader grasps the meaning, stores it in his/her memory for later retrieval, filters it through his/her experience to judge its veracity or relevance, weighs it, evaluates it, accepts it, rejects it, or otherwise reacts to it in one way or another. This is what goes on when we read.

All this may seem rather basic, but it is useful to look at reading in rather basic terms before examining reading as it relates to classroom instruction and particularly as it relates to instruction for children with special needs.

TOWARD A DEFINITION OF READING

Reading has been defined in a number of different ways, and anything as complex as reading does not lend itself to any sharp definitional boundaries.

In the broadest terms, reading has been defined as the interpretation of any observable phenomenon.[1] In this view, the astrologer "reads" the future in the stars, the sailor "reads" a storm in the clouds, and the infant "reads" the look of love in a mother's eyes. Reading in this sense is older than writing; it is as old as humankind itself. In a school sense, however, the act of reading involves a process of dealing with print.

The more traditional and conventional view of reading defines it primarily as a meaning-getting process: "the recognition of important elements of meaning in their essential relations."[2] In this view, meaning remains the alpha and omega of reading instruction. The words that children learn to read are seen merely as stepping-stones to arriving at meaning, and comprehension is the part of reading that receives the heaviest emphasis from the very beginning.

The 1960s brought a shift in emphasis. Reading came to be viewed or defined primarily as a decoding activity; that is, a process of translating printed symbols into their equivalent spoken sounds.[3] In this sense, we can read words like *wob, gribe,* and *infractaneous,* even though these words have no meaning (because they are nonsense words). The meaning dimension of reading was certainly not ignored in this definition, but it was seen as something that came after the child's ability to crack the sound-symbol code.

More recently, a psycholinguistic view of reading has emerged. With this definition or orientation, reading is viewed as a step in the continuing development of language learning and information processing.[4] Psycholinguistics covers the crossroads between thought and language. The psycholinguist sees reading as a process by which the reader draws on previous experience with language, decoding skills, and expectations, and uses semantic and syntactic clues in making logical predictions or "guesses" at words and meanings that s/he encounters in print.

There is, of course, no single or unitary definition of reading. Reading is a process of moving through printed language to meaning. How one achieves mastery of this complex human behavior—or fails to do so—is a process not yet fully understood.

Coming to grips with a definition of reading is more than an academic exercise, more than a polemic introduction to a book such as this. The way reading is viewed often determines the approach one chooses in teaching children how to read. Definitions are translated into instructional techniques and materials, particularly in the beginning stages of reading instruction and with children who have reading problems throughout the grades. From different views of reading come different approaches to teaching reading in the classroom.

READING: DIFFERENT APPROACHES

A number of different approaches to beginning reading are used in schools. We know them by name: the look-say method (sometimes referred to as "the basal approach"), the phonics approach, linguistic programs, the language experience approach, reformed alphabets, and other programs intended to get each child off on the right foot in learning to read. Aukerman[5] has reviewed over 100 of the commercially prepared beginning reading programs that are available in the marketplace. The ultimate aim of all these programs is the development of reading competency. There are, however, basic differences among the various approaches, and in order to make intelligent decisions on the choice and use of instructional materials in reading, it's important for teachers to be aware of some of these basic differences among reading programs and the approaches they take.

Look-Say

The "look-say" or sight method is basically a meaning-oriented approach; that is, comprehension is the major emphasis from the beginning. The words selected for beginning reading are those sure to have meaning to the children—words like *come, go, see, look, mother, laugh,* and all the other stereotyped "primerese" of Dick and Jane. Reading in "meaningful" context is stressed from the beginning. Whole words are learned by sight. Each word is repeated over and over again—as many as ten or more times in two or three pages—so that through repeated exposure, children will learn to recognize the words on sight.

As the name itself indicates, the *sight* method requires a high degree of visual retention. Context clues are important to help the child get meaning from the print. So are elaborate pictures and other illustrative clues to meaning. With the stress on meaning, comprehension questions demanding the use of the higher mental processes are an important part of beginning reading instruction. Basic reading skill development is highly structured throughout typical look-say programs.

Language Experience

Another meaning-oriented approach to beginning reading is the language experience approach. In this method, the children dictate stories that are then transcribed on experience charts. Thus, the children's own experiences and language become the vehicles in their learning to read.

The language experience and the look-say method have a lot in common. Meaning is the starting point, major emphasis, and expected end-product of reading. A high degree of visual retention is required in remembering the written forms of the words that the children have dictated. Context and configuration clues are stressed. The approach to teaching reading is basically the same. However, these approaches differ greatly in the nature of the reading material itself. Instead of choosing words selected by the publisher to be spoken by Dick and Jane, children learn to read words that they've used in recounting their own experiences. The content and language are unique to each child's experience and cultural background. Speaking, listening, and writing are closely integrated in the process of learning to read. Basic reading skill development, which is provided through the children's reading experience, is necessarily less tightly sequenced than in a more structured basal program.

Phonics Approaches

In a phonics approach, the conscious concentrated teaching of letter-sound relationships is the starting point and major emphasis in beginning reading instruction. The primary focus is on decoding printed words rather than on memorizing words as a whole. The approach may be synthetic; i.e., children learn the "sound" of individual letters and letter combinations, then synthesize these sound elements into words. Or the approach may be analytic; i.e., starting from a core of familiar sight words, children learn to analyze these words into their component phonetic elements. Whatever the orientation, however, the major instructional focus is on helping children link letters to their equivalent sound features in learning to decode written language. Rules become important in "sounding out" words. Materials are constructed to contain the basic sound elements to be learned. Comprehension is expected to result once the written language is pronounced.

Linguistics

A closely related decoding approach to beginning reading is the linguistic method. It is similar to phonics in that both stress the decoding of sound-symbol relationships as the road to mastery in beginning reading. They go about this decoding approach in a different way, however. Linguistics programs typically control sounds *and* symbols in beginning reading materials. While a phonics program may introduce a sound element (the "long o" sound, for example) together with its variant spellings (as in *go, note, goat, toe*, and *blow*, for instance), linguistics programs also control the spellings that represent these sounds. Thus, children learn one written representation of a certain sound before variant spellings of the same sound are introduced. The basic beginning reading vocabulary is restricted to phonetically regular words—words in which letters consistently represent the same sound. Common irregular words (like *the, is, was*, etc.) are learned by sight in order to allow for meaningful sentences in beginning reading materials. Phonics programs are largely deductive in their approach; i.e., children learn rules in order to figure out the sound or pronunciation of a word. The linguistics approach is more inductive; children learn to recognize spelling patterns without necessarily ever consciously learning the rule governing these patterns.

Other Approaches

Other approaches to beginning reading have been promoted and used effectively in classrooms, and new programs are published all the time. A few examples of these approaches follow.

Reformed alphabets

Reformed alphabets—such as the initial teaching alphabet, UNIFON, and others—augment the traditional alphabet with additional symbols to represent the more than twenty-six sounds in our language.

Programmed reading

Programmed reading became popular with the rising interest in technology in education, and programmed materials are still used effectively for different aspects of beginning reading instruction; one example is the Sullivan Reading Program (McGraw-Hill).

Color codes

Color-coded systems used colors as cues in helping children learn to associate sounds and symbols as an initial step in learning to read; for example, *Words in Color* (Learning Materials, Inc.)

Rebus

Rebus programs try to help the process of learning to read by systematically including pictures in place of certain written words; for example, *Peabody Rebus Program* (America Guidance Service).

Perceptual approaches

Perceptual approaches have been used for some time, particularly in teaching children with special learning needs. Such programs as the Slingerland method, the Dubnoff program, the Frostig program, and others place heavy emphasis on the perceptual factors that are basic and essential components in the initial stages of learning to read. Although these programs are not really approaches to reading per se, they promote the development of skills essential in learning to read. Thus, developmental exercises and structured patterning designed to strengthen visual, auditory, kinesthetic, and tactual perception are integral parts of such programs.

In considering these different approaches to beginning reading, two factors are important to remember:

1. Approaches are characterized by differences in *emphasis* and they don't concentrate exclusively on one aspect of reading instruction or another. In other words, code-emphasis programs don't completely ignore meaning any more than meaning-emphasis programs ignore word skills. Different programs do, however, emphasize different aspects of learning to read. Though there may not be a total look-say program on the market today, and though most basal readers attempt to incorporate a combination of methods, programs are usually oriented toward one approach or another, and identifying the major or essential orientation of the program is important.

2. These approaches apply primarily to the beginning stages of reading instruction. There are fewer observable differences among programs at the fourth- and fifth-grade levels, for example, than at the primer or first-grade levels.

A host of new reading programs have emerged in the past twenty years. Each of these approaches—the ones briefly described in the preceding pages and those not even mentioned—has merit. Each has earned its share of objective attention and classroom trial, because each has been designed and advanced in the hope that it will provide early reading mastery for all children. Yet each has fallen short of this noble goal.

The proliferation of the past is likely to continue, and every new program will demand its share of attention for the promise it holds. But if history repeats itself—and chances are it will—then the success or failure of each approach will continue to rest in the hands of the teacher. Research has proven 1) that it's the teacher rather than the program that produces successful reading instruction; 2) that there's more difference from teacher to teacher in the same program than between one program and another; and 3) that a poor method in the hands of a good teacher produces better results than a good method in the hands of a poor teacher.[6] The hope that good teachers will continue to search out and try good methods makes the future reasonably bright.

The Happy Combination Called "Eclecticism"

Out of the pluralism that has marked beginning reading programs has developed an approach that has come to be known as "the eclectic approach." Eclectic, by definition, means "selecting or choosing from various sources; not selecting one system but using the best elements from all systems." An eclectic approach to reading is more than a cafeteria style of teaching, randomly taking a little from this approach and a little from that and then feeding an instructional potpourri to children. Nor does it involve a melding of all the methods, using color-coded symbols from a reformed alphabet to record phonetically regular words to be learned by sight from individualized experience charts. The eclectic approach to reading instruction involves the careful selection of different aspects that will help different children achieve success in the initial stages of learning to read.

Method-learner matching

In practice, eclecticism involves matching the method to the learner and to the task involved. Some approaches to beginning reading may be incompatible with others. To emphasize sound-symbol relationships with a sentence such as *Mother will see Fred here,* a sentence containing words in which the grapheme *e* represents several different phonemes, would be counterproductive. But it is possible to look at individual children's learning styles and select both materials and techniques that will build on children's perceptual and learning strengths, to adopt a program that works well for the special-needs child.

Variety

An eclectic view of reading instruction allows the teacher to shift gears and use a variety of programs and techniques according to the specific children and their learning styles. Some children will master beginning reading whatever approach is used. For children who don't learn so easily, the flexibility of eclecticism is important. An eclectic approach might involve using a look-say program for children whose visual perceptual skills are strong, a phonics approach for children whose auditory modality is dominant, and a modified language experience approach for children whose language comprehension skills are weak. It may involve a multibasal system, with different series chosen not only according to pupils' ability levels but with an eye to their variety of learning styles as well. Eclecticism in teaching beginning reading allows the teacher to choose an approach, or aspects of an approach, that will meet *all* (or at least as many as possible) reading-learning needs of the children in any class.

Individuality

An eclectic approach allows not only for individual differences in children, but also for individual differences in teachers, since it permits the latter to use their own special talents. Teachers can use a variety of methods and materials with which they are familiar and comfortable, and which they know will meet the needs of the children in their classes.

Recently, many of the published programs have attempted, with varying degrees of success, to build a measure of eclecticism into their materials. For example, the name of a "linguistic advisor" or strong early decoding components can be found in otherwise heavily meaning-oriented programs. The noble or commercial aims of the publisher notwithstanding, no reading series can be all things to all children. This is why the key to successful reading instruction rests—and will remain—in the hands of the teacher rather than in any program itself.

READING: FOUR PROCESSES

No matter how one views or defines reading or what approach one chooses to teach it, there are four essential processes that compose the reading act. They are just as essential in a look-say program as in a phonics approach, and just as important to the beginning reader as to the mature literate adult. These processes are sensory, perceptual, linguistic, and cognitive. Breakdowns or deficits in these areas are often the root cause of reading problems for children with special needs.

Reading is an interaction between a reader and a piece of written material, one that involves the reader's sensory, perceptual, linguistic, and cognitive processes. (Photo by John A. Malnati)

Reading as a Sensory Process

The senses are the pathways to the brain. The dominant senses in reading are sight and sound, and reading involves a close integration of the two. Reading is an intersensory rather than an intrasensory activity; that is, it requires the ability to integrate sensations across the visual and auditory modalities.

Visual

Reading is, first of all, a visual activity. It involves the split-second fixation of the eyes on sequential elements in segments of print. The symbols on the page are flashed to the brain, where meaning is attached. When the reader encounters a problem in recognizing or understanding what s/he reads—whether individual symbols in a word, single words on a line, or longer segments in larger printed passages—s/he "regresses"; i.e., the eyes flash back to make another fixation on the same written element or on an element earlier in the passage. As skill increases, the reader makes fewer and fewer fixations and thus speed and ease of reading increase.

Auditory

The sense of hearing is also very important to the reading process. In order to translate written symbols into their equivalent spoken sounds, the reader must learn these sounds through the auditory sense. Hearing also provides a means of feedback, a check to insure that the meaning of the message is clear. This is why even the capable reader often reads a particularly difficult or technical piece of writing (a legal document, for example) aloud.

Learning to read depends upon the normal functioning of the auditory and visual systems. When the sensory mechanism of the eyes and/or the ears is damaged or impaired, the sense of touch is employed as part of the reading process. This accounts for the use of Braille for severely visually impaired readers, for example, and for the use of kinesthetic and haptic inputs in teaching reading to children with visual and/or auditory deficits.

Reading as a Perceptual Process

Volumes have been written in an attempt to define or describe the perceptual process. In a nutshell, perception is the recognition of incoming sensory stimuli. It involves the manipulation of sensations in order to achieve a mental or neurological impress. "In perceiving, the brain selects, groups, organizes, and sequences the sensory data so that people perceive meaningful experiences that can lead to appropriate responses."[7] Perception is the process that occurs in the millisecond between the reception of a stimulus and the response to that stimulus. It can be encapsulated as "information extraction."

Recognition

Perception in reading involves the accurate recognition of the sounds and symbols of language. The general inventory of perceptual skills related to reading includes discrimination, figure-ground, memory, sequencing, and synthesis. In other words, reading requires the ability to distinguish between different symbols and groups of symbols, to correctly associate the appropriate sounds with the symbols, to sequence these sounds in the proper order, to synthesize these sounds into words and these words into larger ideas and images, and to attend to all these visual and verbal stimuli in the face of similar competing stimuli (such as other letters on the page and other sounds in the environment).

Background

One's general perceptions differ according to one's background and experience, and these differences will influence the meaning dimension of reading as well. One child's perception of a *furry white animal* might be a cuddly bunny, while another child's perception might be a frightening rat. The general perceptions, associations, and meanings that the reader brings to the printed page will largely determine what s/he receives from it.

Reading as a Language Process

Being deeply rooted in language, reading is part of the communication process. It is one of the language arts, preceded in the learning sequence by listening and speaking and followed by writing. It is impossible to view reading without dealing with the broader topic of language.

Symbol System

Learning to read involves learning to deal with a secondary language symbol system. Humans invented language to represent or symbolize objects, experiences, ideas, emotions, and other concrete and abstract phenomena in the world around them. The language they created consists of sequences of vocal sounds. Eons after the invention of language, humans devised ways of representing these sounds in a written form so that language could be recorded and preserved over space and time. Only after the advent of writing did the need to read arise.

Speech is still the primary form of language. Writing is used to represent speech. Written language is, in essence, a graphic representation of spoken sounds. The sounds of spoken language make up the primary symbol system; the letters that represent that system constitute the secondary symbol system.

Sounds and Letters

The English writing system is based on the alphabetic principle; that is, individual written symbols (or graphemes) are used to represent individual speech sounds (or phonemes). Although the overall sound system of American English has approximately forty-four phonemes, we have only twenty-six letters of the alphabet to represent these sounds. The resulting mismatch between sounds and symbols is familiar to all of us. We have the same symbol used to represent different sounds—the letter *o*, for example, in the words d*o*, n*o*tice, *o*ne, s*o*n, w*o*man, and w*o*lf. And we have the same sound represented by different symbols or combinations of symbols—the phoneme /uw/, for instance, in the words tw*o*, gn*u*, gr*ou*p, d*o*, m*o*ve, n*ew*, t*u*ne, fr*ui*t, cl*ue*, can*oe*, *cool*, and man*eu*ver. This inconsistency has been the bane of teachers and learners alike for years.

Some words conform perfectly to the alphabetic principle: that is, the phoneme-grapheme relationship is regular and consistent. The word *pin*, for example, has three graphemes, *p-i-n*, that represent three phonemes, /p/, /i/, /n/, in a highly consistent and regular way. For other English words, the sound-symbol relationship is considerably less regular. Words like *laughed*, *said*, and *mother*, which are commonly used words in many beginning basal programs, are considerably less regular in their sound-symbol relationships. Based on a careful analysis and detailed computer programming, the staple of English words we use has been shown to be about 85 percent regular and consistent in its phoneme-grapheme relationships. [8]

Recognizing groups of printed symbols is, then, the first step in learning to read. Different beginning reading programs handle the sound-symbol mismatch in different ways. Some programs choose to largely avoid or bypass the alphabetic principle and present whole words to be memorized by sight. Other programs build upon the considerable regularity that does exist in our writing system and include only words in which the sound-symbol relationships are regular and consistent. Certain programs add additional symbols to our twenty-six–letter alphabet to create a one-to-one sound-symbol relationship in beginning reading materials. Others use color coding to help children master the writing system. No matter which approach one takes, it's impossible to learn to read without mastering the sound-symbol system of our language.

The child learns to speak years before s/he learns to read. In beginning to read, s/he learns to translate graphic symbols into spoken sounds and to recognize printed words according to their spoken equivalents. In order to obtain meaning from print, the child must be able to recognize the corresponding meaning in oral language. That is, the reader must know the meaning(s) of the words he reads and be able to determine the language meaning(s) that groups of words carry in phrases, clauses, sentences, and longer passages of written material. Understanding language is the key to understanding in reading.

Language is, then, an essential underpinning in any view of reading. An adequate definition of reading is impossible without taking language into account.

Reading as a Cognitive Process

Reading is also a cognitive activity, an activity that involves the use of the higher mental processes. Reading demands thinking at all stages, from the basic levels of association and memory necessary in mastering sound-symbol relationships through the highest levels of reasoning and evaluation that characterize critical reading. All these processes operate as the act of reading is taking place. The lines between these levels of thinking are not sharply defined, nor do they follow in a fixed order every time we read, but cognition remains a crucial dimension of the reading act at all stages.

Because the ultimate goal of reading is understanding, the cognitive component is viewed by most teachers and experts as the most important part of the reading act and thus the most important dimension in any definition of reading.

Interaction in Reading

The four processes that are part of the act of reading—i.e., sensation, perception, language, and cognition—do not provide a total definition of reading. Each act of reading, each interaction between a person and a piece of print, may demand its own definition, depending on the nature of the interaction and the context in which it occurs. A third grader reading a basal story in a reading group will engage in a different type of reading from a graduate law student reviewing a moot piece of legislation in preparation for an important examination. And even two people reading the same piece of material will read it in different ways. The school board member, for example, will read a local newspaper article on declining school enrollment differently from an unemployed teacher, even though both are mature, capable readers.

What happens during the act of reading is determined in large measure by the nature of the reader and the type of material that s/he is reading. Every act of reading, however, whatever the context or situation in which it is done, demands the involvement of language, sensation, perception, and cognition. Problems in learning to read can often be linked to problems in these areas.

These four processes inherent in the reading act cannot be viewed as separate, independently operating functions. Each process goes on in close conjunction with the others. The brain is in motion as the eyes fixate on the language symbols printed on the page. All four processes blend closely together as the reader interacts with print, and combine in various ways to produce the product called "reading." All are essential components in any view of reading.

READING: BASIC SKILLS

As an inherent part of any act of reading, there exists an inventory of identifiable skills that are included in reading instructional programs. These are the skills you are now using while you read and the skills the child acquires in learning how to read. The skills are broadly classified as word recognition, phonetic analysis, structural analysis, context clues, and the general area of comprehension. Reading-study skills we use when we put reading to work for us are also included as basic skills.

These reading skills are handled differently in different reading programs and in different approaches to reading instruction. In most programs, the skills are systematically built into a carefully developed scope and sequence for presentation to children. They may be included in a different order and with different degrees of emphasis. In some programs, for example, phonetic analysis is the starting point and concentrated phonics instruction is the major emphasis throughout the early grades. In other programs, phonics may be introduced later and more incidentally. But in all approaches, the skills are included because they are essential to the act of reading. While many psycholinguists see the traditionally strict adherence to the "skills model" as an overreliance on separate parts of reading, the skills are what enable the reader to make the predictions and "guesses" needed to arrive at meaning contained in printed passages.

In the process of learning to read, the development of these skills begins at the readiness stage and continues until reading competency has been achieved.

Readiness

Readiness has been defined as a state of maturity and development that will allow a person to begin to learn to read. It consists of a broad spectrum of highly complex and interconnected human traits and qualities. The areas important to readiness are physical, emotional, intellectual, and linguistic. The development of factors in these areas enables a person to learn to read; these factors are the foci of readiness training programs.

Physical factors

Since reading involves the use of our physical facilities, it is axiomatic that physical factors are important elements in readiness. The physical factors most commonly associated with reading readiness are visual and auditory acuity, eye-hand coordination, large- and small-muscle development, and generally sound health. When problems in reading develop later, the problem can often be traced back to a physical factor at the readiness stage.

Emotional factors

Personal and social adjustment are closely tied in with the development of the individual. Emotional factors thought to be important to reading readiness are personal confidence and security; and the ability to maintain attention, to stick with a task until completion, to work independently, to accept responsibility, and to adjust well to a learning situation. These factors also include social readiness: willingness to participate in social activities; the ability to work well with others, to cooperate, and to share responsibility in a learning task. Included here also are the essential affective factors of interest or motivation in wanting to learn to read. Though emotional-social readiness is important, these factors are generally considered more global than other factors at the stage of reading readiness.

Intellectual factors

Since reading is also a cognitive activity, intelligence plays a role as a readiness factor. The general intelligence factor—i.e., a child's mental age—was once considered the primary component in reading readiness. While intellectual maturity is still considered an important dimension in the process of learning to read, intelligence alone does not guarantee success.

Children with a low mental age can learn to read and intelligent children can experience reading problems. More important than a general intelligence score are the concomitant intellectual abilities of perception and thinking.

Perception involves an awareness of similarities and differences in the size, shape, orientation, color, and other relationships in objects and visual symbols. It also involves an awareness of auditory stimuli; the ability to recognize similarities, differences, and relationships in sounds; and the recognition of separate sounds in spoken words. Activities to develop visual and auditory perception are major parts of reading readiness training programs.

Cognition is also an important readiness factor. At the readiness stage, children are trained in the ability to interpret pictures and experiences, to recall ideas and details, to see relationships and predict outcomes, to think logically and reasonably, and to grasp ideas. Since language and thinking are so closely tied together, cognition also includes the ability to know the meaning of words, to understand and interpret verbal messages, to express thoughts, and to otherwise manipulate verbal concepts.

Linguistic factors

Reading is a language activity, and therefore linguistic factors are primary readiness factors as well. One must be able to understand oral language before being expected to deal with that language in print. In readiness programs, general language-thinking factors are developed through popular oral language activities like show-and-tell, discussion, listening exercises, poetry and story telling, creative dramatics, conscious vocabulary development, conversation, and all the other formal and informal encounters with language that are typically a regular part of a child's early educational experience.

In addition to developing general language power, readiness training deals extensively with the language codes—the sounds and symbols of our language. Here, the specific focus is on learning letter names and sounds as the most immediate steps leading from the readiness stage to actual reading. Readiness training in this area also involves an awareness of—and practice with—the left-to-right directionality of our written language code, a dimension that is also part of the physical and perceptual phases of reading readiness training and development.

Experience

Experience is a crucial dimension that underlies these other aspects of reading readiness. A child whose sensory environment has been rich, who has been to many places and seen many things, will likely be more physically, and love, who has listened to stories and retold them to others, who has witnessed reading as an important part of the lives of those around him, who has been to many places and seen many things will likely be more physically, emotionally, intellectually, and linguistically ready to read than one whose background has not been so rich. Intelligence, language, and experience are interactive. In the final analysis, experience that nurtures intelligence and language may be the most crucial reading readiness factor.

Though we usually associate reading readiness with the preschool and kindergarten years, readiness continues long beyond these early grades. The adult with problems in perception and language deprivation may lack the same readiness factors as a young child, and this will interfere with his/her development of reading ability. When a mature and capable reader attempts to read about a topic with which s/he is totally unfamiliar, s/he will likely have "reading problems" because of lacking the vocabulary meaning, the concepts, and the background—the readiness factors—necessary to deal effectively with the topic.

The special-needs child   For children with special needs, readiness is particularly important. The special needs themselves are often defined in terms of the physical, emotional, intellectual, or linguistic factors that the child lacks. For example, when we say that a child is "visually impaired" or "perceptually handicapped" or "emotionally disturbed" or "mentally retarded" or "language disordered," we are defining the disability in terms of a developmental factor the child lacks. Meeting this special need may center extensively (or even exclusively) on the readiness level in learning to read.

Word-Recognition Skills

Word recognition is the skill that allows the reader to instantaneously identify words upon visual contact. Word recognition involves learning words by sight, then building a store of "sight words" that can be instantly recognized in written form. It is a skill that involves not only being able to recall and pronounce the word, but knowing the meaning of the word as well. Through word recognition, the reader associates the visual form with the pronunciation and meaning of a word.

Word recognition requires repeated exposure to familiar words. We learn to recognize people by seeing their faces and attaching names to those faces. The more we see a person in a variety of situations, the easier it is to recognize and greet him/her. So it is with words. The child learns to recognize a word by sight, and to attach meaning to that word, by seeing it over and over. The more s/he sees the word in different contexts, the easier it becomes for him/her to recognize and read the word.

For good readers, word recognition becomes almost automatic. They can recognize whole words at a glance—either in isolation or in the context of a written sentence—based on visual memory of the word. When the whole word is not immediately recognized, children often resort to other visual clues to word recognition. These include configuration (i.e., word shape or form) or distinguishing characteristics (the *oo* in *look*, for example, or the initial and final letters) as aids to recognition. While these visual clues can often be useful in the beginning stages of learning to read, their utility is limited in learning the large number of words necessary for reading mastery. Often, the child depends on context in recognizing unknown words; i.e., s/he recognizes the word on the basis of expectancy in a verbal passage or by attaching the word to a picture clue provided. These techniques become the focus of classroom exercises in helping children develop word-recognition skills.

In a look-say program, word recognition is the primary skill emphasized in beginning reading instruction. Even in code-emphasis programs, a certain number of words are learned by sight, either prior to or as part of the process of learning to decode printed language. No matter which beginning approach is used, word recognition is a skill essential to the act of reading as long as a person continues to read.

Word Analysis

Because there are 600,000 or more words in the English language, and because our writing system is based on the alphabetic principle, learning to read by sight alone—i.e., learning to recognize each word as a separate entity—is a highly inefficient way to achieve reading mastery. In our reading, we all occasionally encounter words that we don't automatically recognize. When faced with such words, we analyze them to get the pronunciation and meaning. Word analysis or word attack, then, becomes an essential part of the act of reading and an important component in reading instruction. These word-attack skills are phonetic analysis and structural analysis.

Phonetic analysis

The process of analyzing unknown words on the basis of letter-sound relationships in the words is called phonetic analysis. The amount of phonics taught and the way it is included differ from one reading program to another. But whether learned early or late, directly or incidentally, phonics is an essential reading skill. It is impossible to read without a knowledge of the letter-sound relationships of our language.

Phonics begins at the readiness stage with an awareness of separate sounds in spoken words and a knowledge of the written symbols that represent these sounds. Included in the inventory of phonetic elements of our language that are part of reading instruction are:

- consonants—singly in various positions in words;
- consonant digraphs—two consonant letters that represent a single sound (or phoneme) as in *ch*in, *sh*ip, *th*in, *wh*en, etc.;
- consonant blends or clusters—two or three consonant letters that represent closely related but separate phonemes, as in *cl*ap, *br*ag, *st*op, *str*ap, etc.;
- vowels—short vowels represented by the letter-sound relationships in words like *a*pple, g*e*t, and f*i*t; long or "glided" vowel sounds in words like *o*pen, c*u*te, and b*y*; r-controlled vowels as they occur in words like *a*rm and f*u*r;
- vowel digraphs—two vowel letters representing a single vowel phoneme, as in s*ea*t and r*ai*n. In more and more phonics programs, *w* is included as a vowel letter since it functions as a vowel in digraphs like gro*w* and pa*w*;
- vowel diphthongs or blends—two vowel letters representing closely related sounds in sequence, as n*oi*se and *ou*t.

Instruction in phonics also includes attention to so-called "silent letters" (the *k* in *k*now, for example, or the *b* in clim*b*), phonics rules, syllabication, and other elements that help the reader to attack, analyze, and "sound out" unknown words.

These phonetic elements are the focus of phonics instruction throughout the grades. They are more easily identified than taught, however. Not all phonics programs include them in this order (some start with long vowels while others tackle short vowels first), but all reading programs include these phonetic elements because they are the basic sound elements of our language.

Normally, a great deal of attention is devoted to phonics instruction in schools. The overall aim of this instruction is to give children the tools they need to read the words they cannot recognize on sight.

Structural analysis

The process of identifying meaningful units in words is called structural analysis. While phonetic analysis concentrates mostly on individual sound-symbol relationships, structural analysis deals with larger meaning-bearing units in words. Some words are meaningful units in and of themselves—the word *dog*, for example. Other words are built from a combination of two or more meaningful units; *dogs*, for example, consists of the base word *dog* (meaning a canine creature) and the inflectional suffix *-s* (meaning more than one). The ability to identify these structural units or meaningful word parts— "morphemes"—is the skill of structural analysis.

Structural analysis usually begins with the identification of independent word parts in compound words. It extends to the recognition of other meaningful units from which words are built—roots and affixes (word endings, prefixes, and suffixes). Some programs include syllables as part of structural analysis. Syllables, however, are pronounceable units, whereas roots, prefixes, and suffixes are morphemes or meaning units in words.

A knowledge of roots and affixes contributes significantly to word analysis. A limited number of roots and affixes are used to build thousands of English words. The more knowledge the reader has of these meaningful word parts, the better will be his/her chances of analyzing words s/he does not recognize by sight, and of getting meaning from words that s/he can "sound out."

Phonetic and structural analysis are closely related aspects of word attack. Both involve a coordination of skills needed to unlock unknown words. While phonetic analysis concentrates on sound units, structural analysis deals with meaning units in words. Taken together, the two skills enable the reader to analyze the pronunciation and meaning of words.

Context Clues

Using context clues is another helpful skill in the total act of reading. When a reader encounters an unknown word, s/he uses the surrounding language as a clue to figuring out what the word may be. Using context clues involves successful and calculated guessing; i.e., inferring the appropriate pronunciation and meaning of new words encountered in reading on the basis of expectancy or anticipation.

Using context clues requires a knowledge of surrounding words and an understanding of the syntactic structure of the entire phrase or sentence in which the word is used. It's a skill that's taught from the beginning stages of reading instruction, and as reading competency grows, we continue to depend more and more upon clues in the verbal context to infer both pronunciation and meaning of unknown words. While context itself can be a useful way of figuring out unknown words in reading, it must be used in conjunction with other word analysis skills.

A combination of word skills

All the word skills mentioned above—word recognition, phonetic analysis, structural analysis, and context clues—operate in close conjunction with one another during the total act of reading. For example, let's assume the child is called upon to read the sentence

Jack walked up the hill to get a bucket of water.

If the child can readily and instantly recognize each word by sight, then s/he should be able to read the sentence. If s/he doesn't visually recognize the first word, *Jack* (or any other word in the sentence), s/he has the opportunity to sound out the word on a sound-symbol basis. If *walked* is unfamiliar, s/he can look at the base word *walk* and use a combination of phonetic and structural analysis to decode the word. If s/he stumbles on *bucket*, the context of the sentence suggests the word. But the context here also suggests *pail*, so the child reverts to phonics to see that *pail* does not begin with *b*. Having identified the initial sound in *bucket*, s/he is on the way to decoding the word.

And so it goes. Mature readers jump back and forth, using a combination of the word-attack skills they have at their disposal. These word skills enable the reader to identify different elements in printed language and to translate these language elements into their equivalent spoken forms. Word skills, then, lead up to the component that completes the act of reading—i.e., comprehension or understanding messages presented through print.

Comprehension

Comprehension—the ability to derive meaning and understanding from printed language—is the consummation of the act of reading. Reading is a language activity. Since language is a tool of communication, and communication involves the reception as well as the expression of ideas, then the act of reading is not complete until comprehension has taken place. Reading comprehension has long been a primary fundamental goal of reading instruction.

*Product and
process*

It is important to distinguish between the product and the process of reading comprehension. The product is easily identifiable through the conventional multiple-choice, true-false, or fill-in-the-blank items on objective tests. It is observable through the child's ability to retell a story in his/her own words, act out the events of a story, recount the major points of a passage, or follow a set of written directions. These products are easy to observe and measure. The process of comprehension is more difficult to get at since it goes on inside the child's head. It's how the child comes to understand, interpret, store, and react to what s/he reads. These processes are not observable and not as easy to measure.

*Views of
comprehension*

One can view reading comprehension from a number of theoretical perspectives. Conventionally, comprehension is viewed in terms of a number of specific factors that include understanding the author's use of language, locating and recalling information, finding main ideas, seeing cause-and-effect relationships, drawing conclusions, making generalizations, sequencing events, distinguishing fact from fancy, determining the author's purpose, evaluating the veracity or value of a written passage, applying information to one's own experience, identifying with characters and events, and a number of other reading/thinking processes. Taken together, these factors—which can be itemized in a list of 200 or more—are said to make up the total entity called reading comprehension.

Many authors and reading programs arrange these factors by a classification system based on the level of mental operation required. Such taxonomies of reading comprehension typically include levels of: (1) *literal meaning*—understanding and interpreting what the author has to say; (2) *inferential comprehension*—reading "between the lines" to infer meaning not specifically stated in a printed passage; and (3) *critical-creative reading*—extending beyond the lines to evaluate, relate, or apply what is read.

More recently, comprehension has come to be viewed in more general terms, as something that is related to reading but apart from the reading act itself. In other words, processes like deriving meaning, forming conclusions, and seeing cause-effect relations—and all the other specific factors identified as part of "reading comprehension"—are no more involved in reading than in any other area of the curriculum or of life itself. For example, the farmer working in his field looks at the clouds and determines the wind direction. He then makes inferences, sees cause-effect relationships, draws conclusions, and predicts outcomes, even though he is not reading. After word skills are used to decode written language, reading comprehension becomes largely a function of the reader's background of experience, his/her language, his/her mental operations, and other factors.

*Dimensions of
comprehension*

In reading instruction, the crucial dimensions of reading comprehension are these:

- mastery of basic word skills. It's axiomatic that the child won't be able to understand what s/he reads unless s/he is able to read it; that is, unless s/he is able to identify the words and see them in their essential relationships to one another.

- the nature of the reading material. Materials are particularly important. Different materials demand different degrees and types of comprehension. Reading a poem, for example, requires interpretation and imagery; reading a set of directions demands more literal comprehension and careful attention to details. Some materials are written primarily to inform; others are written chiefly to entertain; still others are written for the primary purpose of helping children master basic reading skills. The type of comprehension demanded will vary according to the nature of the material and the purpose for which it was written.

- the reader's background and experience. The more a reader brings to a printed page in terms of knowledge and background, the better s/he will be able to understand what s/he reads. Concepts built through experience will enhance concepts gained through reading.

- the reader's understanding of language. Reading comprehension involves understanding the linguistic elements that make up reading passages: the words, phrases, sentences, paragraphs, and chapters (in longer reading selections). Comprehension involves not only understanding each of these language elements as a unit, but also how each relates to all the other elements.

- the reader's purpose or motivation. Our reason for reading has a lot to do with how well we understand what we read. Comprehension in pleasure reading, for example, is different from the comprehension demanded in studying for an important examination. If we are truly interested in what we are reading, we will likely comprehend it better than if we couldn't care less about the topic. Interest or motivation is an important factor in determining how hard readers will work at trying to understand what they read.

- the reader's thinking ability. Since reading is a cognitive operation, the reader's ability to think will have a significant effect on comprehension, particularly at the critical-creative level. It's unlikely that children will be able to predict outcomes or draw conclusions from what they read unless they can predict outcomes or draw conclusions from pictures, events, or oral language. In other words, these cognitive skills are prerequisite to reading comprehension. General cognitive functioning is bound to affect cognitive processing (or comprehension) in reading.

Each of these factors serves to enhance or delimit a person's ability to comprehend what s/he reads. "Teaching comprehension" involves attention to each of these dimensions as part of reading instruction.

Reading-study skills

Another group of skills usually included as part of reading instructional programs are the reading-study skills. These include skimming, scanning, using different reference sources, seeing organization in a piece of written material, summarizing, and the related research skills of locating information, notetaking, and outlining. Such skills are particularly important in reading in content areas of the curriculum.

In one sense, these reading-study skills are "basic," since they are important to reading throughout the grades and beyond, and since the skills are developed through instruction. In another sense, however, they are based upon more basic word and meaning skills in reading. Skimming, for example, requires quick recognition of words, and notetaking requires a host of prerequisite comprehension skills.

Study skills involve the effective use of reading. They are more part of the "reading-to-learn" aspect of reading than of the "learning-to-read" phase. These skills are, however, part of reading instruction, even from the early years.

READING: THE AFFECTIVE DIMENSION

In addition to the cognitive and psychomotor demands of learning how to read (like learning sight words or mastering sound-symbol relationships or recalling what is read), there are important affective dimensions to reading as well. These include the attitudes, needs, interests, feelings, and values that the child develops before, during, and after learning how to read.

Krathwohl, Bloom, and Masia classify the categories of the affective domain as receiving, responding, valuing, organizing, and characterizing a complex of values.[9] Each category involves the child's emotions in learning to read.

Receiving

Receiving is the basic level of this affective taxonomy. At this level, the child becomes aware of reading and is willing to receive and attend to instruction. At a very early age, through reading in the home, children become aware of the existence of reading. This is especially true when parents read to them, when they are surrounded by books, and when they see parents (and others who are important to them) reading. Even in the preschool years, the child becomes conscious of reading and begins to see it as something pleasurable and important. In such cases, the child comes to school more ready and willing to

Learning to read begins long before school entrance, with positive affective reading experiences in the home. (Photo by John A. Malnati)

give his/her attention to the job of learning to read. In the normally busy environment of the kindergarten classroom, the child will be willing to listen to a story in the face of competing stimuli, and will be aware of the readiness activities designed to build the basic foundational skills necessary for reading.

Responding

The second level involves response. Reading involves a pattern of responses that are seen by the child as pleasure or pain. In the home, pleasant experiences with reading produce positive and satisfying responses; that is, positive association with reading. For example, the child looks forward to a nightly bedtime story and may even prefer to hear a story read than to watch a cartoon on television. In school, the pattern of effective responses continues to develop. For children who learn to read "on schedule," reading is accompanied by a sense of satisfaction, an emotional response of enjoyment. Reading becomes a voluntary activity that proceeds from the child's own choice. For children whose initial attempts at learning to read are met by failure, reading produces a feeling of frustration accompanied by a sense of emotional pain. If affective responses are unfavorable—if the tasks demanded of learning to read are beyond the child's level of ability or stage of development, and if learning to read becomes too difficult a chore—then negative feelings start to develop and emotional blocks to reading begin.

Valuing

With positive experiences at the awareness and response levels, reading becomes a value. It is incorporated into the child's value system as a pleasant or satisfying activity, one that has worth. The child accepts reading as a value and responds accordingly by demonstrating a preference for reading over other activities. With negative experiences, the child learns to shift attention elsewhere and, in the extreme case, begins to engage in behaviors to avoid reading. Here is where the affective response leads to behavior problems like acting out or withdrawing.

Organizing

At the organizational level, reading is organized as part of the child's broader value system. It is integrated into a relationship with the other values the child holds. If emotional blocks and negative feelings have developed, reading is assigned a low priority in relation to other values.

Characterizing

The highest level of this affective schema is characterization, or the organization of a value as part of one's whole value complex. Values at this level are all-encompassing and become part of one's philosophy. Our value complex determines our way of life. With internal consistency in one's system of attitudes and values, reading is reflected as a lifelong interest or a lifelong aversion.

While this taxonomy of the affective domain identifies five separate categories: receiving, responding, valuing, organizing, and characterizing, there's an obvious overlap and close relationship among all five areas. Commonly used terms such as "interests," "attitudes," and "values" have a wide range of meanings and are subject to various interpretations. The chart below shows how each fits into the different categories of the affective continuum.

The affective dimensions of learning to read are vitally important. Attitudes influence behavior on a lifelong basis. Continuing to provide favorable affective responses in reading instruction for all children will greatly facilitate the whole process of learning to read.

CONCLUSION

When carefully analyzed, the act of reading appears to be an intricately complex form of human behavior. It is an activity not easy to define. It has been

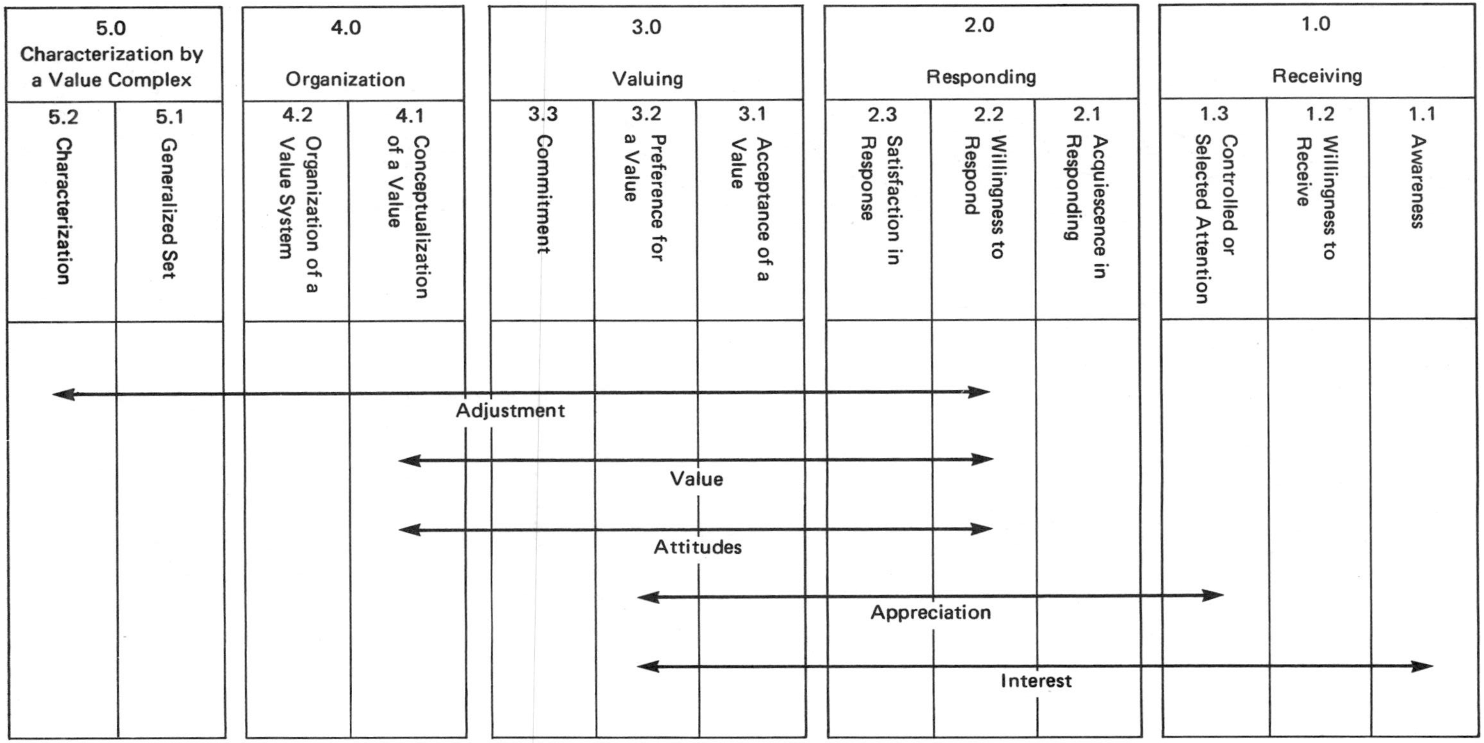

1.0 Receiving	1.1 Awareness	
	1.2 Willingness to Receive	
	1.3 Controlled or Selected Attention	

2.0 Responding	2.1 Acquiescence in Responding	
	2.2 Willingness to Respond	
	2.3 Satisfaction in Response	

3.0 Valuing	3.1 Acceptance of a Value	
	3.2 Preference for a Value	
	3.3 Commitment	

| 4.0 Organization | 4.1 Conceptualization of a Value | |
| | 4.2 Organization of a Value System | |

| 5.0 Characterization by a Value Complex | 5.1 Generalized Set | |
| | 5.2 Characterization | |

Interest

Appreciation

Value

Attitudes

Adjustment

(From Taxonomy of Educational Objectives: The Classification of Educational Goals: Handbook II: Affective Domain, by David R. Krathwohl, et al. Copyright © 1964 by David McKay Company, Inc. Copyright © 1977 by Longman Inc. Reprinted by permission of Longman Inc.)

Figure 1.1   The range of meaning typical of commonly used affective terms measured against the Taxonomy continuum.

viewed as primarily a meaning-getting process, as primarily a decoding process, and as a psycholinguistic activity that includes thought and language. However it is defined, reading involves the process of arriving at meaning through printed language.

From different conceptions or definitions of reading come various approaches to reading instruction. The look-say method, the language experience approach, phonics, linguistics, and various other approaches have been used in an attempt to help children learn how to read in school.

Understanding the rationale or underlying assumptions of these approaches is important for the teacher. The methods, techniques, books, worksheets, tapes, kits, and other gimmicks and gadgets designed for reading instruction are just the tip of the iceberg. Understanding the orientation or foundations upon which these methods and materials are based is essential to making intelligent decisions in the selection and use of reading materials for classroom instruction.

No matter which approach or program is chosen, the act of reading involves the use of the reader's sensory systems, organization of those sensations into accurate perceptions, language, and his/her thinking ability. When all these systems are "GO," most children learn to read without undue difficulty. An impairment in any of these systems, however, causes trouble and creates a special need for some children in the classroom. The teacher who can identify and isolate problems in these four areas is often in a position to avoid or correct the problems before they get in the way of successful reading for the child.

The teaching of reading involves helping children develop basic skills: 1) the ability to identify words in print (word recognition); 2) the ability to "sound out" unknown words by attaching equivalent spoken sounds to written symbols in words (phonetic analysis); 3) the ability to look for meaning in the morphemic elements in words (structural analysis); 4) the ability to figure out the pronunciation and meaning of a word from the surrounding printed language (context clues); and 5) the ability to understand the meaning of a message conveyed in print (comprehension). These are the skills that the good reader masters and automatically applies when reading. They are as important to the special-needs child as to the so-called "regular" child in the classroom. Whatever the nature of the child's special needs, s/he needs these skills in learning how to read.

Finally, there is also an important emotional side to reading. The affective response to reading develops systematically, from awareness that there is such a thing as "reading" to the integration of reading into a value system that governs one's life. Everything we do in the classroom in the name of reading instruction has an emotional consequence—positive or negative—that will have an effect in forming a child's attitude toward reading.

Reading development is a lifelong proposition. Indirectly, it begins with language acquisition in the early-childhood experiences of the very young preschooler. It becomes a major focus and concern in the life of the school-age child. And it continues as long as a person continues to read. Each time you read—each time you encounter a new word or relate to a new character in a story or search out new information from a page of print—you practice and thus further develop the basic components that are part of the act of reading. From the beginning stages through reading maturity, the basic elements of the reading process don't change. The mature reader who encounters a word like *morphophonological,* or who grapples with a new and difficult concept in a text, performs the same operations as the first grader who encounters a word like *grandfather* for the first time, or who tries to understand a sentence about ducks swimming in a pond. Reading, once mastered, is a never-ending process.

ACTIVITIES FOR PRESERVICE TEACHERS

1. Examine a basal reader and a teacher's edition from a beginning reading program. Does the approach primarily maintain a code emphasis, a meaning emphasis, or is there a balance between the two? How can you tell? Compare the program you examine with other basal reading programs on the market.

2. Analyze a lesson plan from the teacher's edition that you examine. What skills are included? What techniques are suggested for helping children master these skills? What provisions are suggested for those children who don't master the skills "the first time around"? What provisions would you suggest for these children?

3. A child who is reading the following sentence stops at the underlined word:

    The creeping <u>kudzu</u> spread across the hills.

    Assuming s/he can read all the other words in the sentence, how might s/he decode the unknown word through phonics and context clues? Describe the steps you would follow in helping the child read the word.

4. Reading comprehension is a broad and complex area. List what you consider the three most important factors that influence comprehension and briefly describe how each influences your own ability to comprehend what you read. How might these factors influence a child's ability to understand what s/he reads in the classroom?

5. Analyze your own reading experiences from an affective perspective. Where does reading fit into your own value complex? What types of reading material do you prefer? Why? Under what circumstances do you

choose reading over another activity, and vice versa? How can your own affective experiences with reading be translated into instructional terms for teaching reading in the classroom?

ACTIVITIES FOR IN-SERVICE TEACHERS

1. Carefully and critically examine the reading program you use in your classroom. Would you consider it primarily a code-emphasis or a meaning-emphasis program? Why? What supplementary materials do you find necessary for reading instruction?

2. Identify a child in your class who has difficulty learning to read. What can be said about his/her reading with regard to the sensory, perceptual, language, and cognitive processes identified in this chapter as part of the reading act?

3. Identify two or three components from a reading-skill area that you teach every day in the classroom (beginning consonant blends, long vowels, prefixes, literal recall of details, etc.). What techniques do you find particularly effective in helping children master these specific reading skills? What alternative techniques can you suggest for children who have trouble with these skill areas?

4. A number of factors that influence reading comprehension were identified in this chapter. Analyze the responses of children to the comprehension questions you ask to determine which help or hinder your pupils in comprehending what they read.

5. Examine the reading of your children from an affective perspective. What types of favorable responses do the good readers derive from reading? What types of negative responses do poor readers exhibit? What types of activities do children seem to prefer over reading? Where does reading fit into the hierarchy of your own value complex?

NOTES

1. Frank G. Jennings, *This Is Reading* (New York: Bureau of Publications, Teachers College, Columbia University, 1965).
2. William S. Gray, *The Teaching of Reading, A Second Report, Part I of the 36th Yearbook of NSSE* (Bloomington, Ind.: Public School Publishing Co., 1937.)
3. Charles Fries, *Linguistics and Reading* (New York: Holt, Rinehart and Winston, 1963.)

4. Frank Smith, *Understanding Reading* (New York: Holt, Rinehart and Winston, 1971.)
5. Robert Aukerman, *Approaches to Beginning Reading* (New York: John Wiley and Sons, 1971.)
6. Guy L. Bond and Robert Dykstra, "The Cooperative Research Program in First-Grade Reading Instruction," *Reading Research Quarterly* 2 (Summer 1967): 5–141.
7. Albert J. Harris and Edward R. Sipay, *How To Increase Reading Ability*, 6th ed. (New York: David McKay Co., 1975), p. 250.
8. Paul R. Hanna, Jean S. Hanna, Richard E. Hodges, and Erwin H. Rudorf, Jr., *Phoneme-Grapheme Correspondences as Cues to Spelling Improvement OE* - 32008 (Washington, D.C.: U.S. Department of Health, Education, and Welfare, 1966).
9. David R. Krathwohl, Benjamin S. Bloom, and Bertram B. Masia, *Taxonomy of Educational Objectives, The Classification of Educational Goals. Handbook II: The Affective Domain* (New York: David McKay Co., 1964.)

REFERENCES

Burns, Paul C., and Roe, Betty D. *Teaching Reading in Today's Elementary School*. Chicago: Rand McNally, 1976.

Durkin, Dolores. *Teaching Them To Read*. 3rd ed. Boston: Allyn and Bacon, 1978.

Guszack, Frank J. *Diagnostic Reading Instruction in the Elementary School*. New York: Harper and Row, 1972.

Harris, Albert J., and Sipay, Edward. *How To Increase Reading Ability*. 6th ed. New York: David McKay Co., 1975.

Heilman, Arthur W. *Principles and Practices of Teaching Reading*. 4th ed. Columbus: Charles E. Merrill Co., 1977.

Karlin, Robert. *Teaching Elementary Reading: Principles and Strategies*. 2d ed. New York: Harcourt Brace Jovanovich, 1975.

Smith, Frank. *Psycholinguistics and Reading*. New York: Holt Rinehart and Winston, 1973.

Smith, Richard J., and Johnson, Dale D. *Teaching Children To Read*. Reading, Mass.: Addison Wesley Publishing Co., 1976.

Spache, George D., and Spache, Evelyn B. *Reading in the Elementary School*. 4th ed. Boston: Allyn and Bacon, 1977.

Walcutt, Charles, Lamport, John, and McCracken, Glen. *Teaching Reading: A Phonics-Linguistic Approach to Developmental Reading*. New York: Macmillan Co., 1974.

Zintz, Miles V. *The Reading Process: The Teacher and The Learner*. 2d ed. Dubuque, Iowa: Wm. C. Brown Co., 1975.

2

Learning Problems

Preview

*Children experience difficulty in learning for a variety
of reasons. Over the years, special schools and
programs have been established to meet the needs of
children with specific problems, e.g., blindness
deafness, mental retardation, etc. The newest field of
special education is that of learning disabilities. Since
children with learning disabilities in no way conform
to any specific set of behavioral characteristics or
academic difficulties, specialists in the field have
developed approaches to assessment and instruction
that focus on identifying individual learning needs
and selecting appropriate teaching strategies. These
techniques of individualized assessment and instruction are equally applicable to children with other types
of handicaps. The concept of a "learning problem"
implies the application of learning-disability approaches to a wider population.*

Any child in school faces a multitude of learning situations. He learns in different ways and in different places. In the classroom he learns about words and numbers; on the playground he learns to play games, fight, and make up; in the gym he learns to tumble and run and wait his turn. On the school bus he learns to survive. For centuries, theorists have attempted to define and describe the process of learning—its prerequisites and conditions, what contributes and what detracts, what facilitates remembering and what does not. There is no universally accepted theory of learning and there probably never will be.

The difficulty in constructing a precise theory of learning is compounded when attempting to formulate an acceptable definition of learning disorders. Quintilian spoke about individual differences in the first century A.D. and educators have continued to ponder the question ever since. Over the years, children who were very different were excluded from school. They were kept busy around the farm, in the village, or, in severe cases, hidden away in the house. The world has been aware of the accomplishments of certain handicapped individuals; Beethoven was deaf, Homer was blind, and Helen Keller was both deaf and blind. However, society has tended to view their successes as miraculous. Until the nineteenth century, very little recognition was given to the rights of all children to an appropriate education, or to the wisdom of providing a means for handicapped children to become contributing members of society. Beginning with the work of Itard, Braille, Seguin, and Binet in France, and Gallaudet, Howe, and later Adler in the United States, a body of knowledge started to accumulate that provided the foundation of various disciplines in special education. Once special schools for the deaf, blind, retarded, and disturbed children were established, specific and special techniques for children with those handicaps evolved as the result of the hard work—and trial and error—of the teachers and children during those early years. Educators discovered what worked, and contributed greatly to the knowledge of curriculum design and accommodation for children with special needs. Other work followed for children with less dramatic handicaps. Drawing from the fields of medicine, psychology, and education, professionals devoted attention to the unique training needs of children who had physical handicaps, communication disorders, brain damage, and emotional problems. The field is now immense.

THE MORE SUBTLE HANDICAPS

During the time when people were reexamining theories about the best way to educate children who were slow in learning, the field of learning disabilities was established. In 1963 a group of parents and professionals met in Chicago to unite in the common interest of children with developmental deficits of various kinds. The largest representations at that conference were from the Associations for Brain Injured Children and the Fund for the Perceptually Handicapped. In the major address at the conference, Kirk[1] suggested that in their search for a term that could apply to the very diverse population of children who experience difficulty in learning, they resist the temptation to use the traditional terms with biological or psychological significance like "minimal brain damage" or "perceptual disorder," and adopt one more descriptive of the behavior that is the cause for concern. Kirk told the group:

> Sometimes names block our thinking. I would prefer that people inform me that they have a child that does not talk instead of saying to me their child is dysphasic. People apparently like to use technical terms. I have received letters from doctors and psychologists telling me that "we are referring a child to you who has strephosymbolia." I would prefer that they tell me that "the boy has been in school two years, and he hasn't yet learned to read even though his intelligence is above average."[2]

He suggested the term "learning disabilities" as being both accurate and comprehensive in describing children who have failed to learn because of problems in "language, speech, reading and associated communication skills needed for social interaction."[3] The term was adopted and the Association for Children with Learning Disabilities was formed.

The field of learning disabilities has had considerable impact on the changing philosophy in special education. The learning-disabled child has been traditionally defined as one who fails to learn in spite of normal intelligence and the absence of any significant sensory, emotional, or physical problems. Because the problems children experience are so diverse, the field has become a synthesis of work done in other disciplines. Much of the early work was done by educators interested in children who presented rather specific problems. Strauss and Lehtinan[4] and Cruickshank[5] worked with brain-damaged children who showed excessively high activity levels; Kephart,[6] Getman[7] and Barsh[8] identified children with perceptual motor problems; Wepman[9] and Myklebust[10] moved from a concern for deaf and aphasic children to concern for those who had normal hearing but showed some of the same receptive and expressive problems in language development. Their mutual concern for the various groups of children with subtle, often hidden, handicaps created the initial contributions to the growing body of knowledge in the field.

A commonly recognized characteristic of a child with a learning disability is the fact that s/he shows specific strengths as well as weaknesses, and the assessment of skills has become an important part of the prescriptive process. The determination of an individual learning profile and the selection of appropriate teaching strategies and accommodations is the closest any discipline has come to a rational basis on which to individualize instruction.

As assessment techniques and approaches to remediation were developed and refined, prescriptive teaching became recognized as appropriate for all children with special needs, not just for the child who fits the traditional criteria of learning disabled. In the mid-sixties, Bateman[11] and Wiseman[12] suggested that the "learning disability approach" would lead to better and more individualized education for children classified as mentally retarded. Further support of this point of view was provided by Sabatino[13] in a study of children in San Diego County who had been identified as educable mentally retarded (ERM) or learning disabled. He found that although the ERM children as a group showed more generalized cognitive deficits, they demonstrated the same kinds of perceptual-motor, receptive, and expressive language disorders (and wide variances of them within each child) as the children serviced in learning disability programs. The notion that special education for retarded children implied a special curriculum had to be abandoned in the face of the mounting evidence that no one curriculum could meet the needs of children with such diverse learning profiles. Indeed, as special educators, psychologists, and teachers began to take a closer look at children who had been classified as educable mentally retarded, they discovered that some of them were not retarded at all, but experienced significant learning disabilities. Because the initial evaluation was inadequate or occurred before appropriate assessment techniques were available, the children had been inaccurately diagnosed.

The rather obvious need to alter approaches to identifying, describing, and educating retarded children prompted a closer look at other populations of children. It became apparent that educators had been programming children according to the most obvious handicaps (i.e., vision, audition, behavior, etc.) and failing to recognize commonalities across groups. Schools are now learning to do a better job for *all* children who have trouble learning. The major focus has become the educational need rather than a medical grouping like blindness or deafness. Therefore, this text will deal with a broader definition of a learning problem as one that includes any factor—physical, intellectual, or social-emotional—within the mild-to-moderate range, that interferes with learning to read.

SPECIAL EDUCATION AND MAINSTREAMING

In the beginning, the trend was for special and separate education for children fitting into specific categories of handicapping conditions, usually defined according to the medical label. Since special education began with the more dramatic, less frequently seen handicaps, the validity of the approach seemed obvious. As work began with other groups like the educable mentally retarded and the learning disabled, the trend continued. By the late sixties, researchers in special education began to look at the effect of segregation on the academic, social, and emotional growth of children assigned to special classes. Although some of the research seems equivocal, many studies[14,15,16] supported the notion that special and separate education did not serve the needs of children in

The teacher's willingness to use and adapt a variety of teaching devices allows many handicapped children an opportunity to participate in a regular education program. (Photo courtesy of Borg-Warner Educational Corp.)

the mild-to-moderate range of retardation. In 1968 an article by Dunn[17] had a remarkable impact on the field of special education. Dunn questioned the efficacy of special-class placement for children in the mild-to-moderate range of retardation and noted the overrepresentation of minority children in such classes. Although Dunn did not advocate the complete abolition of special-class programs, but rather the more careful selection of the population, practitioners reacted as though he had. School systems and state departments of education began altering policies and procedures for educating retarded children. Since the research available for review at that time was not without problems—i.e., sampling biases, poor assessment devices, and the lack of longitudinal data—the abrupt shift in direction may have been premature. The decade of the seventies has seen a rather frantic effort to formulate a sound and sensible system of services for children with problems in learning. Out of these efforts, the concept of "mainstreaming" evolved.

"Mainstreaming" is a term applied to the process of integrating handicapped children into regular educational programs. The rationale for doing this is largely the result of the efficacy studies in retardation already cited. In a way, these studies exploded the myth that special teachers had been trained to do special things, and that these special things allowed a retarded child to succeed better than s/he would if left in the regular classroom. The field of special education had for some time encouraged the "fix-the-kid" philosophy, which is based on the notion that a child found lacking in learning ability for one reason or another should be sent off to a class for children of a similar condition to be repaired for return or retained until the end. The truth of the matter is, as Deno suggests, "whatever distinctions can be made between regular education and special education are mainly organizational and not substantive, that is, the manner in which learning experiences need to be presented is the main basis of distinction. Whatever learning principles apply to handicapped children apply to all children and end goals are the same in their most essential aspects." [18]

Mainstreaming does not mean, however, that all handicapped children should be assigned to regular classrooms on a full-time basis. On the contrary, it recognizes the need for a broad range of services and encourages the assignment of a child to the "least restrictive" program. The least restrictive program means the one that is closest to the regular education program but still allows the child all the help s/he needs. For some children the degree of special need is such that a substantially separate program is the most appropriate. However, the philosophy of mainstreaming implies flexibility of placement so that children may be moved along the continuum of services from the most to the least restrictive programs.

Figure 2.1 represents the cascade system of special educational services as described by Deno.[19] The largest number of children are in the regular education class and may not require direct services from support personnel. These are children with mild problems who can profit from participating in a regular classroom with consultation provided to the teacher.

Level II represents the children who are removed from the classroom for a certain percentage of the school day for special training provided in an alternative setting. Level III is designed for children with significant difficulties in learning which require that the largest percentage of their time be spent in a special educational setting. Levels IV and V involve full-time placement in substantially separate programs. Levels VI and VII represent the placement of children outside the school district. As can be seen here, the regular classroom teacher can be involved with children in Levels I, II, and III. This includes problems across the mild-to-moderate range of a handicapping condition.

When one considers the job of teaching such a variety of children how to read, it becomes apparent that the limits of the curriculum must be extended to include a wider range of skill levels than would normally be attended to at a given grade level. In fact, the magic associated with "grade-level achievement" had best be dispelled altogether. It serves no child's needs, least of all those at either end of the normal curve. Teachers need to become adept at identifying where the child is on the continuum of reading skills, how s/he learns best, and what to do to get him/her to the next level. This is not the exclusive responsibility of the classroom teacher, however, and no teacher should be made to feel that it is. It should be a team effort, with adequate support provided for the teacher as well as for the child.

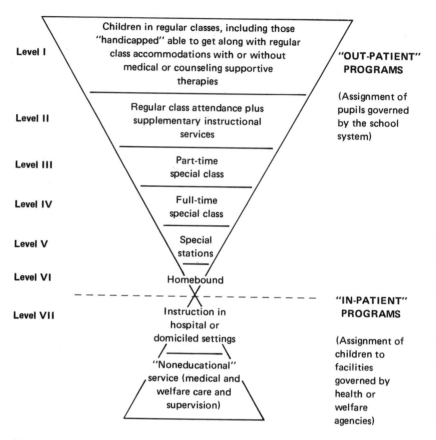

Level I — Children in regular classes, including those "handicapped" able to get along with regular class accommodations with or without medical or counseling supportive therapies

Level II — Regular class attendance plus supplementary instructional services

Level III — Part-time special class

Level IV — Full-time special class

Level V — Special stations

Level VI — Homebound

Level VII — Instruction in hospital or domiciled settings

"Noneducational" service (medical and welfare care and supervision)

"OUT-PATIENT" PROGRAMS

(Assignment of pupils governed by the school system)

"IN-PATIENT" PROGRAMS

(Assignment of children to facilities governed by health or welfare agencies)

(From Deno, E., "Special Education as Developmental Capital," Exceptional Children 37, 1970, p. 235)

Figure 2.1   *The cascade system of special education service. The tapered design indicates the considerable difference in the numbers involved at the different levels and calls attention to the fact that the system serves as a diagnostic filter. The most specialized facilities are likely to be needed by the fewest children on a long-term basis. This organizational model can be applied to development of special education services for all types of disability.*

THE CONCEPT OF DISCREPANCY

The concept of discrepancy is basic to an understanding of approaches to the identification and treatment of learning problems. One of the characteristics observed across the various categories of children with learning difficulties is the uneven rate of growth in the various physical, intellectual, and social-emotional skill areas. Although normal child growth and development allows for variation in rate, the child with a learning handicap may show disparity beyond normal expectation.may have decided strengths and weaknesses. When one looks at intellectual potential (as measured by an individual intelligence test), academic chievement, and interpersonal skills, one sees a marked disparity between estimations of his/her potential for intellectual development and his/her actual achievement. Figure 2.2 shows the learning profile of eight-year-old Bobby, a third-grade boy who has been identified as an underachiever. At the beginning of third grade, this boy was eight years

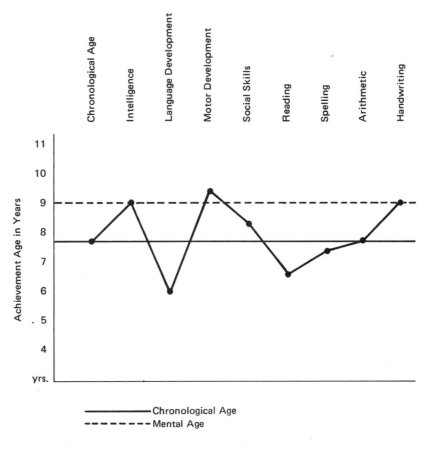

Figure 2.2   Learning profile.

and two months in age. The psychologist reported a mental age of nine years and one month, placing him in the "bright normal" range of intelligence. On a motor inventory used by the physical education department, he performed better than the average nine-year-old. A teacher rating scale and other sociometric measures judged his social skills to be a bit better than those of most children his age. On an achievement test given in the fall, his overall performance was at the middle of the first grade in reading and the middle of the second grade in spelling. In arithmetic he was right at grade level, although computation skills were a bit unreliable. His handwriting was considered excellent for a third grader. An analysis of Bobby's learning profile shows him to be well above average in intellectual and motor development, developing nicely in social-emotional and mathematical skills, but considerably below his mental age and grade level in speech and language, reading, and spelling. Compared with the average third grader, he is a year and a half below grade level in reading. Considering his mental ability, he is two and a half years below his expected achievement level. This child would be considered an excellent referral for a multidisciplinary evaluation to identify the factors interfering with the achievement of his full potential.

The concept of discrepancy does not apply to all children with problems in learning. There are children with generalized cognitive deficits in whom patterns of growth in various areas are relatively even. That is, all areas of skill development lag behind those of age mates to about the same degree. These children will be discussed in Chapter 7 on The Slow Learner.

SOURCES OF PROBLEMS

Children fail to learn for a variety of reasons and combinations of reasons. Some of these reasons are understood; some are not. Frierson[20] lists fifteen points of view for looking at the sources of learning problems (see Fig. 2.3). One group of factors are medically based, involving such things as inborn traits (genetic), brain damage, and certain biochemical and nutritional problems that interfere with the efficient functioning of the brain. Another group of factors are more psychological in nature and include the concept of a developmental lag, emotional distress, and motivation. Sociocultural and educational issues are also seen as the source of significant underachievement and, indeed, one must always ask the question, "If he can't do it, has he ever been taught?"

The whys and wherefores of learning problems are complex and highly technical issues that are the subject of numerous projects of research and investigation. The returns are just beginning to come in. It is already obvious that there is no single cause and that the search for the specific culprit for any given child may well be futile. Knowing that a child's problem is due to a genetic factor, lack of oxygen at birth, or a developmental lag will tell little, if anything, about teaching him how to read. Teachers still have to look at the

Table 2.1   Learning abilities/disabilities—five frames of reference.

Point of viewing	Diagnostic procedure	Descriptive terms	Information
1. Anatomical (genetic)	Family history	Dyslexic Hyperkinetic	Critchley Bannatyne
2. Behavioral (environmental)	Behavior analysis	Nonattending Disruptive	Skinner Haring Lindsley
3. Biochemical (nutritional)	Metabolic evaluation	Hypoglycemia Anemia	Cott Kretch Davis
4. Constitutional (pathological)	CNS testing EEG	Brain damaged Hyperactive	Orton Strauss Cruickshank
5. Developmental (maturational)	Case history	Language-delayed "Late bloomer"	Gesell DeHirsch Piaget
6. Educational (situational)	Achievement testing Diagnostic teaching	Underachiever Educationally handicapped	Holt Page
7. Functional (inferential)	Motor-perceptual testing "Symptoms"	Cerebral dysfunction Perceptually handicapped	Clements Frostig Kephart
8. Psychoanalytical (clinical)	Projectives Structured interview Psychoanalysis	Phobic Depressed Anxious	Bettelheim Axline
9. Modal (integrational)	Optometric exam Audiogram	Visile Audile	Getman Rosner Wepman Kirshner
10. Model (linguistic)	Language evaluation I.T.P.A.	Auditory decoding deficit	Osgood Kirk Bateman
11. Neurological (physiological)	Neurological exam	Disorganized Confused dominance	Delacato Fay Ertl
12. Personal (aneodotal)	Graphoanalysis Autobiography Drawings	Unmotivated Creative Dependent	Guilford Goodenough

13. Psychological (statistical)	Psychometric profile W.I.S.C. Rating Scale	High Risk	Wechsler Myklebust
14. Sociocultural (experiential)	Social maturity scale Community analysis	Culturally different Bilingual confusion	Meade, etc. Riessman Doll
15. Speculative (miscellaneous)		Sociopathic Delinquent	Krippner Poremba

(From Frierson, E.C., "Edward C. Frierson," in Kauffman, J., and Hallahan, D., Teaching Children with Learning Disabilities, Columbus, Ohio, Charles E. Merrill Publishing Company, 1976)

child's reading skills and decide what to do about them. One hopes that the diagnosticians are sufficiently trained and sensitive to these issues to make good use of medical personnel when needed. Good medical management is essential to the progress of some children. For the child with low blood sugar, a graham cracker provided at ten in the morning may be a simple (and inexpensive) treatment for his inattention and poor performance. For the child with a hearing loss, good medical treatment and amplification, if necessary, can reduce the effects of the loss on academic achievement. One should never underestimate the value of good medical supervision of children with learning problems. However, the medical diagnosis may not define the variables of educational management.

TYPES OF LEARNING PROBLEMS

The ultimate objective of any educational assessment procedure is to discover what a child can and cannot do in order to decide what to do about it. One of the first and most important steps in the process is careful observation of behaviors. The classroom teacher must be actively involved at this level since the conditions surrounding the failure in learning are of vital importance to the formulation of rational conclusions as to interfering factors.[21] Learning failure does not occur in a vacuum. It occurs within specific subject areas within a regular classroom. It is important for any assessment team to consider why a classroom teacher has determined that a child is not learning up to his capacity and that something should be done about it.

Cognitive Deficits

Many authors writing in the field of special education have their own system for identifying the kinds of problems children can have, and the impact of these problems on learning. Kephart[22] and Barsch[23] identify clusters of perceptual-motor skills which they see as key factors to the acquisition of skills in other areas. Frostig[24] has done significant work with children who experience difficulty in various aspects of learning. She has made a significant contribution to the understanding of problems in visual perception. Chalfant and Scheffelin,[25] Johnson and Myklebust,[26] Kirk, McCarthy, and Kirk[27] deal with language classifications. Hewett[28] has focused on the impact of maladaptive behavior (or emotional disturbance) on the learning process.

A hierarchy of learning   Johnson and Mykelbust have the broadest view of the hierarchy of skills involved in the learning and language process. They include sensory deficits as a problem area, which, for the purposes of later discussion of the problems of the low-vision and hearing-impaired child, makes their model particularly appropriate for consideration. Overall, the Johnson and Myklebust approach can be considered developmental, as it recognizes that learning occurs in a natural, sequential, and lawful fashion. They suggest that the following systems must be fully operational if efficient learning is to take place.

Sensation—Sensation is the most basic level of behavior in the learning hierarchy and refers to reception of sensory information. Problems at this level include problems in vision and hearing.

Perception—Perception involves the ability of the central nervous system to organize incoming sensory information in such a way as to distinguish the unique features, relate it to past perceptions, and come to an awareness of what it is.

Imagery—Imagery is a type of memory function that involves the ability to recall information already received and perceived. The ability to reauditorize and revisualize are skills at the level of imagery.

Symbolization—Symbolic behavior refers to the ability to represent experience. It can be done in a verbal form (words) and a nonverbal form (pictures). Skills at this level include understanding and using speech, reading, and writing.

Conceptualization—Conceptualization is the highest level of learning. It involves the ability to abstract and categorize. It includes those mental processes involved in problem solving.

For example, in reading the simple word *cat,* the child must see the symbols and be able to hear the sounds most commonly associated with these symbols. At the perceptual level, he must recognize the symbols as letters of the alphabet and/or recognize the entire word as a meaning-bearing unit. Imagery allows the child to recall the visual form and sound features of the word as a language unit. Through symbolization the child is able to attach the word to the object (animal) that the word represents. At the highest level, the child attaches meaning and significance to *cat*, recognizing it as a different animal from *dog*, associating it with a feline family that includes lions and other animals, and attaching the appropriate meaning when s/he encounters it in such expressions as "cool cat."

These processes are hierarchical, so a disruption at one level disrupts what lies above it. If a child has a hearing loss, the basic input is incomplete. This incomplete information leads to incorrect perceptions that are later recalled for comparison with new perceptions. These defective perceptions contribute to problems in symbolization, since vital pieces of a symbol may be missing or altered.

This construct can be very useful in the assessment process. When a child is referred for evaluation, the first area to be checked should be hearing and vision, since these areas are basic to higher-level functioning. Skills in perception and memory should be assessed for possible contributions to problems in language. At the symbolic level, auditory (listening and speaking) language skills should be evaluated in order to determine whether there is a sufficient auditory language base to support success in visual language (reading and writing). Conceptual development depends on the efficient functioning of lower levels. Some children show difficulties at certain levels and in only one modality. For example, Bobby (Fig. 2.2) has very good skills at all levels of learning when he is asked to deal with visual information. However, due to a hearing loss, he has considerable difficulty processing auditory information. Children who are below average in intellectual ability may simply be slower in dealing with skills at every level. Other children in this group may show specific deficits that interfere with their reaching their fullest potential.

Psychosocial Problems

In addition to the cognitive deficits that have been described, children with learning problems exhibit certain social and emotional problems that almost invariably accompany, if not contribute to, poor performance. It is very difficult to fail for any length of time and not have it affect one's feeling of self-worth. The emotional overlay to problems in learning is considerable. It is sometimes difficult to separate the primary from the secondary disability areas, since there is considerable interplay among them. If Bobby in the third grade has had three years of failure in reading and spelling, has been teased in school and scolded at home, his self-image may have suffered enough to affect his relationships with peers and adults. He may be on his way to becoming a troubled young man.

Several authors[29,30,31] have attempted to categorize behaviors that call attention to the child as being disturbed, and those that appear to accompany problems in learning. This is a difficult task, since the two groups cannot be separated neatly. For the clinician, the problem is compounded because teachers have different tolerance levels for certain behavior and may respond differently. Ms. Jones may view Mary as hyperactive because she has a short attention span, is frequently out of her seat, and is continually tapping her foot. Ms. Smith may vary assignments frequently enough so that Mary's attention is held, and "out-of-seat" behavior may not be unusual in her more flexibly arranged classroom.

In the absence of any well-documented list of emotional and social correlates to learning problems, it may be useful to note the few that tend to appear on numerous lists.[32] While these characteristics are often mentioned, they cannot be considered descriptive only of children with learning problems. Children who are achieving well may also exhibit one or more of these traits. The list is by no means complete, but simply representative of the behaviors most often attributed to children with difficulties in learning.

1. Activity level

A common complaint of teachers of children with learning problems relates to the child's activity level. An overly active child is very difficult to live with (for parents as well as teachers) and is apt to be referred for help ahead of the child who is hypoactive or lethargic. Both children require attention because such problems are sometimes physiological and may respond to medical treatment.

2. Attention

Lack of attention and distractibility are frequently seen in children with learning and/or behavior problems. For some of these children, the presence of a highly stimulating auditory (the band rehearsing in the gym) or visual (wall decorations, drapes, etc.) environment reduces their ability to attend to a specific task.

3. Interpersonal relationships

Getting along with people can be very difficult for a child with a learning problem. Some children learn to expect failure and dread the ridicule that comes with it. They prefer to withdraw from social interaction in order to reduce the risk of being found deficient. For children who experience memory deficits, remembering the rules of games is difficult. They make mistakes and are called cheats. Children with language problems have difficulty making their thoughts coherent enough to make sense. Some, if they cannot control the world verbally, tend to want to push it into place. Others give up and withdraw.

4. Maturity

Growing toward independence and self-reliance can be a slow process for children with learning problems. There is often a tendency on the part of adults to do for them what they cannot do for themselves. There is an even greater tendency on the part of the children to look to adults for help. Fostering a proper balance of assistance and self-reliance is an important contribution adults can make to children with problems in learning.

While these behaviors do not, in themselves, constitute learning problems, they are often observed in children who have difficulty learning and can be disruptive influences on learning experiences the children are expected to engage in.

Motor Problems

Children can experience problems in gross and fine motor development and both can lead to difficulties in school. Since it is difficult to consider motor skills as separate from the visual skills that help to guide movement, most of the literature on the subject considers visual-motor skills as a single entity. Children with problems coordinating visual-motor movements are observed to be awkward in such motor skills as climbing, running, playing ball, etc. In the fine motor area, problems are likely to affect handwriting, cutting, buttoning, tying, etc. Whatever the problem, it is apt to be obvious to anybody who observes the child going about his business at home and in school. Failure in this area has considerable social repercussions.

In addition to problems in visual-motor skills, some children show motor problems due to muscle weakness. This can affect a rather specific part of the body like one arm and hand or a leg. Although the eyes and hand may work in coordination with one another, the muscles are weak and the effort to use the hand may be considerable. The results are often fatigue when writing, unusually light pencil marks, and even illegible writing. Another problem may occur as a result of the child's inability to recall motor plans for movements. For example, the child may recognize the word *cat* and be able to spell it from memory, but may be unable to write the word independently because s/he is unable to remember the motor plan for forming a *c* and an *a* and a *t*. These children also have trouble learning the motor plans for drawing geometric shapes, opening bottles, tying shoes, etc.

Many school systems offer remedial physical education programs for children who experience difficulty with gross motor skills. Not only do these children become more efficient users of their bodies, but they often feel so much more comfortable moving through space.

PRESCRIPTIVE TEACHING

Mainstreaming involves more than the physical placement of children in the regular classroom. It involves a new approach to instruction, one that may be termed a "diagnostic and prescriptive approach." The objective of this approach is to provide the child with an instructional program based on a thorough assessment of his/her individual needs as a learner. That is, teaching techniques are chosen according to the determination of how the child learns. What the child can do is as important to this process as what s/he cannot do. In order to move the child ahead, good educational planning provides for the full use of those skills that are intact as well as for the remediation of those that are deficient.

Assessment

A formal assessment procedure is often done by a team of specialists and revolves around their mutual concern for identifying factors that interfere with learning. The psychologist is concerned with intellectual functioning and personality variables. The special educator focuses on identifying the nature of the learning problems and the implications for instruction. The reading specialist evaluates various reading skills through diagnostic testing. There may be other specialists involved as well (e.g., speech therapist, guidance counselor, etc.). In the early days of special education, there was a tendency on the part of assessment teams to use a prescribed battery of formal tests. Such a procedure lacked precision and often led to overassessment. Today the trend is to use careful observation of behavior by the classroom teacher and appropriate specialists in order to formulate initial hypotheses on which to base test selection. If a child has performed in the superior range on the Performance Scale of The Wechsler Intelligence Scale for Children (WISC), there is little point in putting him/her through numerous measures of visual motor skills, particularly if observation of his/her performance in school has shown him/her to be quite good at sports, art, handwriting, etc. An assessment should be done for the purpose of answering specific questions relative to observed difficulties.

There is no single way to evaluate children with learning problems. Informal or formal assessment techniques can be used. Specialists may use either or both in assembling the necessary information on which to base educational-management decisions.

Informal

Informal assessment includes such devices as skill inventories, informal language samples, and structured observation sheets. Many of these informal procedures can be used by classroom teachers, who may find the information useful in identifying areas of difficulty as well as providing necessary preliminary input for a multidisciplinary evaluation.

Formal

Formal assessment includes the use of certain criterion-referenced or norm-referenced tests for the purpose of measuring intelligence; achievement in academic areas; perceptual, motor, and memory skills; and language development. There are hundreds of such instruments available. The most commonly used in each area will be presented within the chapters dealing with specific learning problems.

The final exercise in the evaluation process is the synthesis of assessment information and the determination of priorities for special services. For the child with multiple problems, such a determination is essential if s/he is to escape being pulled in several directions at once. In school systems where numerous special services are available, there is always the danger of providing too much at one time. It is the responsibility of the team to decide what the most critical needs are, provide for those, and defer the rest. When this is not done, children can spend most of their time bouncing from one specialist to another, leaving very little time for the regular curriculum. In this situation, the classroom teacher becomes the social secretary whose job it is to see that the child arrives at appointments on time and in possession of whatever equipment is required. Too much is perhaps as bad as not enough.

Synthesis of assessment information can be tricky and requires very competent and secure professionals. When conflicting observations are noted, it is important that the decision be the result of careful review and resolution so that the disposition of the case does not reflect the point of view of the strongest member of the team.

Educational Planning

The assessment procedure is useful only to the extent that it contributes to the formulation of an appropriate educational plan. Prescriptive teaching has been uniquely identified with the field of learning disabilities and the concept has been adapted to educational management of children with numerous other learning problems. As a process, it can easily be used for children across the entire range of intellectual endowment, from the profoundly retarded to the gifted, and with the variety of specific problems in learning; i.e., hearing loss, language disabilities, behavior disorders, etc. It has much to offer the classroom teacher and specialists concerned with children who are not learning to read as easily as they should. Public Law 94–142 requires that an "individualized education program" (IEP) be written for each handicapped child. The major components of such a process are as follows:

1. Areas of strength

It is essential to identify those areas in which the child has proved to be an efficient learner. It is from the knowledge of the child's success that we gain the clues as to what s/he is capable of learning and under what conditions. For Bobby, the child represented in Figure 2.2, an evaluation revealed that he had considerable strength in gross and fine motor skills. Although his spelling was not at grade level and he showed considerable difficulty applying phonic rules, he could recall visual patterns rather well, and his ability to re-visualize accounted for his moderate success in spelling. In reading, the words he had been able to learn were acquired through a sight method.

2. Areas of deficit

The variety of assessment techniques used by the evaluation team has been primarily aimed at discovering what systems are "go" and which ones are "out of whack." Knowing precisely what the difficulties are and, hopefully, finding sufficient evidence of why they are occurring, assist in the determination of what to do about them. For Bobby, the evaluation revealed significant difficulty in his ability to discriminate, sequence, synthesize, and recall auditory information. The nurse's records showed a history of middle-ear infections during the preschool years, which have left him with a mild-to-moderate hearing loss. His articulation had improved but was not yet adequate for his age. His vocabulary had improved considerably. What these problems meant for his reading and spelling was an inefficient system for dealing with word attack skills. He had trouble discriminating similar-sounding consonants like *p* and *b*, *t* and *d*, *k* and *g,* and was totally unable to distinguish long and short vowels. He could not reliably recall the sequence of sounds in words in order to attach the visual code, and blending more than three phonemes at a time was impossible. He also had trouble following directions.

3. Teaching strategies that failed

All too often an assessment procedure leads to some very hard looking at what is wrong with the child. An equally important factor is looking at what approaches have failed the child. Learning is an interactive process of learner and materials to be learned. Some strategies are more favorable to a learner than others. At some point in the evaluation process, consideration must be given to the match between the learner and the strategies used. There are some children who have no learning disability but possess a strong cognitive preference for certain styles of learning. If such a child is forced into a reading approach that is unfavorable to him/her, progress may be slower than it would have been given an approach more appropriate to his/her own unique system.

4. Learning style

Learning style is an interesting construct that has received considerable attention in recent years. It recognizes that people learn in different ways. Researchers have looked at such variables as divergent and convergent thinking,[33] impulsivity and reflectivity,[34] auditory and visual learning.[35] Most likely, our own unique learning styles are the result of the interaction of many variables and cannot be defined in terms of a single dichotomy. While lacking a precise definition of the variables involved in styles of learning, a good assessment team learns a great deal about how a given child organizes him/herself for learning—what works and what doesn't. Since this information is absolutely essential to a classroom teacher responsible for curriculum modifications and instructional alternatives, a clear statement of conditions that facilitate learning for the child should be included in every summary of assessments.

5. Remedial strategies

An educational plan should include annual goals as well as specific short term objectives for each area of deficit identified as requiring special training. The individual specialists responsible for providing the services list these objectives in written form so that all professionals, as well as parents, are aware of the sequence of skills to be developed. The value of the entire process is very closely related to the quality of *written* communication. Merely assigning a child to a special education or remedial reading program leaves the objectives of such a treatment plan totally undefined. A precisely written plan allows for the careful monitoring of progress by all concerned, including the child himself. Appendix A suggests a useful format for such a remedial plan. The instructional objectives are stated in understandable and measurable terms. The materials and techniques appropriate to the child and the objectives to be met are specified. The date of mastery and a comment on the success of the strategies are provided. Over the course of a school year, as objectives are met and new ones are written, a complete history of the therapeutic process is maintained. A change in personnel does not require anything more than a quick reevaluation of achievement levels. Trial and error (along with considerable wear and tear on the child) can be avoided because of the careful documentation of what worked and what didn't.

6. Classroom accommodation

One of the most important and frequently omitted components of an educational plan is the portion written with and for the classroom teacher. Accommodation is not remediation. When significant remedial education is prescribed, it is clearly the responsibility of the appropriate specialists to provide it. A classroom teacher cannot be expected to accomplish all of the specialized training a child may need in order to improve his efficiency in learning. Accommodation involves those modifications of regular class curriculum and alterations in the learning environment which provide the child with the maximum opportunity for success. Although the identification of appropriate strategies should be the result of the team effort, implementation is clearly the responsibility of the classroom teacher. Accommodation involves using approaches that will allow the child to use his strengths. For Bobby, the teacher can use a reading approach that capitalizes on his ability to remember word configuration and make use of picture clues. S/he can provide a quiet place to work, reduce the number of work sheets to be accomplished in a day, and allow a friend to help him recall oral directions. The teacher can also use materials provided by a remedial specialist that will reinforce skills being trained in the support program. Bobby's special training focuses on strengthening his auditory skills so that he can begin to deal with phonics.

7. Ancillary services

In addition to the educational services to be provided, an evaluation team may need to consider services within the community that can supplement what the school is able to provide. Family counseling centers, social service agencies responsible for child welfare, medical clinics, and recreational programs are examples of the kinds of services that can be mobilized on behalf of children with special needs.

Once all the necessary information has been assembled and the educational planning has been completed, any prescribed remedial services and curriculum modifications within the regular classroom can begin. The process of assessment and remediation is circular. Both the regular and the special educational components should be closely coordinated and monitored so that alterations can be made on the basis of continual evaluation of the child's academic progress. At any point the cycle may be reentered in order to make the necessary corrections in the educational plan. (See Appendix A)

APPROACHES TO REMEDIATION

Since problems can occur at various levels of learning, in different curriculum areas, in social-emotional and motor as well as cognitive development, the treatments implied and applied must be equally diverse. A variety of techniques and approaches have been developed over the years to teach children in specific problem areas. Several strategies will be presented here. There are many others and new ones are continually appearing. What is conspicuously absent is the type of longitudinal research that would help us determine the effectiveness of various treatments for specific problems.

Perceptual-Motor Training

Throughout the study and investigation of child growth and development, there seems to be a theoretical consensus on the importance of the early developmental period when the child learns to integrate incoming sensory information with motor activity. In the early months of a child's life, all senses are fully exercised. For example, the baby explores the ball placed within his grasp by manipulating it so that s/he may see it from all sides; shaking it to hear the bell in the center; chewing on it to confirm its roundness, hardness, and absence of taste. The baby's early exploration of the world is primarily through the coordination of sensory inputs with motor responses. There are certain theorists and educators who see this learning as basic to all other learning. Of these, Barsch and Kephart were influenced by their work with Strauss, whose background in Gestalt psychology, which stresses the importance of perception in learning, led him to the development of techniques to improve the efficiency of the various perceptual motor systems.

Barsch   The essence of Barsch's work is the Movigenics Curriculum[36] based on eight constructs relating to the importance of movement patterns to learning efficiency. This approach provides a sequence of planned activities that promote the child's awareness of himself in space and flexibility in movement as he learns to shift from one movement pattern to another. The prescribed environment calls for an open-space room with all windows occluded to allow for complete control of light. Indeed, some activities, like tracking an object with a flashlight, are conducted in total darkness. Stimuli are presented in a systematic fashion—i.e., first to one eye, then to the other eye, and then to both eyes—while the child is in various body positions.

Kephart
Kephart also stresses the importance of perceptual-motor abilities to success in development in other areas. His theory is primarily derived from a notion of feedback mechanisms in perception based on the influence of muscular response on the alteration of basic input. As the child engages in motor activity involving visual information such as copying a word on a piece of paper, his motor responses are guided by what his eyes are telling him. Like those of Barsch, Kephart's techniques (described in his widely read book *The Slow Learner in the Classroom*[37]) include the use of walking rails, tracing, chalkboard activities, etc.

Getman
Getman,[38] an optometrist, has developed a training method for visual-motor skills. In a book called *The Physiology of Readiness,*[39] he outlines practical strategies for helping children develop visual-perceptual and visual-motor skills. These activities include gross motor exercises to promote the coordination of head, arms, and legs, as well as eye-hand exercises to develop fine motor skills. Getman also stresses the importance of training in eye movements in order to develop efficiency in fixating and tracking.

There have been numerous studies of the usefulness of the various approaches in promoting growth in perception, school readiness, and reading. Reviews of the research[40,41] suggest that although there may be benefit to motor development, there is no demonstrated relationship between perceptual-motor training and academic achievement. This is not meant to imply that these techniques are of no value whatsoever. They can do a great deal to improve the child's motor coordination. To a child, riding a two-wheeler or connecting a bat with a ball may rate an even higher priority than learning to read.

Special Reading Approaches

Since many children with learning problems have difficulty in learning to read, specialized techniques have been developed for use with such children. Two of the most widely used of these approaches are the Gillingham and Stillman Program[42] and the techniques developed by Fernald.[43] Both approaches were the result of work with disabled learners at a time when few people understood their problems.

Gillingham and Stillman
Gillingham worked extensively with Orton[44] in his monumental work with children who failed to learn. Since Orton's chief concern was with the development of language skills, reading was the focus of much of their work.

The Gillingham and Stillman program is a highly structured synthetic phonics (sounding and blending) approach designed for children in the third grade and above. The program progresses through a sequence of increasingly complex phonetic exercises beginning with individual letters, then words, sentences, and paragraphs. The exercises use six combinations of visual, auditory, and kinesthetic modalities. For example, the child might be given the word (auditory) and asked to identify it on a card (visual), or he might be given a word on a card (visual) and asked to say it (auditory).

Fernald

Fernald's[45] approach is equally structured and multisensory. However, it does not involve phonics. It is essentially a look-say approach but with certain features of language experience. At first, words the child chooses are written in large letters on cards. The child traces the letters with his/her finger while saying each letter. S/he then uses words in sentences and later in a story. Fernald believed that children should learn to read what they have written themselves. Tracing is an important feature of the technique. Later, the tracing is dropped and the child is expected to reproduce the word from memory. Eventually, the child is encouraged to read whatever he likes. Words he does not know are taught through a see it, say it, write it approach.

Although there have been objections to the highly structured nature of both approaches and to the fact that no materials or workbooks are provided, some children have succeeded with Gillingham or Fernald techniques when other methods have failed.

Assessment Models

Certain remedial approaches have developed as a direct result of an assessment instrument. Instructional techniques are designed for the specific skills measured on the test.

The Developmental Test of Visual Perception[46] identifies five specific functions of visual perception: 1) eye-motor coordination, 2) figure-ground, 3) form constancy, 4) position in space, and 5) spatial relations. *The Frostig Program for the Development of Visual Perception*[47] is designed to develop skill in each of these areas. It includes the basic program and intermediate and advanced pictures and patterns.

The Illinois Test of Psycholinguistic Abilities (ITPA)[27] attempts to measure certain language skills we consider important to the development of speaking and reading. (The ITPA is presented in detail in Chapter 6). Several remedial programs have been developed around the basic-skill areas involved in the test. Programs such as the MWM Program[48] and the GOAL program,[49] as well as techniques outlined by Bush and Giles[50] and Karnes,[51] are all based on the ITPA model.

One of the basic premises on which the above tests were developed is that some children process information better in one modality than another.

For example, a child may understand auditory information more easily than visual information. Another premise is that weaker modalities must and can be strengthened through training. The value of such training has been questioned in its relationship to academic learning. In a review of numerous studies using the Frostig program, Spache[52] concluded that the program did not produce significant gains in reading. However, he does suggest that there are studies which used other approaches to perceptual training that produced good results.[53] The ITPA-based programs have been similarly questioned.[54,55] At this point, it is difficult to know where the field stands on the issue of psycholinguistic training. Minskoff[56] points out that the review of research fails to take into account the variation in the samples used, the content of the treatment, and the experimental design. She suggests that, so far, the research has been inadequate and inconclusive.

Approaches to remediation are many and varied. In addition to the perceptual-motor and special reading approaches and the remedial strategies based on specific lists, there are special techniques based on environmental control systems, language development, and applied behavioral analysis. The attempt here has been to present a sample of approaches. Other reading-related approaches and techniques will be described more fully in later chapters on specific areas of learning problems.

In the absence of the kind of research that would allow a proper evaluation of the effectiveness of specific training programs, it seems safe to assume that no one strategy or method is appropriate for all children who experience difficulty in learning. Minskoff[57] states that the major question to be answered by the research is, "What types of remedial methods are most effective with what kinds of learning disabled children under what conditions?" In the area of reading, this is particularly crucial due to the great importance of that skill and the fact that there are so many methods from which to choose.

CONCLUSION

In the past, special education usually meant separate-school or separate-class placement for children with learning problems. In examining the effectiveness of various models for working with special-needs children, it has become apparent that many of these children with mild-to-moderate needs may be better served within the regular classroom. The idea of "mainstreaming" mildly handicapped children into regular classrooms has required the formulation of a team approach to the educational management of such children. Out of this come a new role and responsibilities for the classroom teacher.

The clinical point of view, based on a multidisciplinary evaluation of the child, has been introduced to education. It requires the coordination and collaboration of professionals from a variety of fields; central to this collaborative effort is the classroom teacher.

Out of the general area of special education has emerged the field of learning disabilities, which has had considerable impact on both regular and special education. It has introduced the variable of the child as a learner into the educational decision-making process. It suggests that instruction be individualized according to the child's own unique style of learning and not according to programmatic features of certain materials. This implies the use of a broad range of options, with techniques selected on the basis of a careful assessment of learner needs, interests, and motivation. This approach can be applied to children who would not be included in the learning disability category according to the traditional definition, which excludes children with sensory deficits (hearing and vision), mental retardation, physical handicaps, and behavior disorders. These children need the same form of rational decision making and careful monitoring that children with less involved problems require. They may, in fact, need it more.

Since most children with learning problems have trouble learning how to read, the question is often asked, "Is it a reading problem or a learning problem?" For many children it is not an either/or proposition. It is both. For example, the child's problem in processing auditory information makes it difficult for him/her to discriminate sounds, sequence sounds in words, and recall which sound goes with a particular symbol. Bobby (Fig. 2.2) had all these problems. A hearing loss affected his ability to receive the incoming sounds clearly, so that he had difficulty organizing them into correct perceptions. This affected his speech, his basic vocabulary, and his reading. The speech therapist worked on his auditory discrimination skills in order to help him learn to identify the correct auditory features of different sounds so he could learn to produce them correctly. She helped him become aware of the differences in the way various sounds feel and look in the mouth so he could make use of the tactile, kinesthetic, and visual clues to strengthen the weaker auditory ones. Learning to monitor his own speech helped him to monitor the speech of others and become a better listener. Learning to speak better did not help him to read better. He still required special help in reading so he could learn to apply his more efficient auditory skills to phonics. No one person or discipline could insure Bobby's success in school. It required a team effort of classroom teacher, speech and language therapist, and reading specialist. Bobby's reading difficulty could not be viewed as a separate entity, but rather as a part of the Gestalt of his language disabilities. When reading is taught in isolation, the results may be disappointing.

As teachers struggle to find new and better ways to help children learn and love to read, they find more and more people involved in getting the job done. There are classroom aides, parent volunteers, reading specialists, special educators, counselors, speech and language therapists, and others. The issue should never become one of "whose child is he" but rather "what can we do together?" Our resources and expertise are growing. Now we must learn to blend them in a variety of ways to help a variety of children.

ACTIVITIES FOR PRESERVICE TEACHERS

1. Review the laws in your state that pertain to the education of children with special needs. How is the school-age child defined? Under what conditions can a child be placed in a special educational setting? What types of services are required?

2. What was the best thing that ever happened to you in school? What was the worst? Share your experiences with classmates. Was it easier to identify the best or the worst experience? What were some of the common features of the unhappy experiences that were recalled by the group? Of the happy experiences?

3. Review some of the literature on learning styles. How many different variables have been identified? What additional ones can you think of that might be important to consider when making educational decisions? Describe yourself as a learner.

4. Assume you are a classroom teacher who has agreed to accept two mildly retarded children into your class for 40 percent of the school day. A group of parents of children in your class protest that their own children will suffer because you will have to give too much time to the new children, and they will slow the progress of the group as a whole. What would you tell them?

5. This chapter has suggested that there may be an emotional overlay to learning problems. For Bobby, described throughout the chapter, what would you expect to be his difficulties in developing good peer relationships?

ACTIVITIES FOR IN-SERVICE TEACHERS

1. Review four behavior rating scales or checklists for identifying children with learning problems. What categories of behavior does each tap? What additional categories would you like to include? Use one of the scales on five children in your class.

2. Choose a child in a middle grade who has a severe reading problem. Review his folder in order to identify the sources of the data. What decisions were made on the basis of this information? What additional information do you feel is missing? What services have been provided? Has the degree of underachievement in reading been reduced?

3. Identify the various specialists who operate in your building. How are referrals made? What kinds of assessments are done? What do you judge to be the quality of the written reports? Do you have a copy of any educational plans developed for children with special needs in your own classroom? What procedural changes would you recommend for your school?

4. React to the statement, "In the educational life of the child, the classroom teacher is the star performer; the specialists are the supporting cast."

5. Develop a learning profile on a child in your class who shows decided strengths and weaknesses. Carefully observe his behavior in a variety of situations. Identify any behaviors that appear atypical for his age level. What concerns you most about this child? Prepare an anecdotal record that could be used to accompany a referral request.

NOTES

1. S. Kirk, "Behavioral Diagnosis and Remediation of Learning Disabilities" in *Exceptional Children: Educational Resources and Perspectives*, S. Kirk and F. Lord (Boston: Houghton Mifflin Co., 1974) p. 76.
2. Ibid., p. 78.
3. Ibid.
4. A. Strauss and L. Lehtinan, *Psychopathology and Education of the Brain Injured Child* (New York: Greene & Stratton, 1947).
5. W. Cruickshank et al., *A Teaching Method for Brain Injured and Hyperactive Children* (Syracuse, New York: Syracuse University Press, 1961).
6. N. Kephart, *The Slow Learner in the Classroom* (Columbus, Ohio: Charles E. Merrill, 1971).
7. G. Getman, "The Visuomotor Complex in the Acquisition of Learning Skills," in *Learning Disorders,* ed. J. Hellmuth, Vol. I (Seattle, Washington: Special Child Publications, 1965).
8. R. Barsch, *A Movigenic Curriculum,* Bulletin No. 25, 1965, Wisconsin State Dept. of Public Instruction, Wisconsin Bureau of Handicapped Children.
9. J. Wepman et al., "Studies in Aphasia: Background and Theoretical Formulations," *Journal of Speech and Hearing Disorders* 25 (1960) : 323–332.
10. H. Myklebust, *Auditory Disorders in Children: A Manual for Differential Diagnosis* (New York: Greene & Stratton, 1954).
11. B. Bateman, "Implications of a Learning Disability Approach for Teaching Educable Retardates," *Mental Retardation* 5 (1967) : 23–25.
12. D. Wiseman, "A Classroom Procedure for Identifying and Remediating Language Problems, *Mental Retardation* 3 (1965) : 20–24.
13. D. Sabatino and D. L. Hayden, "Information Processing Behaviors Related to Learning Disabilities and Educable Mental Retardation," *Exceptional Children* 37 (1970): 21–29.
14. H. Goldstein, J. W. Moss, and L. Jordan, "The Efficacy of Special Class Training

on the Development of Mentally Retarded Children," U.S. Office of Education Cooperative Research Project No. 619 (Urbana: University of Illinois, 1965).

15. J. H. Meyerowitz, "Self-derogations in Young Retardates and Special Class Placement," *Child Development* 33 (1962): 443–451.

16. E. Welch, "The Effects of Segregated and Partially Integrated School Programs on Self Concept and Academic Achievement of Educable Mental Retardates" (Ph.D. diss., University of Denver, 1965).

17. L. M. Dunn, "Special Education for the Mildly Retarded—Is Much of It Justifiable?" *Exceptional Children* 35 (1968): 5–22.

18. E. Deno, "Strategies for Improvement of Educational Opportunities for Handicapped Children: Suggestions for Exploitation of EPDA Potential," in *Exceptional Children in Regular Classrooms*, M. Reynolds and M. Davis (University of Minnesota, Dept. of Audio-Visual Extension, 2037 University Ave. S. F., Minneapolis, Minn.).

19. Ibid., p. 15.

20. E. C. Frierson, in *Teaching Children with Learning Disabilities*, J. Kauffman and D. Hallahan (Columbus, Ohio: Charles E. Merrill, 1976), pp. 142–143.

21. There are numerous lists of characteristics of children with learning problems. Since these characteristics tend to be diverse across the broad range of handicapping conditions, these will be discussed within each chapter.

22. Kephart, *Slow Learner*.

23. Barsch, *Movigenic Curriculum*.

24. M. Frostig, D. Lefiver, and J. Whittlesey, *The Marianne Frostig Developmental Test of Visual Perception* (Palo Alto, Calif.: Consulting Psychology Press, Inc., 1964).

25. J. C. Chalfant and M. Scheffelin, *Central Processing Dysfunctions in Children: A Review of Research.* (National Institute of Neurological Diseases and Stroke Monographs, 1969, No. 9).

26. D. Johnson and H. Myklebust, *Learning Disabilities, Educational Principles and Practices* (New York: Greene & Stratton, 1967).

27. S. A. Kirk, J. J. McCarthy, and W. Kirk, *Examiners Manual, Illinois Test of Psycholinguistic Abilities* (Urbana, Ill.: University Press, 1968).

28. F. M. Hewett, *The Emotionally Disturbed Child in the Classroom* (Boston: Allyn and Bacon, Inc., 1969).

29. W. Gardner, *Children with Learning and Behavior Problems* (Boston: Allyn and Bacon, 1974).

30. H. D. Quay, "Dimensions of Problem Behavior and Educational Programming," in *Children Against Schools*, ed. P. Graubard (Chicago: Follett, 1969).

31. L. Wright, "Conduct problems or learning disability?" *Journal of Special Education* 8 (1974): 331–336.

32. There are numerous behavior checklists and scales for classroom teachers, such as:
J. Schleichkorn, "The teacher and recognition of problems in children," *Journal of Learning Disabilities* 5 (1972): 55–56.
H. Myklebust, *Pupil Behavior Rating Scale* (New York: Greene & Stratton, 1971).
H. Quay, W. Morse, and R. Cutler, "Personality patterns of pupils in special classes for the emotionally disturbed," *Exceptional Children* 32 (1966): 297–301.
M. Serio, "Know the child to teach the child," *Academic Therapy* V (3) (1970).

33. H. A. Witkin, R. B. Dyk, H. F. Faterson, D. R. Goodenough, and S. A. Karp,

Psychological Differentiation: Studies of Development (New York: John Wiley, 1962).

34. J. Kagar, "Impulsive and Reflective Children: Significance of Conceptual Tempo," in *Learning and the Educational Process*, ed. J. Krunibolz (Chicago: Rand McNally, 1965), pp. 133–161.

35. B. Bateman, "Reading: A Controversial View—Research and Rationale" in *Learning Disabilities*, L. Tarnopol (Springfield, Ill.: Charles C Thomas, (1969).

36. Barsch, *Movigenic Curriculum*.

37. Kephart, *Slow Learner*.

38. Getman, "Visuomotor Complex."

39. G. Getman, *The Physiology of Readiness: An Action Program for the Development of Perception for Children* (Minneapolis, Minn.: Programs to Accelerate School Success, 1964).

40. D. Hammill, L. Goodman, and J. L. Weiderholt, "Visual Motor Processes: Can We Train Them?" *Reading Teacher* 27 (1974): 469–480.

41. G. Spache, *Investigating the Issues of Reading Disabilities* (Boston: Allyn and Bacon, 1976): pp. 407–408.

42. A Gillingham and B. Stillman, *Remedial Training for Children with Specific Disability in Reading, Spelling and Penmanship,* 7th ed. (Cambridge, Mass.: Educators Publishing Service, 1965).

43. G. Fernald, *Remedial Techniques in Basic School Subjects* (New York: McGraw-Hill, 1943).

44. S. Orton, *Reading, Writing and Speech Problems in Children* (New York: Norton, 1937).

45. Fernald, *Remedial Techniques*.

46. Frostig, Lefiver, and Whittlesley, *Frostig Developmental Test*.

47. M. Frostig, and D. Horne, *The Frostig Program for the Development of Visual Perception* (Chicago, Ill.: Follett, 1964).

48. E. H. Minskoff, D. E. Wiseman, and J. Minskoff, *The MWM Program of Developing Language Abilities* (Ridgefield, N.J.: Educational Performance Associates, 1973).

49. M. Karnes, *GOAL Program Language Development Game* (Springfield, Mass.: Milton Bradley, 1972).

50. W. J. Bush, and M. Giles, *Aids to Psycholinguistic Teaching* (Columbus, Ohio: Merrill, 1969).

51. M. Karnes, *Helping Young Children Develop Language Skills: A Book of Activities* (Washington, D.C.: Council for Exceptional Children, 1968).

52. Spache, *Reading Disabilities*, p. 421.

53. Ibid., p. 413.

54. D. Hammill and S. Larsen, "The Effectiveness of Psycholinguistic Training," *Exceptional Children* 41 (1974): 3–15.

55. P. Newcomer and D. Hammill, "ITPA and Academic Achievement: A Survey," *Reading Teacher* 28 (1975): 731–741.

56. E. Minskoff, "Research in the Efficacy of Remediating Psycholinguistic Disabilities: Critique and Recommendations," in *Psycholinguistics in the Schools*, P. Newcomer and D. Hammill (Columbus, Ohio: Charles E. Merrill Co., 1976), p. 103.

57. Ibid., p. 110.

REFERENCES

1. Charles, C. M. *Individualizing Instruction*. St. Louis: The C. V. Moseley Company, 1976.

2. Gearheart, B. R., and Weishahn, M. W. *The Handicapped Child in the Regular Classroom*. St. Louis: The C. V. Mosby Company, 1976.

3. Hammill, D., and Bartel, N. *Teaching Children with Learning and Behavior Problems, Second Edition*. Boston: Allyn and Bacon, Inc., 1978.

4. Hewett, F. M., and Forness, S. R. *Education of Exceptional Learners*. 2d ed. Boston: Allyn and Bacon, Inc., 1977.

5. Johnson, S. W., and Morasky, R. L. *Learning Disabilities*. Boston: Allyn and Bacon, Inc., 1977.

6. Kirk, S. A., and Lord, F. E. *Exceptional Children: Educational Resources and Perspectives*. Boston: Houghton Mifflin Company, 1974.

7. Sperry, L. *Learning Performance and Individual Differences*. Glenview, Ill.: Scott, Foresman and Company, 1972.

8. Stephens, T. M. *Teaching Skills to Children with Learning and Behavior Disorders*. Columbus, Ohio: Charles E. Merrill Publishing Company, 1977.

3

Assessment

Preview

Assessment is a vital dimension of reading instruction for the special needs child. It involves both evaluation and diagnosis through formal and informal means. Assessment is not an end in itself. Rather, it is a means of gathering information that will help provide as complete and accurate a picture of the child as possible. Assessment is always directed toward instructional improvement. A wide variety of assessment instruments and techniques can be used for different purposes. Assessment remains, however, essentially a human function and while the input of specialists can be expected, the classroom teacher retains a central role in the assessment process.

The starting point in reading instruction for the special-needs child, as it should be for all children, is assessment. Assessment is the process of measuring or estimating the amount or status of a given quality. In reading, it includes *evaluation* to determine the child's level of achievement or ability, and *diagnosis* to identify areas of strength and weakness and to determine the underlying causes of the child's reading disability. Both formal and informal assessment is a necessary part of instruction in reading.

EVALUATION

Evaluation has long been an important part of education and an integral dimension of instruction. In essence, evaluation is the process by which we determine the extent to which our objectives have been met. In most schools, standardized evaluation measures are administered annually and evaluation is a daily concern of the teacher in the classroom.

Formal Evaluation

Formal evaluation measures the status or level of achievement in reading of a pupil, a class, or a school. It provides information, not only for judging the level of achievement of individual children, but also for continuing evaluation of the adequacy of instructional programs.

Formal evaluation in reading involves the use of norm-referenced and criterion-referenced measures.

Norm-referenced tests

Norm-referenced tests have been used for many years to measure pupil achievement in reading. In norm-referenced tests, a child's performance is judged on the basis of comparison with the average performance of pupils at the same grade level, age, and/or similar educational experience. "The point of reference is not the task per se, but the performance in some more general reference group . . . the norm of acceptable performance is set by group comparison." [1] These tests yield scores that are translated into an age- or grade-level equivalent that is reported to the year and month, and they indicate a child's percentile or stanine ranking relative to his/her performance in comparison with others in some well-defined comparison or norm group.

Norm-referenced standardized tests commonly used to measure reading achievement are the *SRA Assessment Survey* (T.1,)* the *Iowa Test of Basic Skills* (T.2), the *Stanford Achievement Tests* (T.3), the *Cooperative Progress Tests* (T.4), the *Metropolitan Achievement Tests* (T.5), and the *Sequential Tests of Educational Progress* (T.6). These six tests by no means constitute an exhaustive list. There are many other standardized instruments that are widely used with a similar purpose and format. In measuring pupils' abilities in major

*Test note reference.

areas of reading—word skills and comprehension—these tests are designed to assess a level of achievement.

Although norm-referenced measures do provide evaluative information about pupils and programs, they have long been the object of criticism and concern. These tests differ in purpose, length, difficulty, and components of the reading process that they measure. Factors of guessing, the appropriateness of material for culturally different children, the methods of measurement used, and the accuracy of the tests in measuring children's functional reading ability are the questions and limitations most often identified. Perhaps the most serious concern is the overreliance of many teachers, administrators, and parents on the test results.

There are particular dangers in relying on norm-referenced measures in judging the reading ability of the special-needs child. The personal, social, and learning characteristics of special-needs children often make them untypical of the "mythical average" population upon which standardization norms are set. Special-needs children frequently defy comparison according to the relative standards used in norm-referenced measures. Such instruments typically have strict time limits for completing the test, and since children with learning problems may have difficulty finishing the test in the prescribed time, scores will be depressed. Language impaired children may not have the vocabulary required in such tests, and children with visual-motor disorders may have trouble getting the line in the right spot, thus making answers that are accurate appear to be wrong. This is why, in many schools, norm-referenced testing as an indication of reading achievement is giving way to criterion-referenced tests.

Criterion-referenced tests

Criterion-referenced tests are measures designed to assess children's mastery of specific skills. Rather than comparing a child's performance to that of others in a standardized sample, criterion-referenced tests focus on the child's ability to reach a stated level of performance on the skills that the test measures. These tests yield results in terms of specific performance standards. Explicit instructional objectives are stated—for example, "The child will identify the vowel sounds in a list of words with 90 percent accuracy" or "The child will identify the topic sentence that summarizes the main idea of a paragraph with 80 percent accuracy"—and assessment is conducted to determine whether the child can meet the objective at the criterion set. Performance is related to the standard or criterion for success. Because criterion-referenced tests are less concerned with whether the child is better or worse than other children, they provide less global measures, and they are more closely related to a child's skill development in reading.

Formal criterion-referenced tests are part of management systems (described later in Chapter 9, pp. 305–308). Other criterion-referenced achievement tests in reading that are available for use in the classroom are *Customized Objective Monitoring Service* (T.7), *Diagnosis: An Instructional Aid Series* (T.8), and *Prescriptive Reading Inventory* (T.9). Item banks for the construction of criterion-referenced tests are also available from some test publishers, from the Educational Testing Service, and from the university of California.

Though criterion-referenced tests are being more widely accepted and used as objective-based evaluation measures in schools, these tests have received their share of criticism. The overisolation of reading skills, the rigid sequencing of these skills, the arbitrary level of the criteria set, and the whole notion of what constitutes "mastery" are the questions and criticisms most often raised.

Criterion-referenced tests offer one major advantage over norm-referenced measures: they provide a breakdown that conventional achievement tests do not. For the special-needs child (as for all children), it's far more important to know in which area(s) the child needs help than to know what his/her reading level is. The more precise information that criterion-referenced measures provide can be the foundation for more precise instructional planning based on the child's needs in reading.

In considering the merits of norm-referenced and criterion-referenced tests, it's important to remember that they are similar in that both are evaluative devices for measuring pupil achievement in reading. Both can be used by the same teacher in the same classroom with the same children. They are different, however, in that one provides a comparative rating whereas the other provides an objective-based measure of mastery. Normed tests are survey tests, while criterion-referenced tests are more diagnostic in nature. The former give a "bigger picture" of the highs and lows of the class and how the child compares with other pupils across the nation, while the latter focus specifically on reading skills. Both are appropriate as formal evaluative devices and both will likely continue to be used as long as formal evaluation remains part of the educational process in our schools.

Informal Evaluation

Most teachers don't need the grade-level score of a standardized reading achievement test or a formal report that "the child has achieved 80 percent mastery in determining cause-effect relationships" in order to judge a child's reading ability. Listening to the child as s/he reads a story in *One To Grow On* is a way of judging his/her level of reading achievement, and asking the child comprehension questions about what s/he has read provides indications of his/her state of skill development. These informal evaluative measures are important parts of the assessment process. In fact, most of the evaluation that we teachers conduct is of an informal nature.

Informal evaluation is a daily activity of teachers. It takes many forms. It occurs when we observe children in functional reading situations. It includes the brief tests we administer to check children's mastery in word recognition, decoding, and comprehension skills. It's a focus of the basal reader and supplementary worksheets we administer for skill development. And it involves quick checks we make on an individual basis. In short, informal assessment involves anything we do in the classroom to help us answer the question, "Howz 'e doin'?"

The informal devices that teachers use at different times during the school week, while they may not be as efficient as a one-shot standardized achievement test, are often more valid, dependable, and complete. Informal assessment involves a variety of measures administered over periods of time.

The steps suggested for informal assessment are:

1. decide exactly what information is desired and what this means in terms of observable behavior; 2. devise new or adapt existing test items, materials, or situations to sample the behavior to be evaluated; 3. keep a record of the behavior evoked in the test situation; 4. analyze the obtained information; 5. make judgments as to how the information fits the total picture and how it fills the gap for which it was intended.[2]

For the special-needs child in the regular classroom, informal evaluation is especially important. It supplements and confirms data that are available from norm-referenced or criterion-referenced tests. Individual educational plans designed for the special-needs child require constant evaluation to determine whether instructional objectives have been met. Informal evaluation thus becomes an integral part of the instructional process each day.

Evaluation is important, but knowing the child's reading level or level of mastery in reading skills is not enough. This is why evaluation quickly leads to the second step in the assessment process—diagnosis.

DIAGNOSIS

The nature of the diagnostic process is suggested by the origin of the word diagnosis itself. Diagnosis is derived from two Greek word parts: *dia-*, meaning "completely or thoroughly," and *-gnosis,* meaning "knowledge." Diagnosis is an information-gathering process that aims at providing as complete and accurate a picture of the child as possible in order that sound instructional decisions can be made.

Qualities of Diagnosis

Diagnosis has (or should have) three essential qualities. It should be *complete,* and *continuous,* and it should *lead to instructional improvement.* These three characteristics encapsulate the nature of the diagnostic process.

Complete

The learner is a complex human organism. The many facets of his/her personality and experience affect the way in which s/he learns. Since many factors influence a child's learning to read, thorough diagnosis demands a multidimensional assessment, one that extends well beyond the child's reading ability and skills alone. And since learning to read is a complex process involving a constellation of skills, even reading diagnosis in the narrow sense demands an intensive and detailed assessment.

Avoiding one-dimensional assessment

Too often, the assessment of children tends to be one-dimensional. That is, we look at one aspect of learning and base decisions on a single designation. We say, for example, that the child is a "slow learner" or that s/he is "hyperactive," without exploring further areas of learning strength or specifying areas of weakness in reading skills. Thorough diagnosis involves looking beyond the obvious to explore many avenues through which effective instruction can be provided.

Amount of diagnosis necessary

The exact amount of diagnosis that should be conducted is often difficult to determine. For children without special learning problems, schools typically do too little diagnosis. When children arrive in school in September, their reading program has already been determined, the books have been ordered, and the teacher is ready to go. This is roughly analogous to the physician who has already prescribed the drugs even before s/he has seen the patient. For the child with special needs, such a situation is usually not the case. The more serious the child's learning needs are, the more extensive the diagnosis is likely to be. This is understandable. To use a medical analogy again, the person with a health problem usually requires more extensive diagnosis than a healthier counterpart. The healthy individual normally has a physical checkup once a year, just as the child making normal progress has a standardized reading achievement "checkup" once a year. Extensive diagnosis is required to determine the nature and cause of a person's health problem, just as more extensive assessment is typically required for the child with special learning needs.

Critics often maintain that children are tested so much that too little time is left for treatment. Perhaps a key word in this respect is *efficiency*. Diagnosis should go as far as it needs to go and no farther. If one considers assessment as a continuous process that always leads to instructional improvement, then the ongoing nature of the process will provide for completeness.

Success oriented

Diagnosis is success oriented as well as failure oriented; that is, it seeks to identify areas of ability as well as disability. Very often, diagnostic assessments are based on failure; for example, a child is required to read a list of words until s/he makes seven errors; or read paragraphs with increasing levels of difficulty until s/he can no longer understand what s/he reads. Errors are recorded and areas of weakness identified, with the major focus on the problems that the child has. Success and areas of strength should not be ignored, however. Analyzing where the child does well, in addition to his/her areas of weakness, can provide very valuable information as an aid in planning instruction.

Open-minded

Assessment should be objective and open-minded. It accepts no biases before the fact. It is broad enough to accept all possible causes for learning difficulty, not just those the diagnostician believes to be the most promising. A few years ago, we visited a school and asked the learning specialist, "What provisions are being made for children who have weak auditory abilities but are strong visual learners?" "There are no such children here," we were told. "All our pupils have good auditory skills." The specialist's view was colored by the belief that phonics was *the* treatment strategy for all children with problems in learning to read. Honesty in exploring all areas and accepting even those causes of difficulty that we may be uncomfortable with are essential to complete diagnosis.

Team approach

Because assessment needs to explore many areas of potential strengths and weaknesses, a team approach is usually required. Specialists with expertise in many disciplines are needed to search out information that will have a bearing on the child's problem. Because the results of complete assessment will be multifaceted, the diagnostic process must also involve the tying together, integration, and translation of all the diagnostic information in such a way that practical carry-over from assessment to instruction will result. By its nature, diagnosis involves assessment in many different areas. Often, there is a tendency to fractionate diagnostic information into areas that may be minute. Complete assessment demands putting all the information together again. Assessment is more than a list of test scores. Rather, it involves the interpretation and application of information that can be directly translated into treatment.

Continuous

Diagnosis is a continuous process. It's not a one-shot gathering of information for the purpose of making permanent instructional decisions. Rather, it is ongoing and involves the constant formulation, testing, and reformulation of hypotheses about the child and his learning. The process is often time-consuming and difficult.

In essence, diagnosis may be described as a calculated guessing game. That is, it samples a certain set of behaviors at a given point in time. We test and assess, and our conclusions give us a picture of the child and where s/he stands. But as new conditions prevail and as new learnings are acquired, the picture often changes. For example, the statement, "Johnny does not know the sound-symbol relationships in the initial blends *bl, br*, and *cl*," may be an accurate assessment. However, as Johnny masters these phonetic elements, the statement is no longer accurate. Instructional decisions always need to be flexible and open to revision on the basis of further information.

Assessment is predicated on patterns of repeated evidence. There's a danger in the practice of basing decisions on one-time performance. We know that a child's physical or mental condition at the time of testing, the interaction with the examiner, the nature of the instrument itself, and a host of other factors can influence a child's performance on a test. Without continued, repeated evidence, diagnostic information can give a distorted and inaccurate picture of the child, a picture that can lead to inappropriate instructional decisions.

Instructional improvement

Assessment is not an end in itself. All the diagnostic information in the world, no matter how accurate, is of little use unless it leads to some instructional benefits for the child. It doesn't do much good to know that the child has a low IQ score, for example, unless the pace of instruction is adapted to his/her rate of learning, or that the child can't discriminate between long and short vowel sounds in words unless a prescriptive program is provided. Assessment is useful only when something is done about it. By its nature, diagnosis should provide direct suggestions for the implementation of a plan of specific treatment strategies. Diagnosis and remediation are inseparable, in that diagnosis is directly related to corrective and remedial strategies.

The diagnostic component of the assessment process may be represented as a spiral. (See Figure 3.1) It starts with determining children's instructional needs. This information is used as the basis for setting instructional objectives, which lead, in turn, to instructional activities. Evaluation to determine the effectiveness of teaching activities follows. The evaluative information provides additional data from which further diagnostic leads can be drawn, and suggests the need for further assessment. Like a spiral, the process comes back to the same beginning point but at a higher level. The process is a continuing one for the special needs child in the regular classroom.

Dimensions of Diagnosis

Assessment is a multifaceted process. The types of diagnosis appropriate for the special-needs child in the regular classroom are an important dimension of the process. Also important are the devices available for use in schools.

Types of diagnosis

Bond and Tinker[3] identify two major types of diagnosis: etiological and therapeutic. Special educators typically refer to these types of diagnosis as "the medical model" and "the diagnostic-prescriptive model," and add a third approach, "the task analysis model."

Etiological diagnosis

"Etiological diagnosis is concerned with finding out what caused a child to get into difficulty." This is the type of case study assessment that looks at the child's records and previous experiences in an attempt to uncover the causes for reading difficulties. Etiological diagnosis (or the medical model) typically extends beyond reading ability and skills. For example, it may reveal that a child was absent for long periods of time or suffered temporary hearing loss due to an ear infection in the first grade, or that the child was placed in six different (and unhappy) foster homes during the first two years of school.

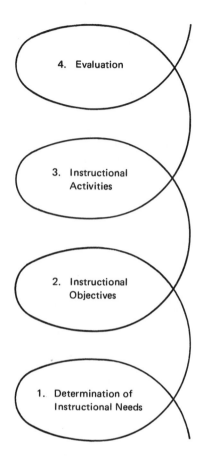

Figure 3.1   *The spiral of assessment.*

These factors may account for some of the child's reading and related learning problems in later school years.

Etiological diagnosis can help the teacher get to the root of a child's problem so that the difficulty can be better understood. However, the effect of such assessment may not be immediately applicable to teaching. It may be useful, for example, for the teacher to know that Joey is brain damaged, but an EEG won't tell the teacher which reading approach to use or how to plan phonics instruction or how to handle Joey in a reading group. Knowing the "why" of a problem is valuable to the extent that something can be done about it.

Therapeutic diagnosis   Therapeutic diagnosis is more immediate. It "is concerned with the conditions that are now present in the child in order to give direction to a program of reeducation." Therapeutic diagnosis involves the child and his/her present environment to determine how current factors may influence progress and/or problems in learning to read. It deals with such constant factors as the child's cognitive strengths and weaknesses, skill weaknesses, and other factors immediately relevant in planning a program of remediation in reading. It is typically more analytical and focuses more closely on the skills involved in reading. It may involve, for example, determining whether the child has difficulty in dealing with vowel diphthongs and digraphs in decoding words, or whether new words should be introduced primarily through the auditory or visual modality to facilitate mastery.

Task analysis   Task analysis is a third model that can be used in addition to the medical model (etiological) and the diagnostic-prescriptive model (therapeutic). This approach involves taking a task apart to determine what is required for the successful performance of that task. "Two ways to think about task analysis are (1) the *modality-processing* approach, to evaluate and analyze the processing abilities that underlie the learning task; and (2) the *skills-sequence* approach, to analyze and evaluate what is to be learned—the task itself. The first analyzes the child, while the second analyzes the content to be learned."[4]

The modality-processing approach to task analysis aims at answering the essential question, "What kind of processing demands does this activity place on a child?" It considers the cognitive demands as the child takes in information, the system used to process this information, the type of response required, and other factors inherent in the completion of the task. The focus is constantly diagnostic, because "the ability to analyze the informational processing demands of tasks we present to students allows us to systematically detect trends of weaknesses and strengths in their ability to meet our demands."[5]

The skills-sequence approach to task analysis is directed more toward the task itself in an attempt to answer the essential question, "What subskills are required for the successful completion of the task?" It identifies component parts of tasks in order to identify where potential breakdowns occur. Isolating these component parts can allow the teacher to make very specific diagnostic decisions on where the child may be having a problem.

In addition to being a major model of an approach to diagnosis, task analysis is an appropriate daily diagnostic activity for the classroom teacher, and it will be treated as such later in this chapter.

For the special-needs child, each type of diagnosis is appropriate. Etiological diagnosis helps the teacher understand some of the background and underlying causes of reading difficulties the child may be having. Therapeutic diagnosis provides the very specific information that is essential in prescriptively planning for reading instruction. The on-the-spot information provided by task analysis is feedback the teacher can use every day in the classroom.

Diagnostic Devices

There are many reasons why children have difficulties in learning to read: physical factors, perceptual problems, social-emotional problems, intellectual limitations, and educational or instructional factors. Any or all of these can interrelate in a complex fashion to create problems for the child in his/her attempts at reading. A major purpose of diagnosis is to determine possible sources of children's problems so that barriers to progress can be removed and appropriate instruction delivered. The diversity in the causes and nature of children's reading disabilities demands a corresponding diversity in assessment devices.

As with evaluation, both formal and informal diagnostic assessment is appropriate for the special-needs child in the regular classroom. Diagnosis should include a balance of diagnostic approaches that will reflect the many potential causes of problems in learning to read.

Observation

Under normal school circumstances, observation should precede the onset of testing and should be prerequisite to the selection of tests. In some cases, once it has been determined that a child may have a learning problem, a total preselected battery of tests covering all areas of functioning is immediately administered. In these cases, there's danger of overassessment, because even with a balanced testing battery, many of the tests may be inappropriate for a given child. Careful observation prior to testing allows for the judicious choice of assessment instruments and saves a lot of unnecessary wear and tear on the child.

The classroom teacher plays a key role in the observation process. Teacher observation can be the first indication that something is wrong. For example, it may be observed that the child is turning his head as s/he reads, squinting or rubbing his/her eyes while looking at the printed page, or losing the place frequently. A check may reveal that the child's vision has been measured by a Snellen chart, a device that does not adequately measure near-point vision required in reading nor the ability of the child to move his/her eyes together along a line of print. In this case, the teacher's observation is the basis for referral for more accurate and detailed visual screening as part of the diagnostic process.

Observation following testing

Observation is no less important following formal testing. It is a means of checking the validity of assessment information gathered on the child. A reportedly diagnosed "auditory discrimination problem" can be confirmed by monitoring the child's performance on auditory discrimination exercises in the classroom. The source of the "problem" for the child may have been the dialect of the tester, extraneous noises present in the testing situation or the fact that the child did not understand directions for the test ("which words rhyme," for example). Children are often more at ease in the familiar surroundings of the classroom than in a formal testing situation, so the way they use language in the classroom may be different from the language capacity they demonstrate on a test. Thus, classroom language performance can be used as a check on the reported results of language tests. Patterns of errors observed in classroom situations can also confirm the accuracy of conclusions drawn from assessment.

Ongoing observation can add to the information gathered through more formal assessment. Each time a child reads aloud in a reading group or in a one-to-one conference with the teacher, opportunities exist for observing strengths and weaknesses in functional reading. Watching how the child attacks a new word, noting the types of errors made in comprehension, or watching how the child goes about forming letters during handwriting can supplement and complement diagnostic data gathered through formal assessment.

Knowing what to look for

Intelligent observation requires knowing what to look for. Observation does little good unless useful information results. For example, most teachers are familiar with children who hurriedly guess at unknown words versus those who painfully attack new words on a sound-by-sound basis. These contrasting types of behaviors may indicate an impulsive versus reflective learning style that needs to be addressed in teaching. As another example, the teacher observed that while first graders were playing with the telephone in the play area, Tommy could remember seven unrelated digits in sequence (i.e., he could recall and repeat an unfamiliar telephone number like 437-8926 when he was asked to dial it), yet he couldn't recognize the numbers on the dial when he tried to "make a call." This observation gave the teacher some awareness of Tommy's strong auditory memory but weak visual recognition skills, a piece of information that could be applied when introducing new words to Tommy. Conclusions based on observation need to be as tentative as those drawn from formal testing, but they can provide instructional leads that are useful in helping children develop reading skills.

In addition to being a source of information, observation provides a personalized dimension to the diagnostic process, an indication of behavior that no objective instrument can provide by itself. Observation puts assessment in a human perspective and extends the process beyond a cold objective list of test scores—it is a way of humanizing the diagnostic process.

Formal testing

In addition to observation, formal tests provide a data base for instructional decisions about the child. The range of tests available for assessment includes physical examinations, IQ measures, standardized achievement tests, group diagnostic reading tests, individual reading diagnostic batteries, specific reading subskills tests, and tests of perceptual/learning abilities. Although not all of these assessment instruments would be administered to all children, these tests provide potential sources of information about the child's abilities and disabilities in areas directly related to reading. These are the types of tests that the classroom teacher has to deal with, either as a diagnostician or as a consumer of diagnostic information.

Physical examinations

Since reading is in part a physical activity, physical factors are a focus of assessment. In addition to generally good health that will allow the child to cope effectively with the normal demands of learning, the ability to see and hear are important in learning to read. Visual deficiencies like the inability of the eyes to focus on a visual symbol, nearsightedness, farsightedness, ocular motor problems, and other visual deficiencies have been linked to reading disabilities as causative factors. Along with the Snellen Eye Chart, which has been used as a visual screening device for a long time, instruments like the School Vision Tester (Bausch and Lomb), the Visual Survey Telebinocular (Keystone), and the Reading Eye Camera (Educational Development Laboratories) are used to diagnose visual problems related to reading. Learning to read also requires accurate hearing, the ability to hear sounds of different degrees of loudness and varying levels of pitch. Auditory acuity is most often formally measured by a pure-tone audiometer.

Physical problems can be a root cause of reading problems, so the results of visual and auditory screening are important dimensions of the diagnostic data base for the special-needs child in the regular classroom.

IQ tests

The diagnostic significance of intelligence tests has long been a subject of question and debate. Nevertheless, IQ tests are typically part of the normal assessment process for the child with special needs, and the results of these tests are part of the data available to the classroom teacher. The usefulness of this information rests more in the analysis of the information than in the overall test score itself. For example, a child's performance on the vocabulary subtests on the *Stanford-Binet* (T.10) or the *WISC* (T.11) can indicate language ability (or disability) that may affect learning to read, or a low performance on the Block Design or Object Assembly subtests of the *WISC* may indicate visual motor problems that need to be addressed in the classroom. This type of information has diagnostic value, because when it is "teased out" from the child's overall performance, it can suggest instructional leads for the classroom teacher.

Standardized reading achievement tests

Achievement tests are not, by nature, diagnostic. Nevertheless, through interpretation and analysis of results, these tests can often provide general assessment information. If, for example, the child achieves a grade score of 3.2 on word meaning and 1.2 on paragraph meaning on a norm-referenced achievement test, the teacher has some indication that comprehension may be the source of the reading problem. In the reverse case (grade scores of 1.2 on word meaning and 3.2 on paragraph meaning subtests), the teacher recognizes that decoding and vocabulary problems may need to be a major focus of instruction.

Criterion-referenced achievement tests typically provide information that is readily translatable for diagnostic purposes. A criterion-referenced test provides a breakdown of strengths and weaknesses in reading skills areas, and thus provides an indication of areas of instructional needs that is an important part of the diagnostic process.

Reading readiness test

Not to be forgotten in the category of standardized tests are reading readiness tests. The instructional requirements of the special-needs child in the regular classroom may be so basic that formal assessment of readiness factors (auditory and visual discrimination, listening comprehension, auditory and visual memory, word knowledge, and knowledge of letter names and sounds) may need to be part of diagnosis. Besides, a pupil's performance on various subtests of a reading readiness test may provide specific instructional leads for the teacher. For example, this child's scores on the subtests of the *Gates-MacGinitie Readiness Test* (see box) indicates more than adequate auditory processing abilities but weaknesses in visual and visual-motor areas. Thus, from a diagnostic point of view, the test scores suggest the need for a phonics approach to beginning reading instruction.

Subtest	Stanine
Listening Comprehension	8
Auditory Discrimination	9
Visual Discrimination	5
Following Directions	8
Letter Recognition	7
Visual-Motor Coordination	3
Auditory Blending	9

Frequently used reading readiness tests are the *Murphy-Durrell Reading Readiness Analysis* (T.12), the *Gates-MacGinitie Reading Readiness Test* (T.13), the *Lee-Clark Reading Readiness Test* (T.14), and the *Metropolitan*

Readiness Test (T.15). Though designed primarily as evaluative measures, these readiness tests can be the source of very valuable diagnostic information on the special-needs child.

Group diagnostic reading tests

Instruments like the *Stanford Diagnostic Reading Test* (T.16) and the *Doren Diagnostic Reading Test* (T.17) can be administered to large groups of children at once, yet they include a more detailed breakdown of reading subskills than do norm-referenced reading achievement tests. Group diagnostic tests contain subtests on word attack skills like syllabication, sound discrimination, and word blending. These tests provide information that can be useful to the teacher in more accurately pinpointing specific areas of skills needs. While designed to be administered on a group basis, they are diagnostic in intent; i.e., they indicate more specific areas of strengths and weaknesses in reading subskills and provide the basis of a more detailed diagnostic profile on the child.

Reading diagnostic batteries

The most detailed reading diagnostic instruments available are individually administered batteries like the *Durrell Analysis of Reading Difficulty* (T.18), the *Gates-McKillop Reading Diagnostic Test* (T.19), and the Spache

Individual assessment is an important dimension of reading instruction for all children. (Photo by John A. Malnati)

Diagnostic Reading Scales (T.20). In addition to oral and sometimes silent reading measures, these tests provide for detailed assessment of a range of subskills involved in reading: word recognition, word analysis, a variety of phonics competencies (like auditory discrimination, knowledge of letter sounds, sound blending, and syllabication) necessary for decoding words, and reading-related skills like spelling and handwriting. Though they differ in some of the subtests they include, and in the standards and guidelines for interpretation that they use, these instruments are generally similar in nature and purpose. All provide a diagnostic profile on the child and indicate his/her strengths and weaknesses in reading skills areas.

Reading skills tests   While individual reading diagnostic batteries assess areas of reading subskills, separate tests are also available to measure specific aspects of reading ability. Tests like the *Gray Oral Reading Test* (T.21) and the *Gilmore Oral Reading Test* (T.22) include graded paragraphs that can help the teacher determine the child's level of reading ability, as well as his/her accuracy and comprehension in oral reading. The *Rosewell-Chall Diagnostic Reading Test* (T.23) is a short series of tests that can be used specifically to assess phonic skills. The *Botel Reading Inventory* (T.24) contains separate subtests for phonics, word recognition, and word opposites. While these tests differ in nature and format from one another, each is designed to measure some specific aspect of reading. Each of these tests provides a potential source of diagnostic information about different aspects of the child's strengths and weaknesses in reading.

"Learning" tests.   Other tests designed to assess children's perceptual/learning abilities can provide additional useful assessment information. While many of these tests don't measure reading per se, they do assess abilities and disabilities in areas that are important foundational prerequisites for learning to read.

Auditory and visual processing abilities, for example, are vital reading readiness skills and they continue to be important aspects of reading beyond the beginning stages. Weakness in the areas of auditory and visual perception is bound to cause reading problems. Auditory discrimination tests like the *Wepman* (T.25) and the *Goldman-Fristoe-Woodcock* (T.26) are individual tests of children's abilities to discriminate sounds in spoken words. Disabilities in visual perception can be diagnosed by tests such as the *Developmental Test of Visual Perception* (T.27), the *Developmental Test of Visual Motor Integration* (T.28) (more commonly known as the *VMI*), and the *Bender Visual Motor Gestalt Test* (T.29). By having children trace and/or copy geometric designs and shapes, these tests also provide measures of visual motor integration, eye-hand coordination, and the ability to determine spatial relations—all essential skills in early reading and writing.

Auditory and visual processing skills can also be assessed through subtests on more wide-range ability tests like the *Detroit Test of Learning Aptitude* (T.30) or the *Illinois Test of Psycholinguistic Abilities* (T.31). The *De-*

troit, for example, has subtests in auditory and visual attention span, and in motor speed and perception. The *ITPA* contains subtests designed to measure auditory and visual reception, auditory and visual sequential memory, and other subtests that measure ability and disability in channels of communication and other areas of perceptual processing.

The nineteen subtests of the *Detroit* allow for flexible selection of assessment tasks for diagnostic purposes. This test can provide a range of information for the classroom teacher. In addition to auditory and visual perceptual skills, the *Detroit* also measures certain reasoning and thinking skills that are essential to reading comprehension. The tests also provide measures of language ability, another important foundation of reading instruction.

The test most often used for determining a child's verbal ability, however, is the *Peabody Picture Vocabulary Test* (T.32), a test designed to measure "verbal intelligence" by measuring the child's vocabulary size. While the *PPVT* concentrates mainly on only one aspect of language (vocabulary), it does provide general diagnostic information that may suggest the need for specific remediation.

Each of these standardized measures (and others not identified) provides assessment data on important areas related to reading. Each can be the source of information that may be useful in planning a program for the special-needs child in the regular classroom.

Obviously, not all of the wide variety of tests available will be administered to any child, no matter how severe or complex his/her needs may be. The reality and practicality of assessment make it impossible and inadvisable to submit the child to every test available in the marketplace. The availability of instruments suggests a flexible choice of tests for diagnostic purposes, because each of these tests is a potential source of information that can help teachers understand the nature of the child's reading problem.

In dealing with diagnosis, there is an inherent danger of becoming too preoccupied with the tests involved. Diagnosis is a *process*, and the process is far more important than the instruments used as components of the process. The tests are a means to an end. Concerns and reservations have been raised about each of the tests identified in this chapter. Any consideration of tests should put them in proper perspective. They are merely the means we use to secure information that will provide tentative programmatic and instructional leads for planning an effective program of remediation for the special-needs child in the regular classroom.

THE TEACHER AS PART OF THE DIAGNOSTIC PROCESS

The classroom teacher is a key person in the whole diagnostic process. In addition to identifying potential learning problems in children, the teacher also serves:

1. as a consumer of diagnostic information
2. as a classroom diagnostician and monitor of progress
3. as an implementor of educational plans based on diagnosis.

Each aspect of the teacher's role is a key ingredient in assessment.

The Teacher as a Consumer of Diagnostic Information

Most of the formal assessment of the special-needs child is conducted by specialists. The use of most diagnostic instruments requires special expertise and training. Thus, formal auditory and visual screening is done by a physician, the school nurse, or another medically related practitioner; the intelligence test is administered by the school psychologist; the diagnostic reading battery is given by the reading specialist; tests like the *Bender-Gestalt* or the *ITPA* are administered by the special educator or the speech and language specialist; and so on. The information gathered by means of these instruments is given to the classroom teacher, and thus s/he becomes a consumer of the diagnostic information. Interpretation is (or should be) normally part of a diagnostic prescriptive report, but when such interpretation is inadequate, incomplete, or incomprehensible, it's up to the teacher to determine what the data mean and what the scores imply.

What the teacher is able to do with information generated by assessment will largely depend on what the data are telling him/her. It does little good, for example, to see the results of the *Detroit Tests of Learning Aptitude* reported as:

Visual Attention Span for Objects:	11.0+
Visual Attention Span for Letters:	9.0
Auditory Attention Span for Sentences:	12.6
Oral Directions:	10.9
Disarranged Pictures:	8.6
Memory for Designs:	6.8
Motor Speed and Precision:	4.9

unless the teacher knows how the scores were obtained and what instructional implications they have. Similarly, a report that says, "Marie's score on the Performance Scale of the *WISC* was two standard deviations below her score on the Verbal Scale," is of little value unless the teacher knows that this "two standard deviations difference" means that Marie is well able to handle receptive and expressive oral language (that is, she can probably understand word meanings and directions), but that visual motor skills may be weak (so that she will probably have trouble with tasks requiring manipulation, like handwriting or putting together a puzzle). The way data are reported is often more important than the data per se.

A good multidisciplinary evaluation requires the participation of everyone concerned with the education of the child. Parents, teachers, administrators, and special-services personnel must maintain close communication in order to facilitate and coordinate the regular and special education programs. (Photo by John A. Malnati)

Without the proper interpretation and supporting information, assessment data can be downright misleading. Oral reading scores provide a good example. The *Slosson Oral Reading Test* (T.33), the *Durrell Analysis of Reading Difficulty*, and the *Gates-McKillop Reading Diagnostic Test* all give an indication of the child's oral reading level. The means used by each test in arriving at an oral reading score is, however, different. The *Slosson* uses lists of single words that the child is asked to read in isolation as the basis for establishing an oral reading level. This test merely involves word recognition and not the ability to read connected language nor the ability to comprehend the meanings of the words. Oral reading level is measured on the *Durrell* by means of time norms and comprehension. That is, the child is said to read at a certain level according to the time it takes him/her to read a series of paragraphs, and on the basis of his/her ability to answer comprehension questions based on the material read. The *Gates-McKillop* counts errors as the basis for estimating a child's level of oral reading ability. It does not include comprehension questions, nor is time a major factor in arriving at the score. Thus, all these tests are instruments that purportedly give the same information—i.e., information about the child's ability to read aloud—but all use different criteria for arriving at an oral reading score.

Questioning

As a consumer of diagnostic information, the teacher becomes a questioner. S/he seeks out the meaning and significance of the information and data presented in diagnostic reports and takes time to examine the instruments by which the data were gathered. S/he asks the tester how scores were arrived at and what they imply for instructional strategies.

As a consumer, the teacher should also be confident enough to question what the diagnostician has to say. Because those who administer assessment instruments usually have special training and expertise, their word is often taken as gospel. The tester's contacts with the child are, however, limited in time and condition. The classroom teacher's contacts are more extensive and can be the basis for correcting a distorted picture the data may suggest. Children with learning problems are often erratic in their performance; that is, the child may do well on an item one day and miss the same item the next day. Diagnosis was characterized earlier as "a calculated guessing" process. The input of the classroom teacher is essential to testing the hypotheses advanced by diagnosis. This questioning process on the basis of the teacher's own observation and experience is a way of validating the assessment results suggested by formal test data.

The Teacher as a Diagnostician

While most of the formal tests administered as part of assessment are given by school personnel other than the classroom teacher, the diagnostic process extends well beyond the administration of formal tests. Diagnosis is a continuous process involving the classroom teacher on a continuous basis. In addition to the types of formal diagnosis described earlier in this chapter, the teacher can engage in more direct diagnostic activity through informal reading inventories and task analysis.

Informal reading inventory

The most frequently used classroom technique for informal assessment in reading is the informal reading inventory, commonly referred to as IRI. An informal reading inventory consists of a series of sequentially graded selections that increase in difficulty from the primer level to the sixth-grade level or beyond. The child reads the selections aloud and answers questions based on what s/he has read. Inventories also include a second set of selections designed to measure silent-reading level, and graded word lists to facilitate initial placement of the child in the inventory. Though the major purpose of the IRI is to indicate a child's reading level through functional performance, this test can provide useful diagnostic information for the teacher.

Reading levels

The reading levels measured by the IRI are designated as Independent, Instructional, and Frustration. Criteria for determining these levels vary from expert to expert, but in general, the standards used are these:

Independent Level

Material that children can be expected to handle adequately on their own; materials like library books or other free reading matter.	99-96% accuracy in Word Recognition At least 90% Comprehension Good reading behaviors

This means that the child makes no more than one to four errors (depending on the criteria accepted) in every hundred running words in a passage, and that s/he can understand almost all of what s/he reads. Good reading behaviors are indicated by fluent and expressive reading, with no signs of physical inefficiencies (like finger pointing or head movement) or evidence of anxiety or nervousness (like a high-pitched voice, overly loud volume, and the like).

Instructional Level:

The Instructional level indicates the level of material that is challenging enough to use in further developing the child's reading skills, yet is not so difficult that it will be a source of frustration for the child.	95–90% accuracy in Word Recognition At least 75% Comprehension Adequate reading behaviors.

In other words, the child makes no more than five to nine errors (again, depending on the criteria set) in every hundred running words, and understands at least three-fourths of the content read. Adequate reading behaviors are reflected by good expression and an absence of physical inefficiencies and nervousness.

Frustration Level:

At this level, the child makes an average of one or more errors in every ten running words and understands only half or less of what s/he reads. Symptoms of stress and/or difficulty are in evidence during the reading.	Less than 90% accuracy in Word Recognition Skills 50% or less in Comprehension Poor reading behaviors.

Material at this level is considered too difficult for the child to handle, even with support and help from the teacher.

At this level, the child makes an average of one or more errors in every ten running words and understands only half or less of what s/he reads. Material at this level is considered too difficult for the child to handle, even with support and help from the teacher.

In addition to the Independent, Instructional, and Frustration reading levels, some inventories suggest a listening comprehension measure that indicates the child's "potential reading level." This level is determined by the child's ability to answer questions based on selections read from the inventory. For example, if the child can answer, with 75 percent accuracy, the fourth-grade selection that s/he listens to, then his/her potential reading level is said to be at the fourth grade. Though listening comprehension and reading comprehension are related, there is a danger of using listening comprehension ability as the primary measure of potential reading ability. Listening comprehension involves the ability to understand oral language, while reading involves the ability to deal with language in print. Listening comprehension focuses on the meaning dimension of language without major regard to the decoding of written language that is essential to reading. Reading demands the ability to recognize (or decode) words as well as to understand them. At best, listening comprehension gives a very rough and global estimate of reading potential. However, using the ability to listen as the sole measure of reading potential is presumptuous and can be dangerously misleading. For most primary grade children, aural/oral vocabulary far exceeds reading vocabulary, so using listening as a measure of potential reading ability at these grade levels is likely to indicate that children are far behind.

Constructing the inventory

Constructing the inventory requires careful attention to the reading material selected. Because of the informal nature of the instrument, teachers often make their own versions of the IRI. Selections are typically chosen from basal readers or from some other carefully graded material (like stories in *My Weekly Reader* or from Smith and Harris's *Graded Selections for Informal Reading Diagnosis*).[6] Passages at the beginning levels are relatively short (20–40 words). For the second- to fourth-grade levels, selections of 100–150 words are usually used, and for the fifth-grade level and above, passages range in length from 175 to 300 words.

In selecting passages, an important consideration is the nature of the material chosen. If, for example, a second grader has learned to read with a highly structured decoding approach that maintains heavy emphasis on regularity in sound-symbol relationships (as in linguistics or synthetic phonics), the child will likely make frequent errors in passages full of high-frequency, but phonetically irregular, words like *said* and *laughed*. By contrast, a child who has been taught from the beginning with a heavy meaning-oriented look-say emphasis, may have trouble with phonetically regular but unfamiliar words. Attention should be given to this aspect of reading in the analysis stage as well as in the construction of the inventory.

In order to reflect a wide and accurate picture of the child's comprehension ability, questions constructed for each selection should include different levels of comprehension (literal, inferential, and critical-creative), as well as different comprehension components (details, main ideas, sequence, cause-effect relationships, etc.). Questions should be specifically related to the content, so that the child cannot answer them on the basis of general knowledge or experience alone. The questions should be short and simple, and a sufficient number should be included so that an accurate level of comprehension can be determined.

The teacher also needs to have a copy of the same material that the child is reading, for "mark-up" purposes.

As a result of the widespread use of inventories as informal reading assessment devices, commercially prepared and published inventories have become more readily available for use in the classroom.[7] While these are professionally constructed and save the teacher time and trouble, they may include more than the teacher typically needs, and they do not have the personalized dimension of being made by the teacher for use with his/her own pupils.

Administering the inventory

Administering the inventory is an individual enterprise. Because of the nature of the instrument, an IRI must be administered to one child at a time. In conducting the inventory, the teacher asks the child to begin reading at an appropriate entry point. This point is usually a grade level or two below the child's expected reading ability, indicated by the child's score on a standardized reading achievement test, performance on a graded word list, and/or the teacher's previous assessment of reading ability.

If the entry selection is at the child's Independent reading level, the child reads the passages at increasing levels of difficulty until the Frustration level is reached. If the entry level paragraph proves to be at or above the child's Instructional level, s/he reads below and above the entry point until appropriate levels are determined.. Some teachers begin administering the IRI at the beginning level paragraphs (primer or first grade), because even if this material is well below the child's level of reading ability, the earlier selections give the child a chance to "warm up" and build confidence with easy reading material.

An IRI usually takes from ten to fifteen or more minutes per pupil to administer. Obviously, the use of supplementary silent reading paragraphs will increase the time.

As the child reads, the teacher marks errors that indicate word recognition difficulties. After each selection, questions are asked to assess the child's understanding of what s/he has read. The coding system used to mark errors usually follows the type of pattern on page 95.

Insertions (the addition of extra words)	. . .it was a nice *and* day to go . . .
Omissions (of words)	. . .when the balloon ~~came~~ down . . .
(or word parts)	. . .he pulled the st~~r~~ing . . .
Substitutions (of easy words)	. . . *these* ~~the~~ girls who were . . .
(of common word parts)	. . .play~~ing~~ *ed* in the park . . .
Words pronounced by examiner (after a 5-sec. pause)	. . .the ~~huge~~ *P* truck . . .
Mispronunciation (of whole words)	. . .in the ~~basket~~ *blanket* . . .
(of word parts)	. . . a ~~precious~~ *pre* . . .
Reversals	. . .the girl ⟨was⟩ *saw* . . .
Punctuation ignored	. . .to the school⁄When they . . .
Repetitions*(of phrases)	*R* . . .David likes . . .
(of word parts)	*R* . . .to fly . . .
(of whole words)	*R* . . .his kite . . .
Inaccurate phrasing or word—by Word reading*	. . .the/man came/along . . .
Hesitations*	. . .the ✓children ✓climbed ✓onto the . . .
Self-corrections	*SC* . . .likes to ~~go~~ to the movies . . .

---

*Whether errors like repetitions, phrasing, and hesitations indicate word analysis difficulties or merely poor oral-reading habits is debatable. These areas of weakness need to be examined from the perspective of two possible areas of difficulty.

Self-corrections are usually marked, but are not counted as errors since the corrections are made by the child. However, a repeated pattern of self-corrections may indicate difficulties in word recognition and word analysis skills.

For marking responses to comprehension questions, a simple check or $+/-$ coding system is normally used. Reading behaviors are also noted and recorded during the administration of the IRI, characteristics like head movement (HM), fingerpointing (FP), volume that is abnormally high or low (H- or L-VOL), lip movement (LM) and subvocalization (SV) in silent reading, and other pertinent signs that may indicate nervousness and/or related reading difficulties.

While administering an IRI, a tape recorder is a useful tool. Tape recording the child during reading relieves much of the pressure and anxiety (and the curiosity too) that the child often experiences while watching the teacher make mysterious marks. Tape recording the reading frees the teacher to devote full attention to the child. It alleviates the problem of trying to record the errors of the child who reads too fast. And the taped record of the child gives the teacher a chance to listen to the reading several times—each time with an ear to a different reading problem—outside the distracting atmosphere of the typically busy classroom. The tape also provides a record that can be the basis of comparison with the child's later reading performance. Tape recording children's oral reading at any time is a useful practice, but it is particularly advantageous in administering an IRI.

Sometimes, silent-reading paragraphs are administered routinely in an informal reading inventory. However, this can be an individual decision for the teacher. Most of the information gathered through an IRI is based on the child's oral reading, because specific abilities and disabilities in word recognition and word analysis skills cannot be assessed while the child is reading silently. Yet many children read better silently than they do aloud. They may struggle with the pronunciation of words and have difficulty with expression in oral reading, yet read silently with speed and comprehension. If there is a discrepancy between the teacher's perception of the child's ability to read and the oral reading performance on an IRI, the silent reading paragraphs should be used. Situations in which serious discrepancies exist—where the child reads well silently but poorly orally—produce diagnostic information; that is, the child needs specific help and practice in the area of oral reading.

Scoring and interpretation

Scoring and interpretation of the IRI are crucial. Scoring involves computing the percentage of word recognition accuracy[8] and the number and percent of comprehension questions answered correctly. These figures give the teacher a global indication of the child's ability to read material at a designated grade level.

The first and perhaps most important question for the teacher to deal with in scoring and interpretation is "What is an error?" In 1969, Kenneth Goodman introduced the term *miscue* into the literature,[9] and since that time the practice of miscue analysis has received considerable attention. Very simply, a miscue is a deviation from print that involves the substitution of a similar or equivalent phonological, syntactic, or semantic language form. For example, if the child reads the sentence *Sally has a little kitten in her hand* as "Sally have a small kitten in her han," the three "errors" here might be considered miscues because 1) *have* and *has* are grammatically similar; 2) *small* and *little* have almost identical semantic meanings; and 3) dropping the final consonant sound on *hand* may be a feature of the child's everyday speech. Miscues can sometimes be linked to dialect variations in children's speech, though they are not limited to these differences.

Miscues don't always interfere with major meaning that the reader derives from print, as children use language cues and expectations to gain meaning from what they read.

Guidelines for analyzing children's miscues in oral reading have been detailed[10] and a published instrument for miscue analysis—the *Reading Miscue Inventory* (T.34)—is available for use in schools.

Though the process of miscue analysis is often complicated and time-consuming, and though there is no universal agreement on what should be considered a mistake and what should be considered a miscue, the process of analyzing errors with an eye to miscues is diagnostically valuable. It often gives teachers some insights into the *whys* of children's performance in oral reading, both as part of an informal reading inventory and while the child is reading aloud in the classroom.

Using the IRI for diagnostic purposes involves more, however, than the simple tabulation of mistakes or miscues. It involves analyzing the child's oral reading performance to determine patterns that will indicate areas of weakness. It includes, for example, noting whether the errors are made more often in basic sight words or in trying to sound out phonetic elements, whether decoding errors are more prevalent in consonant or in vowel elements in words, and whether the comprehension questions the child is unable to answer correctly indicate literal or inferential difficulties. The results of this type of probing can suggest the need for further assessment that will verify suspicions aroused by the child's performance on an IRI and it can provide the basis for appropriate instructional follow-up.

There are legitimate criticisms and practical problems with the theory and use of the IRI as an assessment instrument. Some think the criteria for determining levels are arbitrary, rigid, and (for the Independent and Instructional levels) too high. Making an occasional error in reading aloud is not uncommon even for the most capable reader, yet just a simple slip on a word can bring the child down a level when the "99% criterion" is used. The IRI assumes that readability measures applied to selections are firm and accurate, yet both research and practical experience suggest that this assumption is questionable. Interpretation can be subjective. Two teachers may not always agree on what is considered an "error"—a question related to the "mistake vs. miscue" issue, nor on what might be considered a trivial versus a significant departure from the text. Also, a child's performance on material contained in the IRI may not reflect his/her ability to deal with other types of printed materials (content area textbooks, for example).

What sometimes happens in practice is that a child reads a second-grade selection with no errors and perfect comprehension, begins to make errors at the third-grade level, yet reads the fourth-grade paragraph perfectly. In this case, determining a specific instructional and independent level is difficult, because the child's performance may be based on familiarity with the content of the material at different levels. Levels can also vary according to the criteria of accuracy that one accepts. For example, if the child scores 97% on word recognition (that is, makes three mistakes in a 100-word passage) at the third-grade level, this is considered his Independent level with the "96% criterion," but it would be considered the Instructional level if one accepts a criterion of "99% accuracy in word recognition." For these reasons, teacher judgment and common sense are important ingredients in interpretation. The inventory is an *informal* measure and needs to be balanced with other measures in assembling a total diagnostic picture of the child.

Another practical problem that occurs is a discrepancy between the child's word recognition score and his/her comprehension score. With any paragraph, a child's performance may indicate an Independent level in word recognition and a Frustration level in comprehension (or vice versa). Although the lower score is thought to be the more accurate one for placement, the teacher must be able to interpret reasons for the discrepancy. Three pupils can serve as examples:

> *Allan* scores 92% in word recognition and 80% in comprehension with third-grade reading material, so this would be considered his Instructional level.

> *Billy,* however, scores 99% on word recognition but only 50% in comprehension with the same third-grade reading material. For Billy, this would be considered his Frustration level because of his low comprehension score.

> *Carol*, on the other hand, scores 85% on word recognition and 100% on comprehension with the third-grade paragraph. Despite her ability to understand what she reads, third grade would be considered Carol's Frustration level because of word recognition problems. (Carol would be a prime candidate for a supplemental set of silent-reading paragraphs.)

In interpreting the results of the inventory, Allan's balanced score makes interpretation "neat" and orderly. Billy, however, is a "word caller"— someone who can decode words but has some basic comprehension problems. Carol uses context or general thinking skills that allow her to understand what she reads, but word recognition and word attack problems indicate an Instructional level below third grade. In interpretation, the *pattern* of errors needs to be taken into account.

Despite its limitations, the IRI can serve as a viable assessment tool. It's an on-the-spot device that the teacher can construct and administer according to his/her own needs and schedule. It gives a focused measure of the child's functional reading ability that filling in the bubbles or circling items on a standardized reading achievement test does not. And it's a manageable tool that the teacher can use in placement, selection of reading materials, and prescriptive planning for children with special needs. Even when not used in their entirety, the criteria for determining levels can provide a thumbnail indicator of how well the children can handle materials used in the reading group, as well as reading materials used for related curriculum and recreational purposes.

Making and using inventories has a potentially valuable spin-off effect for the teacher:

> A teacher who has constructed and used reading inventories can hardly ignore the minute-by-minute, day-by-day opportunities for informal evaluations of his pupils' performances. Thus, each lesson becomes a part of a continuing diagnosis of existing strengths and weaknesses. When this occurs, truly appropriate instruction can be planned and provided with ever decreasing need for individual testing.[11]

The results of an IRI are, by nature, informal. They provide an estimate of the level of material a child can deal with comfortably. But they need to be balanced with other assessment tools and test results in planning reading instruction for children with special needs in the regular classroom.

Task analysis

Task analysis, identified earlier in this chapter as a major approach or type of diagnosis, is also an appropriate assessment activity for the classroom teacher. Children's daily classroom experiences typically include many reading-related tasks. Failure to successfully complete these tasks can occur for a number of reasons. Pinpointing where the breakdown occurs is an important diagnostic activity.

A useful model for approaching task analysis in the classroom is to examine tasks according to the modality processing demands that the task make upon the child. This model may be represented schematically thus:

Input	Cognitive Processing	Output
Auditory		
Visual	Conceptualization	
Tactual	Symbolization	Vocal
Kinesthetic	Perception	Motor

Credit: *Junkala, "Task Analysis."*

Input

Input involves the reception and organization of information. Earlier, the senses were described as "pathways to the brain." The sensory channels of input for most reading-related tasks are auditory, visual, tactual, and kinesthetic. In other words, reading involves the intake of information primarily by seeing the symbols in print and hearing the language sounds represented by the symbols. When these primary channels of input are impaired, children are taught to use the sense of touch (as in Braille) or movement (as in tracing sandpaper letters) as a means of compensating for, or supplementing, the primary sensory channels. We also gain information through the gustatory and olfactory channels of input, but these senses are normally not used in reading-related tasks.

Output

Output is the means the child uses to generate a response. The response may be vocal, as when the child uses his/her organs of speech in answering a question or imitating a nonlanguage sound; or it may be motor, as when the child writes an answer or responds by underlining an item or by raising his/her hand. Whatever mode of response is involved, output is what the child generates in response to a task and what allows the teacher to judge the child's success or failure at the task.

Cognitive processing

Cognitive processing is the remaining component of this task analysis model. Processing is what goes on inside the child's head while s/he switches from input to output. Since it is not observable, it is more difficult to deal with and to describe than the input or output functions. Processing essentially involves the mental manipulation of information. It occurs at three hierarchical levels: perception, symbolization, and conceptualization. The lines dividing these levels of the cognitive hierarchy are not sharply defined, and there is considerable overlap from one area to the next.

Perception, the first level in the cognitive processing component, involves the ability to integrate incoming sensory information into an awareness of what one is seeing, hearing, and feeling. It is a process of recognizing and differentiating symbols and objects.

Symbolization involves language, the ability to attach verbal symbols to referents. It requires not only the ability to get meaning from what one senses, but also the ability to name objects and actions and to describe these objects and actions with appropriate language.

Conceptualization, the highest level in this model, involves the development of meaningful relationships, the ability to recognize patterns and arrive at broader meanings. Conceptualization extends upward to include inferential thinking, analysis, systhesis, evaluation, and the other cognitive operations that are characteristic of higher mental processing.

Memory is an important cognitive operation that underlies each of these processes. It represents the ability to store and retrieve information. The perceptual, symbolic, and conceptual levels of processing all demand the ability to store information for immediate recall (short-term memory) and to maintain the information for retrieval at a later time (long-term memory). This dimension is extremely important when one is involved in analyzing a task. Memory can spell the difference between success and failure for the child, because if the child can't hold the information available long enough to deal with it, or can't remember information from past learning, then s/he will not be able to complete the task.

How can this model of task analysis serve a practical diagnostic function for the classroom teacher? When a child consistently fails or does poorly on a series of reading-related tasks, the pattern of error can often reveal useful information. Take, for example, a visual discrimination task typically found in reading readiness programs, one in which children are directed to match and mark figures on the basis of shape and size:

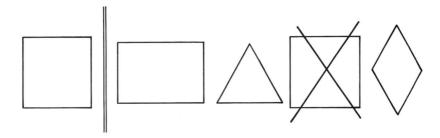

Applying this model of task analysis to this example, it's apparent that the *input* is primarily visual; that is, the child is asked to visually match two non-language symbols. Auditory input would have been used if the child had been asked to respond to an auditory stimulus. There would have been tactual/kinesthetic input had the child been directed to trace the figures. *Cognitive processing* is at the perceptual level; that is, the task demands that the child match the figures on the basis of similar shape and size. Had the task demanded naming the objects (square, triangle, rectangle, etc.), symbolization would have been involved. Had it involved having the child explain the relationship between the shapes or make statements about them ("The shape has four equal sides with four right angles"), processing would have been raised to the level of conceptualization. *Output* in this task is motor; that is, the child is asked to respond by marking an X on the appropriate figure.

If the child responded to this example incorrectly—if, for example, s/he marked the rectangle instead of the square—task analysis could provide the classroom teacher with a framework for determining where the breakdown may have occurred. If the child was successful with the task using blocks (tactual/kinesthetic input), then the teacher would have reason to suspect problems with the visual input channels. Assuming input channels are in order, task analysis suggests examining the child's perceptual abilities. This may be done by reducing the level of complexity of the task by presenting more grossly different configurations; for example:

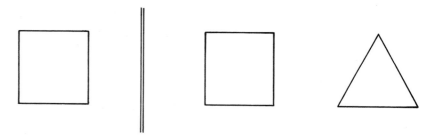

Task analysis also suggests that the output function be scrutinized to determine whether the child may have a visual motor problem that would cause him/her to locate the X on the wrong figure, or some other problem that would influence the visual motor response demanded. For example, the teacher should manipulate the task by having the child point to, rather than mark an X on, the figure. If the child fails this task, s/he likely has trouble with visual information at the perceptual level. Since reading involves visual perceptual processing in the finer discrimination of letters, a potential reading disorder is apparent.

Memory

The memory demands are an important part of the cognitive processing component as well. Some children, for example, have trouble when given a simple verbal direction like "Open your reading book to page 83," yet they can easily find the page when the page number is written for them. In this case, task analysis suggests that the child may have difficulty revisualizing the graphic form of the numeral *83*, or s/he may not be able to hold the auditory information in mind long enough to respond or carry out the task. In either case, short-term memory is involved. Providing the model reduces the memory demands. Long-term memory is especially crucial in reading comprehension, as children are so often called upon to remember what they read.

Sometimes, a child will do well with intrasensory tasks; that is, processing information with similar input-output channels (like tasks with auditory input and vocal output, or with kinesthetic input and motor output.) However, the child may have trouble crossing modalities; that is, with tasks involving auditory input and motor output. Since reading is an intersensory task requiring the child to cross modalities (from visual input to vocal output), task analysis provides a framework for spotting potential reading problems that other diagnostic procedures do not.

In addition to providing a useful dimension to diagnosis in the classroom, this model of task analysis can be used to analyze pupils' performances on more formal assessment measures.[13]

*Alternative
instructional
strategies*

Task analysis can also suggest alternative instructional strategies in the classroom. Sally is a case in point. Sally was referred to a learning specialist because she was thought to have "auditory problems." She could not correctly identify sounds as high or low according to their appropriate frequencies. Sounds with two extreme pitches were "beeped." When asked whether the sounds were high or low, Sally would either respond, "I don't know" or respond incorrectly. On the basis of task analysis, the specialist tried another approach.

"Sally," the specialist said, "when you hear this sound (high), I want you to put your hands in the air like this. When you hear this sound (low), I want you to put your hands down like this. Ready?" When the sounds were "beeped," Sally responded beautifully with this approach. She could consistently respond correctly to sounds at different levels. The specialist had given Sally an alternative means of response. Instead of a verbal output (naming the sounds as "high" or "low"), the specialist suggested a motor response (raising or lowering the hands). The specialist found that Sally had, in fact, no auditory problem, but rather a language problem. She did not know the words *high* and *low* in relation to the sounds.

The teacher who suggests alternative input channels (having children trace or copy sight vocabulary words for reinforcement), or alternative output responses to tasks (having children who cannot write words from dictation on a spelling test identify the correct spellings in a multiple-choice fashion), is using the results of task analysis as a means of putting assessment information to work for the special-needs child in the classroom.

*A diagnostic
"mind-set"*

In addition to using informal reading inventories and task analysis, the teacher as diagnostician develops what might be described as "a diagnostic mind-set." That is, the teacher is constantly on the alert for information that may be helpful in prescriptive planning. In most elementary school classrooms, children do some reading every day, complete worksheets and other activities related to reading skill development, and engage in other reading-related tasks. Rather than just listening to the children read, correcting the worksheets, and checking off the completion of other activities and tasks, the teacher with a diagnostic mind-set listens carefully to see where errors in the reading occur and where strengths and weaknesses are apparent. Is the reading material too difficult for the child? Where does the major area of reading difficulty seem to be? Does s/he often miss familiar sight words? Can s/he sound out unknown words? Where are his/her word analysis problems? Phonics? Consonants or vowels? Long or short vowels? Consonants at the beginning or the end of words? Can s/he understand what is read? Can s/he infer and draw conclusions about what is read? Can s/he write answers to simple questions? If not, can s/he respond successfully with another mode of response? Can s/he remember what I tell him/her? If not, what kind of visual backup to my instructions can I provide? And so on. These are the questions that constantly race through the teacher's mind while dealing with the children in the day-to-day business of teaching reading in the classroom. This constant questioning makes assessment an ongoing process. A diagnostic mind-set keeps the teacher questioning, probing, seeking out information about the child and his/her reading that will help the teacher plan successful reading experiences.

The Teacher as Implementor

The third general principle of diagnosis identified earlier—i.e., that diagnosis should lead to instructional improvement—suggests the third role for the teacher in the assessment process. Assessment is not complete until something is done with the results. The teacher is the one who puts assessment information to work in the reading instruction of the special-needs child in the regular classroom.

Implementation involves considering all the available data in planning reading instruction for the child. Assessment data will indicate areas of instructional need. Addressing these areas of need is the basis of prescriptive instruction.

Accommodation

Considering diagnostic information in planning instruction may involve relatively simple adjustments or accommodations in the classroom; for example, insuring that children with visual acuity problems be seated where they can see clearly, or arranging for children with poor auditory memory to have "buddies" whom they can ask "What did the teacher say?" whenever they can't remember a verbal direction. These accommodations, aimed at helping children with diagnosed learning problems to survive in a regular classroom setting, are suggested in the chapters that follow and are summarized in Appendix C.

Most instructional accommodations will extend beyond this simple level, however. Prescriptive instruction involves such provisions as: 1) choosing a systematic phonics program as the approach to beginning reading for the child whose diagnostic test scores indicate auditory strengths and visual weaknesses, while providing plenty of games for the teaching and reinforcement of sight words; 2) providing many listening comprehension exercises to build thinking skills for the child whose diagnostic test scores indicate that comprehension is a weak area of reading; 3) choosing books that may have some therapeutic effect in helping children in emotional distress deal with their problems; 4) using plenty of language experience charts for children with problems in the area of expressive language; and so on. In sum, basing instruction on diagnostic information involves making instructional adjustments and accommodations for the special-needs child in the regular classroom. These accommodations are part of the entire assessment process, just as much so as the tests that the specialist administers. Implementation makes the diagnostic process complete.

The implementation of educational plans based on assessment results for every child is not an easy operation. Human beings are complex organisms, and instructional accommodations may need to be made in several different areas, even for the same child. Prescriptive instruction requires individualization, a process that is never simple for the teacher responsible for the instruction of twenty-five or more children in the classroom. But prescriptive instruction is important, especially for the special-needs child. The child's needs are such that an "off-the-rack" reading program just won't fit. The success provided for the child by a truly prescriptive reading program makes the rewards of such a program well worth the effort.

CONCLUSION

Assessment is a broad term that covers both evaluation and diagnosis. It involves formal evaluation through the use of both norm-referenced and criterion-referenced instruments, as well as informal observation and testing. It includes diagnosis through the use of formal diagnostic devices and informal processes. It is a multi-dimensional operation that is an integral and ongoing part of the instructional process. Assessment extends into many areas. Physical, intellectual, perceptual, language, and emotional areas are explored, as are the specific skills areas that must be mastered as part of learning to read. Through formal testing and informal observation, each area contributes a piece of the puzzle for the child with reading problems.

Assessment necessarily involves testing, and tests have long been a regular part of children's school lives. This is especially true for special-needs children. Unfortunately, parents and educators alike often put too much faith in test results. Assessment is never absolute. As a process, it is as dynamic as the subjects being assessed. Tests provide *estimates* of human qualities, not absolute measures on children.

Assessment extends well beyond a collection of test scores and records of observations. It is a means of arriving at an instructional plan that will enable the child with special needs to progress in reading in the way that is best for the child and as far as his/her characteristics will allow. Assessment should always be carried on with the aim of building on human strengths and remediating weaknesses.

Assessment is not a mechanical function; it is a human function. And the person most crucial in the assessment process (apart from the child) is the teacher. S/he is the one who participates in the synthesis of information that assessment produces, who carries on the assessment as an ongoing part of instruction in the classroom, and who, most importantly, puts his information to work through prescriptive teaching. Though assessment may involve a wide variety of special-services personnel on an interdisciplinary team, the teacher maintains the central role through the whole assessment process.

ACTIVITIES FOR PRESERVICE TEACHERS

1. What is your reaction to the following critical statement: "We spend too much time and money on testing in schools these days. We should forget about all the assessment and get down to the business of teaching."

   Do you agree or disagree with the statement? On what do you base your position? What can be said in response to the statement from a diagnostic point of view?

2. Examine two or three of the tests identified on pp. 73–88. Compare these tests on the basis of what each measures. What value do you think these tests have as assessment instruments? Given a free choice, which ones would you use and for what purpose?

3. Listen to a child read orally. Compute percentages for word analysis and comprehension accuracy suggested by the criteria of the Informal Reading Inventory. What's the level of the material in relation to the child's reading ability? What does your analysis suggest in choosing future reading material for the child?

4. Do a task analysis on the following sample exercise designed to teach syllabication:

   Directions: Write the number of syllables in each word.

_____ pond	_____ sometimes	_____ elephant
_____ apartment	_____ took	_____ morning
_____ into	_____ typewriter	_____ drive

   What channel of input is involved? What level of cognitive processing is required? What mode of output is demanded? If a child failed in completing this exercise, what alternatives might task analysis suggest?

5. Describe some of the things you might do as a consumer, as a diagnostician, and as an implementor as part of the diagnostic process in the classroom.

ACTIVITIES FOR IN-SERVICE TEACHERS

1. Select two or three children in your class and determine what assessment data are available on them (reading scores, IQ scores, etc.). What instructional implications does this information suggest? Test these implications

in practice and report the results in terms of the child's success and/or mastery in some aspect of reading.

2. On pp. 79–80, the diagnostic process was represented as a spiral involving the steps of determining instructional needs, setting instructional objectives, planning instructional activities, and evaluating. Using one aspect of reading (phonics, comprehension, etc.), design and follow this spiral with a child in your classroom who has a reading problem. What means of determining instructional needs might be appropriate? How ought the instructional objectives to be stated? What instructional activities will follow? What means of evaluation should be used? Report your results after you implement this "diagnostic spiral" with the child.

3. Listen to one of the poorer readers in your classroom read aloud. Using the Informal Reading Inventory criteria suggested on pp. 92–93, determine the level of the material in relationship to the child's reading ability. Besides the difficulty of the material, what other diagnostic information can you gather from listening to this child read aloud?

4. Task analyze a segment of a reading lesson you teach—for example, the way you introduce vocabulary, conduct comprehension practice, suggest follow-up activities. What channels of input do you use the most? What levels of cognitive processing are usually required? What mode of response is most often used? On the basis of the task analysis you conduct, what types of alternative strategies might be appropriate for children who have difficulty?

5. In practical classroom terms, describe how you function as a consumer of diagnostic information, as a classroom diagnostician, and as an implementor in the diagnostic process. What conditions need changing to help you function more effectively in these roles?

NOTES

1. Robert L. Thorndike and Elizabeth P. Hagen, *Measurement and Evaluation in Psychology and Education,* (New York: John Wiley & Sons, 1977), p. 6.
2. Albert J. Harris and Edward R. Sipay, *How To Increase Reading Ability,* 6th ed. (New York: David McKay Co., Inc., 1975), p. 166.
3. Guy L. Bond and Miles A. Tinker, *Reading Difficulties: Their Diagnosis and Correction,* 3rd ed. (Englewood Cliffs: Prentice-Hall, 1973), p. 153.
4. Janet W. Lerner, *Children with Learning Disabilities,* 2nd ed. (Boston: Houghton Mifflin Company, 1971), p. 108.
5. John Junkala, "Task Analysis: The Processing Dimension," *Academic Therapy* 8 (Summer 1973): 408.

6. Nila Banton Smith and Anna Harris, *Graded Selections for Informal Reading Diagnosis* (New York: New York University Press, 1963).

7. The most popular commercial inventory is *Classroom Reading Inventory* (3rd ed.) by Nicholas J. Silvaroli (Dubuque: William C. Brown Company, 1976). Others available are: Robert A. McCracken, *Standard Reading Inventory* (Kalmath, Ore.: Kalmath Printing Company, 1966); *Informal Evaluation of Oral Reading Grade Level* (New York: Book-Lab, Inc., 1973); Thomas C. Potter and Gwenneth Rae, *Informal Reading Diagnosis: A Practical Guide for the Classroom Teacher* (Englewood Cliffs: Prentice-Hall, 1973): Margaret LaPray, *Teaching Children to Become Independent Readers* (New York: Center for Applied Research in Education, 1972). Also, basal reading programs often provide supplementary paragraphs that can be used as material for constructing Informal Reading Inventories.

8. Elton E. Ekwall presents a useful chart for translating the number of word recognition errors into percents for passages of varying length in *Diagnosis and Remediation of the Disabled Reader,* p. 276.

9. Kenneth S. Goodman, "Analysis of Reading Miscues: Applied Psycholinguistics," *Reading Research Quarterly* 5 (Fall 1969): 126–135.

10. Kenneth S. Goodman, ed. *Miscue Analysis* (Urbana, Ill.: National Council of Teachers of English, 1973); Yetta M. Goodman, "Reading Diagnosis—Qualitative or Quantitative," *The Reading Teacher* 26 (Oct. 1972): 32–37; Carolyn M. Burke and Kenneth S. Goodman, "What a Child Reads: A Psycholinguistic Analysis," *Elementary English* 47 (Jan. 1970): 121–129.

11. Marjorie Seddon Johnson and Roy A. Kress, *Informal Reading Inventories* (Newark, Del.: International Reading Association, 1965), p. 43.

12. This model is adapted from one designed by John Junkala, "Task Analysis and Instructional Alternatives," and "Task Analysis: The Processing Dimension," *Academic Therapy* 8 (Fall 1972 and Summer 1973).

13. Clifford Hakim, "Task Analysis: An Alternative," *Academic Therapy* 10 (Winter 1974): 201–209.

TEST NOTES

Tests cited in this chapter are marked with the letter "T" to indicate *Test*. The tests cited are intended as a representative sample. Other tests are available and are widely used.

T-1. *SRA Assessment Survey.* A battery with separate tests at different grade levels that contain vocabulary and comprehension subtests. Science Research Associates.

T-2. *Iowa Test of Basic Skills.* Test battery with different tests at different grade levels from grade 1 through junior high school. Provides measures of vocabulary, word analysis, comprehension, and word study skills. Houghton Mifflin.

T-3. *Stanford Achievement Test.* Tests reading levels from primary grades through junior high school. Contains subtests on vocabulary, comprehension, and (at the primary levels) word study skills. Psychological Corporation.

T-4. *Cooperative Primary Tests.* A battery of tests for the primary grades containing assessment measures for listening, word analysis, and reading. Educational Testing Service.

T-5. *Metropolitan Achievement Tests.* Contains subtests to measure word knowledge, comprehension, and (at the primary level) word analysis. Psychological Corporation.

T-6. *Sequential Tests of Educational Progress* (STEP Tests), Tests for grade 4 through adult level that include measures of reading comprehension. Educational Testing Service.

T-7. *Customized Objective Monitoring Service.* A data bank containing criterion-referenced items for elementary-grade reading objectives that schools can select. Schools using this service can specify the number of items to be included and tests are custom-made. Houghton Mifflin.

T-8. *Mastery: An Evaluation Tool.* A system for building objective-based, criterion-referenced tests in reading for grades K–9. Contains customized tests based on objectives that schools select, or catalogue tests made up of preselected items. Science Research Associates.

T-9. *Prescriptive Reading Inventory.* A series of criterion-referenced tests to assess reading objectives, grades 1–5. Objectives are classified according to skills areas and levels. CBT/McGraw Hill.

T-10. *Stanford-Binet Intelligence Scales.* An individually administered test of general intelligence. Requires special training for administration. Houghton Mifflin.

T-11. *Wechsler Intelligence Scale for Children* (WISC). An individually administered test of general intelligence for ages 5–15. Requires special training for administration. Psychological Corporation.

T-12. *Murphy-Durrell Reading Readiness Analysis.* A readiness test assessing ability in auditory and visual discrimination and letter names. Contains component for measuring learning rate. Psychological Corporation.

T-13. *Gates-MacGinitie Reading Readiness Test.* A readiness measure containing subtests on listening comprehension, auditory and visual discrimination, the ability to follow directions, letter recognition, visual-motor coordination, and word recognition for beginning readers. Teachers College Press.

T-14. *Lee-Clark Reading Readiness Test.* Includes measures of letter discrimination, selection of pictures based on verbal directions, discrimination of printed word forms. CTB/McGraw Hill.

T-15. *Metropolitan Readiness Test.* Measures word meaning, listening, and alphabet knowledge, along with math readiness. Psychological Corporation.

T-16. *Stanford Diagnostic Reading Test.* A three-test series (primary through junior high school levels) measuring decoding skills, vocabulary, reading comprehension, and reading rate. Psychological Corporation.

T-17. *Doren Diagnostic Reading Test.* A group test for children grades 2–8 measures a variety of word attack components (beginning sounds, rhyming, blending, final sounds, etc.) as well as word recognition and spelling skills. American Guidance Service.

T-18. *Durrell Analysis of Reading Difficulty.* A battery for detailed diagnosis of reading problems for children grades 1–8. Measures oral and silent reading, listening comprehension, word recognition and analysis. Optional tests are included for hearing sounds in words, letter recognition, visual memory, and phonetic spelling. Psychological Corporation.

T-19. *Gates-McKillop Reading Diagnostic Test.* An individually administered diagnostic reading battery with subtests for oral reading, word recognition, word analysis, phrase reading, syllabication, letter names and sounds, word blending, and spelling. An optional oral vocabulary test is included. Teachers College Press.

T-20. *Diagnostic Reading Scales*. Contain subtests on word recognition, oral and silent reading, and a variety of decoding components (letter-sound matching, recognition of common word parts, auditory discrimination). Assesses levels grades 1–8. CTB/McGraw Hill.

T-21. *Gray Oral Reading Test*. Assesses oral reading level and types of errors (mispronunciation, omissions, insertions, etc.) with paragraphs from first grade through high school. Bobbs-Merrill Co.

T-22. *Gilmore Oral Reading Test*. Assesses oral reading performance of pupils grades 1–8. Provides measures of accuracy of oral reading, comprehension, and rate. Psychological Corporation.

T-23. *Roswell-Chall Diagnostic Reading Test*. A brief word analysis test specifically designed to measure knowledge and application of phonetic elements (consonants, short and long vowels, vowel combinations, and syllabication). Essay Press.

T-24. *Botel Reading Inventory*. Includes subtests for word recognition, vocabulary, and a range of phonics skills. Follett Publishing Co.

T-25. *Wepman Auditory Discrimination Test*. Measures auditory discrimination by having child identify whether pairs of words are the same or different. (See Chapter 4 for a fuller description.) Language Research Associates.

T-26. *Goldman-Fristoe-Woodcock Auditory Discrimination Test*. Uses taped stimulus to measure child's ability to discriminate speech sounds in quiet versus noisy environment. (See Chapter 4 for a fuller description.) American Guidance Services.

T.27. *Developmental Test of Visual Perception*. Measures five aspects of visual perception: eye-motor coordination, figure-ground, form consistency, position in space, and spatial relationships. (See Chapter 5 for a fuller description.) Consulting Psychological Press.

T-28. *Beery Developmental Test of Visual-Motor Integration*. Assesses visual-motor integration by having child copy a series of geometric forms. (See Chapter 5 for a fuller description.) Follett Publishing Co.

T-29. *Bender Visual-Motor Gestalt Test*. Tests visual-motor integration by having child copy designs presented on cards. (See Chapter 5 for a fuller description.) Psychological Corporation.

T-30. *Detroit Test of Learning Aptitude*. Nineteen subtests include assessment of auditory and visual processing abilities, motor speed and precision, oral language, social adjustment, and number ability. The use of nine to thirteen subtests from the instrument is recommended for complete diagnosis. Provides mental-age norms. (See Chapters 4 and 5 for fuller description.) Bobbs-Merrill Co.

T-31. *Illinois Test of Psycholinguistic Abilities*. A clinical instrument containing twelve subtests designed to assess children's ability to comprehend visual and auditory symbols, to organize information, and to use verbal or manual symbols to transmit ideas. (See Chapter 5 for a fuller description.) University of Illinois Press.

T-32. *Peabody Picture Vocabulary Test*. Assesses verbal ability by having child match spoken words with pictures. Reports an intelligence score. American Guidance Service.

T-33. *Slosson Oral Reading Test.* Reports an oral reading grade score (grades 1–12) on the basis of children's ability to read lists of words presented in isolation. Slosson Educational Publications.

T-34. *Reading Miscue Inventory.* Oral reading selections, grades 1–7, with procedures for analyzing miscues in reading. Macmillan Publishing Co.

TEST PUBLISHER ADDRESSES

Addresses of the publishers of the tests cited in this chapter are:

American Guidance Service, Inc.
Publishers Building
Circle Pines, MN 55014

The Bobbs-Merrill Co., Inc.
4300 West 62nd St.
Indianapolis, IN 46268

Cooperative Tests and Services
Educational Testing Service
Princeton, NJ 08540

Consulting Psychologists Press, Inc.
577 College Avenue
Palo Alto, CA 94306

CTB/McGraw-Hill
Del Monte Research Park
Monterey, CA 93940

Essay Press, Inc.
P.O. Box 5
Planetarium Station
New York, NY 10024

Follett Publishing Co.
1010 West Washington Blvd.
Chicago, IL 60607

Houghton Mifflin Co.
One Beacon St.
Boston, MA 02107

Language Research Associates
Box 95
950 East 59th St.
Chicago, IL. 60637

Macmillan Publishing Co., Inc.
866 Third Ave.
New York, NY 10022

Psychological Corporation
(A subsidiary of Harcourt Brace Jovanovich)
757 Third Ave.
New York, NY 10017

Science Research Associates
259 East Erie St.
Chicago, IL 60611

Slosson Educational Publications, Inc.
140 Pine St.
East Aurora, NY 14052

Teachers College Press
1234 Amsterdam Ave.
New York, NY 10027

University of Illinois Press
Urbana, IL 61801

Western Psychological Services
12031 Wilshire Blvd.
Los Angeles, CA 90025

Manufacturers of visual screening devices identified in this chapter are:

(School Vision Tester)
Bausch and Lomb, Inc.
565 Commonwealth Ave.
Boston, MA 02215

(Visual Survey Telebinocular)
Keystone View Co.
2212 East 12th St.
Davenport, IA 52803

Reading Eye Camera)
Educational Development Laboratories, Inc.
1221 Avenue of the Americas
New York, NY 10020

REFERENCES

Buros, Oscar K., ed. *Reading: Tests and Reviews*. New Brunswick, N.J.: Gryphon Press, 1975.

Buros, Oscar K., ed. *The Seventh Mental Measurements Yearbook*. New Brunswick, N.J.: Gryphon Press, 1972.

Bush, Wilma J., and Waugh, Kenneth W. *Diagnosing Learning Disabilities*. 2d ed. Columbus: Charles E. Merrill, 1976.

Ekwall, Elton E. *Diagnosis and Remediation of the Disabled Reader*. Boston: Allyn and Bacon, 1976.

Farr, Roger, and Anastaslow, Nicholas. *Tests of Reading Readiness and Achievement: A Review and Evaluation*. Newark, Del.: International Reading Association, 1969.

Gearheart, Bill R., and Willemberg, Ernest P. *Application of Pupil Assessment Information for the Special Education Teacher*. Denver, Colo.: Love Publishing Co., 1970.

Lerner, Janet W. *Children with Learning Disabilities*. 2d ed. Boston: Houghton Mifflin Co., 1971.

Martuza, Victor R. *Applying Norm-Referenced and Criterion-Referenced Measurement in Education*. Boston: Allyn and Bacon, 1977.

Spache, George D. *Diagnosing and Correcting Reading Disabilities*. Boston: Allyn and Bacon, 1976.

Spache, George D. *Investigating the Issues of Reading Disabilities*. Boston: Allyn and Bacon, 1976.

4

Problems in Auditory Learning

Preview

Problems in auditory processing can interfere with school achievement, particularly in the area of reading. Hearing loss and auditory perceptual deficits require careful attention from specialists and appropriate instructional accommodations within the regular classroom. Teachers must become sensitive to the kinds of behavior that may indicate a problem, as well as to issues of individualizing reading. It cannot be expected that the classroom teacher will assume the full responsibility for remediation; it is presumed, however, that s/he will modify the learning environment and reading instruction to provide the child with the maximum opportunity for success.

With our eyes we take in the world in all shades of the spectrum and in all variations of size and shape. With our ears we scan the world through the range of frequencies available to the human ear. What we see is restricted to specific fields. We hear, however, in all directions. Through the auditory channel comes knowledge of the world as it is perceived by man, with all the sounds that identify things—those auditory symbols that allow us to code and store our experiences. A disturbance in this channel alters that symbol system at some point. Since all sensory avenues are crucial to the development of language, an auditory problem has significant influence on learning to read.

DISORDERS OF HEARING

As described in Chapter 2, the first level of learning is sensory; therefore, the first breakdown that can occur in the auditory channel is due to hearing loss. Since reading is also partially a sensory process, hearing loss can have a serious effect on learning to read. The severity of the loss very much determines the components of the educational process required to provide a child with the maximum opportunity for acquiring language.

Historically, children with a severe or profound loss of hearing have been educated in substantially separate programs in private or state schools for the deaf. In some parts of the country, however, attempts are being made to establish regional day classes for young deaf children, who need and will enjoy an opportunity to participate in regular classroom activities with hearing children. Since it is highly unlikely that this participation will include instruction in the language arts, it is not within the scope of this book to discuss techniques for developing language skills in the deaf child. Language instruction for the deaf requires the attention of a teacher trained in deaf education as well as a specially designed acoustic environment. When deaf children are integrated into regular classrooms for specific activities, classroom teachers should maintain close contact with the specialists in order to insure the most appropriate accommodations to the children's needs. There is another group of hearing-impaired children, however, who are very much within the mainstream, and their unique learning problems may or may not be recognized. These children experience a loss of hearing less severe than that of the totally deaf child, but sufficiently severe to cause problems in understanding and using language.

Conductive Hearing Loss

The mechanism for hearing is divided into three parts: the outer, middle, and inner ear. A dysfunction in the outer and/or middle ear (with a normally

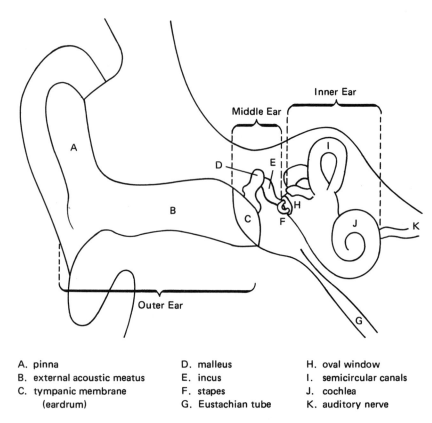

Inner Ear

Middle Ear

A

D

E

I

B

C

F

H

J

K

G

Outer Ear

A. pinna	D. malleus	H. oval window
B. external acoustic meatus	E. incus	I. semicircular canals
C. tympanic membrane	F. stapes	J. cochlea
(eardrum)	G. Eustachian tube	K. auditory nerve

(From Phyllis P. Phillips, Speech and Hearing Problems in the Classroom *[Lincoln, Nebr.: Cliffs Notes, 1975], p. 114. Reprinted by Permission.)*

Figure 4.1   *The hearing mechanism.*

functioning inner ear) is considered a conductive hearing loss—that is, the result of difficulty in the conduction of the sound to the auditory nerve endings in the inner ear. In other words, the signal being delivered is diminished through an obstruction in the outer ear canal or middle chambers (e.g., by wax), or a malfunction in the activity of the tiny bones in the middle ear. Most hearing loss of this type is acquired during early childhood due to otitis media (middle-ear infection). Upper respiratory infections often travel the open pathway from the nasal passages and throat along the Eustachian tube to the middle ear.

The result can be the distention of the eardrum due to the accumulation of fluid and this may be very painful. The presence of fluid also prevents the eardrum and the ossicles (tiny bones called malleus, incus and stapes) from vibrating normally, thus causing a hearing loss. Without prompt medical treatment the pressure can build to the point where the drum ruptures spontaneously to release the fluid. Repeated ruptures of the drum may cause scar tissue to form, and this has a more permanent effect on the mobility of the drum. Tonsils and adenoids are a prime source of infection that may be communicated to the middle ear. When the condition becomes chronic, with recurring infections in the middle ear, there is a real danger of permanent damage.

The symptoms of a conductive hearing loss are quite obvious in the elementary classroom. Runny nose, draining ears, mouth breathing, and the general look of an unwell child are signals that hearing may be (or may become) a problem. In some cases treatment with antibiotics may not be sufficient to correct the condition. A minor surgical procedure involving the insertion of tiny Teflon tubes into the eardrum may be necessary to achieve good and complete drainage. Of course, some of these same problems can occur when children poke things into their ears and rupture the drum. Foreign objects usually cause ragged tears and, again, scar tissue may form. In any event, the condition and its treatment may stretch out over several weeks or months. During this time, hearing levels may fluctuate depending on the amount of fluid built up in the middle ear. Following successful treatment of a chronic ear infection, it is always wise to ask for an audiological evaluation in order to determine whether a hearing loss still exists and, if it does, the educational significance of the loss.[1]

A conductive hearing loss results in the fairly equal reduction in loudness of all frequencies of sound. Children with this condition have trouble with the transmission of sound waves to the organ containing the auditory nerve endings. The nerve functions properly but the input is weaker than normal. The problem is mechanical.

Sensorineural Hearing Loss

A sensorineural hearing loss is the result of damage to the inner ear and/or to the auditory nerve itself. This loss is also called a perceptive or nerve loss. Nerve endings of the auditory nerve are contained in tiny hairlike projections within the cochlea in the inner ear. These projections respond to different sound frequencies, the differentiation being a systematic progression from the lowest to the highest frequencies along the length of the membrane. These highly sensitive structures are vulnerable to certain internal and external agents. Most babies born with a hearing problem have this type of loss. Hereditary factors and prenatal conditions in the mother, e.g., German measles (rubella) during early pregnancy, are known contributors to auditory nerve damage. Other factors, such as high febrile diseases; toxic effect of drugs, particularly the mycins; head injury; acoustic trauma; or merely growing old, may lead to an acquired sensorineural loss at any time of life.

Unlike a conductive loss, the sensorineural loss cannot be treated surgically or medically. The damage is irreversible. The overall effect of a sensorineural hearing loss is different from that of a conductive loss, which reduces sounds rather evenly. A sensorineural loss tends to affect high-frequency sounds more than the low. The reason is not fully understood, but the result is that the child hears certain speech sounds better than others. High-frequency sounds like s, th, f, sh and ch are more difficult for him/her to discriminate than k, d, l, m, which have lower frequencies. S/he does not hear consecutive speech clearly. Discrimination exercises are very difficult when the stimulus words contain high-frequency sounds. Pairs like sheep-cheap, some-thumb truly sound alike, since the initial sounds may not be received at all.

Classroom Accommodation for the Child with a Hearing Loss

An important factor to remember in planning for any child with special needs is that the most obvious cause of learning problems may be secondary to other less evident but more significant factors. Social, emotional, and intellectual variables may be operating against the child as well. A good multidisciplinary evaluation is essential to the formulation of an appropriate educational plan.

In the classroom, the hearing loss can account for much of the fatigue the child may exhibit as a result of the effort to hear. Failure to understand directions and instruction is most likely related to his/her missing parts of the communication or to his/her lack of certain vocabulary. Being at a disadvantage in social and instructional settings can often lead to feelings of insecurity. The urge to withdraw becomes rather strong. Mistakes made in public reinforce those feelings. The child is obviously at greatest risk during school activities involving oral language, his/her own or that of the teachers. Most often the child with an educationally significant hearing loss has articulation problems as well as language problems. S/he articulates and uses language differently from other children. In the early years this may not be a problem, since many children have immature speech and language patterns; however, in the middle and upper grades the problem is particularly noticeable and often embarrassing.

There are certain issues of classroom accommodation for the hearing-impaired child that require the special attention of the classroom teacher. Careful consideration of instructional and environmental modifications can provide the child with the greatest comfort and opportunity for successful participation in the regular educational program. The following are of major importance.

Advantageous seating

Children with sensory impairments (hearing and vision) need to be close to the source of instruction. Since this is not a privilege that can be extended to all class members without complete chaos, the children in the class must understand the reason for this special permission. Flexibility of placement in any instructional setting, but particularly in those dealing with the development of skill in the language arts, is important to the academic success of children with hearing loss. It is of additional benefit to seat such children next to a window so that the speaker's face, as well as any visual aids, remain in good light.

Amplification Amplification may be a critical factor in the education of a child with hearing loss. Although a hearing aid may not be required for the child with a mild loss, it would usually be prescribed in cases of moderate, severe, or profound loss. Although hearing aids are very sensitive instruments, they in no way compare with prescription glasses. The latter can correct a visual image to within normal limits of vision. No hearing aid allows a child to hear as he would with normal hearing. No hearing aid is completely free from distortion. In spite of their shortcomings, however, these devices help considerably to compensate for damage to the hearing mechanism, particularly in the instance of conductive loss. Some children have difficulty in developing a tolerance for wearing an aid. A good amount of cooperation may be necessary between parents and teachers in order to work out a program of adjustment. The benefits are worth the effort. Since batteries are apt to run down and cords may become detached, teachers can help by making sure the aid is fully operational before beginning a lesson, particularly in the area of language arts. For some children, a desk model auditory trainer may be more beneficial than an ear level aid. One becomes concerned about asking a child to use such an obvious piece of equipment; however, with so many electronic devices being used in classrooms today, this is not the problem it once was.

Lipreading Lipreading is a great help to the child with a problem in hearing. Unfortunately, not all speakers are easy to read. The easiest are those who speak clearly, rather slowly, and with good eye contact. The hardest are those with limited lip movements, rapid speech, or a tendency to move about. It may be necessary for a teacher to interpret class speakers if they are not easily seen and heard. The speech patterns of the teacher are even more crucial than those of the class members, since s/he is the source of the greatest amount of communication. In addition to facilitating the child's ability to lip-read, the teacher serves as a model for the child's own speech. Volume should be held normal. For the child with a hearing aid, shouting may blast him out of his seat.

Vocabulary Learning new vocabulary is often difficult for the child with a hearing loss. S/he may need the visual reinforcement of seeing the words written on the chalkboard as well as seeing and hearing them spoken. Spelling words are more easily identified when dictated in the context of a sentence. The child with a sensorineural hearing loss may not hear two or three of the sounds in a word causing him to make numerous errors. For example, in the sentence

The thief stole some shoes

the child may actually hear only

ŭ ē tōl ŭm oo.

Spelling tests are more fairly administered individually or through a recorded tape so that words or sentences may be replayed.

Fatigue and distractibility

A great deal of concentration is required of a child who must attempt to acquire verbal information using a hearing mechanism that is inefficient. The child must expend more energy to attend to what is being said than children with normal hearing. The difficulty experienced is similar to that of anyone sitting in the second balcony at the theater or trying to follow a conversation in a busy restaurant. It can be very tiring. Children with hearing losses should not be exposed to prolonged periods of oral instruction. Reading activities should be alternated between group exercises requiring careful attending and independent work on skills.

Factors of fatigue, in addition to the developmental differences in children's attending behavior, contribute to problems of distractibility for children with hearing loss. Teachers must provide periods of relief from heavy listening demands along with well-planned, highly motivating lessons that are "attention holding." The child him/herself will provide the best feedback as to the conditions that promote ease of listening, particularly during reading instruction.

Participation

Some children with hearing loss prefer to be as inconspicuous as possible in order to avoid calling attention to any difficulties they have. The classroom teacher's sensitivity to these feelings, and his/her attitude toward the children, will influence the degree to which they participate in classroom activities. When the environment is accepting of individual differences and supportive of all efforts to learn, children feel free to get involved and attempt new things.

Since some hearing-impaired children are reluctant to socialize with other children at the risk of being misunderstood or rejected, the classroom teacher may need to provide opportunities for the child with a hearing loss to work comfortably and successfully with small groups of peers. Reading activities; creative dramatics; projects in social studies, science, art, etc., can be reinforcing of social as well as academic skills.

The amount of accommodation required by any child with a hearing loss depends on the degree of the loss and the child's own ability to use other systems to compensate. Classroom teachers should be careful to observe signs of stress, inattention, and confusion in order to take the appropriate steps to relieve the problem.

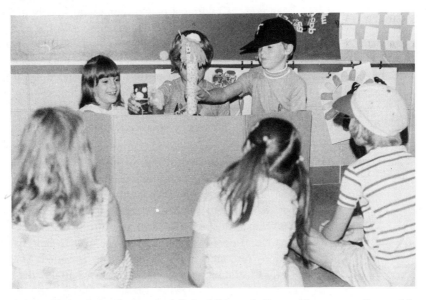

Creative dramatics and puppetry delight children of all ages. They are excellent activities for developing self-confidence along with self-expression. (Photo by John A. Malnati)

DISORDERS OF AUDITORY PERCEPTION

Problems in auditory perception relate not only to the child with a hearing loss, but also to the child with a breakdown at the perceptual level. Indeed, it is often difficult to distinguish between these two groups. Problems in sensory input and problems in the organization of that input into adequate perceptions both place a constraint on the ability to acquire auditory information. The impact on the development of language and reading is significant.

There are certain auditory perceptual behaviors involved in the development of receptive and expressive language. Auditory discrimination has long been recognized as an important skill in learning to speak and to read.[2] The ability to blend sounds is another. Reading readiness programs pay much attention to both skills in attempting to prepare a child for the auditory demands of the decoding process. Although such training is necessary and important at this stage, it does not cover the full range of auditory perceptual tasks. In addition, a child must be able to detect a sound source, separate relevant from irrelevant stimuli, and observe the order in which sounds occur. Problems in auditory perception can be detected in a number of areas.

Awareness

The most basic auditory skill involves the recognition that sound is occurring. In infants one can see this through the startle reflex following a sudden noise. Children at play respond immediately to the first sound of the ice-cream truck even before it comes into view. For some children, this behavior is absent or at best inconsistent. They do not tune in or respond to sound—for example, the word "Go" to start a race—but respond to the sight of children running. A child who has difficulty responding to gross sounds will have greater difficulty attending to the distinction between phonemes as similar as p and b.

Localization

By five to six months an infant can turn toward the source of a sound. Being able to respond to a sound source is, at times, necessary to our survival. Negotiating through rush hour traffic can be hazardous whether on foot or in a car, and success depends not only on a quick response to a horn or whistle but on the ability to identify the direction as well. For the child who has not fully developed this skill, life can be difficult. S/he feels the need to localize the source of every sound by using the eyes to help the ears. The child is constantly distracted by the need to "see" a sound. Spelling dictation is particularly frustrating when the teacher moves around the room while dictating.

Figure-ground

Most educators are more familiar with figure-ground as it relates to the visual modality. The detection of a figure hidden in the background of a picture is often used as a puzzle in children's magazines. This involves the ability to attend to the details of a specific stimulus while ignoring all other stimuli within the field. In the auditory modality, this skill is a bit more difficult. Vision has the rather natural boundaries of the visual fields. We do not see what is behind or above us. The world of sound has no such limits. We hear in all directions—through doors, walls, and windows. The sources of distraction are countless, particularly in the classroom. Children who cannot screen out extraneous stimuli attend to all of it—the traffic outside, the reading group in the corner, the custodian's cart in the hall, and the numerous other everyday sounds. Selective listening is difficult. Phonic exercises requiring the discrimination, sequencing, or blending of sounds can be confusing to the child who cannot isolate the stimuli presented from other auditory signals.

Discrimination

Auditory discrimination involves the ability to detect differences among sounds. Templin[3] suggests that children have developed adequate auditory discrimination skills by the age of eight. In the early school years, skills are still in the process of evolving. Children who fail to develop them or who develop them at a slower-than-normal rate are usually in difficulty with language by the time they start school. Articulation errors are often associated with poor discrimination of speech sounds. In severe cases, vocabulary and comprehension are affected to the point where the child may appear to be a

Direct auditory input through the use of headsets and taped material eliminates distracting sound and allows children to work independently. (Photo by John A. Malnati)

slow learner, when in fact the problem may be one of auditory discrimination. In addition to being able to distinguish the individual sounds in words, the child must also be capable of discriminating linguistic units or segments within a sentence. The inability to do this can disrupt verbal communication.

A kindergarten teacher may first suspect difficulty with auditory processing when the child fails to progress in the reading readiness program. S/he may show adequate performance in exercises involving visual skills but poor performance on those requiring auditory skills. Later, this child experiences difficulty with a phonic approach to reading and spelling.

Sequencing   In addition to the child's ability to receive, locate, and differentiate an incoming auditory signal, s/he must attend to the order in which the sounds occur. S/he must listen to the temporal order of the individual segments of each auditory configuration. Identifying sequence depends on the child's ability to analyze the individual components of a word. This involves knowing that words are composed of parts, recognizing what parts are present in a given word, and relating one part to another. The ability to observe serial order is a skill required in multiple systems. Children must recall the sequence of sounds in words in order to speak (auditory), the sequence of letters in words in order to spell (visual), and the sequence of motor movements of individual letters in order to write (kinesthetic). Children who cannot sequence properly have great difficulty learning to read and spell. They frequently omit or reorder sounds in words. Attaching the correct order of visual symbols to the phonemes in dictated spelling words is difficult when the phonemes are not recalled in correct order. If visual skills are strong, the child may compensate by monitoring him/herself visually. S/he may know how the word should look, and s/he can then revisualize the sequence s/he could not reauditorize.

Synthesizing

Identified sound segments must be blended together to form the whole. Children demonstrate this skill at an early age when they begin speaking in whole words, then in phrases and sentences. Many beginning decoding programs rely heavily on the child's ability to synthesize phonemes in learning to read. Children are expected to learn new words by carefully observing the total auditory gestalt, by identifying the individual units and the order in which they occur, and by blending these units together through an accurate auditory-motor match. Children with problems at the perceptual level cannot take individual sounds and blend them together easily. The segments remain fractionated and without meaning.

Memory

Underlying all auditory perceptual behavior is the capacity to store and retrieve auditory information. The memory process may be more important in auditory than in visual perception. Visual stimuli remain constant. They remain available to the perceiver for as long as it takes to separate, differentiate, and sequence individual elements. In the auditory channel this is not so. An auditory signal occurs and then disappears. For the human information-processing system to operate upon it, the stimulus must be stored and reauditorized. As children become more and more adept, the behaviors become more and more automatic; that is, the discrimination of elements, identification of sequence, etc., become instantaneous. The system becomes highly efficient. Reaching this point, however, very much depends on the capacity of the system to store and get at previously presented stimuli.

Short-term memory involves the child's holding information in mind for a short time before responding. Memory span indicates the amount of material a child can retain at a given time. Binet was one of the first to recognize that memory span increases with age, and he used memory span tasks as indicators of intellectual maturity. Problems in the ability to retain auditory information even for a short time interfere with the performance of the various perceptual functions, since the information does not remain available. A child may lose the first two steps of an instruction, or the sequence of sounds in a word or of words in a sentence. Material that has not been stored cannot be retrieved for future use, and learning is seriously disturbed.

Long-term auditory memory involves the ability to retrieve information stored over a period of time. Although research goes on, there is, as yet, no clear definition of the nature of the memory process. However, we are sure that there are numbers of children who have difficulty with retrieval. They store information on a short term basis, but either the process for long-term storage fails to take place, or once it takes place, the retrieval mechanism fails. The result is the same: what the child learns today, s/he may not remember tomorrow; what s/he read in the first paragraph may not be recalled by the time the story is finished. In reading, then, the problem is the inability to recall the sound a letter makes, the sounds within words, or the details of a story just read, in order to answer questions.

Children with auditory deficits are truly disabled in learning basic decoding and comprehension skills. The symptoms can be very subtle and often go unrecognized, especially if visual skills are intact.

Observable Classroom Behavior

Children experiencing problems in auditory processing show a variety of symptoms in the elementary classroom. These symptoms may seem more apparent at certain times than at others. The differences are most likely due to changes within the environment and not within the child. The following list is by no means an exhaustive inventory of behavior, and certainly each child will not exhibit all of them. The list is provided as a basis for formulating a hunch that hearing or auditory perception may be involved in a child's difficulty in learning to read.

A child with poor auditory processing:

1. often appears not to hear (is slow to respond to auditory information).
2. is distracted by other activities going on in the classroom; therefore, rarely finishes his work.
3. works better by him/herself in a quiet corner.
4. often approaches the teacher to repeat directions or assignments.
5. usually watches the other children before following through.
6. overreacts to a change in acoustic environment such as entering the gym or cafeteria.
7. has low tolerance for noisy environments.
8. seems to tire easily, particularly during listening activities.
9. has difficulty attending to the order in which sounds occur.
10. is unable to recall simple information like his home address, phone number, etc.
11. cannot march in step to music or beat a simple rhythm with a drum.
12. mispronounces words.
13. can discriminate better visually than auditorily.
14. has great difficulty in distinguishing long and short vowel sounds.

15. may have difficulty with phonetic analysis.

16. cannot readily identify initial, medial, and final consonants.

Once again, it is important to remember that the child with an auditory perceptual problem probably will not exhibit all of these behaviors. It is also important to realize that one or more of these behaviors do not necessarily indicate an auditory problem. Teachers should not deal with isolated symptoms as much as with clusters of behaviors taken together. It is the recognition of the specific manifestations, as well as of the interaction between and among the behaviors, that has implications for instructional management. The child with auditory perceptual problems is highly distractible, slow to respond to auditory information, has difficulty discriminating sounds and tends to stop processing altogether when too much information is coming in at one time, and requires an environment devoid of extraneous auditory stimuli, as well as reading instruction that is carefully segmented and presented. This child presents a greater demand for individualization than the child who attends very well but has difficulty distinguishing between long and short vowels. A classroom teacher should be a careful observer and alert to any signs that a child is experiencing problems in auditory learning.

Classroom Accommodation for Children with Auditory Problems

For the child with hearing, perceptual, and/or memory problems, environmental and instructional adjustments are necessary if he is to learn to read. The following suggestions are aimed at providing for his comfort and well-being within the regular classroom.

1. Avoid space with a free flow of sound in all directions.
2. Provide a quiet corner for independent work.
3. Use carpets and drapes to help absorb sound.
4. Make sure instructional areas are well lit.
5. Allow the child to move to the most advantageous position for seeing and hearing.
6. Give clear, concise directions.
7. Use visual aids to reinforce auditory features of sound and to facilitate memory.
8. Provide visual drill and reinforcement of new vocabulary.
9. Assign a "buddy" to assist with directions, assignments, etc.
10. Make sure that seat work is throughly understood before leaving him/her to work independently.

ASSESSMENT OF PROBLEMS IN AUDITORY PERCEPTION

Observation of Behavior

Careful observation and recording of a child's performance in the classroom are among the most important steps in the assessment of individual problems in learning. The behaviors described above may make a classroom teacher suspect that a child is having difficulty dealing with auditory information. Confirmation or rejection of that suspicion depends on the teacher's ability to determine the conditions under which the child functions efficiently, and to identify what tasks s/he can and cannot perform. This information contributes to the determination of the need to refer the child for assessment. When a more thorough evaluation is considered necessary, the information provided by the classroom teacher is used to help formulate the questions the evaluators will attempt to answer. Chapter 3 presented the various approaches to assessment. Although there is a trend toward the greater use of criterion-referenced measures, there is still widespread use of standardized norm-referenced tests. Evaluations made at hospital clinics or agencies outside the school may report the results of standardized measures.

Tests of Auditory Discrimination

Although the type of formalized test procedures will vary from one evaluation team to another, there are certain tests that are used more frequently. It is not expected that classroom teachers will actually administer these tests. Descriptions of the most commonly used instruments are presented to help classroom teachers become familiar with the format and composition of the various measures in order to become good "consumers" of assessment information.

The *Wepman Auditory Discrimination Test*[4] is often used to evaluate a child's ability to detect differences in words that vary on one phoneme, e.g., *web-wed*. The child must make the judgment of same or different for the forty pairs of words. Norms are provided for ages five to eight. The test was re-standardized in 1973 and includes a method of scoring different from that of the 1958 edition.

The *Goldman-Fristoe-Woodcock Test of Auditory Discrimination*[5] measures a child's ability to discriminate one-syllable words by correctly identifying a picture of the stimulus word presented on an audiotape. The child must select the correct picture from the four possible choices. There is a preliminary training procedure which insures that the child knows the vocabulary involved. When the child has indicated his ability to identify all stimulus words, two subtests are administered; the first, Auditory Discrimination Quiet, presents the words without competing noise; the second, Auditory Discrimination Noise, presents the same task in the presence of background noise. Norms are provided for age four and above.

Although both the Wepman and the Goldman-Fristoe-Woodcock are called tests of auditory discrimination, they do not correlate and therefore must be viewed as measuring different skills.[6] It is possible that a poor performance on one would not mean a poor performance on the other. For this reason, interpretation of tests of this type is difficult.

Detroit Test of Learning Aptitude[7]

There are certain subtests of the Detroit Test that are useful in observing problems of auditory sequential memory.

Subtest #6: Auditory attention span for unrelated words

This task presents a series of unrelated words (from two to eight in the series) and requires the child to say them back. The number of items remembered and the order in which they are recalled can be observed. Some children fail the task because of poor discrimination of the individual words.

Subtest #13: Auditory attention span for related syllables

This involves the ability to repeat sentences of increasing length. Children may have difficulty with this test because they cannot retain information long enough to recall it, or because they are unable to deal with the syntactic complexities of the sentences themselves.

Wepman and Morency have recently published the Auditory Memory Span Test,[8] which is similar to Subtest #6 of the Detroit. Since the norms are from 1973, this test might be a better choice for assessing memory for unrelated words.

Illinois Test of Psycholinguistic Abilities[9]

There are certain subtests of the ITPA that assess skills in auditory processing.

Auditory sequential memory

This is a digit repetition task similar to the one included as part of the WISC. The child is required to repeat a series of numbers. Since digit span is likely to be a child's best memory span,[10] interpretation must be done with caution. When a child is suspected of having a problem recalling verbal information, his/her ability to remember meaningful language—as well as digits—should be assessed.

Auditory closure

This subtest evaluates the child's ability to identify words that are presented with missing syllables. For example, the child hears da e and must recognize it as "daddy." The child is required to recall the missing information.

Sound blending

In this subtest the child is required to synthesize sounds that are presented in segments. Sounds in both actual and nonsense words are used. Children who have difficulty learning phonics often have difficulty with blending tasks.

In addition to the tests described here, Chapter 3 presented numerous other instruments that may identify problems in auditory perception. A task analysis of many of the reading tests can reveal a child's difficulty in responding to, and organizing, incoming auditory information. When these problems are identified, careful consideration must be given to the child's instructional needs.

TEACHING TO STRENGTHS IN READING

Although there are many good beginning programs available for teaching children to read, the choices narrow somewhat when instructing a child with auditory problems. In reading programs based on a phonics approach, success depends on good auditory perceptual skills, and on the ability to discriminate, to sequence, and, for some programs, to blend sounds. For the child who cannot perform these perceptual functions, phonics programs may be a source of great frustration. In beginning reading, it may be best to choose those instructional materials that teach to the child's strength. The learning profile of the child with a hearing loss and/or auditory perceptual problems often shows strength in the visual modality. A visual approach to beginning reading may best serve his/her needs. Matching reading approach to learning strengths does not imply that a phonics approach should never be used or that phonics will never be taught. It means only that work on auditory skills and their application to the sound-symbol relationship needs to be provided in a program personalized to the child's need. In the meantime, the child can experience success in reading by using those systems which function best.

Careful evaluation of the specific features of a reading program can eliminate the need for trial and error. Chall[11] and Aukerman[12] provide extensive analyses of the most widely used approaches to reading. For programs not reviewed, it is possible to use the same criteria to identify program characteristics. Those approaches which emphasize meaning using whole words set for diversity with low vocabulary and phonics load are appropriate for the child with auditory problems. The high-frequency vocabulary, along with picture clues, allows the child to gain basic sight vocabulary through visual analysis. This sight vocabulary can be reinforced through the use of such devices as a card reader or simple flash cards. Children enjoy operating electronic equipment as well as making their own materials to use. Once the child has acquired a basic vocabulary, creative writing with illustrations, cartoon stories, and picture dictionaries can be used as additional language exercises for reading reinforcement.

WORKING ON AUDITORY SKILLS

There is mounting evidence to support the notion that reading is more related to audition than was previously believed. In looking at the differences between a group of boys with severe reading problems and a group of boys who read well, Zigmond[13] presented both groups with six tests of auditory functioning, four tests of visual functioning, and five tests requiring both auditory and visual processing. The results showed the poor readers to be inferior to the good readers on all tasks involving auditory skills but on only one task involving visual skills. Bateman[14] reports her attempt to match teaching method to style of learning defined in terms of preferred modality. The results show, first, the superiority of the auditory approach (Lippincott), and second, the superiority of readers who were identified as auditory learners. In other words, children who process well auditorily may have the edge in beginning reading.

The above seems to suggest that careful consideration must be given to developing good auditory skills in all young children. Since the child with hearing and/or perceptual problems is at greatest risk in this area, auditory training is essential to his success as a reader.

The Child with a Hearing Loss

Adequate readiness

A great deal of the preparation for reading occurs long before the child enters school. It begins when s/he learns to use the auditory symbols that mark life's experiences. The oral vocabulary s/he acquires during these early years serves as the language base for his/her learning the visual code later on. For the child with a hearing loss, the basic problem occurs when s/he is unable to acquire sufficient vocabulary, or when the vocabulary s/he does acquire is inaccurate in its auditory features. Early identification and intervention are obviously necessary to his/her survival in school.

Reading readiness programs for the hearing-impaired child should pay particular attention to the auditory language base. Vocabulary development through structured programs such as the Peabody Language Development Kits[15] allows a teacher to observe the degree of language deficit in relation to other children in the group, the rate at which new words can be acquired, and the consistency with which individual speech sounds are misarticulated. Such observations are an essential part of a multidisciplinary evaluation of the child's special needs. Preschool programs are rich in the kinds of experiences that stimulate language development. Field trips, classroom pets, storytime, show-and-tell, and other classroom activities provide an excellent opportunity for the development of verbal expression. Within the context of these activities, it is possible for a teacher to reinforce both new vocabulary and the child's attempts at forming sentences. These activities are equally appropriate for reinforcing those skills in lipreading, articulation, and language that are being developed with the assistance of a speech and language therapist.

More specific skills related to reading can be developed through the reading readiness curriculum. The child with a hearing loss needs the same preparation for discriminating letter shapes and word configurations as do children who hear well. Indeed, attention to visual details and clues is a mechanism of compensation that may need to be stressed if the child has not begun to acquire it on his/her own. Introduction to the auditory features of words must be based on the child's maximal use of his remaining hearing. Taped material, using a cassette player with a headset, is particularly effective in the presentation of individual sounds and words. First of all, it screens out all competing noise through direct auditory input (via headset); second, it allows the stimulus words to be repeated if necessary; and third, the volume can be set at a level comfortable for the child.

Instructional approaches for word attack skills

Auditory training for the child with a hearing loss may well be the responsibility of a hearing therapist. If so, then work in the classroom will be geared to providing the drill and reinforcement for the developing auditory skills. When such specialized support services are not available, however, auditory training may rest largely with the classroom teacher. The following suggestions are provided for the teacher who must operate with limited resources.

When one modality is impaired, we look to other modalities to compensate. In the instance of hearing loss, this means highlighting those visual, tactile, and kinesthetic features of language which accompany the auditory signal. This is particularly important to the child with a sensorineural loss, since there may be high-frequency sounds that cannot be perceived at all. Initially, major emphasis needs to be placed on speech sound discrimination; that is, the child must learn to detect physical differences in sounds. Before the introduction of the grapheme, the child should be encouraged to explore certain phonetic and acoustic characteristics of sounds. A good place to start is with the sounds /f/ and /v/, since the differences are more physically observable. The formative movements of both are the same, and therefore look the same on the lips of the speaker. The basic difference is in voicing. The phoneme /v/ is voiced because the vocal cords vibrate when we articulate the sound. The phoneme /f/ is unvoiced; the vocal cords do not vibrate as the sound is made. Children can "feel" the differences in the sounds by placing their fingertips on the larynx (the Adam's apple) as they articulate and prolong the sounds. Calling the child's attention to the "motor" in his throat helps him to know more about the way sounds are made and the way they feel when he makes them himself.

The place or point of articulation is another important clue that provides proprioceptive (tactile-kinesthetic) feedback. Consonant sounds are grouped according to the point of contact or placement of the tongue within the oral cavity and the manner of articulation. For example, /t/, /d/, and /n/ are called lingual-alveolar because they are made by the tongue tip coming in contact with the alveolar ridge (behind the front teeth). The summary of research by Sanders[16] suggests that a listener may perceive speech only after he has mimicked the articulatory patterns that he associates with the auditory signal. Young children can be seen doing this in an overt manner. It helps them to mediate between the acoustic signal and the final perception of speech. Making use of these placement clues can contribute additional information in sound discrimination. The /p/ and /b/, also among the most visible sounds, are bilabial, formed by exploding the air pressure built up behind the lips. It is possible for the child to feel the exploding air on his hand, and to observe and feel the movement of the lips as well as the vibration of the vocal cords for /b/. Programs such as *Auditory Discrimination in Depth*[17] assign descriptive names to sound clusters based on the manner of articulation; /p/ and /b/ are called "lip poppers" or "lip stops." The emphasis is on the total perceptual experience prior to the time when the child must associate sounds with symbols. A child with a hearing loss may need to spend a considerable amount of time identifying the distinctive physical features of each sound first, before the introduction of letters.

Oral reading

There are certain special problems that can occur for the hearing-impaired child in the process of learning to read. Problems observable in oral reading reflect the child's difficulties in using oral language.

Voice modulation is often a problem for the child with a hearing loss. Some children shout, but many speak with inadequate projection. Oral reading can become a cause for concern when the child reads with poor articulation and a low monotone voice. Attempts at correction during the course of a reading group are rarely helpful and usually contribute a great deal of anxiety to having to read at all. The therapist providing speech and auditory training may well be working on voice quality and projection. If so, efforts should be coordinated to avoid inconsistencies of instruction. Drill and reinforcement can occur within the classroom with the aim of promoting more rapid progress. With a very young child, however, voice quality may not be a priority of the remedial program because of more critical language and communication needs. In this case, it is wise to accept the child's best efforts at oral reading so that the act of reading remains as pleasurable as possible.

Stress and intonation patterns

Children who proceed through the normal sequence of language development tune in to stress and intonation patterns at a very early age. A toddler will use stress and phrasing while babbling. This ability to recognize and imitate these patterns of language depends on normal hearing. The child with a hearing loss is very slow to acquire these features of language. A certain amount of intervention is necessary. There are techniques that can be used quite successfully and appropriately in a classroom setting. For example, choral reading provides a good opportunity to read aloud without notice while experiencing the normal rhythm and flow of the language. It helps all children

Choral reading allows children to experience the rhythm and flow of language while reading aloud. (Photo by John A. Malnati)

recognize the use of voice as an instrument to develop mood and characterization. Books like Bill Martin's *Sounds of Language*[18] series contain numerous passages of prose and poetry to delight and entertain children of all ages. The old rhyme "Over in the Meadow"[19] uses simple vocabulary with beautiful picture clues.

> Over in the meadow in the sand in the sun
>
> Lived an old mother turtle and her little turtle one.
>
> "Dig," said the mother.
>
> "I dig," said the one.
>
> So they dug all day in the sand in the sun.

It is possible for the children to tap out the rhythm of the verses as they read. This series also provides visual emphases for certain other language features such as sentence structure, grammatical markers, and punctuation. All of these help the child develop reading fluency.

Along with the problems of rhythm, even more disturbing problems relate to the learning of morphological and syntactical rules. The child with sensorineural hearing loss misses plural endings (s and z are high-frequency sounds) and has a tendency to drop word endings altogether in oral reading and in written work. The lack of awareness of these features causes difficulty in structural analysis and in comprehension when the child is faced with passages containing fairly complex sentence structure. Children often miss the clues of verb tense, subject-predicate relationship, etc., and come to wrong conclusions. Formal instruction in grammar must begin early for the child who cannot learn it him/herself through listening to adult speech. If s/he is to be able to write after s/he reads, then s/he must learn the rules in a systematic fashion using the visual features to reinforce the auditory ones. Teaching the basic sentence patterns with color coding of nouns, verbs, adjectives, etc., provides a visual reinforcement of those features that may be missing in auditory input.

The Child with Auditory Perceptual Problems

The child with a hearing loss may have problems in perception as well. The following instructional techniques are, therefore, appropriate to both groups of children and should be used as a result of careful assessment of strengths and weaknesses.

Perceptual training and skills training

The distinction is often made between perceptual training and skills training. Since learning to read requires the accurate intake and organization of auditory and visual stimuli, perceptual training forms an important foundation for the development of reading skills. When the content of perceptual training involves elements of the language code (sounds and letters), then the areas of perceptual training and skills training overlap. For example, an exercise in differentiating between and identifying two nonverbal sounds (a bell and a whistle, for example) may be considered a perceptual training exercise; when this extends to differentiating between the vowel sounds in the words *rob* and *robe,* it takes on a reading skills dimension as well. Similarly, a visual-dimension activity like this:

Mark the same shape in the line

is an exercise in visual perception. But when the exercise extends to letter forms as in

B | **B**   **G**   **T**   **B**   **D**

the activity is part of reading readiness training too.

Perceptual training is part of a development process. The young child learns to distinguish among the myriad of auditory and visual stimuli that are part of his/her environment. Perceptual training is a vital dimension of reading readiness programs. The problem comes when children progress beyond the readiness stage. If the second grader lacks basic perceptual skills, the teacher faces a decision of whether to continue with reading skills activities or "drop back" into more basic skills training. The answer to the question rests in the determination of how far the child has come in the developmental process. If s/he lacks basic readiness skills, skills that support success in reading, then perceptual training may be in order. Wherever possible, this training in the deficient perceptual skills should be provided in conjunction with reading instruction. Perceptual training and skills training are not an either/or proposition; there is considerable overlap between the two.

Word attack skills and problems in auditory discrimination As suggested in the previous section, the child with problems in detecting the differences in sounds may need to learn the distinctive features of speech before attempting to associate sounds with visual symbols. Before being expected to learn the sound-symbol correspondence and pronunciation principles, the child must develop the skill of detecting which speech sounds are present. Detecting the similarities and differences between two words should begin with words that vary on two phonemes. For example, it is easier for children to identify *week* and *meet* as being different than it is to distinguish between *week* and *weep*. The progression should be from simple to complex. In distinguishing between single sound features in words, auditory discrimination practice should begin with initial consonant sounds (the difference between *fat* and *pat,* for example), since initial consonant sounds are usually easier for the child to hear and identify. Children with auditory problems will need auditory discrimination practice with initial consonant sounds before final (*rat* and *rack*) and medial (*ladder* and *latter*) ones.

Identifying and sorting out consonant sounds is a great deal easier than discriminating vowel sounds. Except for the phonemes /r/, /h/, and /w/, there is a precise point of contact for the tongue, teeth, and lips that provides a tactile feature to reinforce the auditory one. Vowel sounds are formed through adjustment of the size of the oral cavity. There is very little proprioceptive feedback. Monitoring depends, for the most part, on hearing the difference. Activities such as the playlets suggested in *Picnic of Sounds*[20] are a delightful way of putting vowel, as well as consonant, sounds in the ear first before attaching the symbols. For the child with hearing loss and/or auditory perceptual problems, discrimination of short vowel sounds is the appropriate beginning point. The sound-symbol relationship is more consistent in words with short vowel sounds. That is, when a long vowel sound is represented in writing, chances are that it will be spelled in a number of different ways (the long [i] sound in *sigh, ride, die, eye,* etc.). The spelling of short (i), as in *rid* and *bit,* is more regular and consistent. Children with auditory problems require much practice in discriminating between spoken minimal pairs like:

pit	:	pat	ham	:	hem
pet	:	pot	him	:	home

When learning to discriminate between long and short vowels, children need to hear the difference between pairs of words like:

rob	:	robe	plan	:	plane
set	:	seat	cot	:	coat

words in which the sound features differ for a specific vowel. For children with severe problems, it may be necessary to provide exercises in sound duration using nonverbal sounds first. Buzzer boards are very appropriate and highly motivating for this type of training.

Word attack skills and problems in analysis and synthesis of sounds

Certain facts concerning perceptual functioning must be considered when teaching word attack skills involving analysis and synthesis of spoken sounds. The total perceptual gestalt is more than the sum total of its individual parts. In other words, each individual sound is influenced by those that surround it. Research in experimental phonetics has led to the conclusion that distinctive features of speech sounds are significantly less recognizable when spoken in isolation than when spoken in words. It seems to follow, then, that approaches to auditory analysis and synthesis that rely on auditory input alone are inappropriate for children with problems in auditory perception. While the child with good auditory skills is usually able to identify a match between phonemes uttered in isolation and his/her recollection of previous experiences with the sounds in sequence, the child with poor perceptual skills cannot. S/he needs to experience the total auditory and visual pattern in order to recognize the nature of the relationship between sound and symbol. In reading, the conclusions support a linguistic approach to beginning reading or an analytic approach to phonics.

Although the many linguistic reading programs available in today's market differ in emphasis and techniques, they are similar in their structuring of the phonemic elements of reading in a systematic, developmental sequence. The fact that most of these approaches are confined, at the beginning stages, to phonemically regular words is important for children who have a great need for a well-defined system of rules before facing the challenge of exceptions. Most of the programs provide concrete experiences with the language patterns through workbook exercises.

In most linguistic programs, the fact that sounds are not taught in isolation but are initially presented in monosyllabic words is a distinct advantage to the child with auditory problems. The acoustic characteristics of individual phonemes remain unaltered and easily recognizable, particularly within the limited field of selected word families. In addition, the presentation of the visual pattern along with the auditory one allows the child an opportunity to observe the integration of all component stimuli.

There are certain specific advantages of the linguistic approach for the child with auditory problems.

1. Words are selected for phonic consistencies.
2. Only the most regular patterns are introduced to insure early mastery.
3. Programs typically provide carefully ordered sequences of instruction from simple to complex.
4. Success does not rely on the child's ability to blend sounds.
5. Sentence patterns in reading material are more consistent with the sentence patterns in children's spoken language.
6. The primary early emphasis and focus are on decoding elements of print and not on the higher thought processes associated with reading.

In a nutshell, not only is a linguistic program consistent with mastering the alphabetic principle of our written language code, but it also includes features consistent with the learning style of the child with auditory problems.

Word attack skills and auditory sequencing

Sequencing involves the ability to retain sound patterns in mind long enough to identify individual elements and observe the order in which they occur. Most reading programs draw attention to the visual patterns of individual words. These patterns are more easily identified due to the nature of the stimulus, which remains fixed and available. Auditory patterns are equally important but considerably more difficult to deal with. Children who have difficulty observing and recalling auditory sequences usually have problems in speaking, reading, and spelling. At the root of these problems is short- and long-term memory. Short-term is involved in those tasks requiring an immediate response to the order of sounds, as in a spelling test; and long-term in the recalling or reauditorizing of sound patterns that have been stored, as in the task of creative writing.

For some children who have problems sequencing auditory information, it is necessary to begin with rather simple nonverbal sound patterns to allow them to experience initial success in determining the order in which sounds have occurred. Simple rhythm patterns beaten on a drum or with rhythm sticks are easy to identify and fun to reproduce. Equally simple are hand claps. Buzzer boards are a bit more sophisticated but infinitely more motivating. The teacher can persent patterns of long and short buzzes to a child, or two children can present sequences to one another. Visual sequence cards can be made to accompany the auditory patterns on the buzzer board in a manner that resembles the Morse code:

• — — • — •

When beginning training on speech sounds, it is sometimes helpful to use the auditory and visual stimuli together. Using two-syllable words helps the child to identify that each word has two beats or parts. When the child can successfully identify the two parts of words, increase the complexity of syllables within words, having the child tap the number of syllables. Once s/he can correctly identify the order of syllables, attention can be drawn to the sequence of individual sounds within each syllable.

Young children can use colored blocks to indicate sound sequences and shifts in sounds from one pattern to another. This helps children to note likenesses and differences in sound sequences. The colored blocks or chips are helpful in initial sound tracking exercises, because the children are not distracted by trying to identify words and their meaning.

The ability to sequence sounds is a skill essential to reading success. Kass[21] found auditory and visual sequential memory tasks to be an area of significantly different performance between a group of good readers and a group of poor readers. Obviously, sequencing properly depends in great measure on the ability to store and retrieve. Therefore, sequencing and memory exercises need to be considered together.

Comprehension and auditory problems

The ultimate goal of reading is the ability to understand what is written. Problems in auditory processing weaken the foundation on which visual language is based. For the child with a hearing loss, the difficulty may be basic vocabulary.

A child may miss the point of a paragraph or story because s/he doesn't know the meaning of certain words that are used. For the most part, however, the problem arises from the child's inability to translate the visual symbols into their auditory counterparts. Misreading initial, medial, or final segments of words can alter meaning. *Contempt* may be read as *content* and *thrifty* as *thirty*. In each case, meaning is altered. At this point it becomes critical that the reading material be well within the child's reading level. Books that appeal to a child's individual interests—i.e., animals, sports, etc.—put him/her in safe territory, since s/he is most likely well acquainted with the vocabulary and can make good use of contextual and picture clues. Giving him/her stories to title helps to focus on the important words that convey meaning. Such stories can also present "sillies" (absurdities) to be detected, such as:

Karen and Jane wanted to make a birthday cake for mother. They mixed flour, sugar, eggs, milk, and turpentine in a pan.

Memory contraints are a major factor in listening and reading comprehension. In addition to the ability to understand the communication in a sentence and paragraph, the child must be able to recall specific details—names, events, and the order in which they occurred. The child with a memory deficit is usually in great difficulty when reading for meaning. Although s/he may be capable of the kind of thinking involved in understanding events and relationships, and in drawing conclusions and evaluating solutions, s/he makes errors because s/he is unable to recall the specifics of characters, place, time, and events.

For beginning training in listening comprehension, there are many techniques to facilitate auditory recall. Activities such as playing, "I packed my trunk and in it I put . . . ," adding items in alphabetical order; listening to stories on a record, with immediate reenactment through creative dramatics or puppets; watching a cartoon filmstrip and later drawing pictures of events in the order in which they happened, provide experience in attending to events in the order of occurrence. In reading comprehension, the child should be made aware of the fact that information remains available through the printed word. Techniques like outlining and underlining may be helpful in highlighting important information. Providing the questions first helps the child to structure his/her thinking and to recognize material to be remembered. Since problems in storing and retrieving have serious implications for learning in all areas of the curriculum, it is impossible to overemphasize the need to provide the necessary memory training.

CONCLUSION

Deficits in auditory processing at the sensory and perceptual levels interfere with a child's ability to learn language, both spoken and written. In order to facilitate the learning process in general and learning to read in particular, the classroom teacher must be willing to provide the necessary environmental and instructional accommodations. The observable classroom behaviors of children with hearing loss and of those with perceptual deficits are very similar. Although modifications of the learning environment may be more extensive for children with hearing loss than for children with perceptual problems, teaching strategies may be the same. The willingness of the classroom teacher to teach to strengths in beginning reading offers the child the best chance for experiencing satisfaction and success. Initially, this means capitalizing on more efficient modalities. If visual skills are adequately developed, a look-say approach will allow for a greater amount of success. As remedial or developmental instruction is provided in the basic auditory skills involved in reading, a phonics approach can be introduced. The approach selected should take into account the fact that sounding and blending place the heaviest demand on the child's auditory system. The better match between learner and method appears to be analytic phonics or a linguistic approach to beginning reading.

As the child with hearing and perceptual problems struggles to compensate for his/her poor ability to process auditory information, the classroom teacher may well be his/her most important ally. The teacher's sensitivity to the child's unique needs as a learner can contribute immeasurably to his/her academic and social-emotional growth.

ACTIVITIES FOR PRESERVICE TEACHERS

1. Obtain an anthology of children's poetry. Find a poem suitable for choral reading by third graders. Choose a poem for its rhythm, stress, and intonation pattern as well as its appeal to children.

2. Make a list of "minimum pairs" to be used by students working on sound discrimination.

3. Form two teams of three members each plus a moderator. Prepare and debate the issue: "Auditory perceptual training should be included in all programs of reading readiness."

4. Choose a linguistic series found in your media center. Analyze it according to the criteria presented by Chall.[11]

5. Design a game to provide drill and reinforcement of auditory sequential memory for letters.

ACTIVITIES FOR IN-SERVICE TEACHERS

1. Prepare a PTA presentation on "Auditory Problems and their Relationship to Reading."

2. You have a child in your room who is unable to sound-blend. Identify six subskills that support success in sound blending.

3. Listen to side I of the record *Breaking Through* (Zenith Corporation). Take the dictation test at the end of the record. After identifying the missing high-frequency sounds that gave you the most difficulty, review the spelling lists for your grade level and underline the words that would be missed easily by the child with a sensorineural hearing loss.

4. Design an informal assessment procedure that would help you decide whether a child's difficulty with word attack skills is due to auditory perceptual problems.

5. Given your own school situation, identify three ways you could accommodate for a child who is very distracted by sounds in the environment.

NOTES

1. A loss measured at 25 decibels or more is considered educationally significant.
2. M. Templin, *Certain Language Skills in Children: Their Development and Relationship* (University of Minnesota, Institute of Child Welfare, Monograph Series No. 26, 1957).
3. Ibid.
4. J. Wepman, *Auditory Discrimination Test* (Chicago: Language Research Assoc., Inc., 1973).
5. R. Goldman, M. Fristoe, and R. W. Woodcock, *Goldman-Fristoe-Woodcock Test of Auditory Discrimination* (Circle Pines, Minn.: American Guidance Service, 1970).
6. J. Schultz, "Four Measures of Auditory Discrimination: A Factor Analytic Determination of Their Relative Equivalence" (Ph.D. diss., Boston College, 1974).
7. N. J. Baker and B. Leland, *Detroit Test of Learning Aptitude* (Indianapolis: Bobbs, Merrill, 1967).
8. J. Wepman and A. Morency, *Auditory Memory Span Test* (Chicago: Language Research Assoc., Inc., 1973).
9. S. Kirk, J. J. McCarthy, and W. D. Kirk, *The Illinois Test of Psycholinguistic Abilities*, rev. ed. (Urbana: University of Illinois Press, 1968).
10. J. Mooney, "Digit Span as a Measure of Short Term Auditory Memory in Children" (unpublished research, Boston College, 1976).
11. J. Chall, *Learning to Read: The Great Debate* (New York: McGraw-Hill Book Co., 1967), p. 336.
12. R. C. Aukerman, *Approaches to Beginning Reading* (New York: John Wiley & Sons, Inc., 1971).
13. N. Zigmond, "Auditory Processes in Children with Learning Disabilities," in *Learning Disabilities*, L. Tarnopol (Springfield, Ill.: Charles C Thomas, 1969), p. 196.
14. B. Bateman, "Reading: A Controversial View—Research and Rationale," in *Learning Disabilities*, L. Tarnopol (Springfield, Ill.: Charles C Thomas, 1969), p. 289.
15. Peabody Language Development Kits (Circle Pines, Minn.: American Guidance, Inc.)
16. D. A. Sanders, *Aural Rehabilitation* (Englewood Cliffs, N.J.: Prentice-Hall, 1971).
17. *Auditory Discrimination in Depth* (Boston: Teaching Resources).
18. B. Martin, *Sounds of Language Series* (New York: Holt, Rinehart and Winston, Inc., 1970).
19. B. Martin, *Sounds of a Powwow* (New York: Holt, Rinehart and Winston, Inc., 1970), p. 62.
20. L. Buckley and A. Cullum, *Picnic of Sounds* (New York: Citation Press, 1975).
21. C. Kass, "Psycholinguistic Disabilities of Children with Reading Problems," *Exceptional Children* 32 (1966): 541–553.

REFERENCES

Birch, J. W. *Hearing Impaired Children in the Mainstream*. Reston, Va.: The Council for Exceptional Children, 1975.

Ekwall, E. E. *Diagnosis and Remediation of the Disabled Reader*. Boston: Allyn and Bacon, 1976.

Durrell, Donald D. *Improving Reading Instruction*. New York: Harcourt, Brace, Jovanovich, 1967.

Gearheart, B. R., and Weishahn, M. W. *The Handicapped Child in the Regular Classroom*. St. Louis: The C. V. Mosby Company, 1976.

Phillips, P. P. *Speech and Hearing Problems in the Classroom*. Lincoln, Neb.: Cliffs Notes, Inc., 1975.

Zigmond, N. K., and Cicci, R. *Auditory Learning*. San Rafael, Calif.: Dimensions Publishing Co., 1968.

5

Problems
in Visual
Learnings

Preview

Reading involves the learning of the visual symbol system that allows us to put ideas into print. The visual aspects of reading are fully as complex as the auditory features, and require careful teacher observation and attention. Children who have problems with eyesight often require adaptations of printed material as well as special lenses and devices for use in the classroom. Children with adequate vision but with problems in differentiating and integrating visual stimuli (perception) also require modifications and accommodations in order to learn to read. The degree to which a classroom teacher is flexible and open to consultation with appropriate specialists has a direct influence on the success of the child in the reading program.

Our eyes bring us initial contact with the printed word. The very first process involved in reading is purely sensory and, unlike the perceptual system, is unalterable. Just as the auditory nerve is the only structure in the human body sensitive to sound waves, the optic nerve is the only structure sensitive to light waves. The rods and cones of the retina respond to the incoming visual information, which is then transmitted through the optic nerve to the visual cortex (occipital lobe) for differentiation and interpretation. The term *visual acuity* refers to the efficiency with which the structures of the eye can respond to incoming visual stimuli. Visual perception occurs as a result of the differentiation, organization, and interpretation of those stimuli within the brain. Bishop[1] defines the visually limited child as "one whose visual condition is such that it interferes with his efficient learning unless curriculum adaptations are made."

Within the visually handicapped group, totally blind children require the most significant alterations, due to complete dependence on other sensory systems. In reading, they require a totally tactile symbol system, making all conventional printed reading materials inappropriate, or they must use readers, tape recordings, talking books, etc., for the acquisition of printed material. Some visually handicapped children are educated in private or public residential schools. Most of this group, however, are educated in public school programs, the majority in regular classrooms with support services provided by an itinerant teacher of the visually handicapped. These children present a considerable challenge to classroom teachers who must devise curriculum accommodations to meet individual needs.

THE LOW-VISION CHILD: IMPAIRMENTS IN THE SENSORY SYSTEM

There are many conditions and eye diseases that occur congenitally or in the early years and contribute to problems in learning. Only the most common ones will be described here, with the understanding that the more complex and unusual problems would be identified by qualified medical specialists before the child starts school.

Of the conditions described, farsightedness and nearsightedness are not considered pathologies of the eye, but they are nevertheless troublesome to children in school. It must be kept in mind that both conditions can be present developmentally and cannot be regarded as abnormal. For example, children in the primary grades are normally farsighted to some degree, whereas nearsightedness increases during the teen years. However, it is important to recognize that either condition can be serious enough to cause concern and require correction. Children with low vision may experience nearsightedness or farsightedness along with a more serious eye condition.

Common Problems in Vision

Farsightedness
(hyperopia)

The child who is farsighted sees better at a distance, making board work more comfortable than seat work. In reading, s/he may be seen constantly adjusting the distance of a book in an attempt to see it more clearly. Attention span for close work may be short and the child may easily become restless and fatigued by the visual demands of academic tasks. In extreme cases, s/he may experience headaches and/or nausea during prolonged near-point work.

Nearsightedness
(myopia)

The nearsighted child cannot see well at a distance. S/he may squint, lean forward, and show other signs of attempted accommodation for poor distance vision. This type of visual problem may cause no undue difficulty in learning to read. Since close work presents no problem, his/her seat work may be well done and s/he will show no unusual signs of fatigue when working independently at a desk. S/he may not do well in sports or other physical activities without corrective lenses. However, a child who is myopic and also classified as having low vision *will* have difficulty with near-point work and require considerable adjustment within the regular classroom. The kinds of adjustments are best determined in consultation with a teacher of the visually handicapped.

Regular checkups are important for both conditions so that any associated eye conditions can be detected and treated promptly.

Astigmatism

Astigmatism results in the blurring of vision due to an uneven curvature of the cornea. It affects visual images at any distance, and therefore there are no visual demands that are more comfortable than others. The child may experience frequent headaches and poor visual discrimination. Because visual configurations are distorted, the child may confuse similarly shaped symbols such as o and c, m and n, t and f. Reading is difficult and the child may be seen holding printed material quite close in an attempt to see it more clearly. Although there is a wide variety of types and severity of astigmatism, most cases can be corrected with glasses, which should be worn constantly.

Muscle imbalance

Muscular imbalance can cause serious problems in vision when left untreated. The symptoms of the incoordination of eye movements are readily observable in the child whose eyes are crossed (as in strabismus), deviate upward or downward, or turn in or out. When the eyes do not function together in a coordinated fashion, the result is double vision; that is, separate images are recorded. In order to compensate for the difficulty in processing incoming visual stimuli, the weaker eye may cease to function in favor of the stronger single image. When this occurs, vision is permanently lost in the "unused eye." Obviously, early diagnosis and treatment are essential to preserve vision in the weaker eye. During the course of treatment (usually "patching" of the good eye), special reading materials and accommodations may need to be made on the recommendation of the specialists involved.

Nystagmus

Nystagmus involves jerky, rapid eye movements. Although it usually occurs in association with other eye disorders, it can also occur alone. Unfortunately, there is no treatment that has proven entirely effective so the child must learn to adjust as best s/he can. Since s/he is unable to fixate on a visual target, s/he tends to see fragments of words or phrases, making reading very difficult. A teacher must be creative in his/her exploration of the most efficient devices to help the child move more smoothly across a line of print. A "window card," a marker, or a finger are obvious aids, but not necessarily the most effective. The child should be encouraged to experiment with a variety of techniques in order to determine what is most comfortable.

Other conditions

Congenital cataracts (a clouding of the lens), albinism (lack of pigmentation in skin, hair, and iris of the eye), glaucoma, and certain other diseases that affect visual functioning are also inhibitors of good visual acuity. These conditions are usually recognizable at birth and most such children have been following a course of treatment prior to school entrance. In some locations, preschool programs are available to provide early training in the maximal use of vision. In any case of known eye defect or disease, the classroom teacher should remain in contact with a trained teacher of the visually handicapped who can translate information provided by eye specialists into appropriate educational strategies. An accurate assessment of the disorder and of the degree to which it may affect academic progress, as well as recommendations for classroom management techniques, can be of immeasurable benefit to the teacher and the child.

Identification of Visual Problems in the Classroom

There are certain observable behaviors and symptoms that can alert classroom teachers to the possibility of visual problems. The following list is by no means exhaustive and no child would exhibit all of them. However, observation of a cluster of symptoms would be sufficient to justify a referral for evaluation.

Physical appearance

eyes in constant motion

crossed eyes

red-rimmed or swollen eyelids

crust near lashes

red or watery eyes

Behavior

frequent rubbing of eyes

constant blinking

tilting of head to one side when reading

covering one eye when reading or copying from board

       losing place on page

       confusing o and a, e and c, n and m

       screwing up face

       frequently changing distance of book

       crossing of eyes during reading

       sensitivity to light

       stumbling and tripping over objects

       poor alignment in writing

       difficulty with eye-hand coordination

The age of onset of visual problems has implications for the degree to which an individual may be handicapped. The congenitally visually handicapped child has no reference point from normal sight by which he may judge the world. The child whose sight is lost or diminished through accident or disease after beginning school is less apt to suffer severe effects from the condition, because s/he has already developed an awareness of space and configuration. As in any potentially handicapping condition, early detection and treatment of visual problems are essential. Unfortunately, not all screening programs are well managed. Since most screening procedures are confined to the ability to see at twenty feet (distance vision), no attention is given to the child's ability to see at eighteen inches (near vision). Farsightedness is apt to go undetected; in fact, many visual problems remain undiscovered until the middle grades when the visual demands of academic tasks increase and print size becomes smaller.

Reading and Visual Problems

The research concerning the relationship between visual problems and reading has been inconclusive. In a recent review of the literature, Spache[2] states that the major variations in research findings are due to the facts that 1) vision tests purporting to measure the same functions do not yield precisely the same indications; 2) most tests used are relatively brief and therefore not reliable; 3) the ages or stages of visual development of the population studied are not comparable; and 4) individuals vary in their ability to make internal adjustments to compensate for defective systems. Most of the work so far has studied specific visual problems in limited populations. The one major longitudinal study[3] has provided rather substantial evidence that certain types of visual difficulties and combinations of problems do, in fact, relate to poor reading skills. For example, overconvergence of the eyes at both near and far point was clearly related to poor reading and academic performance. Farsightedness with associated muscle imbalance showed a negative influence on reading ability. What must be remembered, however, is that research results describe populations studied. Although the findings can alert us to what might be expected, they can in no way provide accurate predictions for any given child. Only a precise diagnosis, effective treatment, and good communication between the classroom teacher, parents, and professionals involved, can eventually determine the degree to which a visual problem may be educationally limiting.

Classroom Accommodation for the Child with Low Vision

Since the partially sighted child is quite likely to be educated in a regular classroom with special services provided by an itinerant or resource teacher for the visually handicapped, attention must be given to providing optimum conditions for learning. The physical features of the room, as well as specific alterations of materials and techniques of instruction, are important considerations in providing the greatest opportunity for success.

Environmental considerations

A constant, relatively unchanging environment is important to the child with low vision. Once s/he has learned the location of his/her desk, the pencil sharpener, crayons, scissors, etc., s/he needs to be able to count on their being there. An open classroom can be rather upsetting to a child with severely limited vision because the flexibility of space and materials requires constant readjustment. Also, the noise level in such classrooms can be distracting for a child who must rely so heavily on auditory input.

Illumination is another urgent consideration in the management of the learning environment. Adequate lighting without glare is important in highlighting the contrast of print on a page. Even distribution and adequate diffusion are significant. For children whose eyes are light sensitive (as in albinism), attention must be given to the control of glare through adequate shielding of the light source, whether artificial or daylight. Skylights in classrooms or libraries present a particularly difficult problem. In order to avoid unnecessary stress, particularly during activities requiring reading, the child's eye specialist and/or vision specialist should be consulted for recommendations concerning lighting.

An important thing to remember when teaching a child with low vision is that the use of vision will not hurt the eye. Looking, seeing, and reading help the child to use the vision s/he has with greater efficiency. However, fatigue is a factor to be considered, since straining to see, like straining to hear, creates tension within the body that requires periods of relief. The child with low vision may not be able to complete all assignments within an allotted time period, making adjustments necessary. The extension of time limits or the reduction of work load should be determined after a realistic appraisal of the child's capacity to perform. However, excessive adjustments should be avoided in order to prevent the child's using his/her disability as an excuse for underachievement, and to insure that s/he has maximum opportunity for developing good academic skills and work habits.

Verbal directions should be carefully given, with full descriptions of media beyond the child's visual field. Freedom to move about the room in order to locate him/herself close to the site of instruction offers the best chance of getting the information through all channels. Overhead projections as instructional media can be a problem. Providing printed copies of the transparencies before or during a lesson will allow the child to follow a discussion quite comfortably.

Printed materials

For the child with low vision, the nature of the printed materials themselves can influence the degree of success in reading. Although some children can handle regular readers and workbooks, other children require larger print. In most locations these books can be obtained or borrowed from agencies providing services to the visually handicapped. For other classroom assignments involving reading, teachers must be careful of the quality of the inking. The child should receive the first or darkest copy of a ditto sheet. For some children, a worksheet might need to be gone over with a black marking pen in order to provide the right contrast. Black on white may be better than any other combination. Felt tip pens may be preferred for writing assignments, since pencil lead on paper may be too light for the child to read what s/he has written. In all instances, the child him/herself will provide the most reliable feedback as to what s/he can see best.

Low-vision aids ·

There are certain magnification and projection devices that can be of great benefit to children with low vision in increasing the efficiency of the vision they do have. Special lenses that clip on the regular glasses, or lenses that can be hand held (similar to a magnifying glass), are easy to use and helpful in dealing with print. Fixed-focus stand readers are also useful and can be viewed from a normal reading distance when used with regularly worn glasses. A closed-circuit TV system has proved efficient for some children with low vision. The printed material is placed on a scanning mechanism and is projected onto a TV screen magnified up to approximately fifteen times. There are several types of distance magnifiers, e.g., telescopic devices that can be used for reading from the chalkboard, overhead projections, etc. At the secondary level, these are particularly important as the student faces the various reading demands in a variety of learning environments. Since very few texts, manuals, workbooks, etc., are available in large print, the low-vision aids allow a student to use conventional materials. Selection of such devices is usually done by the opthalmologist or optemetrist with the assistance of a specialist skilled in working with children with visual problems. The classroom teacher should encourage the child to make optimum use of any devices prescribed, including his/her glasses.

PROBLEMS IN VISUAL PERCEPTION

The perception of visual stimuli involves the discrimination and interpretation of incoming sensory information. Although more research has been done

Fixed-focus stand readers are low-vision aids that are portable and easy to use for both reading and writing assignments. (Photo courtesy of Vision Systems, Peekskill, N.Y.)

in the area of visual perception than in auditory perception, present knowledge is far from conclusive in identifying the various dimensions of visual perception or their influence on reading difficulties. According to Barraga,[4] "visual perception involves the examining of an object, distinguishing the essential features, understanding the relationship between the elements and integrating the information into a meaningful whole." Since reading involves the visual representation of auditory language, the ability to receive and perceive the distinctive features of orthographic symbols is essential to success as a reader. There are certain visual perceptual behaviors that have been suggested as component skills[5,6,7] of the perceptual process. The major components considered here are form perception, figure-ground, position in space, visual closure, and visual sequencing.

Form perception   The ability to discriminate or respond to the differences in visual form is the first skill developed in a hierarchy of skills that leads to the ultimate recognition of an object. By the time a normally sighted child reaches school, s/he has a wealth of experience in dealing with the visual attributes of the world. The very nature of academic tasks places increased demands on his/her ability to discriminate spatial features of objects and symbols. The alphabet presents the initial challenge in the act of reading. Gibson[8] suggests that the child's progression from spoken to written language involves three types of learning that are more or less sequential: 1) learning to differentiate graphic symbols; 2) learning to decode letters to sounds; and 3) using progressively higher-order units of language structure. The first very clearly involves visual perception. Children who experience difficulties in form perception cannot recognize differences in visual configurations of letters and words. At the preschool level, they are unable to do matching and sorting activities involving size, shape, color, etc.; and later, they cannot identify likenesses and differences in letter and number shapes. Problems at the first level prevent the smooth transition to the more complex tasks of associating sounds to symbols and ultimately recognizing words and their meanings.

Figure-ground

A skill related to the discrimination of form is figure-ground, which Frostig and Maslow[9] define as the ability to attend to one aspect of the visual field while perceiving it in relation to the rest of the field. When children are unable to screen out irrelevant stimuli, discrimination becomes very difficult. They become lost in visual details. The result is poor judgment of visual features of letters, words, and phrases. Although they may learn to associate a sound with an isolated symbol, the recognition of letters combined into words and sentences is difficult. Many children persist in using a finger, marker, or "window" to reduce the number of competing stimuli. In their great efforts to identify each word, they lose the continuity and meaning of a story.

Position in space

The ability to detect the orientation of objects in space is necessary if the child is to discriminate letters that differ in position only, like m and w, p and b, d and q, n and u. Although letter reversal is a developmental phenomenon in young children, teachers have recognized the symptom of reversal of letters as part of a constellation of perceptual problems that can affect the development of skill in reading. Gibson et al.[10] found that children in the primary grades have a tendency to reverse letters; however, by the third grade those children for whom this was a developmental problem have ceased to do so. They also found that discriminating letters involving reversal transformations (p and q) was more difficult than discriminating open and closed forms such as ɑ and c. In reading, it seems, the left-to-right orientation is crucial.

Visual closure

Whole and part perception is a skill that develops with age. Gollin[11] studied the ability of children to identify objects on the basis of incomplete configurations. The younger children required more complete pictures than older children. Although it may seem to be an obscure skill where reading is concerned, it must be remembered that the efficient reader does not fixate on every detail of every word or phrase. As the eye scans a line of print, the reader recognizes words with a minimum amount of attention to detail. The child who has difficulty with visual closure reads slowly and less smoothly than other children and tends to focus on one or two letters at a time until recognition comes.

Visual sequencing

After the child has become aware of incoming visual information—that is, has discriminated essential features and the relationships among the elements—s/he must be able to observe the order in which these elements occur. In reading, the ability to identify the sequence of letters from left to right is essential to the child's ability to recognize one word as different from another and to ultimately write words by being able to recall how they look. For the child who has difficulty revisualizing the sequence of letters in a word, learning basic sight words is very difficult. Spelling is equally (or more) difficult. For example, a child might write *widnow* for window. The correct letters are present but in an incorrect order. Children who experience these problems tend to rely on their auditory skills and the application of phonic rules in order to decode and encode words.

Identification of Visual Perceptual Problems

Since children who experience problems in vision have difficulty in organizing sensory information into accurate perceptions, there is considerable overlap in observable symptoms. Again, no child would exhibit all of the behaviors, nor would a single behavior be indicative of a problem. Children with visual perceptual problems may show some of the following behaviors:

1. reversal of letters and numbers
2. lack of interest in picture books
3. poor visual discrimination of similar letters
4. loss of place in reading; skipping line or words
5. difficulty finding a word or section on a page
6. not distinguishing between words with similar shapes, like boy and dog
7. difficulty copying from the board
8. poor handwriting, cutting, and drawing

When a teacher recognizes a group of these behaviors and/or the behaviors that tend to accompany problems in vision, a referral for evaluation is indicated. In many states, assessment teams are required and this multidisciplinary group does the initial evaluation. When poor vision is suspected as being a source of difficulty, an outside referral for an ophthalmological evaluation is usually suggested to the parents.

Classroom Accommodation for the Child with Visual Perceptual Problems

For children with vision and visual perceptual problems, environmental and instructional adjustments are necessary if they are to learn to read. The following suggestions are aimed at providing for their comfort and well-being within the regular classroom.

1. Encourage the use of a marker or finger to hold place in reading.
2. Code the left side of the desk with colored tape so s/he is constantly reminded of the left-to-right orientation.
3. Copy the print from the "busy" page of a reader onto a chart or separate piece of paper if child has a figure-ground problem.
4. Use dark lines on writing paper to facilitate proper alignment and spacing.
5. Allow him/her to trace over new visual configurations.
6. Use auditory clues or patterns to facilitate the recall of visual sequences.
7. Use color coding to highlight visual features of printed material.
8. Reduce the amount of printed material on work sheets.
9. Don't overload with seat work.
10. Allow him/her to move about the classroom in order to find the best position for following instruction.

In the normal development of reading, using a marker or a finger to hold the place in reading is a behavior that teachers want to eliminate as the child acquires ease and fluency with words in print. For most children this is not difficult, since the normal maturation of the ocular motor process, as well as increased skill in decoding, reduces the need for such devices. However, children with visual problems (low vision and/or perception) may need to use these aids long after other children have given them up.

Assessment of Problems in Visual Perception

Observation of behavior

Any good diagnostic procedure begins with the careful observation of the child's learning behaviors. It is therefore essential that the classroom teacher observe and record all relevant information. Recognition of some of the observable symptoms of difficulty in visual processing will allow the teacher to decide that the child should be considered for referral and assessment. Careful documentation of the specific tasks that are proving difficult, in addition to those the child can perform well, provides a data base from which appropriate decisions can be made as to the type of assessment required.

Although the type of formalized test procedures will vary from team to team, there are certain tests that tend to be used most frequently; some of these have already been identified in Chapter 3.

*Developmental
Test of Visual
Motor
Integration
Test* (VMI)[12]

This test is often used with children (ages three to fift en) suspected of having visual perceptual problems. Although its specific purpose is to measure the child's ability to integrate what s/he sees with the motor patterns necessary to reproduce it, the child who has difficulty with form recognition and spatial relationships will be unable to perform well on this test. Since many children with visual perceptual problems also experience difficulty with eye-hand coordination, this test is very effective in detecting problems in visual-motor integration.

*Detroit Test of
Learning Aptitude*[13]

Certain subtests of the Detroit Test are useful in identifying problems in visual perception. Norms are provided for ages three to nineteen.

Subtest #9: Visual Attention Span for Objects. This task presents a sequence of pictures (from two to eight in a series) for one second per picture in a given sequence and asks the child to name the pictures he saw. Although this is viewed as a task of short-term visual memory, it involves short-term auditory memory as the child uses the auditory symbols (names of the objects) to facilitate visual recall. A child may have difficulty with this task because of auditory, as well as visual, problems.

Subtest #12: Memory for Designs. This test is similar to the VMI in the measurement of the child's ability to integrate visual input with the appropriate motor patterns for reproduction of the designs. This test, however, makes slightly varying demands. Group A presents a geometric figure and provides space for the child to reproduce the figure. Group B presents the outline of a geometric figure on the test booklet. The completed design is presented to the child for five seconds. He must draw the internal features of the figure in the test booklet. Group C requires that the child view a design stimulus for five seconds and then reproduce the entire design from memory. Children who are able to integrate visual and motor systems do very well on Group A. Children who have difficulty remembering visual configurations show greater difficulty with Group B, and the greatest difficulty with Group C where no outline or model is provided.

Subtest #16: Visual Attention Span for Letters. This task presents a sequence of letters (from two to eight in a series) and asks the child to name the letters s/he saw. Again, it is a task that depends on short-term visual memory with auditory sequential memory as the additional factor in a successful performance.

*Developmental
Test of Visual
Perception
(DTVP)*[14]

The DTVP has been widely used with children from five to eight and, with some adjustments in scoring, for children up to ten. The test has five distinct tasks:

1. *Eye-Motor Coordination*—asks the child to draw a continuous line to a specific target or within confined space. Children who cannot do this show problems in handwriting, cutting, coloring, etc.

2. *Figure-Ground*—asks the child to outline specific figures, i.e., triangles, squares, stars, etc., embedded within a background of irrelevant stimuli.

3. *Form Constancy*—asks the child to identify specific shapes (circles, squares) that vary in terms of size, shading, orientation, etc.

4. *Position in Space*—asks the child to evaluate a series of similar forms and identify the one that is reversed or rotated. This task is similar to many found in reading readiness workbooks under the title of visual discrimination.

5. *Spatial Relations*—asks the child to reproduce a design by linking dots with a line. This task attempts to measure the child's ability to see the relationship of one object to another.

The ability of the DTVP to measure five discrete components of visual perception has been questioned.[15,16] It appears that it may be better to view a child's performance on a composite of the five subtests as an indication of his visual perceptual development rather than considering each subtest as a valid measure of discrete skills.

Illinois Test of Psycholinguistic Abilities (ITPA)[17]

Certain subtests of the ITPA involve aspects of visual perception.

Visual Sequential Memory. This test requires the child to view a sequence of nonmeaningful designs for five seconds and reproduce the series using corresponding chips. It does not lend itself to the use of the auditory code (the names of designs) as does the task described from the Detroit Test of Learning Aptitude. Children who perform poorly on this subtest tend to have difficulty revisualizing sequences of letters in words for reading and spelling.

Visual Closure. This test asks the child to identify common objects from incomplete representations embedded within a busy visual field. Success on this task depends on the child's ability to distinguish foreground from background, as well as closure.

There are numbers of other tests that a psychologist or special educator might use to assess a child's visual perceptual and visual motor skills. Portions of individual intelligence tests give this kind of information. The Performance Scale of The Wechsler Intelligence Scale for Children[18] taps numerous visual skills and can provide a comparison of these skills with language skills assessed on the Verbal Scale. A psychologist might also use the Bender Visual Motor Gestalt Test,[19] which is very similar to the VMI although it uses fewer designs and provides less structure. This test requires a certain degree of sophistication to evaluate, since the scoring procedures allow for the forming of inferences as to emotional adjustment.

Informal assessments can also be used in identifying difficulties in visual processing. A task analysis approach that looks at the input demands of an academic task can be used to show a child's pattern of error when he is required to deal with incoming visual information. Regardless of the approach to assessment—formal or informal—the results should be synthesized by the examining team into a clear statement of how the child learns. Appropriate teaching strategies and curriculum modifications should be identified for the classroom teacher.

Auditory-Visual Integration

There are some children who show no problems in visual or auditory processing. These children may experience reading difficulties, however, due to problems in integrating information from the auditory and visual modalities. For these children, the results of formal testing show no problems in dealing with tasks that make a single sensory demand—for example, identifying words that look alike or discriminating between words that vary on only one phoneme. However, these children may have difficulties in tasks that require crossing modalities; for example, writing a written symbol based on a spoken sound (moving from auditory to visual) or being able to identify the sound represented by a letter symbol (moving from visual to auditory). Reading is an intersensory task. It involves the integration of visual symbols (printed words) into auditory symbols (spoken words). The conversion is from a spatial (left-to-right) dimension to a temporal (first-to-last) order. Since there are very few tests that measure integrative skills, problems in this area may go undetected in the assessment process. This is an area where teacher observation and task analysis is useful.

TEACHING TO STRENGTHS

When planning reading instruction for the child with diagnosed problems in visual acuity, one must keep in mind that the visual problem may be the most obvious but not necessarily the primary cause of reading difficulties. Children with low vision are susceptible to the same kinds of problems in learning as other children. One cannot assume that a problem in vision will necessarily affect reading, or that the low-vision child's problem in reading is necessarily due to his problem in vision. There is a tendency on the part of educators to assume that if the child wears glasses and cannot read well, his problems are due to poor vision. This is not a safe assumption. When difficulties become obvious, the differential diagnosis must consider all requisite areas of learning and not merely those involving visual processing. Since it seems sensible to use auditory approaches for children with visual problems, the presence of good auditory skills should be evaluated (formally or informally) before an approach is prescribed.

When selecting appropriate reading materials for children whose primary problem is low vision and/or visual perception, it should be kept in mind that there are certain reading materials that provide a more comfortable fit between learner and strategy. For these children, reading programs based on a phonic approach may provide the greatest opportunity for success. Their need to depend on other, more reliable modalties requires that the instructional materials give low priority to visual features in favor of stressing auditory and tactile-kinesthetic features. In reading, there are many choices of programs that include early attention to the grapheme-phoneme correspondences, with difficulty controlled according to phonic elements. Programs that select words primarily on the basis of spelling regularity provide the least amount of confusion for the child who must rely on auditory cues. It has been suggested in the previous chapter that analyses of the features of various reading programs presented by Chall[20] and Aukerman[21] can be very useful in selecting an approach to meet an individual need.

When selecting a phonic approach, one must choose between a method that relies on sounding and blending (synthetic phonics) and one that presents a whole word and requires the child to analyze its parts phonemically and structurally (analytic phonics). At the moment, there is no research evidence to help us make that choice. Many approaches have been used; many have been successful. The approach making the heaviest demand on the auditory system is synthetic phonics. Since children with visual problems have not developed skills in what might be described as "gestalt" learning—that is, the ability to recognize the whole through the interrelationship of the parts—an approach which takes individual graphemes of a word and blends them into the auditory whole accommodates to their learning preference or strength. Hay-Wingo,[22] Gillingham,[23] Spalding,[24] Lippincott,[25] and Sullivan[26] provide examples of programs that use a synthetic approach to phonics.

WORKING ON VISUAL SKILLS

As stated before, teaching to strength in beginning reading does not mean to suggest that visual skills should be neglected or deemphasized in the total educational experience. Children with low vision will almost certainly qualify for special assistance from the teacher of the visually handicapped. Children with visual perceptual difficulties may be scheduled for remedial programs in a special resource room or tutorial program. For children receiving such services, the classroom teacher can provide the drill and reinforcement of the specific skills being stressed in these programs. Coordination of efforts among all those servicing the needs of an individual child is essential to his progress in reading. For children with visual problems who are not in special educational programs, the classroom teacher can provide appropriate learning experiences through the careful selection and adaptation of regular reading materials. For example, when a phonics approach to reading is being used, particular attention must be given to the fact that the visual discrimination of the letters that represent vowel sounds is difficult for the child with poor visual skills. The letters *a o u e* are very similar in shape. In order to decode well, the child must be able to recognize the correct visual form before attaching an appropriate sound to it.

The Child with Low Vision

A major emphasis in the preschool curriculum is readiness for reading. All children need an opportunity to develop the constellation of skills that have come to be recognized as prerequisites for developing the ability to read. For children with low vision, these experiences are crucial, since they must develop skills in a major sensory system that is functioning at a minimal level. They need to develop their fullest potential by using systems available to them, as well as compensatory techniques to accommodate for visual limitations. It is in this area that a close collaboration is required between the classroom teacher and the teacher of the visually handicapped. Helping children to make the most efficient use of the vision they have must be a major focus of both the regular and the special educational programs.

Pittam[27] suggests that certain skills should be given special emphasis in the learning experiences for the child with low vision:

Tactual perception

The ability to identify and discriminate among objects through touching is very important to the child who may not have a complete concept of objects in terms of their visual-spatial dimensions. The visually limited child may need to develop the ability to determine likenesses and differences among objects according to size and shape by feeling them first and then assessing the visual features of each. Some children need to manipulate actual objects before they can use pictures of them. Eventually, the alphabet can be introduced through the use of "textured" letters made of velvet, sandpaper, or some other substance with a degree of coarseness. Children can be encouraged to reproduce letters and shapes using clay or Play-Doh.

Left-right orientation

The left-to-right orientation is a necessary skill in reading. Initially, children may need to distinguish left from right through gross motor activities involving their whole bodies. Singing games like Hokey Pokey give a child the opportunity to feel the right hand shaking as s/he uses the language of the experience, "I put my right hand in, I put my right hand out. . . ." Colored tape or mitts can be used to distinguish the right hand from the left so that children will not be in error while playing the game. Once the child has learned body orientation, s/he can begin to identify the left and right sides of his/her desk and papers. A strip of colored tape on the left side of the desk or table can provide a clue as to where to begin.

Auditory perception

Since the child with visual problems will need to rely heavily on auditory information, it is important to give special care to the developmental aspects of auditory perception during the preschool years. Although most con-

Musical instruments can be used to promote the development of auditory discrimination skills. The color-coded notes on this xylophone can serve to teach visual skills as well. (Photo by Edward Thomas)

ventional reading readiness programs stress skills in identifying and tracking sounds, some children may need to begin with discriminations that are not quite as fine as the likenesses and differences between phonemes. Discrimination of gross environmental sounds, loudness and softness in musical instruments, low and high pitch, can be important subskills that prepare the child for the finer discriminations required in reading. Rhythm games are another excellent and fun activity that provides training in listening to the distinctive features of sounds.

The key factor in developing an appropriate and well-balanced readiness program for the child with low vision is the careful assessment of his/her developmental levels in various aspects of perception. Instruction should begin at the level where the child is experiencing at least partial success, so that expectation levels are not too high.

During these early learning experiences, it is essential that the teacher tie vision into all activities. The integration of seeing with hearing and feeling may be difficult for the young visually limited child, since the use of his/her eyes has never yielded much information about the world. As s/he works to develop the efficient use of the vision s/he possesses, the teacher should remain aware of his/her continual need to look as well as to listen and feel.

Since reading involves the learning of the visual code that is used to represent the auditory one, good language development is essential to success in reading. The process of language acquisition is the same for the child with low vision as with the sighted child, except that the rate may be slower. The sighted toddler who is busy exploring his/her environment is constantly stimulated by the sight of what is within and beyond his/her reach. S/he learns the names for these things. The visually limited child lacks the basic interactions with the environment that serve to prompt the development of vocabulary. S/he misses most of the visual stimulation that motivates exploration, and therefore requires some carefully structured experiences in order to learn a meaningful vocabulary. Bishop[28] suggests that the teacher give particular attention to the following areas of vocabulary comprehension:

1. *Noun Classifications*—Providing activities and toys that encourage the naming of objects and groups of objects facilitates language and higher-level conceptual skills through classification and categorizing.

2. *Verb Meaning*—Learning the names of actions helps the child to describe what s/he has done or intends to do. Later, this vocabulary will allow the child to follow directions at home and at school.

3. *Physical Expression of Adverbs*—Becoming aware of descriptive words used to qualify actions (softly, loudly, slowly, badly, etc.) gives the child greater proficiency in making his/her thoughts known and in understanding those of others.

4. *Descriptive Words*—Adding descriptive words allows the child to become more precise in his use of language to manipulate the world.

5. *The Language of Direction*—Manipulating objects and using the prepositions to denote the spatial relationships—i.e., *under*, *over*, *above*, *below*, *beside*, etc.—are important to the child who cannot see enough of the word to become aware of these relationships on his/her own.

Opportunities for verbal expression are important for all young children, but particularly important for the visually limited child who may be slower in expressive skills as well. Until the child has assimilated the full meaning of words, s/he will not begin to use them. It is important for a teacher to provide the language appropriate to any new experience and to encourage the children to share news of events at home. Experience stories based on field trips, family outings, or school projects can make the children aware of the use of printed words to communicate their thoughts.

Formal reading instruction for the visually limited child is not essentially different from that for the sighted child. The child will need to develop the same sequences of skills in the same fashion. Although modifications may be required in the size of the print and the way s/he manipulates the materials, most partially sighted children can profit from reading instruction in the regular classroom. It must be remembered, however, that problems in vision may lead to problems in visual perception. The following suggestions on techniques for the child with visual perceptual problems can apply to the partially sighted child as well.

The Child with Visual Perceptual Problems

The distinction between perceptual training and skill training has been discussed elsewhere in relation to auditory skill development. The factor of overlap is equally true in the visual modality. In fact, reading readiness programs have traditionally paid more attention to visual perceptual training than to auditory perceptual training. For this reason, children with visual perceptual problems are apt to have more attention paid to their area of deficit than are children with auditory problems. Kindergarten teachers may be quicker to recognize visual problems, since much of the daily activity centers around tasks requiring visual-motor integration, i.e., cutting, coloring, pasting, etc. When work begins on sound-symbol relationships, visual problems become even more apparent in the form of letter reversals, inversions, and the inability to distinguish one letter from another. Early identification is essential if the child is to be provided the best opportunity to develop his/her skills before experiencing serious academic failure.

Although the child with visual perceptual problems may feel more comfortable with a phonics approach to reading, the visual aspects of the process must receive full attention as well.

Visual discrimination and form recognition

The basic visual perceptual problem in reading is the inability to distinguish among letter shapes. The distinctions between m and n, o and c, b and d, p and q are subtle, and require the ability to analyze component parts and recognize likenesses and differences. Before introducing the two-dimensional symbol on a page, it may be helpful to use large wooden letters that can be manipulated and traced. Tracing with a finger in sand or clay is fun, as well as useful for reinforcing the visual pattern of a letter. Felt and sandpaper letters can be made quite easily, stored in the child's desk, or taken home for periodic review and reinforcement.

Older children who have difficulties in visual perceptual areas may require some remedial help in order to deal more effectively with visual symbols. Their difficulty is not confined to letters alone, but involves numbers, the signs in mathematics ($+ - \times \div$), illustrations in science, etc. For these children, it is important that the remedial strategies be appropriate to their age levels and particular interests. One teacher was able to teach a child discrimination of letters by using his passion for sports cars. The words Alfa Romeo, Porsche, Jaguar, Corvette, Mercedes-Benz, Sting Ray, Datsun, and Triumph contain all but four letters of the alphabet.

Figure-ground

The child with difficulties in figure-ground perception needs to attend to one letter at a time in learning letter shapes. When letters are combined into words, they must be well spaced and lines of print must not be too close together. This may require the preparation of special forms of printed material until s/he is able to use conventional print. Sorting exercises can be helpful in providing experience in picking out specific objects or symbols within a group. Boxes of buttons, farm animals, crayons, etc., can be kept available for free-time activity. Once the child has experienced success with objects that differ in color and shape, a bowl of alphabet cereal or plastic letters can be used to provide the more direct work on letters.

Older children can use things like maps and graphs related to social studies or science for improving their ability to detect specific visual stimuli within a visual field. For them, it is important to use academic skills and content areas for developing perceptual efficiency.

Position in space

In the first few grades, children experience difficulty in identifying the orientation of objects in space. As they begin to deal with the letters of the alphabet, there are certain reversals and inversions that occur. Whether this is

Working at the chalkboard is a good way to reinforce the visual discrimination of letters, and it also helps children learn motor patterns associated with letter formation. (Photo by John A. Malnati)

due to developmental factors or perceptual problems, there are certain strategies to facilitate the discrimination of symbols that differ in direction only. One of the important subskills of the correct identification of position in space is the language of spatial relationships. The child must acquire the concept of above, below, front, back, under, over, etc., in order to verbally mediate the actual production of each letter. Spalding,[24] in the *Writing Road to Reading*, uses an auditory pattern to teach the formation of letters. The technique uses the face of the clock with the numbers as points of orientation. For example, for the letter C children are taught to begin at 2, go up and around the clock, and stop at 4. Gillingham[23] uses another approach that integrates the writing with the sound and symbol. For some children, the combination of the visual, auditory, kinesthetic, and tactile features of a letter or of words assists in distinguishing characteristics of the individual graphemes.

Closure

Certain activities can contribute to the child's ability to identify words on the basis of a minimum amount of information. For young children it is best to begin with picture identification. The Peabody Language Kit (Primary Level)[29] provides pictures of objects in numerous categories along with a series of templates that can be used to partially obscure a picture. The child can progress from identifying the object on the basis of nearly complete information to the identification of an object from a minimum amount of information. The templates can be used in the same way with letters. A more advanced task would require the child to recognize words with missing letters, providing picture or context clues at first and then words alone.

Sequencing

Difficulty in visual sequencing leads to difficulty in the recognition of sight words and in spelling. As has been noted elsewhere, memory for sequences of stimuli involves short-term storage and long-term retrieval; that is, the child must observe the order of the letters and store that sequence. Later, s/he must be able to revisualize or retrieve that pattern in order to recognize the word in reading or to write the word in spelling. Exercises in short-term recall may be a necessary first step to developing good facility in retrieval. At the readiness level, young children enjoy playing games with objects or pictures in which the teacher presents a series and asks the child to hide his/her eyes while one or more are removed. The child must then be able to identify the missing objects. Presenting a series and then mixing the order so that the child has the task of reassembling the initial sequence, can be done with objects and later with letters. The intent of this type of activity is to develop and strengthen the child's visual sequencing abilities so that by the time s/he becomes involved in learning to read, s/he has a natural tendency to observe the order in which visual patterns occur.

For older children, visual monitoring can be encouraged through proofreading texts that contain spelling errors. Each exercise can yield an overall score so that the child can compete with him/herself in bettering his/her score.

When sufficient skill has developed in the spelling of regular and irregular words, dictionary skills can be introduced as an application of the ability to sequence visually. While some children have difficulty in the spelling of irregular words due to an inability to recall the order in which letters occur, other children have difficulty due to poor short-term memory. These children fail to identify and store letter patterns. For example, a child may be presented with the word *neighbor*. When writing the word, s/he may write *nabor*, using a phonetic pattern indicating failure to recall the individual letters as well as the word length. Another child presented with the same word may write *niegbhor*, indicating an ability to recall the individual letters but not the order in which they occur. The latter child may have a sequencing problem.

Sight vocabulary   Ekwall[30] states that "in teaching any sight word, one of the most basic things to remember is that for any normal child without problems in reading, a word is not likely to become a sight word until the child has encountered the word many times." He further suggests that the time required for a child to develop instant recognition depends on such factors as "the potential of the child for word learning tasks, the meaning or relevance of the word for a child, the configuration of the word, and the context in which it is used." For the child with visual problems, learning sight words is especially difficult. Since his visual disability operates against the efficient use of visual cues, i.e., the shape of letters and words, he must rely heavily on word meaning and context. For the partially sighted child, this can also be a problem, since vocabulary may develop at a slower rate. If the normal child requires repeated presentations of a word in order to recognize it, the child with visual problems not only needs even more presentations but specific exercises to strengthen his ability to attend to the visual features of words.

With young children, block designs can be used to develop an awareness of visual configuration. Later, blocks can be used to depict word shape.

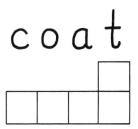

Attention can be focused on the special features of words such as double consonants or vowels, and letters that extend above or descend below the line. Older children can outline the shape of a word in order to highlight those aspects of the visual pattern that facilitate recognition.

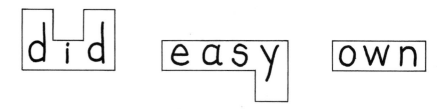

While training in visual configuration is useful, it can be used only with a limited vocabulary, and other aids to independence should be quickly developed. For children with visual problems, however, attention to configuration can provide one more clue to the identification of certain words.

Writing words while saying them out loud helps to reinforce the way they look. Children should also be encouraged to use the words in sentences so that meaning is firmly associated with the sight and sound. In view of the need for repeated exposure to sight words, this exercise can become rather tedious unless it is approached creatively. The words should be presented in the context of the children's own experiences with life. A group can be encouraged to use specific sight words in dictating or writing a story about an event in the neighborhood or community, a TV show, or a field trip. Card games using the same words can provide the drill and reinforcement necessary to the development of easy recognition.

Tachistoscopes and controlled readers can also be used effectively as long as the objective of such activity is kept clearly in mind. For children experiencing visual problems, such devices should not be seen as a means for increasing reading speed (for the visually limited child this may not be possible), but as motivational devices to provide practice. Ekwall[31] suggests that several children be allowed to work together and yell out the words as they appear. It's a bit noisy but great fun.

Color coding has been used in a variety of ways to differentiate letters and sound. For children with visual problems, this technique should be used with caution, since adding a visual dimension (color) may only add to the confusion. When such a technique is contemplated, it is best to rely on feedback from the child as to whether or not it is helpful.

Comprehension and Visual Imagery

Imagery is an aspect of cognitive functioning that involves information already perceived, stored, and available for retrieval. Frostig and Maslow[32] state that "whereas language represents the environment through the use of verbal symbols (words), imagery represents the environment through remembered auditory, kinesthetic, and visual images." The auditory language system has provided the child with the code for the stored perceptions so that much of his/her knowledge of words is associated with appropriate images. If a group of young children are asked to draw a picture of Big Bird from

Sesame Street, chances are they will create a rather large yellow creature with beak and clawed feet. They are able to revisualize the features that are unique and specific to him. Written words have the power to evoke images equally vivid. For years readers have been captivated by the adventures of Robinson Crusoe, Gulliver, and Winnie the Pooh. The enjoyment comes from the freedom of the imagination to put together all of the sights, sounds, and other assorted sensations that surround the story. The ability to do this facilitates the recall of events, thus aiding in comprehension.

Children with visual problems usually require some training in the process of forming mental images based on visual information. For the visually limited child, the problem relates to the poor quality of the basic input; for the child with perceptual problems, it relates to the inability to organize and differentiate properly. For both areas of difficulty, initial work should focus on small units of language for which the child must produce an appropriate picture. A teacher might also give the child a picture and ask him to describe what he sees. This can be made more complex by presenting a picture for a short time, then removing it and asking the child to provide the description from memory. There are games like "I'm thinking of . . . ," "Animal, Vegetable or Mineral," and "Policeman Find My Child" that involve the use of visual images and can be enjoyed by everyone. Eventually the transfer can be made to short stories with considerable follow-up discussion of the details of their pictorial representations of events and descriptions. It should be pointed out to the children that the pictures in their minds help them to remember what happened and thus make reading more enjoyable.

CONCLUSION

Children who lack proficiency in a major sense modality are at risk for problems in learning. Since learning to read requires the integration of auditory and visual information, a deficit in one or both areas has implications for the ease with which reading skills can be mastered. When visual problems are identified, consideration must be given to the nature of the difficulty as well as to the implications for instructional management. Although there are many good programs for teaching reading, not all of them can be considered appropriate for teaching children with visual problems. The choice narrows when planning for children who experience considerable difficulty in distinguishing the visual features of letters and words. A complete and thorough assessment is essential to the individualization of reading instruction and the accommodation of a child within the regular classroom.

Assessment should focus on the identification of the conditions that promote the most successful learning. Discovering these factors may be of more assistance to the classroom teacher than a detailed analysis of the handicapping condition. Teaching to strengths in reading may involve using a stronger, more reliable modality. For the child who demonstrates strength in auditory processing, a synthetic phonics approach may lead to the greatest success in dealing with the sound-symbol relationship.

Remedial education for the child with visual problems (both sensory and perceptual) should focus on those strategies which promote the most efficient processing of visual information. Ideally, specialists are available to provide the training and to collaborate with the classroom teacher in attending to the child's individual needs.

ACTIVITIES FOR PRESERVICE TEACHERS

1. Since a multisensory approach to learning is often successful with visually limited children, construct alphabet cards using a variety of textured materials.

2. Using the above cards, design three games that would provide reinforcement of letter recognition through simultaneous auditory, visual, and tactile input.

3. Choose two reading programs that use a sounding and blending (synthetic) approach to phonics. Determine the differences in the order in which consonants and vowels are introduced.

4. Design worksheets to assist children in the discrimination of letters that vary in orientation only, e.g., b d—p q—u n.

5. Fashion three devices to help children maintain their places on a page in a reading book.

ACTIVITIES FOR IN-SERVICE TEACHERS

1. You have a small group of sixth graders in need of work on basic sight vocabulary words. Describe two activities that would be both motivating and reinforcing of this skill.

2. Design an informal assessment procedure to evaluate skill in visual sequential memory.

3. Your school system is using a basal series with heavy emphasis on sight vocabulary. How could you help a visually handicapped child succeed with this material?

4. Identify three strategies for assisting children to develop skill in visual imagery as an aid to reading comprehension.

5. Analyze the environment of your own classroom in terms of illumination, organization of equipment, flexibility of seating, and the nature of printed materials. What accommodations would you need to make for a child with low vision?

NOTES

1. V. E. Bishop, *Teaching the Visually Limited Child* (Springfield, Ill.: Charles C Thomas, 1971), p. 7.
2. G. Spache, *Investigating the Issues of Reading Disabilities* (Boston: Allyn and Bacon, Inc., 1976), p. 46.
3. C. R. Kelley, *Visual Screening and Child Development: The North Carolina Study* (Raleigh, N.C.: Department of Psychology, North Carolina State College, 1957).
4. N. Barraga, "Utilization of Sensory-Perceptual Abilities," in *The Visually Handicapped Child in School*, B. Lowenfeld (New York: The John Day Company, 1973), p. 124.
5. J. Chalfant and M. Scheffelin, *Central Processing Dysfunctions in Children* (Bethesda, Md.: National Institute of Neurological Diseases and Stroke, Monograph No. 9, 1969), p. 26.
6. M. Frostig and P. Maslow, *Learning Problems in the Classroom* (New York: Grune & Stratton, 1973), p. 177.
7. D. Hallahan and J. Kauffman, *Introduction to Learning Disabilities* (Englewood Cliffs, N.J.: Prentice-Hall, Inc., 1976), p. 78.
8. E. Gibson, "Experimental Psychologists Examine the Process by Which a Fundamental Skill Is Acquired," *Science* 148 (1965): 1066–1072.
9. Frostig and Maslow, *Learning Problems*, p. 125.
10. J. Gibson, J. J. Gibson, A. Pick, and H. Osser, "A Developmental Study of the Discrimination of Letter-like Forms," *Journal of Comparative and Physiological Psychology* 55 (1962): 897–906.
11. E. Gollin, "Developmental Studies of Visual Recognition of Incomplete Objects," *Perceptual and Motor Skills* 11 (1960): 289.
12. K. E. Beery and N. Buktenica, *Developmental Test of Visual-Motor Integration* (Chicago: Follett, 1967).
13. N. J. Baker and B. Leland, *Detroit Tests of Learning Aptitude* (Indianapolis: Bobbs-Merrill, 1967).
14. M. Frostig et al., *The Marianne Frostig Developmental Test of Visual Perception* (Palo Alto, Calif.: Consulting Psychologists Press, 1964).
15. L. Boyd and K. Randle, "Factor Analysis of the Frostig Developmental Test of Visual Perception," *Journal of Learning Disabilities* 3 (May 1970): 253–255.
16. N. L. Corah and B. J. Powell, "A Factor Analytic Study of the Frostig Developmental Test of Visual Perception," *Perceptual Motor Skills* 16 (1963): 59–63.
17. S. Kirk, J. J. McCarthy, and W. D. Kirk, *The Illinois Test of Psycholinguistic Abilities*, rev. ed. (Urbana: University of Illinois Press, 1968).

18. D. Wechsler, *Wechsler Intelligence Scale for Children* (New York: The Psychological Corporation, 1974).

19. L. Bender, *A Visual-Motor Gestalt Test and Its Clinical Uses* (New York: American Orthopsychiatric Association, 1938).

20. J. Chall, *Learning to Read: The Great Debate* (New York: McGraw-Hill Book Co., 1967).

21. R. Aukerman, *Approaches to Beginning Reading* (New York: John Wiley & Sons, Inc., 1971).

22. J. Hay and C. Wingo, *Reading with Phonics* (Philadelphia: J. B. Lippincott Co., 1967).

23. A. Gillingham and B. Stillman, *Remedial Training for Children with Specific Disability in Reading, Spelling and Penmanship*, 7th ed. (Cambridge, Mass.: Educators Publishing Service, 1966).

24. R. Spalding and W. Spalding, *The Writing Road to Reading: A Modern Method of Phonics for Teaching Children to Read* (New York: William Morrow and Company, Inc., 1962).

25. G. McCracken and C. Walcutt, *Lippincott Basic Reading Program* (Philadelphia: J. B. Lippincott Co., 1963).

26. C. D. Buchanan and Sullivan Associates, *Programmed Reading Series* (New York: McGraw-Hill Book Co., 1963).

27. V. G. Pittam, "Reading Readiness," *The New Outlook for the Blind* 59 (Nov. 1965): 322.

28. Bishop, *Teaching the Visually Limited Child*, p. 63.

29. Peabody Language Development Kit: Primary Level (Circle Pines, Minn.: American Guidance, Inc., 1968).

30. E. E. Ekwall, *Diagnosis and Remediation of the Disabled Reader* (Boston: Allyn and Bacon, Inc., 1976), p. 74.

31. Ibid, p. 77.

32. Frostig and Maslow, *Learning Problems*, p. 113.

REFERENCES

Barraga, Natalie C. *Visual Handicaps and Learning*. Belmont, Calif.: Wadsworth Publishing Company, Inc., 1976.

Frostig, M. *Selection and Adaptation of Reading Methods*. San Raphael, Calif.: Academic Therapy Publications, 1973.

Hammill, D. D., and Bartel, N. R. *Teaching Children with Learning and Behavior Problems*. Boston: Allyn and Bacon, Inc., 1975.

Hanninen, Kenneth A. *Teaching the Visually Handicapped*. Columbus, Ohio: Charles E. Merrill, 1975.

Lowenbraum, S., and Affleck, J. Q. *Teaching Mildly Handicapped Children in Regular Classes*. Columbus, Ohio: Charles E. Merrill, 1976.

Lowenfeld, Berthold, Ed. *The Visually Handicapped Child in School*. New York: John Day, 1973.

Scholl, Geraldine T. *The Principal Works With the Visually Impaired*. Washington, D.C.: Council for Exceptional Children, 1968.

6

Language
Disorders

Preview

Reading as a language activity must be seen in its developmental relationship to other language skills. Visual language systems (reading and writing) depend on the adequate acquisition of auditory (oral) language systems (listening and speaking). Children who have difficulty developing skills in oral language present a challenge to teachers within the regular educational setting. Although the remedial issues are important and may be attended to by a speech and language therapist, the adaptations of the regular curriculm and learning environment are equally important if the child is to experience success in the classroom. Making use of the child's strengths and interests can contribute to motivation as well as to skill development.

LANGUAGE DEVELOPMENT

Language is the dynamic process of symbolization unique to man. The development of language in the child is the result of his/her being able to know for him/herself what is happening in the environment. The child is not formally taught the elements of language nor the mechanics of speech. S/he has been shaped by nature to pay attention to it, to recall it, and to use it. The capacity for language is innate and may be, as McNeill[1] suggests, the linguistic manifestation of a very general, though still inborn, cognitive capacity.

In developing proficiency in communication, the child must master three aspects of the language system: phonology, semantics, and syntax.

Phonology

Phonology is the system that deals with the sounds of a language. The normal development of speech is an extremely regular phenomenon and follows a certain, almost fixed, sequence of events.[2] The onset of speech is similar across all cultures and languages, and it seems to depend on the maturation of the organism rather than on any external, environmental factors. The mastery of the system proceeds from the birth cry to approximately seven years of age. The first year of life sees the child experimenting with vocalization and the adjustments of the structures man has adapted for the purpose of communication (tongue, lips, teeth, palate, etc.). The following vocal behaviors may be observed in the infant.

Crying— An infant reacts to problems in the environment and/or in his own physical well-being by crying. At first these cries are reflexive and undifferentiated. Later, when the child gains more control over the vocal mechanism, a mother can distinguish differences and therefore the message in his cries. Crying is good basic training for speech.

Cooing— Somewhere between the first and second months of life, an infant begins to make gurgles and vegetative sounds. He usually engages in this vocal play when he is content and happy.

Babbling— By five to six months, infants can be observed in the articulation of consonant and vowel sounds that can be recognized as phonemes in their native tongue. At first, babbling is undifferentiated and random. Later, it is imitative as the child learns to produce the sounds that others make.

First Word—By twelve to fourteen months a child can produce simple recognizable words, e.g., *mama, dada, bye-bye.*

At first, the child uses the sounds that are the easiest to make, requiring the least amount of fine motor coordination. For example, the bilabial (made by the approximation of the lips, i.e., /m/, /b/, /p/) and lingual alveolar sounds (make with the tongue against the ridge behind the upper teeth, i.e., /t/ and /d/) appear first. As the child achieves greater fine motor control and skill in auditory dicrimination, other sounds are acquired.

The following chart suggests the order in which sounds are acquired. Various researchers present slightly different timetables. However, variations in the data are no more than six to twelve months.

Age by which sounds should be acquired	Sounds
3–3½	p b m n w h
4–4½	t d g k y f (ing)
5–5½	sh v r
6–6½	l zh s voiced th
7–7½	ch z j (as in jump) voiceless th
8	all sounds, including blends, should be articulated well in all positions in words

When children enter kindergarden, they are still in the process of learning the sounds of their language. They may omit, substitute, or distort those sounds that are usually acquired at a later age. For example, a five-year-old may ask for a "poon" to eat "toup." /S/ is a sound that is not expected to be mastered until age six. Children who misarticulate sounds that should have been acquired at earlier ages may be referred for evaluation by a speech therapist.

Semantics

Semantics is the study of the meanings of words. Children begin to show understanding of words at an early age. When told to "Go get your hat and coat, we go bye-bye," the toddler will get his hat and coat. The child may not be able to say those words but s/he can understand them. The child's use of words can be observed anywhere from twelve to fifteen months. A review of recent research in cognitive development in relation to language learning suggests that children learn the words and structures that reflect their thinking about the world.[3] For example, the very young child, in what Piaget describes as the sensorimotor stage, is developing conceptual notions about people, objects, and their physical properties. This is what they talk about. Vocabulary development is quite rapid during the preschool years, particularly if the child has been living in a stimulating environment where people talk and read to him/her. The following chart gives approximations of vocabulary development in children from one to six years. Since the data are based on Smith's[4] study in 1941, they can be considered only approximations of vocabulary development in current populations.

Vocabulary Development	
Age	*Approximate Vocabulary*
12 months	2–3 words
18 months	20–50 words
24 months	300 words
30 months	500 words—period of rapid increase in vocab.
36 months	1,000 words
48 months	1,500 words
5 to 6 years	anywhere from 5,000 to 25,000 words

Syntax

Syntax refers to the grammar system of a language. From the time of the first word, between eleven and thirteen months, vocabulary and syntax increase quite systematically. The child's development and use of language at this point are both ordered and purposeful, and proceed according to the set of rules that the child has abstracted independently. The emergence of syntactic structures is most likely the evolution of a series of linguistic systems increasing in complexity, with changes in behavior reflecting changes in the child's syntactical rules. When the young child hears an adult sentence, s/he must hold it in mind long enough to perceive the order in which the words are arranged. Eventually, certain patterns become apparent to the child and s/he begins to use those patterns with his/her own words to convey his/her own ideas.

Brown and Bellugi[5] describe the early patterns, which they term imitation and reduction, and later imitation and expansion. Imitation and reduction refers to the child's ability to listen to an adult sentence and select out the words that convey the meaning. For example, if the mother says: "This coat is very dirty," the child will respond: "Coat dirty." Word order is preserved and the message is reduced to a manageable unit. Imitation and expansion refers to the mother's tendency to take a child's abbreviated utterance and expand it into a full sentence by adding the words the child has omitted, i.e., articles, verbs, etc. For example, if the child says: "Car broken," the mother may respond: "Yes, the car is broken." This does not imply that the child is merely imitating adult speech. The initial acquisition of a word, its phonological and semantic elements, is imitative and conditioned. The use of that word and its combination with others to convey meaning is unique to the child him/herself. The child's first words, used in one-word phrases, may be his first attempts at sentences. These utterances have a much broader and more diffuse meaning for the child than for the adult. The word "cookie" may mean "I want a cookie," "I have a cookie," etc. Following this stage, the child begins to combine words into two-or three-word phrases in what has been described as "telegraphic" speech. This is not to be viewed as an abbreviated form of adult language, but as reflective of the young child's limited memory span. By thirty-six months, with a vocabulary of approximately 900 words, the child is speaking in full sentences. Additional preschool years see the enrichment of vocabulary and the addition of more complex patterns of language. By age five the child has acquired the basic syntactic structures of language. S/he comes to school knowing the meaning of thousands of words, using all of the basic syntactic structures, and able to articulate most of the sounds of his/her language. All of this was achieved without formal instruction.

The acquisition of syntax proceeds according to the following schedule.

12–14 months	first word communicates using single-word phrase
18–24 months	Forms two-word phrases, mostly nouns and modifiers
24–30 months	increased length of utterances from two to five or six words—some children able to form complete sentences
3–4 years	completely intelligible in communication—has acquired simple declarative, negative, and interrogative constructions
5 years	has acquired all basic syntactic structures of his/her native language

The Relationship of Oral Language to Reading

Reading is one facet of the total, dynamic language process. It cannot be developed independent of the auditory system. Myklebust[6] suggests that the nature of this relationship is hierarchical, that is, the development of one level supports the development of those that follow it.

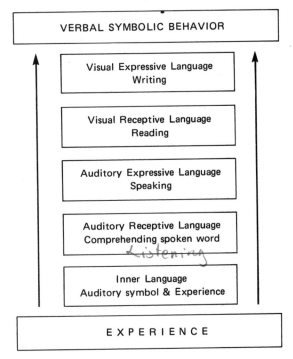

(Reprinted, by permission, from H. Myklebust, *The Psychology of Deafness.*
2d ed. New York: Grune & Stratton, 1965, p. 232.)

Figure 6.1.   *The developmental Hierarchy of Man's Language System.*

Inner language

As Myklebust sees it, inner language is the first acquired process in the
development of language. He has hypothesized that if children are to acquire
the ability to use sounds as symbols in communicative speech, they must first
recognize that the oral communication they hear in the environment is symbolic of the things or events present. The ability to recognize and internalize
these associations precedes the ability to understand. Since the next level, auditory receptive language, includes the understanding of spoken words, it
must be assumed that inner speech is a brief and simple stage of symbol-object
recognition that is somewhat prior to, and later concurrent with, comprehension and executive speech. It becomes the language of thought.

Oral auditory
receptive language
(listening)

Auditory receptive language is the level at which meaning becomes associated with words. This process is essentially one of auditory perception and
association. The ability to represent people, places, and things in their absence makes abstract behavior possible. By ten to twelve months, a baby be-

gins to show his recognition of the use of a specific auditory configuration—a word—to signify an object. If an adult says "Show me the ball," the baby will pick up the spherical object he has come to recognize as being associated with the sequence of phonemes /b//a//ll/. Understanding of new words moves quickly, so that by first grade the average child has a listening vocabulary of anywhere from 2,500 to 25,000 words. The child has learned a considerable amount about the auditory code used in communicating with other people.

Auditory expressive language (speaking)

By the age of about fourteen months, the child begins to use the words s/he has learned in meaningful ways. Although the child may understand the meaning of many words, s/he tends to use the words s/he is able to articulate. Early utterances are characterized by the substitution of certain easily articulated sounds for the more complicated sounds requiring more precise adjustment of the tongue, lips, palate, etc. The child begins to form sentences by combining known words according to the rules that have been abstracted from adult speech. The child is reinforced for the use of acceptable forms of language by gaining control over the behavior of others. S/he uses language as a means of manipulating his/her world. For example, the toddler who announces "Bed, No!" is certainly understood.

Children spend between five and six years acquiring and refining the auditory language system. They come to school knowing the meaning of thousands of words, using all of the basic syntactic structures, and able to articulate most of the sounds of their language. All of this was achieved without formal instruction.

Visual receptive language (reading)

At the magic age of six, our society has determined that it is time to learn the visual code that goes along with the auditory language the child already has. Learning to read will be highly dependent upon the language development that has taken place at the earlier stages. If the child's language has developed "on schedule," all should go well at the visual receptive level. If, however, problems have occurred at the auditory receptive or expressive stages—if, for example, the child has problems in understanding the meanings of words or putting words together to form sentences—then the move from speech to print will likely be difficult. Print is a symbolic representation of speech, and thus problems with spoken language are often the prime basis of problems in learning to read.

The language of print is a standard form of English. Children who have not been exposed to this standard form in the preschool years often have problems making the transition from the language of their homes to the language of their beginning reading books. The bilingual child presents a similar problem. His/her language may be very well developed, but the transition into reading may be difficult because it requires mastery of a visual language system based on an auditory language system the child does not have. This is one reason why recent trends in bilingual education advocate the teaching of reading in the child's native language first, and then teaching English as a second language. It is not within the scope of this book to explore the problems of teaching reading to children who are bilingual or use nonstandard forms of English. Bilingual education is a rapidly expanding field. Since issues of bilingualism or dialect cannot be considered pathologies of language, the reader is urged to refer to the literature in the field of Bilingual Education.

Learning to read involves the ability to cross modalities, that is, to translate visual symbols that are spatially oriented from left to right into auditory symbols that are temporally oriented from first to last. This involves auditory and visual integration. The average six-year-old has already demonstrated readiness for this kind of task. S/he can name (auditory symbol) a picture (visual symbol); and s/he can use language to describe what s/he sees. Under favorable conditions, learning to read progresses in a sequential fashion similar to that which has characterized the acquisition of auditory language. The child learns the sound-symbol relationships, basic vocabulary, and ultimately can derive meaning from printed language.

Visual expressive language (writing)

The highest level of the hierarchy involves the ability to express one's thoughts in written form. This stage is difficult and remains so for quite some time. Throughout the elementary and secondary years, students struggle to improve facility with written language. Although a child may acquire the basic syntactic structures of auditory language independently, without the benefit of formal teaching, the same is not true of written language. One reason may be that the child begins the process after the optimum period of language development (birth to age seven). Another possible reason is that exposure to written language is infinitesimal (two to three hours per day) compared to the child's exposure to oral language. The child does not have the same opportunities to observe the rules and their exceptions. If this were not so, then fluency with the written form would come much earlier, and competence would not be at all dependent on formal instruction.

LANGUAGE DISORDERS

Language is a prerequisite to concept formation and problem solving. Deficits in language have profound effects on all aspects of learning and measured intelligence. The child's inability to acquire language and its structure to his/her fullest capacity is disruptive of intellectual growth. Remediation is possible once a problem has been identified, but there remains the question as to whether remediation is possible beyond certain critical time periods. When the therapy begins during the period of optimum language development, i.e., before the age of seven, there is a greater chance of success. However, early identification has always been difficult. Young children demonstrate varying types and degrees of speech and language problems. In many instances, the causes are purely environmental or maturational and these children fulfill the pediatrician's prediction of "He'll outgrow it." The children who will not improve with age are camouflaged within this population of preschoolers. These are the children who are physically well, intellectually capable, and emotionally stable, yet who fail to follow the normal rate and sequence of language development. These children may, therefore, be considered deficient in the systems that support the development of skill in reading.

There are two types of language disorders: receptive language disorders and expressive language disorders. Each signifies a specific point of disruption in the hierarchical process. Problems in reception, of necessity, imply problems in expression, because a child cannot use language beyond the capacity to understand it. His/her language usage reflects everything s/he knows about word meaning and combining words into sentences to convey ideas. A child with problems in expressive language has an intact receptive system; that is, s/he understands what people say but has difficulty in using the language him/herself.

Receptive Language Disorders

Children can misunderstand what is said for many reasons, among which are: 1) problems in auditory discrimination, 2) poor auditory memory, and 3) the inability to attach meaning to spoken words. The specific aspects of problems in auditory perception and their relation to reading have been presented in Chapter 4. Discrimination and memory are mentioned here as a reminder that in the hierarchy of learning, the development of symbolization depends on the adequate development of perceptual and memory processes.

Problems in auditory discrimination

For the normal development of language, certain sensory and perceptual functions of the auditory channel are essential for the comprehension of the spoken word. An important function is discrimination. Auditory discrimination is the ability to perceive a change in the pattern of acoustic stimuli. In the perception of the sounds of speech, the differences are "just noticeable" and are the function of the central nervous system. It is not enough that the child be able to listen to sounds; s/he must be able to hear differences between and among the intensity characteristics. As listening skills develop, the child becomes aware of specialized sounds and their differences. Defects in auditory discrimination interfere with the child's ability to comprehend spoken language, by rendering inaccurate the perception of individual phonemes. *Cat* becomes confused with *cap, bat* with *pat,* etc. Identification of the semantic unit of a sentence is reduced, and thus the ability to receive and respond correctly to the transmitted message is impaired. For this child the problem is not the ability to acquire word meanings but the misperception of words within a sentence.

Problems in auditory memory

Another important auditory function is memory. To some extent, auditory memory serves every facet of the language process. In the comprehension of language, the phonemes and words that are being emitted or listened to must be stored long enough for the listener to scan back and forth over them to be sure they are in proper sequence or to check the sequence in which they are arranged. In the decoding of the syntactic structure of a particular sentence, for example, both long- and short-term auditory memory are involved— short-term in the memory of the pattern just heard, and long-term in the memory of the rules and past patterns that have been experienced and stored. A deficit in auditory memory, then, can affect the comprehension of spoken language by affecting the listener's ability to derive meaning from the way words are sequenced in a sentence. Auditory-memory deficits also reduce the child's ability to store and recall certain elements of the message. Because reading comprehension is so frequently developed and measured through questions following reading, the effect of auditory-memory problems on reading is especially devastating, since the child is unable to hold in mind the details and events of a story or recall the sequence of sounds in words.

Problems understanding spoken words

The children who have the most serious problems in language comprehension have difficulty learning the meaning of words. The histories of these children characteristically show delayed language development. They do not begin talking at the same age as other children, and often a mother may suspect that her child has a hearing loss as s/he fails to respond to verbal stimulation. When these children do begin to talk, their speech is immature and may include poor articulation as well as a limited vocabulary and immature syntax. Because the child has such difficulty expressing his/her needs and communicating his/her ideas, s/he may experience great frustration. By the time s/he comes to school, his/her language problem can be accompanied by an emotional overlay with accompanying behavioral manifestations that call attention to him/her as a child who is different. Some children become outwardly aggressive in their attempts to get what they want; others withdraw and hope nobody notices their inability to respond appropriately to what has been said. The impact of these problems on social-emotional development is considerable. Peer group relations can be seriously disturbed. The child with a receptive language problem often plays with younger children whose language sophistication is closer to his/her own level. As the child progresses into the middle grades where his/her age mates have acquired much of the idiomatic language of their society, s/he is lost and disconcerted by double meanings and coined words and phrases. S/he is easily confused, makes mistakes, and may be viewed as an "oddball." In its severest form, a receptive language disorder may be termed "receptive aphasia." The term "aphasia" implies a neurological problem that results in an inability to understand and/or express language. Most often, children who have been diagnosed as aphasic have been educated in substantially separate schools and programs. However, with the trend toward mainstreaming and with more supportive services becoming available in the schools, many aphasic children are being transferred back into their district schools. Classroom teachers are already involved in the task of providing for their special needs for whatever time they may spend in a regular classroom.

Identification of Problems in Receptive Language

Unfortunately, the symptoms of receptive language problems are subtle and often not recognized. While the child may be seen as atypical for his/her age group, inability to respond to what is said may cause the child to be seen as immature or a slow learner. In some instances, the parents of a child with language delay will seek help during the preschool years, so that by the time the child starts school, problems may have been identified and appropriate therapy initiated. However, many other children remain undiagnosed, so that the first suspicion that all is not well is the result of poor school performance. Classroom teachers, especially in the primary grades, can play a key role in identifying children who are experiencing serious problems in language development.

Classroom behaviors

In the classroom, children with problems in receptive language may have difficulty:

1. following directions—they usually look to see what others are doing.
2. attending to what is being said—they often appear not to hear.
3. learning the meaning of new words—they have limited vocabularies.
4. understanding what is said—they often repeat what they hear in an effort to decode the message.
5. forming concepts—they do not easily make generalizations.
6. understanding the humor of a situation or story—they fail to get the point.
7. following a lesson that is presented orally—they learn better when visual aids and demonstrations accompany a lesson.

Receptive language problems can also become manifest and directly affect the child in early reading instruction. For example, the child may have great difficulty relating or describing what is happening in a picture. When the time for formal instruction arrives, s/he may have undue difficulty with phonics. When s/he can read simple stories, comprehension will be limited.

Learning sight words may be nothing more than "word calling" if s/he cannot attach meaning to the words. The child will surely have trouble in determining main ideas, in seeing cause-and-effect relationships, in recognizing sequences of events, or in relating present to past learning. Poor listening comprehension will cause him/her trouble with directions that the teacher gives in carrying out reading-related tasks. In short, auditory receptive disorders can cause a range of problems in the process of learning to read.

It should be emphasized that one of these symptoms alone does not automatically indicate a language disorder. All beginning readers have trouble with the comprehension skill of sequencing. A pattern of these problems, however, may reveal the need for further assessment.

Assessment of Receptive Language Disorders

The earliest efforts in the assessment of language skills in young children focused primarily on the development of speech. Standardized tests of articulation evaluated the child's acquisition of consonant sounds in varying positions in words. The evaluation of articulatory skills, however, contributed nothing toward the understanding of the symbolic deficits that were evident in so many children. The evaluation of grammatic competence and vocabulary was more or less a subjective judgment based on a limited sample of the child's speech. Today there are several instruments designed to measure more comprehensive linguistic functioning in children. These tests are by no means infallible; in fact, there has been a great deal of discussion in the literature as to the validity and reliability of some of them. One of the difficulties in test construction and standardization has been the lack of good criterion tests that can be used to establish construct validity. Although these measures cannot be considered absolutely precise, they do represent a more objective approach to assessing language skills than was previously available. In the hands of a good diagnostician, they can yield useful information concerning the nature of the child's difficulty and the requirements of an instructional program.

The tests typically used as diagnostic instruments for children with receptive language disorders are The Peabody Picture Vocabulary Test,[7] The Illinois Test of Psycholinguistic Abilities,[8] The Test for Auditory Comprehension of Language,[9] The Detroit Test of Learning Aptitude,[10] and certain subtests of The Meeting Street Screening Test.[11]

Peabody Picture Vocabulary Test

The Peabody Picture Vocabulary Test (PPVT) is designed to measure a child's receptive vocabulary, that is, the ability to identify objects by their names. The child is presented with a page containing four pictures. The examiner says, "show me . . . ," and the child must point to the picture that represents the word named. It is normed for children from three to eighteen, which makes it very useful for the school population. Although the test provides a table for converting a raw score to an IQ score, this test is not an IQ test and these scores should not be interpreted as such. In fact, to do so would be a serious injustice to a language-disordered child. But it does allow observation of the child's receptive language ability. It tells what the child knows about the words used in an English-speaking school. Unfortunately, some of the vocabulary is inappropriate for children living in the 1970s (e.g., "coal") and many of the items are not within the realm of experience of the bilingual-bicultural child.

The Illinois Test of Psycholinguistic Abilities (ITPA)

The ITPA taps skills considered essential to the development of spoken and written language. The skills sampled are grouped according to the complexity of function. Subtests at the representational level test the child's ability to deal with meaningful symbols (words and pictures); the automatic level looks at the more perceptual functions that tend to be overlearned (or automatic) and contribute to adequate functioning at higher levels. The test is confined to the visual and auditory channels. While other channels are possible, the selection of the auditory and visual ones is based on the fact that these are the channels most related to academic skills. Although this test evaluates certain psycholinguistic components of language, it does not tap all of them. There is no measure of written responses, either as a determination of visual-motor intergration or of written language. Supplementary tests are needed to assess these areas.

The ITPA is a complicated instrument that is often abused and misused. Training in test administration and scoring is necessary to insure that the observations made are accurate for the child being tested. But in the hands of a qualified examiner it can yield a great deal of useful information.

In scoring, raw scores are converted to standard scores, with 36 used as the mean or average score at each age level. Reports and summaries of assessment on the ITPA can vary from very percise, concise statements of the observed areas of deficit to an incomprehensible conglomeration of psycholinguistic jargon that communicates little or nothing. Again, the level of expertise of the examiner makes the difference. For teachers who receive a report that is difficult to understand or interpret, the technique suggested in Appendix D may be of value.

The Test for Auditory Comprehension of Language

This test is normed for children age three to seven, and measures the child's ability to understand four basic language categories: 1) form classes and function words (nouns, adjectives, verbs, and adverbs); 2) morphology; 3) grammar (plurals, pronoun and verb number, tense, voice); 4) syntax (sentence form). The value of this test is that it goes beyond the comprehension of word meaning and takes a look at the child's ability to understand words within the structure of a sentence.

Meeting Street School Screening Test (MSST)

The MSST is designed to screen young children for the purpose of identifying those whose developmental patterns place them in the high-risk group for possible learning disabilities. It is normed for children aged five to eight, and samples behaviors in the areas of motor patterns, visual perception, and language. Although the subtests Follow Directions I and II are not included in the Language area, success on these depends on the child's ability to understand prepositional and spatial language as in the commands "Draw a ball behind the car" and "Take one step forward and two steps backward."

Detroit Test of Learning Aptitude (DTLA)

The DTLA contains several subtests that assess a child's ability to gain meaning from spoken language, as well as his/her ability to use language for abstraction. Since most instruments in this area are standardized for young children, the Detroit is often used with older students because the norms go to eighteen years.

The following subtests are useful as measures of receptive language skill:

Verbal Absurdities— deals with the child's ability to reason and comprehend, based on understanding of what is said.

Verbal Opposites— requires the understanding of basic concepts such as *shut*, and the ability to identify a word meaning the opposite.

Oral Commissions— evaluates the child's ability to follow simple directions such as "Put the book on the table and the pencil on the floor."

Oral Directions— requires the child to listen to oral directions and follow through with a motor response; for example, "Put a one in the circle and a cross in the square box."

Each of these tests can provide a clue to the child's level of functioning in receptive language. Not all of them would be used with any child. A diagnostician would choose those measures appropriate to the child's age that provide the best sample of his/her ability to understand spoken language.

The assessment process begins with good teacher observation and recording of behavior followed by referral to an appropriate specialist. The more formal evaluation attempts to identify the nature of the problem and the degree to which it may be disruptive to academic and social skills. A careful synthesis of all information leads to the determination of appropriate remedial services as well as to the instructional modifications appropriate to the regular classroom.

Instructional Accommodation for the Child with Receptive Problems

Once a child with a receptive language disorder has been identified, all the therapy in the world will make little difference if the regular classroom is not structured for success. Accommodations for a child with visual or auditory problems are important; however, the failure to provide such modifications is, in some ways, less devastating than the failure to make adjustments on behalf of the child with language deficits. In all areas of the curriculum and life skills, this child is disadvantaged more acutely and remains so for a longer period of time. In regard to the area of language development, the child with a visual problem does not experience difficulty until s/he begins to acquire skill in visual receptive language, i.e., reading. S/he has a solid foundation in auditory language on which to build a number of other skills. The child with a receptive language disorder is limited in a major area for gaining understanding of the world. Because language and cognition are so intimately connected, this child is affected in basic mental operations.

The following suggestions are often helpful in accommodating for the child with a receptive language problem.

1. Ask short questions, because elaborate interrogation will leave him/her in a quandary as to what is expected.

2. Use short one-concept phrases. Segmenting directions into specific steps allows the child enough time to process what is being said without having to hold too much information in mind at one time.

3. Do not walk around the room giving directions. The distraction of having to turn to follow, and the loss of direct auditory input, reduce the effectiveness of the communication.

4. Allow the child to choose a classmate or a "buddy" to serve as a "backup" person—the friend can help him/her remember directions, assignments, etc.

5. Seat the child close to the source of instruction so s/he can profit from all avenues of input, auditory as well as visual.

6. Provide for reinforcement of basic skills. In some areas of learning, drill and overlearning are the only way the child will master fundamentals.

7. Prepare the child for shifts in learning. S/he may not shift gears readily; e.g., when the class has moved on to math, his/her mind may still be on social studies.

8. Make generalizations for the child. S/he may not see how present learning relates to past learning.

9. Preteach new vocabulary in science and social studies.

APPROACHES TO READING

Remediation of problems in language should be overseen by a specialist in language disorders. This does not mean that only a person trained in language pathology can provide for the educational needs of a child who has difficulty understanding and using language. It simply means that the instructional objectives and strategies for the remedial program, and their coordination with the regular educational program, should be determined by the specialist together with any other personnel involved in direct services to the child. The actual therapy may be provided by the specialist or by a paraprofessional or tutor under his/her direction. Many language therapists have heavy case loads as well as responsibilities for assessments, so that the time available for any given child is limited. Since the problems of these children tend to be severe and to require rather intensive intervention, some specialists function in a supervisory and consultant capacity with much of the direct work being provided by those who have closer contact with the child, including the regular classroom teacher.

Classroom teachers in the primary grades may be working with children at the time of the identification of language deficits and the initiation of the support programs. The issue of beginning reading will require careful management and a great deal of flexibility on the part of the teacher. Teachers in the upper grades may be working with a child who has been in therapy for some time. Since progress tends to be slow, underachievement in reading is most likely to persist into the secondary level. Again, throughout these years the reading program must be carefully planned and coordinated to meet the needs of the child. Such a child should definitely not be shifted from one approach or one program to another without careful reevaluation of skill as well as cognitive development. Lack of consistency and coordination can be as harmful as not providing help at all.

Since most children with language disorders experience difficulty in auditory perceptual skill areas, these children are likely to have problems in all areas of reading skill development. The strategies suggested in Chapter 4 for children with auditory (sensory as well as perceptual) problems should be considered appropriate for the language-disordered child if the assessment of auditory skills reveals problems in this area as well. Tactile and kinesthetic cues to assist in the discrimination of individual phonemes, choral reading to help him/her experience the rhythm and flow of language, etc., are appropriate for the child with receptive language problems.

Vocabulary Development

The primary consideration in the development of a reading vocabulary is its dependency on the spoken vocabulary. As Johnson and Myklebust suggest, "Reading is a visual symbol system superimposed on previously acquired auditory language."[12] Although with intensive training a child may learn to read words, unless those words have a firm foundation in meaning—that is, the association of the auditory symbol with the experience of what it represents—the child will be a "word caller" and comprehension will not be possible. The development of a speaking vocabulary must therefore be, considered a prerequisite for the development of a reading vocabulary.

Development of Vocabulary in Oral Language

All of life's experiences can be made meaningful for language development. Children whose capacity for learning language is unimpaired acquire the meanings of words at a rapid rate during the second and third years of life. As they interact with the world, they begin to code their experiences. For the child who has difficulty acquiring vocabulary independently, a conscious effort must be made by parents and teachers to provide the language stimulation and reinforcement so that appropriate associations can be made.

Approaches to oral language development

Johnson and Myklebust[13] present the following suggestions for helping children learn meaningful oral language.

1. *Reception before expression.* Since a child must learn what words mean before he can use or read them, work must begin with the semantic process. As comprehension improves, the child will show an increased capacity for using words. Merely repeating words is not an indication of growth in language. The ability to repeat words involves the auditory-motor pattern and does not require an understanding of the meaning.

Show-and-tell encourages children to share experiences through verbal expression. Good oral language supports success in reading. (Photo by John A. Malnati)

2. *Reduction of language complexity.* When providing language stimulation for a child with a language deficit, one must use the child's own language level. The introduction of new vocabulary should be in isolation and in association with a key word or phrase. Once the word has been identified, it can be put into the context of a short sentence. "Thus the task of the teacher is to help him differentiate meaning units and to associate these with appropriate verbal symbols."[14]

3. *Simultaneity.* The spoken word and the experience must occur in close approximation. The variety of sensory impressions that characterize an object, person, or event must be combined with the sound of the word in order that the strongest impression and association be made. Field trips, classroom activities, and family outings provide an excellent opportunity to combine language with immediate experience.

4. *Selection of vocabulary.* Only words that have meaning for the child should be taught. Word selection will be influenced by what is happening in his life at home and at school. If the ZOOMOBILE comes to school, this is a perfect opportunity to increase vocabulary of animal names. If the family takes a camping trip, it is a perfect opportunity to increase his/her vocabulary concerning things to be found in woodlands.

While introducing and reinforcing new vocabulary within the classroom, the teacher should be encouraging the child to talk as much as possible. Since a child with poor language development is often hesitant to communicate before a large group, opportunities may need to be structured for one-to-one or small-group interaction. The child who is unwilling to share with a whole class during Show-and-Tell (or Bring-and-Brag) may easily do so at a small table with one or two other children. Successful communication is the best incentive for learning more about language.

Development of Vocabulary in Reading

Since the child with problems in understanding spoken language needs extensive work on vocabulary development, an approach to beginning reading should be chosen on the basis of its ability to teach meaningful language units using words as a whole. Teaching isolated sounds or syllables is very confusing for a child who has difficulty recognizing the components of language. In view of this, there are two choices that are logical for this child: a word meaning (look-say) or a language experience approach. Of the two, the language experience approach has more to offer in terms of comprehensive language development.

The language experience approach

The language experience approach is described by Aukerman[15] as "an approach to reading that is basically a whole word approach, at the same time utilizing the vocabulary and speech patterns of normal children." The development of this approach was an alternative to basal readers, which use preselected vocabulary and language patterns not typical of the language of six-

and seven-year-olds. There are certain features of this approach that make it particularly suitable for children with language problems.

1. The technique for developing skill in reading promotes the integration of listening, speaking, reading, and writing. This requires the immediate connection of spoken and written language. As the child verbalizes a story or describes an experience, it is immediately recorded in written form so that the child can follow while the teacher reads it, and can later read it him/herself.

2. The technique uses vocabulary that is entirely personal to the child. It comes from the realm of personal experience and thus carries the greatest possible meaning. The initial reading vocabulary becomes sight words the child has selected and used him/herself.

3. The technique is very motivating to a child, both to the beginning reader and to the older one who has failed. It allows the child to read about things that interest, excite, or bother him/her, or in any other way affect his/her life.

Language experience charts

The basic component of this approach is the experience story or chart. Through oral discussion of a story or event, the child dictates his/her thoughts in his/her own words. For the child with language problems, careful questioning may be necessary to help recall the sequence of events s/he wishes to portray. Sometimes it is helpful to have the child illustrate the story first so that s/he will have a pictorial record of what s/he wants to say. After the story has been dictated and transcribed, the teacher can read it aloud and the child can follow along. It is important to call attention to the new words as well as to identify familiar words and the way the words have been put together in sentences to convey meaning. The child should read the story several times until s/he is sure of the vocabulary. Follow-up activities can be used to reinforce basic skill in sight words. Word cards can be used for flash presentation or for matching with words in the story. The teacher can scramble the words in a sentence and let the child assemble them in the correct order. Since the sentence is one the child constructed in the first place, it is important for him/her to learn to assemble it in its visual form.

Word banks

As vocabulary develops, Hall[16] suggests the use of word banks for grouping and classifying words. She offers the following possibilities for group word banks:

Descriptive words	Words for said
Naming words	Compound words

Action words	Words for prefixes
Interesting words	Words for suffixes
Words for sounds	Synonyms
Words for colors	Homonyms
Words for animals	Science words
Opposites	Three-syllable words
Words with more than one meaning	Four-syllable words
	Sports words
Social Studies words	Words for feelings

There are, however, certain cautions that must be exercised in using a language experience approach with a child with language problems. The child must be closely supervised every step of the way. A great deal of teacher time is required to listen, and to record and read what the child has dictated. Follow-up activities must also be carefully planned since there are no workbooks or prepared worksheets to reinforce skills. Close teacher supervision is also required in monitoring sentence structure. The language the child dictates is based on his/her own speech patterns. Since these patterns are limited, the teacher must be sensitive to the child's need to expand sentences and to use a variety of patterns. One of the best techniques for doing this is through oral language activities. As the child's ability to formulate sentences in spoken language improves, the quality of the printed material he reads and writes will improve as well.

Although the language experience approach is an appropriate method for beginning reading instruction for a child with language problems, it cannot provide for all his reading needs. The National First Grade Studies[17] suggest that one approach used exclusively is not as effective as one approach supplemented by techniques associated with other approaches. In the language experience approach to reading, this is especially true. It can provide for initial success in reading, but the development of specific skills in word attack and structural analysis requires the use of materials specifically designed for that purpose. The introduction of these materials, however, should be carefully timed. When the child begins to point out similarities and differences in the visual and auditory aspects of words, s/he is probably sufficiently interested and skilled in reading to tolerate the demands of phonetic analysis. This readiness will be demonstrated as a result of the intensive work on auditory and language skills in the remedial program, as well as of the happy experiences with written language in the regular classroom. The selection of an approach to word attack skills should be a team decision based on what all teachers have learned about the way the child learns best. The use of a linguistic approach for children with auditory problems has been discussed in Chapter 4. This same rationale may hold true for children with language disorders. However, that determination should be based on a careful ongoing assessment of what works and what doesn't. The complicating factor for children with language disorders is that the language deficit may occur with concomitant problems in the visual-motor area. If this is the case, the severity of the child's problems may require placement in a substantially separate program for children with language disorders.

Reading Comprehension

Once the language-disordered child has developed a sight vocabulary of fifty to a hundred words, as well as some beginning word attack skills, direct work on comprehension should begin. In the language experience approach, comprehension is facilitated, since the child has used his/her own words to express ideas s/he understands. This has allowed the child to build confidence as a speaker and a reader. The major objective of developing skill in reading is to be able to understand what someone else has written. The child must be able to extract the meaning from language in print. Developing this skill can be a

New vocabulary should be introduced before reading a story. (Photo by John A. Malnati)

slow and difficult process; therefore, all efforts in the direction of creative and careful teaching will surely affect the degree of success a child experiences in any given school year.

Choice of materials

Reading for meaning requires the ability to understand the vocabulary, sentence structure, and concepts used. Learning basic vocabulary that has been emphasized in the initial stages of learning to read must be continued throughout the teaching of comprehension skills. The choice of materials will directly affect the ease with which the child encounters and learns the meaning of new words, as well as his/her facility in using context clues. Reading materials that focus on an area of interest or on a topic of immediate importance to the child offer him/her the greatest possible chance of success, because 1) the material is motivating, and 2) it has some basis in his/her own personal experience. For younger children, carefully selected stories in a basal reader may be appropriate. For older children, books described as high interest and low vocabulary can be used effectively. In the beginning it is important that vocabulary be taught prior to the reading of the story. Later, the child should be encouraged to make use of context clues in discovering what the words are and what they mean.

The theoretical perspectives of reading comprehension have been presented in Chapter 1. Consideration of the unique problems of the language-disordered child in his encounters with literal and inferential comprehension of language in print is related to his/her basic problems in thinking. For the language-disordered child, the inner language necessary to perform the higher-level cognitive functions is inadequate. Since inner language is dependent on receptive language for its development, the lack of word knowledge and sentence formulation deprives the child of the precise information or concepts that allow him/her to engage in abstract thinking. The child with a receptive language disorder remains at a very concrete level of thought. S/he tends to use descriptive language. S/he may learn to describe what s/he sees in a picture or what s/he has heard or read in a story, but s/he is at a disadvantage in the ability to draw conclusions or in any way evaluate what has occurred.

Science to promote language

Since the basic deficit is in the thinking process, the classroom teacher can do more to promote the development of cognitive skills than the specialist who sees the child on a limited-time basis. All areas of the curriculum provide opportunities for the child to engage in higher-level mental operations. Science is one of the richest areas for developing the ability to see cause and effect, make generalizations, and draw conclusions. Since most newer science programs stress the "hands on," experiential approach to learning, the child receives the multisensory input that helps to develop the new vocabulary, and that facilitates the recall of the sequence of events allowing the formulation of conclusions. Recording the steps of an experiment, and stating the results and laws that govern such a phenomenon, assist the child in recognizing the use of the printed word to preserve and communicate what has occurred. Later, reading reports of scientific experiments that s/he has not observed directly will allow him/her to develop skill in the processes of convergent and divergent

Science activities provide an excellent opportunity for children to develop skills in inferential comprehension. (Photo by John A. Malnati)

thinking. Other areas of the curriculum can also help the language-disordered child develop higher-level thinking skills, as long as the instructional objectives go beyond the knowledge and comprehension levels to include analysis, synthesis, and evaluation.[18]

Inferential comprehension

One of the most difficult skills for the child with problems in receptive language is the ability to make inferences. Since even literal comprehension is not easily acquired, detecting what is not stated but implied is extremely difficult. Preliminary activities to develop skill at this level can include pictorial and then verbal absurdities, such as "Early in the evening, when the sun comes up, I take my dog for a walk." Detecting incorrect information from what is said can be preliminary to drawing conclusions from implied information. Calling the child's attention to each segment of information and how it relates to other segments encourages him to see the relationship of parts to the whole.

SQ3R in the content areas

In paragraph reading, there are several techniques that can provide a logical approach to the question-and-answer procedure. In many upper-grade classrooms, a technique that has proven effective is the SQ3R technique described by Robinson.[19] This Survey-Question-Read-Recite and Review method is most effective with children in the upper grades, since it lends itself so well to the kind of material usually found in textbooks in most content areas. The student learns to survey the content of a chapter through the reading of introductory sentences and all headings and questions provided at the end. Next, these headings are turned into questions— "What did . . . ? Why did . . . ? Who are . . . ?" etc. Students then read the entire passage or paragraph in an attempt to find the answers. In the beginning it is wise to have the student answer the questions orally so that the teacher can immediately identify any wrong conclusions. Finally, once all sections of a chapter have been covered, the student reviews all questions in order to assemble the complete meaning of what has been read. Although this can be done with an entire class or with groups of children, for the child with serious language deficits it is best to provide close monitoring of the process and to prevent errors made in public.

Modified cloze procedure

The cloze procedure typically used to test comprehension of reading material can be modified for use as a teaching technique. Omitting every fifth word (as in the testing procedure) would place the child with a receptive language disorder at a distinct disadvantage, since there is no control of the type of words omitted. A child who does not understand or use structures such as personal pronouns, prepositions, auxiliary verbs, etc., would have no way of identifying them as missing from a sentence. Therefore, omissions should be chosen according to certain form classes such as nouns, adjectives, active verbs, adverbs, etc. The words must be part of the child's speaking vocabulary and the subject matter should be within the realm of his/her own experience. In each instance, the teacher should provide the child with information as to the subject of the passage, and should provide little hints as to what will take place. For example, the teacher might tell the child that s/he will be reading a story about a family who went to the zoo with their father. They saw many kinds of animals and made many new friends. The child reads:

Father said, "Come children. It is a sunny day. Let's go to the _____." Everyone got into Father's _____ for the ride to the _____. When they arrived, they went to the _____ house to see the chimps and a baby gorilla. That was fun. Next, they saw the big cats. There were _____ and _____ and two big black _____. Outside in the yard some men were washing the biggest animal of all. The _____ loved his bath and made funny noises with his trunk. He drank up the water left in the _____ and blew it at the men. It was funny. _____ and the _____ laughed.

The above passage involves noun deletion only. As a first step, a teacher might give a choice of words under the _____. For example, "Let's go to the *zoo school*." Later the choice of words can be eliminated, with the teacher providing only the preliminary discussion of the appropriate vocabulary as assistance in making the selection.

There is an increasing abundance of commercial material designed to promote the development of skill in comprehension. Using packaged material is a great convenience to the busy teacher and, indeed, much of it is appealing and motivating for children. However, selecting appropriate exercises for the language-disordered child must be done carefully. Materials chosen at random without thought to the issue of word knowledge, familiarity of subject matter, or complexity of sentence structure could cause great frustration and ultimate setback. The best approach is through collaboration with the specialists who are supervising the remedial program. Together, these people can coordinate skill development so that the sequence of thought progresses from concrete to abstract and teaching techniques to promote this transition can be consistent and well monitored.

PROBLEMS IN EXPRESSIVE LANGUAGE

The differential diagnosis between receptive and expressive language disorders is based on the determination of adequate skills in understanding language. The child with a receptive disorder cannot understand language very well. The child with an expressive disorder can acquire vocabulary, understand words in connected speech, follow directions, and generally function very well until s/he is required to express him/herself. It is at that point that s/he has trouble.

There are two types of expressive language disorders: word-finding difficulties and sentence formulation problems. Johnson and Myklebust[20] include problems in executing the motor patterns of speech (apraxia) in this category. This will not be included here. Although these are problems in the expressive function, they are more related to the mechanics of sound production and can be considered difficulties of speech rather than of language.

Word-Finding Problems

Word-finding problems (sometimes referred to as dysnomia) are the result of an individual's inability to recall words spontaneously for use in expressing ideas. While we all have words "on the tip of our tongue" from time to time, this phenomenon is, for some children, frequent and severe. The words beyond the child's retrieval are not esoteric words that are seldom used, but the common, everyday words that are used over and over—words that are well known and often needed. The inability to retrieve them in a given situation is temporary. The word beyond reach today may be easily recalled tomorrow. The underlying difficulty accounting for this problem in word retrieval is assumed to be psychoneurological.

Children who experience difficulty in word retrieval may use an elaborate gesture system as they attempt to use body language to compensate for poor oral language. When words cannot be retrieved readily, children often use a sound-associated response such as *pin* for *pen*, or a word in the same category as the word they are looking for—for example, *salt* for *sugar*, *hammer* for *nail*. The inability to recall words for spontaneous use affects their ability to form a cohesive narrative. At times, these children can appear to be nonfluent as they begin a sentence, get stuck, and start again. They often use indefinite words like *stuff, thing, that guy,* etc., to denote what they cannot name. The overall impression is of a child who is unable to organize his/her thoughts and express them well enough to be understood.

Assessment of Word-Finding Problems

There are no standardized tests to measure or identify problems in word finding. The teacher's most reliable instruments are his/her own ears. Careful listening to what the child is saying and how s/he is saying it can provide the best clues as to the nature of the difficulty. Observing and recording the kinds of strategies the child may use to communicate—i.e., gestures, sound associates, etc.—and the conditions under which he communicates best, can provide excellent information to the language specialist, who may attempt a more precise definition of the problem. Certain tasks used to assess other skills are quite sensitive to word-finding problems as well, and can be utilized by the specialist and the teacher. Verbal analogies like those found in the Auditory Association subtest of the ITPA and on the Detroit are difficult for the child who cannot retrieve words well. On the analogy, "Fingers have rings, wrists have _____," one child replied, "Oh yeah, I gave my mother one for Christmas. It was gold and had things that jingle on it. You do the clasp." It was quite clear that s/he had been able to perform the analogy but was unable to label the item that he could see so clearly in his mind. Rapid naming of pictures such as the Dolch Picture Vocabulary Cards can reveal the child's difficulty in recalling vocabulary. Typical responses may be *pie* for *cake*, *dog* for *cat*, *table* for *chair*.

Whatever is at the base of word-finding problems, long-term memory is heavily implicated. The mechanism for triggering the immediate retrieval of required information does not function well enough to be reliable, even for the most basic vocabulary. For the child experiencing word-finding difficulty, the memory deficit may carry over to other skill areas as well. Rarely is this an isolated symptom. Once the problem has been identified, a full evaluation should be considered in order that the problem can be seen it its total perspective.

Sentence Formulation Problems

A second type of expressive language disorder is related to a basic deficit in the child's ability to acquire and use the rules of syntax at a level commensurate with his mental age. In other words, although s/he may understand spoken language very well, s/he has been unable to abstract the rules by which words are strung together to form sentences. S/he sounds rather odd when compared to classmates, and s/he may use an elaborate gesture system in an attempt to communicate. The language s/he does use is marked by incomplete sentence structure and systematic deletion of certain word classes. For example, "My daddy give me two dime" shows incorrect verb tense and use of plurals. "Bike broken" for "My bike is broken" involves deletion of the possessive pronoun as well as the verb. The child may have difficulty forming negatives and interrogatives as well as correct tense, subject-predicate agreement, and the numerous other structures of his/her native language. S/he also has difficulty keeping in mind all that s/he wishes to say, so that oral expression is noticeably immature. Although the child with a receptive language disorder may exhibit similar expressive language behaviors, his/her difficulty is directly related to the fact that s/he cannot understand the words and sentences of others. The child whose language deficit is related only to output has the advantage of being able to understand adequately. For this reason the implications for reading may be less severe.

Assessment of Sentence Formulation Problems

The child who experiences difficulty in language expression has a tendency to withdraw from situations that require a verbal response. S/he rarely volunteers an answer or contributes to class discussion. It is easy to overlook his/her problem on the premise that s/he is shy and shouldn't be pushed to communicate until s/he feels more comfortable. This outlook can contribute to the loss of valuable time in discovering the real nature of his/her difficulty and delay the initiation of appropriate remediation.

The assessment of problems in sentence formulation can be approached somewhat more formally than problems in word finding. Observation is, of course, a most important prerequisite to appropriate assessment. Tape recordings of the child's spontaneous language in the classroom can be of great value to a specialist who may have limited time to establish rapport and complete the necessary assessment procedure. The child may not present a true picture of his/her skills while working with someone s/he does not know very well. The teacher's impressions are therefore very important.

There are certain standardized measures that may be employed to identify problems in sentence formulation. The Grammatic Closure and Verbal Expression subtests of the ITPA,[8] the Northwestern Syntactic Screening Test,[20] and the Tell a Story subtest on the Meeting Street School Screening Test[11] are examples of such measures.

The grammatic closure subtest (ITPA)

This test evaluates the child's ability to use the morphological rules of language. It assesses the use of regular and irregular plurals, pronouns, regular and irregular verb forms, superlatives, and prepositions. For example, the child is shown a divided page with a picture of a dog on one side and two dogs on the other. The examiner says, "Here is a dog and here are two ⎯⎯⎯⎯." The child is expected to respond "dogs." Children who are having difficulty with the grammatical structures of their language will not perform well on a task of this type.

Verbal Expression Subtest (ITPA)

This subtest makes an attempt to evaluate the child's ability to abstract and describe the attributes of four common objects: a ball, a block, an envelope, and a button. It does not measure the child's ability to formulate sentences and in that sense may not live up to its title. However, children with language deficits have difficulty providing adequate responses, and this may be used as one indication of poor language production.

Northwestern Syntactic Screening Test

This test can be used to identify difficulties in the child's ability to understand and express certain language structures. Again, like the Verbal Expression Subtest of the ITPA, it does not evaluate spontaneous language, but relies on the child's ability to repeat sentences the examiner has presented. It is described by Lee as a screening test, and as such can be useful.

At the moment, tests that measure the understanding of language are more numerous and cover a wider age range of skills than those to assess the expression of language. Analyzing a sample of the child's spoken language is probably the most valid measure of all. Most speech and language therapists are trained to do this and can provide valuable insights into the educational significance of disorders of expressive language.

Instructional Accommodations for the Child with Expressive Problems

Problems in language expression have certain implications for the psychosocial as well as the educational success of the child. Like any other child with a specific learning problem, the child with an expressive language disorder requires modifications of the learning environment and curriculum. Although less disabled than the child with receptive problems, the child with expressive deficits may appear to be just as "stupid," since s/he is also unable to express his/her ideas clearly and logically. The following suggestions can provide for his/her comfort and well-being within the regular classroom.

1. Reduce the amount of oral and written work. Since language production is a problem, the work load must be adjusted to something that the child can reasonably handle.

2. Give the child plenty of time to respond. If s/he seems to be having difficulty, say, "Do you mean . . . ?" and not "I don't understand."

3. Resist the temptation to say, "Slow down," "Think before you speak," etc., since this will interrupt communication and reinforce his/her feelings of inadequacy as a speaker.

4. Provide clues when word retrieval is a problem. Don't just say the word. For example, if the child is searching for the word *bag,* the teacher can provide a hint by saying the initial sound: "Is it a *b* . . . ?"

5. Encourage the use of words and not gesture. Ask him/her to *tell* you what s/he means.

6. If the child loses a train of thought, help him/her to get back on the track with careful questioning.

The focus of these suggestions is the reduction of anxiety in a speaking situation so that oral language formulation can develop into a stronger base for written expression.

Expressive Language Disorders and Reading

The impact of problems in oral expressive language is greater for writing than for reading. Since basic auditory skills may be well developed, word attack skills can be acquired without incident. Since receptive language is intact, understanding of vocabulary can be entirely adequate although the child's ability to formulate an adequate response to comprehension questions may be seriously impaired. The inevitable quizzing following a story read in a reading group can present a problem as the child attempts to organize and express his/her ideas in an oral form. If the questions are to be written, the problem may be even more apparent as the visual form depends on an adequate auditory form. Careful questioning by the teacher will reveal the degree of understanding.

The implication of memory

Since memory is involved in the recall of words and the ability to acquire the formula for creating sentences, the memory deficit will have considerable influence on the child's capacity to recall the details and events of a story. The techniques suggested for such problems in Chapter 4 can be of benefit to the child with problems in expressive language. Once s/he has acquired the facts and sequences of events, s/he is capable of identifying the main idea, making inferences, and drawing conclusions, although his/her ability to indicate successful mental operations may be rather limited.

Problems in oral reading

Johnson and Myklebust[21] point out that problems in word retrieval can contribute to problems in oral reading. The child can "associate meaning with visual symbols but cannot call up the correct auditory symbol." As a result, oral reading is filled with substitutions or is significantly below silent reading ability. An eight-year-old girl, asked to read the sentence, "The bird flew back to its nest," could not recall the exact words, so she read it as "The chicken went back to his home." Marshall and Newcombe[22] refer to this problem as "Semantic Dyslexia," that is, a severe reading problem characterized by the child's use of word substitutions that may preserve the meaning but are an inaccurate representation of what is actually written. Once recognized, this problem requires the attention of the language specialist, who can provide exercises to facilitate storage and retrieval. The classroom teacher can encourage the use of word attack skills as a strategy for accurate decoding of words.

CONCLUSION

Learning to read is part of the complex system of verbal symbolic behavior. The acquisition of the system follows a highly systematic sequence of skill development that begins with the child's ability to understand and use spoken language. The visual receptive (reading) and expressive (writing) levels are superimposed on the previously acquired auditory language. The supportive relationship of the auditory to the visual system is critical to the understanding of problems in reading experienced by children who do not acquire auditory receptive and expressive language in a normal fashion.

Problems in auditory receptive language can be related to auditory perceptual and memory deficits as well as to the difficulty of the child in associating meaning with words. The child whose problem in understanding language is due to a lack of facility in associating words with objects, persons, or events is the most disabled learner of the three types, because thinking skills are so closely related to verbal skills. In reading, this child has significant difficulty with comprehension as well as with decoding skills. Therefore, it is important for a teacher to recognize the source of the problem and to make the necessary instructional accommodations.

The approach to reading that can accommodate best for a child's poor understanding of language is the highly personal language experience approach. Although this approach is somewhat demanding of teacher time in terms of preparation and supervision, it pays great dividends in helping the child develop adequate auditory and visual symbol systems. Once the child has demonstrated the ability to tie both auditory and visual symbols to the actual experience with the objects or events they represent, attention can and should be given to basic skills in word attack.

Problems in auditory expressive language are less devastating to the process of learning to read. Expressive problems have greater impact on writing than on reading skills. For children who have difficulty with word finding, there may be a problem in recalling the exact auditory symbol to go with the printed word. They can preserve the meaning of a sentence through the substitution of a word with a similar meaning. For these children, it is important that the teacher stress proficiency in the decoding of words through word attack skills.

The need for careful observation and cooperative decision making in resolving instructional management issues is crucial for the child with a language disorder. Work in the classroom must focus on teaching to strengths wherever possible in order to maximize opportunities for success in reading. The remedial program can provide attention to the deficit areas in an attempt to assist the child in learning the vocabulary and structure of his language, so that they can be available to him/her for comprehending what s/he reads. Progress in this area can be very slow and often frustrating. Good communication between the classroom teachers, remedial staff, and parents can insure that all of life's experiences are made meaningful for language development, and provide the kind of stimulation and satisfaction that keep motivation high.

ACTIVITIES FOR PRESERVICE TEACHERS

1. The mother of a four-year-old boy tells you she is concerned about her child's language development and asks you to listen to him and give your opinion. You meet the child and discover that he distorts *sh* and *ch* and consistently substitutes *t/s*, *d/z*, and *w/s*, in all positions in words. He seems to have a good vocabulary but has difficulty with verb tense, personal pronouns, and irregular plurals. What would you advise this mother concerning the child's language development?

2. The language experience approach to reading can be very motivating to the child with a receptive language disorder. In order to insure the greatest amount of skill development, however, carefully planned follow-up activities are necessary. Outline five activities that could be used for a fourth grader who is just beginning to develop some skill in reading what s/he has dictated.

3. Review two beginning grammar books or workbooks for children in the middle grades. Identify the order in which various structures are presented. Which book appears more adaptable for children with problems in expressive language? Why?

4. You observe a child using word substitutions when reading aloud. S/he can preserve the meaning of a sentence but does not use the words as written. How might you call the child's attention to his problem? What techniques could you use to help the child begin to monitor his/her oral reading?

5. Some children have more than one problem that can interfere with their learning to read. The child with a receptive language disorder as well as low vision presents a unique challenge to a teacher. What are the most important considerations in choosing an approach to beginning reading for this child? What would be your choice? Why?

ACTIVITIES FOR IN-SERVICE TEACHERS

1. You observe a child in your class having considerable difficulty following directions and getting his/her work done. The learning specialist has a backlog of children to be evaluated and will not be able to see him/her for some time. How can you begin to determine for yourself whether his/her problem is due to hearing loss, auditory perceptual or memory deficits, or problems in auditory receptive language?

2. For the above child, what would you expect to find in terms of reading problems? Given the approach you are using in reading, what would be his/her specific problems in dealing with the materials?

3. Receptive and expressive language–disordered children both have problems in formulating language for expression. Identify five exercises or activities for teaching sentence building.

4. The language experience approach to reading requires careful teacher supervision. Given your own classroom situation, what assistance could you provide for a child in addition to yourself, i.e., peer, tutor, etc.? How could you monitor his/her progress within a realistic time commitment?

5. You discover that the mother of a receptive language–disordered child is attempting to teach her child basic word attack skills through sounding and blending. The child is becoming increasingly frustrated and "turned off" to reading. What might you suggest to this mother that would allow her to feel helpful and at the same time permit her child to feel more successful in reading?

NOTES

1. D. McNeil, *The Acquisition of Language: The Study of Developmental Psycholinguistics* (New York: Harper and Row, 1970).
2. E. Lenneberg, *Biological Foundations of Language* (New York: John Wiley & Sons, Inc., 1967).
3. L. Bloom, "Language Development," in *Review of Child Development Research,* F. D. Horowitz (Chicago: The University of Chicago Press, 1975).
4. M. Smith, "Measurement of the Size of General English Vocabulary through Elementary Grades and High School," *Genet. Psych. Monograph* 24 (1941): 311–345.
5. R. Brown and N. Bellugi, eds., "The Acquisition of Language." *Monograph of the Society of Research in Child Development,* 1964, No. 29.
6. H. Myklebust, *The Psychology of Deafness*, 2d ed. (New York: Grune & Stratton, 1965), p. 232.
7. L. Dunn, *Peabody Picture Vocabulary Test* (Circle Pines, Minn.: American Guidance Service, 1965).
8. S. A. Kirk, J. J. McCarthy, and W. D. Kirk, *Illinois Test of Psycholinguistic Ability,* rev. ed. (Urbana: University of Illinois Press, 1968).
9. E. Carrow, *Test for Auditory Comprehension of Language* (Austin, Texas: Urban Research Group, 1973).
10. N. J. Baker and B. Leland, *Detroit Test of Learning Aptitude* (Indianapolis: Test Division of Bobbs-Merrill, 1967).
11. P. K. Hainsworth and M. L. Siqueland, *Early Identification of Children with Learning Disabilities: The Meeting Street School Screening Test* (Providence, R. I.: Crippled Children and Adults of Rhode Island, 1969).
12. D. Johnson and H. Myklebust, *Learning Disabilities: Educational Principles and Practices* (New York: Grune & Stratton, 1967), p. 79.
13. Ibid., p. 85.
14. Ibid., p. 86.
15. R. C. Aukerman, *Approaches to Beginning Reading* (New York: John Wiley & Sons, Inc., 1971), p. 299.
16. M. A. Hall, *Teaching Reading as a Language Experience* (Columbus, Ohio: Charles E. Merrill, 1976), p. 65.
17. G. L. Bond and R. Dykstra, "The Cooperative Research Program in First Grade Reading Instruction," *Reading Research Quarterly* (Summer 1967): 5–142.
18. B. Bloom, *Taxonomy of Educational Objectives: Cognitive Domain* (New York: McKay, 1956).

19. F. Robinson, *Effective Study* (New York: Harper & Row, 1941).

20. D. Johnson and H. Myklebust, *Learning Disabilities*, p. 114.

21. L. Lee, Northwestern Syntax Screening Test (Evanston, Ill.: Northwestern University Press, 1971).

22. D. Johnson and H. Myklebust, *Learning Disabilities*, p. 118.

23. J. C. Marshall and F. Newcombe, "Patterns of Paralexia: A Psycholinguistic Approach," *Journal of Psycholinguistic Research* 2 (1973): 175–195.

REFERENCES

Hall, M. A. *Teaching Reading as a Language Experience*. Columbus, Ohio: Charles E. Merrill, 1976.

Hodges, R. E., and Rudorf, E. H., eds. *Language and Learning to Read: What Teachers Should Know about Language*. Boston: Houghton Mifflin, 1972.

Kleffner, F. R. *Language Disorders in Children*. New York: The Bobbs-Merrill Company, Inc., 1973.

Savage, J. F. *Effective Communication: Language Arts Instruction in the Elementary School*. Chicago: Science Research Associates, 1977.

Schmidt, H. J., and Schmidt, K. J. *Learning with Puppets: A Guide to Making and Using Puppets in the Classroom*. Palo Alto: The Puppet Masters, 1977.

Van Allen, Roach, *Learning Experiences in Communication*. Boston: Houghton Mifflin, 1976.

Weig, E. H., and Semel, E. M. *Language Disabilities in Children and Adolescents*. Columbus, Ohio: Charles E. Merrill, 1976.

7

The Slow
Learner

Preview

*A child whose learning capacity or ability (as
conventionally measured by intelligence tests) is lower
than average, is considered a slow learner. There is a
positive relationship between a person's intellectual
ability and his/her ability to learn, but other factors
besides intelligence affect one's ability in learning to
read. Reading instruction for the slow learner in the
classroom involves adjusting the instructional program to the child's learning capacity, level of achievement, and rate of learning. It includes careful
attention to the choice of materials and to the
techniques used in developing basic reading skills. It
may also involve using expectancy measures as an
indication of a child's reading potential.*

Of all the learning problems conventionally encountered in schools, the one most familiar to the classroom teacher is the slow learner. That's the child who doesn't "catch on" as easily as the other children; the one who is slower to understand; the one who takes longer than others to finish the worksheet—and when s/he does finish, many of the answers may be incorrect; the child whose achievement is below that of the rest of the group; in short, the child who has trouble learning.

Who are the slow learners? Traditionally, slow learners were designated as those pupils whose scores fell within the 75- or 80- to-90 IQ range on an intelligence test. (See Figure 7.1.) These children were generally thought of as a group whose learning ability was above the so-called "retarded" level but immediately below the "normal" range.

This rather strict categorizing and labeling system led to certain problems. The terminology used to serve as diagnostic or prognostic indicators of

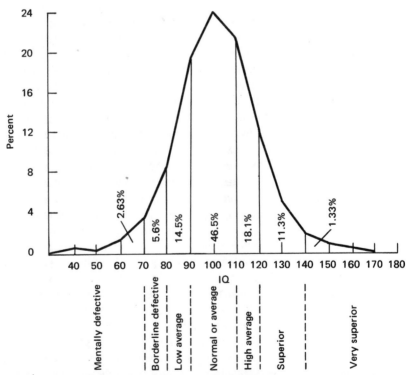

Source: *Adapted from Lewis M. Terman and Maud A. Merrill,* Stanford-Binet Intelligence Scale, Manual for the Third Revision, Form L-M *(Boston: Houghton Mifflin Company, 1960), p. 18.*

Figure 7.1   *Distribution of composite IQs: Form L-M*

children's special needs—terms like "educable mentally retarded," "border-line mental defective," "trainable mentally retarded"—often had the effect of pigeonholing children into hard and fast (and sometimes unalterable) categories. Masked potential and undiscovered strengths were ignored in instructional programs. Some children were thought to be retarded because of undetected problems such as hearing difficulties or language disorders. Early in their school lives, children were sometimes classified as "slow learners" when they were merely slow starters in terms of their developmental learning stages. And because these children often moved ahead more slowly, they were sometimes placed in special classes (or even institutionalized settings) where their instructional needs were bypassed in favor of more basic social needs. Also, because of their IQ scores, these children were often excluded from extra help like remedial reading instruction or other support services available to the so-called "more average" learners.

In this chapter, the rather rigid classification system that has. traditionally been used has been abandoned in favor of a more general view. Slow learners are considered to be those children with generalized cognitive limitations. These are children whose lower academic achievement is linked to limited learning capacity rather than to a specific learning problem. In other words, two children may be at the same level of achievement in reading. But while one (the child with a specific learning problem) may have the intellectual capacity to support adequate grade level achievement, the other (the slow learner) may be achieving up to the limit of his/her capacity, even though the achievement level may be below grade level. Rather than using fixed standards or sharp cutoff points in IQ scores to indicate different groups of below-average learners, the term "slow learner" is used generally and broadly to refer to children whose general mental ability or academic aptitude is limited. Compared with children of the same chronological age, the slow learner's academic performance will be poorer, and this performance is related to the child's general cognitive deficit.

Cognitive deficits, like other learning problems treated in earlier chapters, are viewed on a continuum that ranges from mild to severe. Obviously, the extent of the deficit will reflect the severity of the problem a child may have in learning to read. Children who are severely handicapped cognitively will not be found in regular classrooms, since the mental capacity of these children will limit them to competency in self-care skills and adjustment to an immediate (often sheltered) environment. However, the more flexible way of looking at learning problems on a range from mild to severe allows for the identification of children on the basis of the instructional accommodations and services they need as part of their reading instruction.

Trying to determine a person's native intellectual ability is tricky business. Intellectual ability is a difficult human characteristic to measure, and there are recognized dangers in using intelligence as the primary basis for indicating a child's learning problems. Intelligence is a relative term. Like spatial and temporal concepts and terms, it is difficult to define without some point of reference. How, for example, does one define "a small animal" or "a long time"? A dog might be considered a small animal in comparison to a horse, but one would hardly call a Great Dane "small." And what's a "long time"? An hour is a long time to read the page of a book, but hardly a long time to fly from New York to Los Angeles. Spatial and temporal terms are relative, not absolute. So it is with intelligence. Like size and time, intelligence is a matter of degree. Children are said to be bright or slow according to their ability to function in comparison to those around them.

Educators are on especially risky ground when they use intelligence test performance as the sole criterion for judging a child's learning ability or capacity. Intelligence is a global concept that is difficult to define, academically or operationally. A child's performance on an intelligence test will be influenced by past experience, environment, and physical and cultural milieu. Any group of slow learners may include many potentially normal learners whose level of production has been severely sapped by social and environmental problems. Intelligence tests, despite over half a century of revisions and refinements, are never really "culture fair." The comparatively high incidence of so-called "retardation" among minority groups and people of low socioeconomic status is testimony to this fact.

While many of the slow learner's learning problems may be traced to limited intellectual ability, factors identified in earlier chapters—such as auditory or visual deficits or language disorders—may compound, or be a contributing cause to, the slow learner's difficulties. As a group, slow learners can exhibit the same broad spectrum of learning abilities or disabilities as other children, and slow learners are not equally slow in all aspects of learning. They can demonstrate the same varieties in learning profiles as any other group of learners. Other human characteristics such as physical development, personality, and emotional adjustment may not deviate from the norm. The intellectual functioning of the slow learner does, however, hamper him/her in the process of learning to read.

THE RELATIONSHIP BETWEEN READING AND INTELLIGENCE

There is a simultaneous cause-effect relationship between intellectual ability and learning to read. That is, problems in cognitive processing that are symptomatic of limited mental ability will cause problems in learning to read. At the same time, children who have problems in learning to read are often characterized as "slow learners" because of their reading difficulty. Reading, however one defines it, is at least in part a cognitive operation. Basic mastery of sound-symbol relationships and sight words, for example, requires the mental functions of memory and association. The desired product of reading—i.e., comprehension—falls wholly into the cognitive domain.

Intelligence is related to reading ability. Though controversy and diversity in research exist on the degree of relationship between the two, there is a positive relationship between scores on intelligence tests and scores on reading tests. The correlations between scores on language-based intelligence tests and on reading tests are usually high; correlations between nonlanguage intelligence scores and reading test scores are lower, but nevertheless positive.

As children get older and progress through the grades, the correlations between IQ test scores and reading test scores become progressively higher. The upper-grade emphasis in reading instruction centers heavily on comprehension and critical aspects of reading, tasks that demand higher mental functioning. Low mental ability will affect a child's capacity to recall facts and ideas, to reason logically, to understand relationships, and to perform other operations that are typically part of reading comprehension in the upper grades. Correlations are lower in the early grades, however, indicating that intelligence as conventionally measured on IQ tests is less important than other factors in the process of beginning to learn to read.

That there is a positive relationship between intelligence and reading is not surprising. Reading is a language activity, so the same verbal abilities that influence intelligence test scores will affect children in their ability to read. Factors measured as indicators of intellectual ability—spatial relationships, dealing with symbolic and figural material, memory, symbolization, abstract reasoning, generalization, problem solving, organizing—are also prerequisite skills in learning to read.

Testing Intelligence

Part of the controversy surrounding the question of the relationship between intelligence and reading ability stems from the tests used to measure intelligence. Individually administered intelligence tests like the *Stanford-Binet Intelligence Scale* and the *Wechsler Intelligence Scale for Children (WISC)* contain separate subtests designed to measure different aspects of the child's language and cognitive abilities. Multidimensional intelligence measures can indicate a child's overall developmental pattern rather than a single intelligence score. Administering these tests requires formal training and special arrangements, so other tests are frequently used in school as a measure of a child's mental ability.

Popular among these tests is the *Peabody Picture Vocabulary Test*. While this test purports to furnish an IQ score, the score is based on the child's ability to respond verbally to pictures presented. This is a rather narrow view of intelligence. Verbal ability is an important element in intelligence, but it is not the sole element. In other words, the PPVT measures a child's receptive vocabulary, only one dimension of general mental maturity. Intelligence is a combination of many factors, of which verbal ability is only one (although an important one).

While such tests can provide valuable diagnostic information about the child's ability in many areas related to reading, there are dangers in using these tests as the sole measure of a child's intelligence.

Group intelligence tests, like the *California Test of Mental Maturity,* the *Otis Quick Scoring Intelligence Scales,* the *Kuhlman-Anderson Tests,* and the *Short Test of Educational Ability,* present another problem. Although they contain nonlanguage performance items, group verbal intelligence tests typically involve reading to such an extent that the intelligence score will depend largely upon a child's ability to read. Therefore, the relationship between intelligence (as measured on these tests) and reading is bound to be high.

The faults in these tests rest less with the tests themselves than with the interpretation and use of the results. Educators have a tendency to accept an IQ or mental-age[1] equivalent score as a firm indication of the child's mental capacity or learning potential, without critically examining how that test score was arrived at or what the test measured. Too often, a child's IQ or mental age is derived on the basis of a single dimension of his/her learning capacity. Below-normal intelligence can, to be sure, place a limit on reading achievement, but factors other than mental age influence a child's reading success, particularly in the beginning stages of learning to read. A low IQ score, although it may signal possible reading difficulty, does not assure reading failure. Conversely, a high intelligence test score does not guarantee reading success. Children with perceptual problems whose intelligence is well above average can experience problems in learning to read. One need only deal with articulate, successful adults who are functionally illiterate to realize that the relationship between intelligence and reading ability is not absolute.

In spite of all their limitations, intelligence test scores can serve a useful function in indicating instructional requirements for the special-needs child. If, for example, a child with a high IQ score is experiencing difficulty in learning to read, the need for further assessment is indicated. If, on the other hand, the child has a low IQ score, then special adjustments may need to be made in reading instruction.

TEACHING READING TO THE SLOW LEARNER

At the age of six or so, society in general (and parents and elementary school principals in particular) expect all children to leap into reading. Children are first admitted to school on the basis of their birth date and, with the exception of occasional repeaters, they are promoted from one grade level to the next as they get a year older. Yet among any group of six-, eight-, or ten-year-olds, one finds a variety of heights, weights, hair colors, interests, and other outward manifestations of the range of distinct human qualities making each child unique. The only constant human characteristic found among a group at any grade level is age. Individual differences are indeed a fact of life.

The grade-to-grade procedure followed in most schools promotes the notion that children should progress uniformly. Thus, there is at least an implicit expectation that all nine-year-olds should be reading at a fourth-grade level. However, the procedure ignores one very simple developmental principle—i.e., that children develop at different rates and slow learners develop more slowly. Thus, "the slow learning child does not reach a developmental status comparable to that of the average child in the fourth grade until he is approximately 11 to 14 years of age."[2]

The wide range of learning abilities found in any classroom reflects this irregular pattern of large-group cognitive development. In the very early grades, the range of measured learning ability may span four or more years. In the upper elementary grades, the range widens until it may approach eight years or more.

Children differ in three closely related aspects of learning: learning capacity, learning level, and learning rate.

Learning capacity

Learning capacity is conventionally measured on the basis of IQ test. In any "normal" classroom, one can expect to find 15 or 20 percent of the children below the national average in intelligence. The figure may be higher or lower, depending on the nature of the community, the grouping practices of the school, the economic level of the parents, or a host of other factors. But even within relatively heterogeneous classrooms, there will be a range of learning capacities among children.

Learning level

Learning level follows from learning capacity. After a given period of instruction (a lesson, a week, a month, or a year), children are expected to have attained a certain level of knowledge or competency. Given the same amount and type of instruction as other children, the slow learner will typically not have attained the same level as classmates. The level of learning, judged in terms of the amount of material mastered, is lower than that of his/her more average peers.

Learning rate

Learning rate is the third dimension. A major difference between the bright pupil and the so-called "dull" student is the time it takes each to learn. The bright student is one who catches on quickly. The slow learner (by definition) is one who learns more slowly. Time is the essential ingredient. Given two children of unequal ability with the same achievement test score at the beginning of a school year, it is very likely that their achievement test scores will not be the same at the end of the year.

Thus, in terms of learning capacity, level of achievement, and rate of learning, classrooms typically have bright, average, and slow learners. In most classrooms, instruction is geared to the average learners. Children at the extreme ends of the learning spectrum are too often expected to adjust to the curricular and instructional demands of their educational experience. Given the fact of individual differences in children, however, curriculum and instruction ought to be adjusted to meet the needs of the child. Capable teachers have been making many of these adjustments ever since there have been slow learners in the classroom.

Planning reading instruction for the slow-learning child involves deciding which approach or program to use for beginning reading, and selecting appropriate reading materials. It also includes designing teaching strategies that will help the slow learner master the decoding and meaning skills essential in learning to read.

Selecting an Approach and Materials

In selecting a basal reading program or in determining which approach to beginning reading to use with the slow learner, there is little hard evidence upon which to base a decision. Assuming auditory and visual perceptual skills are intact, neither the decoding nor the meaning-emphasis approach offers total inherent advantages for the slow-learning child. A review of research on instruction for moderately and severely handicapped learners led Kirk to the following conclusion:

> Research on reading methods has not shown the superiority of any one method over others. Some authors found success with the phonic method, some with the experience or other methods. [3]

Similarly, Cawley, Goodstein, and Burrow arrived at the same conclusion, namely, that "the selection of an approach to reading represents only the best thinking at the local level." [4] In short, no one reading approach or program has been found to work best for pupils of low ability any more than with average or above-average pupils.

Advantages can be cited for different aspects of particular programs for use with the slow learner. For example, the slow learner (like any beginning reader) needs a firm foundation in decoding skills. Highly structured code-emphasis programs—basals such as the *Merrill Linguistic Readers,* the Bloomfield-Barnhardt *Let's Read* program, the SRA *Basic Skills* Series, or the McGraw-Hill *Programmed Reading* materials—begin with a heavy emphasis on the most regular letter-sound relationships in our language. The systematic organization of these programs provides a structure for the slow-learning child in the acquisition of the basic decoding skills necessary in learning to read.

For the slow learner, reading comprehension is very often a problem. Typically, meaning-emphasis basal programs have an early stress and focus on pupils' abilities to draw inferences, make generalizations, form conclusions, see cause-effect relationships, evaluate material, and perform other operations characteristic of higher-level cognitive processing. While these are important reading/thinking skills, the slow learner often has trouble performing these operations within the context of the typical basal reader stories. For the slow learner, it's often a good idea to reduce the demands of the reading task by reducing the amount of material to be read. For example, it may be better to use only parts of stories (rather than entire selections), since the

Accounts of everyday experiences provide meaningful material for language experience stories. (Photo by John A. Malnati)

amount of material to be read may be a greater inhibitor of comprehension than the content of the story or the level of cognitive operations demanded.

The language experience approach may be especially appropriate in developing comprehension skills in slow learners. The slow learner will likely be better able to perform the mental operations involved in the comprehension process, because the reading material is generated from the child's own language, thinking, and experience.

Each publisher of basal reading materials will claim unique advantages for its own program over others in providing for the special learning needs of the slow-learning child. And when used well, each basal program does have advantages. But no program can ever hope to meet the needs of every child in any classroom. This is why an eclectic approach—one that combines features of different programs and applies them imaginatively to each problem reader's needs—will ultimately work best. Eclecticism does not involve choosing a little of this and a little of that in order to maintain variety. Rather, it involves intelligent choice and use of materials and techniques to develop basic reading skills according to the child's special learning characteristics and needs.

Whatever basal materials or programs are used with the slow learner, *level* and *pacing* become key words in the use of the materials. That is, the level of reading materials should be appropriate to the child's reading ability, and this material should be presented at a pace that will assure mastery.

Eventually, a reading program must bring the child to a position at which he can independently derive meaning from visual stimuli in word form. This objective is more comfortably attained if the instructional phase of the program takes place in juxtaposition with the developmental status of the child. When the status of the child and the components of instruction are aligned, learning is effective and teaching is effective. When there is significant discrepancy between the two, teaching and learning are reduced to exercises in mutual frustration.[5]

The more severe a child's mental handicap, the greater the adjustments that will be required. Adjusting to the level of reading ability for the mildly handicapped learner may involve using a book that is a year or more below the designated grade level of the class. The slow learner will not learn to read by being "dragged along" or forced to "keep up" with classmates. For the moderately handicapped child, the reading material selected may need to be several years below age or grade placement.

Pacing requires the presentation of material in a manner appropriate to the learning rate of the slow learner. In practical terms, this may mean doubling or tripling the number of presentations of a sight word and increasing the exposure time for each word, allowing five days instead of two to finish a basal selection, or presenting only one library skill at a time instead of three or four concurrently. Appropriate pacing involves extensive practice in mastering skills essential to decoding written language, and it also requires the firm establishment of basic language and concepts upon which reading comprehension is based. Appropriate pacing for all children requires mastery of each step in a sequence of learning before the next step is taken. For the slow learner, it requires moving more slowly, at a rate dependent upon the severity of the child's intellectual deficits.

Supplementary materials

Supplementary materials are important too. Basal reading programs are typically geared to meet the needs of the average pupil, and therefore usually provide only enough practice materials to insure mastery for the average learner. The slow learner, however, will need additional practice in learning to read; hence, many supplementary materials will be needed to meet his/her reading needs at the appropriate level. These supplementary materials should include a classroom collection of simply written trade books, supplementary phonics series to provide practice materials for basic decoding skills, reading kits with appropriate comprehension components, listening tapes and other audiovisual devices designed to add a measure of motivation while providing for essential reading skill practice, and collections of commercially produced and homemade games that can be used for reinforcement and practice. The selection of supplementary materials should be guided by the same criteria as the selection of basal materials—i.e., the materials should be suitable to the child's learning needs, learning rate, and learning level.

For severely handicapped children in the upper grades, supplementary materials should include those aimed at developing pupils' functional reading skills—newspaper ads, road signs, menus, manuals for home appliances, and the like. These practical materials, important for everyday living, can be the vehicles for developing a range of reading skills, since reading can be taught with anything involving printed language. Published programs with this type of reading matter—*Reading 1100–1500 (Steck-Vaughn) and Real-Life Reading Skills Program* (Scholastic), for example—are becoming available for use in classrooms.

Programmed-learning materials

Programmed-learning materials are also especially appropriate for use with the slow learner. In programmed-learning materials, the steps in the reading skills sequence are broken down into small steps (called frames). Each step is carefully arranged for presentation to the learner. Each frame is built upon the previous ones, so that each frame demands prerequisite mastery of those that have gone before. In using programmed-learning materials, an active response is demanded. The pupil must write an answer, press a button, or otherwise react to the material presented. Immediate feedback lets the child know whether answers are right or wrong. In addition to the sound learning principles upon which programmed learning is based, programmed materials—whether presented in book form, in a simple and inexpensive plastic box, or in a sophisticated piece of electronic equipment—allow the pupil to move at his/her own pace without the immediate attention of the teacher. Given the slow learner's need for additional practice and the teacher's responsibility to a whole class of children, programmed materials can be particularly valuable vehicles for independent practice.

High-interest, low-vocabulary materials

Of all the supplementary reading materials available for use with the slow learner, those that demand special attention are high-interest, low-vocabulary materials. The theory behind these materials is as simple as it is sound. Although slow learners may be a year or more behind expected age-grade level in their ability to read, many of them (particularly those near the average range of the learning abilities spectrum) are on a par with their peers in their physical, social, and emotional development. In many instances, slow learners' interests are the same as those of their brighter age-mates. High-interest, low-vocabulary materials, then, are designed to provide reading materials on topics appropriate to an older child's interests, yet they are written in language that the slow learner can read and understand. More and more of these materials are being developed and published annually. They are being presented in series of books with similar and related story content—*The Checkered Flag Series* (Field Educational Enterprises), for example, or *The Cowboy Sam Series* (Benefic Press); in books containing shorter selections on high-interest topics—*The Kaleidoscope Readers* or the *Cornerstone Readers* (Field Educational Enterprises); or in newspaper and magazine format—

Know Your World and *You and Your World* (Xerox Education Publications) or *Sprint* magazine (Scholastic). Often, these materials have specific skill-building exercises and short teachers' guides accompanying them. Some are also supplemented by audiovisual materials like tapes, records, slides, and filmstrips.

While high-interest, low-vocabulary materials have proven to be a boon in teaching the older slow-learning student, there is a practical problem in their use; i.e., most of the materials are written at a high-first-, second-, third-, or higher-grade reading level. Even though topics center about preadolescent, teenage, or adult interests, most of these materials require the ability to read at or above the second-grade level. Thus, at least a minimal competency in basic reading skills is needed.

Developing Basic Reading Skills

There are three underlying factors essential to reading instruction for the slow-learning child.

1. The instructional needs of the slow learner are not essentially different from those of any child in the classroom. That is, the slow learner needs to master the same basic skills as anyone else in the process of learning to read. Instruction does not differ substantially from that provided for children of average or above-average ability. Helping the slow learner develop reading skills, however, requires adjustment of instruction to the child's learning capacity, learning level, and learning rate. The difference is more in kind than in nature.

2. The slow learner is classified as such primarily on the basis of intelligence. Though intelligence is indeed an important factor in learning to read, it's important to remember that, as a group, slow learners exhibit the same range of variation in learning style and learning characteristics as is exhibited by the total population in any school. Some slow learners will demonstrate visual strengths and auditory deficits; for others, the reverse perceptual strengths and weaknesses will be evident. Some slow learners will show a reflective learning style, while others will be more impulsive. The nature of the material and the type of instruction provided for the slow learner should be in line with these perceptual and learning characteristics. In other words, factors besides intelligence must be taken into account.

3. When appropriate instruction is provided, slow learners—even moderately and severely handicapped children—*can* learn to read. In his research review, Kirk found that

> Mentally retarded children do not read up to their mental-age–reading-grade expectancy, probably because teachers emphasize their social adjustment rather than their academic achievement, and also because the child who is most retarded educationally is referred to the special

class . . .. [However] Brain-injured mentally retarded children with perceptual disturbances are able to learn to read as well as non-brain-injured retarded children when emphasis is placed on reading and special methods used.[6]

In sum, when reading is emphasized and appropriate methods are used, handicapped learners *can* learn to read. Low intelligence may place a limit on the level of reading proficiency that a handicapped learner will eventually achieve. However, the ultimate prognosis for moderately handicapped learners may be as high as the upper-elementary-grade reading level, a level high enough to allow the reader to handle most sections of a daily newspaper and read simply written informational and recreational books. Reading instruction for the slow learner—even those children near the lower end of the ability spectrum—is far from futile.

Reading Readiness

Learning to read begins at the readiness stage. But all children don't enter kindergarten with the same mental capacity or language ability or experiential background. Slow learners don't have the same readiness skills as other children their own age. Nor will they respond as quickly or as easily to the readiness training exercises provided during the first years of school.

For a long time in education, mental age was thought to be the major criterion of reading readiness. A widely circulated (and misinterpreted) research study by Morphett and Washburne[7] in 1931 promoted the fallacy that a mental age of 6.6 was necessary for successful beginning reading. Although this conclusion was soon disproved by other reputable researchers, mental age continued to be widely accepted as the single predictor of reading readiness. The unfortunate result of this thinking was that, for decades, slow learners were forced to play a waiting game in beginning to learn to read.

More recently, educators have come to realize that the children who most need intense, specific readiness training are the slow learners. In fact, for the slow learner, structured programs are more effective than informal activities. Slow learners profit from formal training in auditory perceptual skills, visual perceptual skills, language development, spatial orientation, learning letter names and sounds, and other factors that prepare a child for formal reading instruction. If anything, readiness training for the slow learner should be more intense, and the readiness training period may need to be prolonged until a firm foundation of readiness skills has been established. The degree of severity of the child's learning problem will often determine the degree of intensity and the length of the readiness period.

Language development

The first and perhaps most important component of readiness training for the slow learner is language development. The slow learner's receptive and expressive language ability will typically be limited, so developing the power to use language is most often the starting point in readiness training. The readiness period for all children should be saturated with language experiences. For the slow learner, these experiences need to be more basic, more extensive, and extended over a longer period of time. Since language and thought are so intimately related, language deficits are likely a root cause of the child's poor performance on an intelligence test in the first place. Besides, since reading is a language activity, competency in language is a key to reading success.

Listening

Listening is necessarily part and parcel of the sharing, poetry, story time, dramatics, and all the other oral language activities that are a normal part of the child's early school experience. The child who does not have the prerequisite oral receptive language skills is bound to have comprehension problems in dealing with print. The more severe the oral receptive language deficits, the more severe the reading problems will probably be. In listening activities during the readiness period, the focus is not only on listening attentively, but also on the understanding and thinking components that comprise the reading comprehension process: i.e., listening for recall of factual information, for main ideas and details, for sequence of events, for cause-effect relationships, etc. These are exercises in language *and* thinking, since the slow learner typically needs help in both areas.

Expressive language

Expressive language is an equally vital part of readiness training for the slow learner. In oral language activities, the focus is on helping the child expand his/her speaking vocabulary and improving his/her ability to manipulate verbal concepts in narrative and descriptive language.

Visual perceptual training

Visual perceptual training is another necessary part of reading readiness. For the slow learner, this will include puzzles and exercises designed to provide practice in recognizing, identifying, and classifying basic shapes and forms (circle, square, triangle, etc.); and in categorizing simple objects (crayons, glasses, toy telephones, etc.) according to their size, color, function, and other observable characteristics. Such training will also include the development of an awareness of spatial relationships (bigger, smaller, longer, shorter, etc.) and of other basic perceptual-cognitive relationships that are typically part of visual training. Literally thousands of activities designed to help children develop visual perceptual skills can be found in published readiness programs, in resource books for teachers, and in the minds of imaginative teachers.

Auditory perceptual training

Auditory perceptual training is another essential component of reading readiness. Activities that involve the identification of similarities and differences in sounds (a bell vs. a car horn, for example), reproducing similar

sound patterns (from clapping or a buzzer board), repeating words in se-
ence, following simple oral directions, supplying rhyming words in couplets,
and discriminating between sounds in spoken words are important to auditory
readiness training. Once again a variety of these activities is typically found in
published readiness programs and teacher resource books.

Integration

Since reading is an intersensory task involving both ears and eyes, the
integration of auditory and visual stimuli is also an important readiness skill.
Slow learners might process input adequately through one modality but have
trouble when asked to cross modalities. Integration can be promoted by activities like "writing" dots and dashes as visual representations of sound patterns made on a buzzer board (for example, ——•—— or ——•——••),
going from the auditory to the visual stimulus; or making sound patterns (on
a buzzer board or by clapping) based on a visual pattern, going from the visual
to the auditory stimulus. Integration is also involved in activities like visually
identifying sound-producing mechanisms (for example, locating the picture of
a hammer or a saw as the sounds made by these objects are played on a tape
recorder), or holding up letter cards when hearing a consonant sound (either in
isolation or at the beginning of a word). Such activities are designed to help
children use their auditory and visual mechanisms in close conjunction, since
the integration of auditory and visual processing is necessarily part of learning
to read.

Visual and auditory readiness activities for the slow learner are not
dramatically different from those used with average or above-average children. These readiness activities are designed to develop sensory-perceptual
processes that any person needs in learning to read, but the activities must be
adjusted to the needs of the slow-learning child. For example, in arranging
objects in sequence or reproducing sound patterns, it may be necessary to start
with fewer and/or simpler stimuli to assure that the slow learner will master
the skills that the activities are designed to develop. Also, depending on individual children's perceptual strengths and deficits, accommodation and remediation suggested in earlier chapters may need to take place in one area
more than in another.

Directionality

Spatial orientation and directionality are a necessary part of helping
children learn to deal with the left-to-right direction of our written language
code. For any child, this requires learning left from right and developing the
habit of looking at objects, pictures, and words in a left-to-right sequence. For
the slow learner, training in directionality is an integral part of visual perceptual activities and a dimension of the experiences and exercises designed to
develop gross and fine motor control.

*Letter names and
sounds*

Letters of the alphabet are the basic symbols in our written language
code, and dealing with the alphabet is an immediate and specific part of readiness training. Alphabet work at this level includes the identification of letters,
their names, and the sounds they represent.

Matching letter shapes and sounds also requires integrative processing that is essential in reading. Practice with letters and sounds can be woven into appropriate visual, auditory, and motor readiness activities such as matching upper- and lower-case letters, recognizing beginning sounds in words, and learning to copy letter forms. Alphabet training for the slow learner is carried out with essentially the same kind of exercises and activities as are used with any beginning reader. The training does not differ in content, but rather in level and pacing. Depending on the severity of the child's handicap, learning to recognize letters, their names, and the sounds they represent may need to be delayed until relatively late in the child's school experience, after other more basic language and perceptual skills have been established.

When letter symbols are introduced, it's important for the slow-learning child to understand that words are made up of a combination of separate sounds, and that letters represent these sounds. This is an understanding that most children arrive at almost intuitively, but it may need to be taught directly to the slow learner.

Word Recognition

Helping children learn to recognize printed words on sight is usually the first step in reading instruction for the slow learner. The selection of words to be learned by sight can be drawn from a number of sources—label words for objects in the classroom (*door, window, chair, desk, clock, light, floor, wall, book,* etc.), words associated with the regular activities that are part of the daily classroom routine (*run, jump, sit,* etc.), number words, color words, words for parts of the body, direction words (*stop, go,* etc.), words that occur frequently in dictated stories and other classroom language experiences, lists of words frequently used in beginning reading materials (like the Dolch list and picture word cards), and words taught in the beginning basal program being used; all provide a more than adequate pool of words on which to draw. For the slow learner, a file folder of "personal" words—like *swim, love, policeman, swing, truck,* or any other words particularly important to the child in his/her out-of-school life—can be kept as a source for word recognition. These words, appropriately illustrated by the child, can be the beginning of a simple picture dictionary. Meaning and motivation are built-in factors as the child learns to recognize these personal words in written form.

For frequently occurring function words like *the, on, was,* etc., constant drill and repetition are necessary. These words should be presented in context and used repeatedly in phrase practice for oral reading, in language experience stories, in sentence-building activities, and in other classroom reading experiences. They can be added to the child's personal "word bank" for review.

"Knowing a word" involves not only recognizing it by sight, but also knowing the meaning of the word in the context in which it is used. To insure word meaning, it's important that words in print first be a meaningful part of the child's speaking vocabulary. It does little good, for example, for the child to recognize the word *pond* if s/he doesn't know what a pond is or has never seen one in real life or in a picture.

The slow learner will need many concrete experiences in learning to attach meaning to words. The more experiences a child has had with an object or activity that a word represents, the greater will be the child's chances of really knowing the word. Here is where it becomes so important to surround all children's experiences with language, to help children attach linguistic labels to objects and activities in their environment, and to make vocabulary development an ongoing part of each school activity. For all children, and particularly for the slow learner, vocabulary development is an essential ingredient that begins early and continues throughout the entire process of learning to read, as well as throughout life.

When word meaning has been established, the next step is helping the slow learner build a core sight vocabulary, a nucleus of familiar words that the child can use in initial reading experiences. In helping the child recognize words by sight, it may be necessary for the teacher to use multiple channels of input—auditory, visual, tactual, and kinesthetic—to aid mastery.

For example, in presenting the word *tree* as a sight word, the teacher may need to call attention to the visual shape or form of the word and to the phonetic elements represented by the letters of the word. The child may trace or copy the word, noting both the visual and the auditory elements. By using a multisensory approach to word recognition, slow learners can take advantage of all the perceptual strengths they have in learning to instantly recognize words in print.

The ultimate decision on the presentation of sight words should depend on the learning strengths and weaknesses of the individual child. For the slow learner, one modality may be dominant over another, and the dominant modality should be used (with remediation in the weaker area). Sometimes, more than one avenue of input may confuse rather than help the child by overloading the sensory-perceptual channels. The decision on whether to use a multisensory approach or to rely primarily on one avenue of input should be based on how the child seems to learn words best. This decision will necessarily be part of the ongoing diagnostic process in teaching reading. Also, the nature of the word itself may influence the decision of which modality of presentation to use. Emphasizing the phonetic elements in a word like *laughed,* for example, would be counterproductive.

For the slow learner, repeated exposure is usually needed before the child instantly responds to words in print as sight words. The teacher needs to devise a variety of ways to provide for drill without tedium (to him/herself or to the child). Independent and pupil-team practice in reviewing sight words can be provided through games, devices like the Language Master, picture dictionaries, and other tools that will afford repeated exposure for mastery.

Word Analysis

Mastery of word analysis skills—phonetic and structural analysis—is as essential for the slow learner as for anyone who learns to read. The slow learner needs direct and systematic help to catch onto the sound-symbol system of our language.

Phonics

Phonics instruction for the slow learner begins with practice in auditory discrimination and memory, work with letter names and sounds, and other basic activities designed to establish the child's awareness of sound-symbol

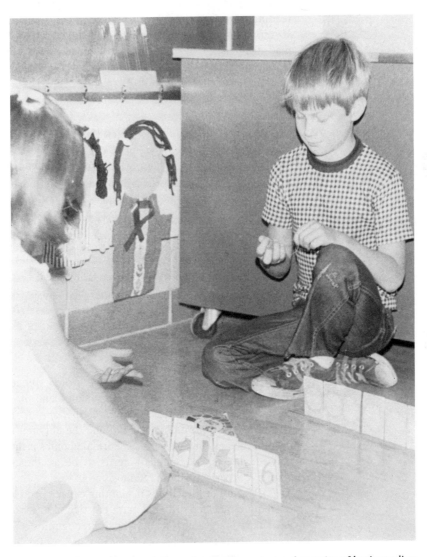

Games provide a motivational dimension for the review and practice of basic reading skills. (Photo by John A. Malnati)

relationships during the early stages of learning to read. It includes work with consonant sounds: single consonants (in initial, medial, and final positions in words), consonant blends or clusters, consonant digraphs, and "silent" consonant letters; vowel sounds: short, long, and r-controlled vowels, vowel digraphs, and vowel diphthongs; and syllabication. These are the elements found in any phonics program. For the slow learner, the presentation of these elements needs to be paced to meet the child's rate of mastery.

Phonics instruction, of course, should not be limited to the content of formally published basal or supplementary programs. It can be part of many reading experiences in the classroom. For example, having read the story *Morris the Moose* to a group of slow learners who were beginning to learn to read, the teacher asked the group to dictate a story based on the one they had just heard. Here's the story that the group composed and the teacher wrote on an experience chart:

Mack the Moose

There was a moose named Mack.
Mack was a happy moose until one day a
spider came along. Mack didn't like spid-
ers so he said to the spider, "Go away."

The spider didn't go away so Mack
spit at the spider. The spider said,
"Thanks, I needed that."

Then the spider went away.

The End.

From this story, the teacher used the words *spit* and *spider* to develop a phonics lesson on the beginning consonant blend *sp*, and the group generated the following list of words: *spin, spot, spy, speed, spank, splash,* and *spell*. Using the story words *spit* and *did* and the children's word *spin,* the teacher developed a lesson on "short i." Formal phonics instruction—the relationship between letters and sounds—needs to be an integral part of all the slow learner's experiences with reading.

Because of limitations in learning capacity and learning rate, slow learners require repeated drill and extra practice in mastering phonics, just as they need extra practice in the area of word recognition. Commercially prepared or teacher-made taped phonics exercises are useful in providing independent practice. Materials such as phonics "word wheels" and "flip charts" of phonograms will provide appropriate manipulative practice materials as well.

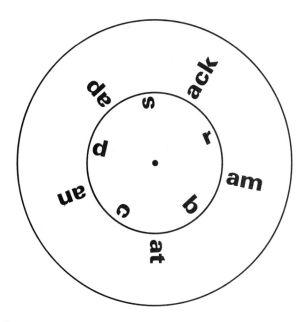

Figure 7.2a   Word wheel.

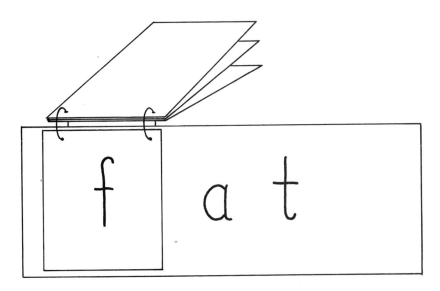

Figure 7.2b   Flip chart.

On the question of "analytic vs. synthetic" approaches to phonics, there are few definitive answers. While a synthetic approach is as effective for the slow learner as it is for other children, slow learners typically take longer to benefit from this type of program.[8]

Phonics instruction for the slow learner—as for any child—is not an end in itself. Rather, phonics is a means of helping children decode unknown words they encounter in print. That's why phonics instruction should be tied directly to reading practice whenever possible.

In more and more programs, nonsense words are being used to develop and/or test children's ability in phonetic analysis. While practice with non-sense words is designed to give a truer or "purer" picture of the child's ability to sound out unknown words, there is a danger in using them with slow learn-ers. The danger is that the child will often attempt to sound out the sequence of sounds in such a way that a meaningful word will result. For example, the slow learner has a tendency to read a nonsense word like *leck* as "lick" or "luck," because even if s/he can decode it correctly, s/he often wants to pro-duce a word that "sounds right." In other words, s/he may be slow to catch onto the idea of using nonsense words as a measure of ability in phonetic analysis. Thus, the use of nonsense words can give a more distorted than true picture of the child's ability to decode unknown words.

Because of a limited learning capacity and learning rate, steps in phonics instruction for the slow learner should be carefully sequenced to in-sure mastery at the beginning stages. Mastery of beginning basic decoding skills will assure a measure of reading (and general school) success later on. Even in the upper grades, reading instruction for the slow learner needs to include a lot of work on basic phonics elements. To master these elements, the slow learner will need much practice and reinforcement, and thus it becomes vitally important for the teacher to have available a wide variety of games, worksheets, and other practice materials for the child to use in mastering the skills essential to phonetic analysis.

Structural analysis

Mastery of the basic structural elements in words—roots, prefixes, and suffixes—is another essential skill in helping children decode words. The be-ginnings of instruction in this area, as in other basic reading skill areas, should be rooted in words that are part of the child's aural/oral vocabulary. When they can recognize component words by sight or by decoding, children should be able to identify the independent word parts or free morphemes in common compound words like *cowboy, fireman,* and *snowball.* Inflectional suffixes— like the plural marker *-s* in nouns and the common *-s*, *-ed,* and *-ing* endings in verbs—can be an early focus of instruction. Words that children know and use, like:

*un*tie	beauti*ful*
*un*cover	power*ful*
*un*happy	care*ful*

can provide a beginning base for learning the function and meaning of common prefixes and suffixes. Further practice can be provided with those elements the slow learner meets in reading materials, as well as in vocabulary development exercises that include words with prefixes and suffixes.

Once again, the slow-learning child will need a great deal of direct help and practice in mastering the inventory of structural word elements in our language. A lot of practice and reinforcement in making structural analysis a functional reading skill will also be essential.

In mastering word skills, the slow learner needs thorough and systematic practice. While independence may be an ultimate goal, close monitoring of skill development and practice is necessary. Directions for independent practice should be clearly understood. If the child interprets the object pictured here ⛅ as "light" or "hills," s/he would be hard pressed to write the intital letter of the word *sun*. A limited number of skills should be presented at a time and the child should work for mastery.

The ultimate payoff in word analysis instruction for the slow learner (as it is for any child) is in the application of these skills in functional reading. It does little good if the child can complete worksheet after worksheet with phonics and structural analysis exercises and then fails to apply these skills when s/he encounters an unknown word in reading. Mastery of word analysis skills is not an end in itself; it is a means to achieve broader goals in reading.

Context Clues

Context clues are important to the slow learner since such clues provide help in both the decoding and comprehension aspects of the reading act. Using context clues in reading requires the use of surrounding words in a written passage to determine the pronunciation and meaning of unknown words. For poor readers, using context clues is a problem because they often stop at the unknown word and don't "read around" or beyond the word to see if they can determine its meaning. The child must be taught to look for clues in written language—definitions of the unknown word, synonyms, comparisons, etc.—that may be provided in the material to help him/her secure the meaning of unknown words. Picture clues can often help the child get meaning from printed language too, although the usefulness of picture clues in reading has recently been questioned by some researchers.

Cloze exercises   In developing the slow learner's ability to use context in reading, cloze exercises are often helpful. The cloze technique involves systematically deleting certain words (usually every fifth word) from a passage and having a child supply the missing word. A simple example of a cloze passage might look like this:

Bill and Pam got __(1)__ the bus. They rode __(2)__ the city and saw __(3)__ things. They saw cars __(4)__ trucks on busy streets. __(5)__ bus stopped at a __(6)__ building and the children __(7)__ out. When they got __(8)__ on the bus, it __(9)__ to the zoo. After __(10)__ ride, Bill and Pam __(11)__ their mother about their __(12)__.

Answers: (1) on, (2) around, (3) many, (4) and, (5) The, (6) big, (7) got, (8) back, (9) drove, (10) the, (11) told, (12) trip.

Cloze passages zero in on context clues, because the context of the entire passage, including semantic and syntactic elements, is necessary to complete the exercise. Very often, more than one word will be appropriate for supplying the missing element—for example, *around*, *through*, *in*, or several other prepositional word choices would be appropriate for #2 in the passage above—and here's where phonics needs to be used as an important "backup" skill. Slow learners will probably need a lot of initial help and instruction on how to use cloze. Practice with multiple choice responses (using first two and then three or four items of choice), or the deletion of easy nouns first (followed by other selected deletions), might help the child catch onto the idea of using cloze techniques.

In addition to using cloze procedures in developing the child's ability to use context clues in reading, the technique has been employed as a measure of comprehension ability and in determining the readability levels of printed materials. Although cloze techniques may be difficult to use until basic reading skills have become well established, the technique has been used successfully with mentally retarded children and young disabled readers.

Comprehension

For the slow learner, comprehension is usually a major area of difficulty in learning to read. Comprehension is a cognitive activity, so it stands to reason that the child whose learning problem is primarily cognitively based will have trouble when this area is applied to reading. When one looks at reading comprehension as a complex process involving thinking, language, and experience, one discovers multiple areas that might be the root of the comprehension problem for the slow learner.

Thinking

Thinking is the first demand of reading comprehension. In fact, comprehension can be defined as a thinking process. "If a reader can translate print into speech—read it aloud as sentences with normal intonation patterns—and still fails to grasp the idea or relate facts or infer or draw conclusions, then he has no *reading* problem; he has a *thinking* problem. . . . (The reading teacher) is made responsible for general mental activities like recalling, inferring, and concluding that belong no more to reading than to any other intellectual activity."[9]

Intelligence involves both a quantitative and a qualitative dimension. An IQ test yields a quantitative score, i.e., we say the child has an IQ of 80 or a mental age of 6.2. But this score tells us little about the qualitative dimensions of the child's thinking; i.e., is the child with an IQ of 140 able to think twice as well as the child with an IQ of 70? The qualitative dimension of thinking—which is the essence of comprehension—involves the child's ability to make associations, see relationships, transfer learning, make inferences, and perform the other thinking operations that are conventionally considered part of the comprehension process.

Several theoretical schemata have been developed in an attempt to describe this qualitative dimension through a hierarchy of cognitive operations. Among these theoretical schemata are:

Bloom (10)	*Sanders* (11)	*Guilford* (12)	*Barrett* (13)
Evaluation	Evaluation	Evaluation	Appreciation
Synthesis	Synthesis	Divergent Production	Evaluation
Analysis	Analysis		Inference
Application	Application	Convergent Production	Literal Recognition or Recall
Comprehension	Interpretation		
Knowledge	Translation	Memory	
	Memory	Cognition	

These taxonomies differ in purpose. Bloom's is a classification scheme for determining overall educational objectives. Sanders's was produced as a criterion for formulating and judging questions. Guilford's model was an attempt to account for our intellectual structure. And Barrett's taxonomy was designed to describe the reading comprehension component in a published basal reading program. Each schema also differs in detail, with different labels attached to different levels of thinking. These differences notwithstanding, the models allow the teacher to begin to examine some of the qualitative dimensions that may affect a child's ability to comprehend what s/he reads. These schemata may also provide a point of reference in trying to pinpoint the comprehension problem of the slow-learning child.

At the lowest level of cognitive functioning is recall or *memory*. Reading comprehension requires both the recognition and retention of information presented in print. Even when they can decode and understand a story in print, slow learners may have "comprehension problems" after reading a story because of deficits in short- and long-term memory. Thus, having read a story about a birthday party, the slow learner may not be able to remember that the children had fun at the party, or what the children in the story did at the party,

the small society   **by Brickman**

© *Washington Star Syndicate. Permission granted by King Features Syndicate Inc.,*
1976.

or the sequence of events from the story, because memory is weak. Similarly,
the child may not respond to the typical opening question, "Do you remember
what happened in the part of the story that we read yesterday?" because s/he
has memory problems.

Memory is a relatively low-level mental skill in the cognitive hierarchy,
and it responds to training and practice. For the slow learner, training will
involve practice in auditory memory through appropriate listening comprehension exercises, presenting only small segments to be read at a time, setting specific purposes *before* reading as an aid in giving children something to
look for while they read, triggering children's recall by providing appropriate
clues, and using oral reading for auditory reinforcement of story content. The
slow learner needs much work at the level of literal recognition and recall before comprehension at higher levels is tackled.

Inference. The higher-level cognitive processes of interpretation,
translation, application, and reasoning are also required in reading comprehension. Inferential comprehension at this level requires that the child read
"between the lines" to determine facts or ideas that the author does not directly state. The basic distinction between literal and interpretative levels of
comprehension can be simply illustrated in the two passages following:

Passage 1   *Passage 2*

Bill was angry. He threw his bat to   Bill threw his bat to the ground and
the ground and yelled at the other   yelled at the other children. Then he
children. Then he picked up his bat   picked up his bat and went home.
and went home.

How did Bill feel?   How did Bill feel?

The two passages present essentially the same information. But in the
first one, the author directly states how Bill felt as the first sentence of the

passage. In the second passage, the reader is left to draw his/her own conclusions on Bill's emotional state.

Because they often function at a concrete and immediate level of operations (not necessarily in Piagetian terms), slow learners frequently have trouble with inferential comprehension tasks that demand abstract reasoning, association, seeing relationships between objects and events, and other factors required to function at the inferential level. The degree of the child's cognitive handicap will govern the degree of difficulty s/he may have in performing these mental operations. The demands of comprehension tasks at the inferential level need to be adjusted to the child's ability to think in inferential ways.

At this level, the teacher needs to work incessantly with thinking processes in the realm of children's oral language in order to develop inferential listening comprehension before (and along with) reading comprehension. If the child cannot see cause-effect relationships or infer main ideas or determine unstated character traits from spoken language, then s/he will hardly be able to perform these operations in dealing with print. Children need to be able to see relationships, to reason logically, and to infer ideas in the concrete world around them before these operations are practiced in reading. In developing comprehension at this level, the teacher must give the slow learner much help through structured questions and verbal clues as aids in inferring ideas and information not directly provided by the author. This often involves building concepts upon which inferences can be drawn. Pictorial material—pictures from which children are asked to infer actions or conditions, or pictures in which children are asked to find errors and absurdities, or comic strips that can be used for main ideas or sequencing—can be useful in helping the slow learner develop inferential thinking skills from visual stimuli.

Critical–creative reading

At the highest level of reading comprehension—the level often classified as critical or creative reading—the child must engage in critical thinking, evaluation, elaborative or divergent thinking, and other operations requiring the use of the higher mental processes. Because of limited intellectual capacity, the slow learner may have particular difficulty operating at this level. Once again, a sound thinking base in oral language must be established. Children need help in evaluating what they hear as fact or fiction, in applying what they hear to their needs and experiences, in predicting outcomes and making up new endings to stories, in raising questions, in drawing conclusions, in making judgments and otherwise reacting to oral language before they perform these mental operations in connection with printed language in reading. In developing critical thinking—which is the essence of reading comprehension at this level—the teacher can draw on children's extensive experiences with television. Questions like

- Could this have really happened?
- Why do you think the character acted in this way?

- How do you think the character will solve his problem?
- Have you ever had an experience like this?
- Why do you think the ending is the happiest part of the story?

apply just as much to television programs that children have seen or stories they have heard as to typical basal reading material. These are exercises in thinking that children must have before they apply these thinking skills in reading. Direct and structured questioning geared to the slow learner's personal experiences are a necessary part of teaching comprehension at this level.

In sum, the factors that cause a child to score low on an intelligence test are the same factors that are demanded in reading comprehension. Helping the slow learner develop and improve these thinking skills is vital to the process of "teaching" comprehension.

Language

Language is another important factor in reading comprehension. Children won't understand what they read if they don't understand the meaning of the words used and the way these words relate to each other in larger sentence structures. Cindy is a good example of how language background may affect reading comprehension. Cindy was a second grader who had a "reading comprehension problem." When she read the sentence:

Can you cup a bud with your hands?   Yes   No

Cindy could not answer the question *yes* or *no* because she didn't understand what she had read. When asked the meaning of the word *cup,* Cindy replied, "It's something my mother drinks coffee from." When asked if she knew what a *bud* was, she responded, "Sure. It's a beer." (Budweiser) In Cindy's mind, then, what she was reading was:

Can you something my mother drinks coffee from a beer with your hands?

It's no wonder she couldn't comprehend the meaning of the sentence! When the meanings of the words *cup* and *bud* were explained in the context of the sentence, Cindy had no trouble understanding it. Cindy's reading comprehension problem in this case was rooted in oral language, in her inability to understand the meanings of the words that she translated from print to speech.

Understanding the syntactic relationships of words in sentences is no less important than understanding the word meanings. In the sentences *John ate the fish* and *The fish ate John,* the words are the same but the relationship of these words to one another makes the meaning of the sentences very different (especially for John!).

For slow learners, practice in identifying the *who, what, when, where* components of sentences is important to developing comprehension ability.

Rearranging scrambled words to construct grammatical sentences, working with materials like *Silly Syntax* (Houghton Mifflin), and engaging in other sentence-building activities are also appropriate. Often, sight words can be used as the "building blocks" for sentences in these activities, since the activity provides for review and reinforcement of basic vocabulary. Matching pairs of sentences with similar meanings (as in *Tom hit the ball* and *The ball was hit by Tom,* or *The ice cream tasted good* and *How good the ice cream tasted*) is another way of helping slow learners recover meaning from sentences, which is the essence of reading comprehension.

Making sure the child knows the meaning of every word (including figures of speech, which cause particular problems for the slow learner), and the relationship of each word in the syntax of the sentence, is essential to insure comprehension in reading.

Experience

The child's experience is the third vital dimension of reading comprehension. The more one brings to the printed page, the more one can expect to take away from it in understanding. For example, a child who has been to the circus—one who has seen the live performers and smelled the circus smells and tasted the cotton candy and heard the circus music and felt the anticipation and excitement that the circus generates—will be better able to comprehend a primary-grade story on the circus. Similarly, when a child's background has been filled with imaginative stories and fables and fairy tales, s/he will be more able to comprehend this type of story material in reading. Lack of experience may be one contributing factor to the child's being classified as a "slow learner" in the first place. This is why it is so important to fill the child's background with a rich variety of direct and vicarious experiences as remote and proximate preparation for reading.

Providing direct experiences for everything the child will read about is, of course, impossible. Before reading a story like *The Elves and the Shoemaker,* for example, the teacher will have to rely on discussion to assure that children understand what elves are, what a shoemaker does (or did in earlier times), what the shoemaker and his wife were like, etc. For the slow-learning child, a solid conceptual background is needed *before* reading. Such discussion will also necessarily include providing a background and understanding in the language the child will need in order to comprehend the story.

Decoding difficulties

For the slow learner, comprehension problems may also be rooted in decoding difficulties. The child may have so much trouble and have to work so hard at decoding the printed language that the broader meaning of what s/he reads is lost. Because decoding precedes comprehension, material for slow learners must be within the range of reading ability level before comprehension can be expected.

If the child can decode what s/he reads—that is, read the words in sentences with normal intonation patterns—and still has trouble with comprehension, then the teacher should begin to look at the three closely related component areas of comprehension

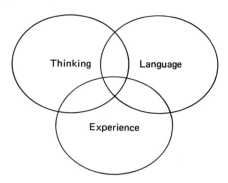

in order to build the slow learner's ability to understand what s/he reads.

Adjustment

In teaching reading to the slow-learning child, there are no magical, mystical answers, just as there are no panaceas guaranteed to insure instant success for teaching reading to any child. If there is a magic word in reading instruction for the slow learner, that word is *adjustment*. The curriculum and instructional program must be adjusted to meet the needs of the slow-learning child. Reading grade level expectations must be set in terms of the child's learning capacity, not in terms of his/her chronological age or actual grade placement. Reading instruction must be paced according to the child's learning rate, a rate that will be typically slower than that of the more average pupils in any classroom. Materials will have to be selected in accordance with the child's learning level, a level at which the slow learner can meet some measure of success.

Making these adjustments early in the child's school life is important. Adjustments made to provide success for the slow learner at the very beginning stages of learning to read will provide a solid foundation in basic reading skills, and will supply early positive learning experiences in reading. But because of the slow learner's typically decelerated rate of development, adjustments need to be made in the upper grades as well. In the middle grades, when average or above-average children are depending more and more on reading and writing for the reception and expression of ideas and information, the slow learner may still have to depend on speaking and listening experiences. Allowing the slow learner to rely more heavily on oral language is not only an appropriate and humanistic accommodation, it is a means of helping the child build the "support system" that s/he will need in learning to deal with language in print.

READING EXPECTANCY

In general, bright pupils can be expected to achieve higher levels in reading than slower learners. But in teaching reading to the slow-learning child, an important question for the classroom teacher is, "Is the pupil reading as well as s/he should?" or "How much success can the child be expected to achieve in reading?" Reading expectancy measures are an attempt to provide an estimate of a child's reading potential.

> Reading expectancy is a predictive term used to express the approximate level on which a pupil should be reading or which he should be able to attain at some designated future time'.[14]

One way of determining a child's reading potential is suggested in Informal Reading Inventories (described in Chapter 3). A series of standardized tests—*The Durrell Listening-Reading Series* (Psychological Corporation)—is also available to provide a specific measure of the difference between actual and potential level of reading achievement. These devices rely solely on the child's ability to understand spoken language to arrive at a potential or expected level of reading achievement.

In an effort to estimate the reading level a child may be expected to reach at a given point in his/her school life, a number of formulae have also been devised to compute reading expectancy. One commonly used is the Bond and Tinker Expectancy Formula:

$$ERG = (\text{Years in School} \times IQ) + 1.\text{[15]}$$

That is, the child's expected reading grade equals the number of years in school (including grades repeated, but not including kindergarten or preschool experiences) times the child's IQ (reported as a decimal), plus 1. The "plus 1" is added because the day the child starts first grade, his/her expected grade score is 1.0, even though s/he has never had a day of instruction. Similarly, the child who is halfway through the second grade has still only had one and a half years of instruction.

Because the use of an IQ score as the primary or sole measure of a child's reading potential is highly questionable, other formulae have been devised, using factors different from (or in addition to) mental age to compute the estimated reading expectancy levels of children.[16] The Harris Expectancy Age Formula uses a combination of mental age and chronological age as the basis for estimating reading expectancy, and the expectancy figure is reported in terms of reading age equivalent (as opposed to Bond and Tinker's reading grade equivalent). The Torgerson and Adams formula also uses mental age

Table 7.1 A Comparison of Reading Expectancy Measures

Igor, Lulu, and Ivan are second graders who have completed half the school year. All are the same chronological age but their other "vital statistics" differ. Igor is a bright student; Lulu, an average pupil; and Ivan is a slow learner.

	Igor	*Lulu*	*Ivan*
	Chronological Age = 7.5 IQ Score = 120 Mental Age = 9.0 Standardized Reading Grade Score Equivalent = 3.0 Standardized Math Grade Score Equivalent = 3.0	Chronological Age = 7.5 IQ Score = 100 Mental Age = 7.5 Standardized Reading Grade Score Equivalent = 2.0 Standardized Math Grade Score Equivalent = 2.0	Chronological Age = 7.5 IQ Score = 80 Mental Age = 6.0 Standardized Reading Grade Score Equivalent = 1.0 Standardized Math Grade Score Equivalent = 1.0
Formula Used for Determining Reading Expectancy			
Bond and Tinker ERG = (Yrs. in school × IQ) + 1	$(1.5 \times 1.20) + 1$ $1.8 + 1$ ERG = 2.8	$(1.5 \times 1.00) + 1$ $1.5 + 1$ ERG = 2.5	$(1.5 \times .80) + 1$ $1.2 + 1$ ERG = 2.2
Harris $RE = \dfrac{2MA + CA}{3}$	$\dfrac{18.0 + 7.5}{3}$ $\dfrac{25.5}{3}$ RE = 8.5	$\dfrac{15.0 + 7.5}{3}$ $\dfrac{22.5}{3}$ RE = 7.5	$\dfrac{12.0 + 7.5}{3}$ $\dfrac{19.5}{3}$ RE´ = 6.5

and chronological age as the basis of estimating reading expectancy, and expectancy is reported as reading age equivalent. In the Monroe Expectancy Formula, a general grade expectancy is first computed by averaging the child's mental age grade, chronological age grade, and arithmetic grade score; then a reading index is computed by dividing the reading grade score by the computed grade expectancy. The results are reported in terms of a ratio between the two measures. Table 7.1 gives examples of how these formulae can be applied in estimating the reading expectancy level of three hypothetical children. By examining the data in Table 7.1, one quickly becomes aware that care must be exercised in interpreting reading expectancy measures. Different formulae use different factors to compute expectancy (years in school, IQ, chronological age, mental age, tested reading ability, and in one instance, the score on an arithmetic test). Expectancy levels are reported in different terms (reading grade equivalent, reading age equivalent, and a ratio between reading test scores and general grade expectancy). Expectancy is reported to the year and the month, as if these measures were absolute indicators of the child's potential. Although the expectancy levels computed using different formulae are fairly consistent in Table 7.1, discrepancies have been found among expectancy levels computed by different formulae; i.e., while one formula may show a great difference between ability and potential, another may show little or no difference. These formulae tend to diminish in validity or as predictive measures towards the upper and lower extremes of the IQ range.[17]

There are other more subtle assumptions to consider. Intelligence (or mental age) is often taken to be the unqualified indicator of reading potential—which it is not. No provision is made for determining how IQ was measured. No distinction is made between verbal and performance aspects of the IQ score. Nor are such factors as the child's background, language, level of interest or motivation, perceptual strengths and weaknesses, or the nature of the material s/he is expected to read, ever taken into account. These formulae assume that all children enter school with readiness skills equally intact. The formulae imply an assumption that one year of growth can be projected for every year of instruction, and any teacher can attest to the fallacy of this assumption.

When properly interpreted and used, however, reading expectancy measures do provide a thumbnail indication or estimate (not an absolute measure) of the child's degree of underachievement or overachievement in terms of his/her mental age, chronological age, and/or grade placement. These measures should be viewed as "floors" rather than "ceilings" of potential reading achievement, because with favorable learning conditions and appropriate instruction, the slow learner can often exceed the expected level of achievement that his/her IQ suggests. As with any other assessment tool or technique, these formulae should not be interpreted as absolute measures. Expectancy formulae do, however, provide objective measures to support other objective data and subjective impressions concerning the reading status and needs of the slow learner. As such, they provide another potential piece of information about the child.

CONCLUSION

Children are usually designated as slow learners on the basis of their performance on an intelligence test. But general intelligence is only one factor in the complex human psyche. The teacher's job remains one of finding out how the child learns best, what his/her reading level is, and where his/her weaknesses in reading skills are. This is part of the ongoing diagnostic process necessary for dealing with special-needs children in the regular classroom.

Most importantly, teaching reading to the slow learner in the classroom involves delivering instruction in such a way that the child will have every chance of success that his/her learning ability will allow. There are no magical, mystical solutions to the slow learner's reading problems. While they have the same diversity of human characteristics found in any group of children, what sets the slow learners apart, as a group, is that they are slow to learn what they are expected to learn. And this includes learning to read. Slow learners learn to read in much the same way as so-called "regular" children, but they do it at a slower pace. Formal reading instruction may need to be delayed, thus prolonging (and intensifying) the readiness period. When instruction begins, it must be adjusted to the child's learning rate. As it progresses, it should include material at the child's reading level.

Slow learners require more than the average amount of review, reinforcement, and practice in mastering basic word skills. In practical classroom terms, this may necessitate introducing sight words more slowly, repeating them more often, presenting them in a greater variety of ways, and using a number of supplementary reading materials containing the same basic vocabulary. It may require spending a lot more time than usual in teaching the basic phonetic and structural elements in our printed language to assure mastery at every instructional step along the way. It involves using the child's perceptual strengths as the primary avenue of input in teaching basic reading skills. All the review and reinforcement that the slow learner typically needs necessitate a wealth of supplementary skill-building material for drill and practice.

In the area of comprehension, adjusting instruction for the slow learner requires that a firm foundation of experience, language, and thinking be established. Instruction needs to be rooted in concreteness. Slow learners often have difficulty generalizing and thinking abstractly about what they are reading. They should be given many opportunities to come in direct contact with objects and experiences that make up the content of reading books so they will have a firm conceptual basis from which to build understanding. They may have to read a written selection several times to fully grasp its meaning. Slow learners typically need a lot of direct help and guidance to fully comprehend what they read. The slow learner will typically require many experiences in listening/thinking tasks before the demands of reading/thinking comprehension tasks can be met.

Teaching reading to the slow learner is not easy. The three essential ingredients in the process are *planning, pacing,* and *patience.* Careful planning is needed, because the slow learner can't be expected to master basic reading skills on the basis of a reading program designed for more average learners. Specific instruction must be carefully planned according to the child's specific learning needs. And the delivery of this instruction must be carefully paced according to the child's rate of learning. This (as most teachers know) requires a large measure of patience, the human quality that enables the teacher to try something one more time and in another way after previous attempts to teach the same thing have been largely unproductive.

With appropriate instruction—thoughtfully planned, carefully paced, and patiently carried out—the slow learner can learn to read.

ACTIVITIES FOR PRESERVICE TEACHERS

1. Examine a teacher's edition for a text from a basal reading program designed for use in the elementary grades. What adjustments do you think would have to be made in the lessons to better gear the material to the learning level and rate of the slow learner in a classroom?

2. Using material from one of the basic reading skills areas of word recognition, phonetic analysis, or structural analysis, design a multisensory lesson that might help the slow learner master the skills you plan to teach. For example, you might use a visual-auditory-kinesthetic-tactual approach to teaching five common sight words, or a multisensory approach to teaching a phonics lesson on the sound-symbol correspondence in the *bl*—/bl/ or *br*—/br/ blends. What evaluative procedures would be appropriate for determining whether or not the lesson has been a success?

3. Write five or six comprehension questions based on a reading selection at the second- or third-grade level. Be sure to include questions that require different levels of thinking. If a slow learner were unable to answer these questions, what adjustments might you make in the types of questions you formulate? What might you do to help the slow-learning child better understand what s/he reads?

4. Using the Bond and Tinker reading expectancy formula, determine whether the following children are reading above or below their expected reading level:

	Grade	IQ Score	Reading Score
Allan	2	100	1.9
Betty	4	68	2.3
Charles	5	133	6.7
David	7	86	4.8
Evelyn	9	92	3.6

How much is each child above or below his/her expected reading level?

5. Do a little research on the relationship between intelligence and reading ability. What conclusions does your research suggest? What are the practical implications of these conclusions for teaching reading to the slow learner in the classroom?

ACTIVITIES FOR IN-SERVICE TEACHERS

1. Identify two or three children in your class who may be classified as "slow learners." How do these children differ from the other children in the class in their learning levels and learning rates? List, for these children, the three most troublesome aspects of learning to read. What specific techniques can you use to help the children over these "trouble spots" in reading?

2. Prepare and administer a simple learning rate test as an informal diagnostic device for the slow learners in your classroom. Select five or ten sight words (the number will depend on the grade level and reading ability of the children) from a source you use for instructional purposes: the basal program, the Dolch or other word lists, lists of label words in the room, words from the children's experience stories, etc. How many visual presentations of the words are required for mastery? Design and test activities and techniques that the children can use for independent review of the words. Which of these techniques seem most effective? How many of the words can the children remember the next day? At the end of the week? After a month? Keep a record of the words that each child most easily remembers. On the basis of the sight words each child remembers and the techniques s/he uses for recall, what conclusions can you draw about each child's learning style and learning rate?

3. On the basis of the child's performance on a worksheet, game, or other piece of instructional material, identify a specific skill area that a slow learner in your classroom has particular difficulty with; for example, learn-

ing letter names, mastering sight words, applying phonics rules, breaking words into syllables, etc. Examine or design alternative materials or devices that the child might use for reinforcement or application of the reading skill you identify.

4. Analyze a slow learner's responses to comprehension questions that you ask as part of a reading lesson. Try to identify problems in the child's responses that may stem from lack of experience, language problems, or inadequate mental processing. What types of aids could you give to help the child develop these dimensions of comprehension as part of tomorrow's reading lesson?

5. Using one of the formulae presented in this chapter, compute the reading expectancy for three or four children in your class. How do the children's scores on standardized reading achievement tests compare with their computed expectancies?

NOTES

1. *Mental Age* is a figure arrived at by multiplying IQ score by chronological age and dividing by 100: $(MA = IQ \times CA).100$ For example, a six-year-old child with an IQ of 100 is said to have a mental age of 6.0. A six-year-old child with an IQ of 70 is said to have a mental age of 4.2, and a six-year-old with an IQ of 120 has a mental age of 7.2. A bright six-year-old may have the same mental age as a slow-learning eight-year old despite the two-year difference in their chronological ages.
2. John F. Cawley, Henry A. Goodstein, and Will H. Burrow, *The Slow Learner and the Reading Problem* (Springfield, Ill.: Charles C Thomas, 1972), p. 22.
3. Samuel A. Kirk, *Educating Exceptional Children,* 2d ed. (Boston: Houghton Mifflin Co., 1972), p. 203.
4. Cawley et al., *Slow Learner*, p. 50.
5. Ibid., p. 12.
6. Kirk, *Educating Exceptional Children,* p. 203.
7. M. Morphett and C. Washburne, "When Should Children Begin to Read?" *Elementary School Journal* 31 (1931): 496–503.
8. Jeanne Chall, *Learning To Read: The Great Debate* (New York: McGraw-Hill Book Co., 1967).
9. James Moffett, *A Student-Centered Language Arts Curriculum, K-6: A Handbook for Teachers*, 2d ed. (Boston: Houghton Mifflin Co., 1973), pp. 16–17.
10. Benjamin S. Bloom, ed., *Taxonomy of Educational Objectives* (New York: Longmans Green, 1956).
11. Norris M. Sanders, *Classroom Questions* (New York: Harper and Row, 1966).
12. J. P. Guilford and R. Hoepfner, "Current Summary of Structure-of-Intellect Factors and Suggested Tests," in *Reprints of Psychological Lab,* No. 30 (Los Angeles: University of Southern California, 1963).

13. Thomas C. Barrett, *A Taxonomy of Reading Comprehension* (Lexington, Mass.: Ginn and Co., n.d.).
14. Eddie C. Kennedy, *Classroom Approaches To Remedial Reading,* 2d ed. (Itasca, Ill.: F. E. Peacock Publishers, 1977), p. 19.
15. Guy L. Bond and Mills A. Tinker, *Reading Difficulties: Their Diagnosis and Correction*, 3rd ed. (Englewood Cliffs, N.J.: Prentice-Hall, 1973), p. 100.
16. These formulae are further explained in John Pescosolido and Charles Gervase, *Reading Expectancy and Readability* (Dubuque, Iowa; Kendal/Hunt Publishing Company, 1971).
17. For a critical comparative analysis of these formulae, see Kathleen Dore-Boyce, Marilyn Misner, and Lorraine D. McGuire, "Comparing Reading Expectancy Formulas," *The Reading Teacher* 20 (October 1975): 8–14.

REFERENCES

Cawley, John F., Goodstein, Henry A., and Burrow, Will H. *The Slow Learner and the Reading Problem.* Springfield, Ill: Charles C Thomas, 1972.

Gillespie, Patricia H., and Johnson, Lowell. *Teaching Reading to the Mildly Retarded Child.* Columbus: Charles E. Merrill Co., 1974.

Kennedy, Eddie C. *Classroom Approaches to Remedial Reading,* 2d ed. Itasca, Ill.: F. E. Peacock Publishers, 1977.

Kephart, Newell C. *The Slow Learner in the Classroom.* Columbus: Charles E. Merrill Co., 1960.

Kirk, Samuel A. *Educating Exceptional Children*, 2d ed. Boston: Houghton Mifflin Co., 1972.

Payne, J., Palloway, E., Smith, J., and Payne, R. *Strategies for Teaching the Mentally Retarded.* Columbus: Charles E. Merrill Co., 1977.

Wilson, Robert M. *Diagnostic and Remedial Reading for Classroom and Clinic*, 2d ed. Columbus: Charles E. Merrill Co., 1972.

8

Problems in Attitude and Behavior: The Emotional Dimension

Preview

Attitude and behavior, the emotional or affective dimensions of learning, can directly influence the process of learning to read. The child's attitude toward self (the self-concept), the relationship s/he maintains with others, and his/her attitude toward the entire school experience will spill over to affect reactions to an instructional program. Treatment strategies recommended for dealing with troubled children in the classroom can be adapted and directly applied to reading instruction, for the dual purpose of improving both social skills and reading skills. Other school professionals and parents can be agents for treatment of the child's problems as well.

"The emotionally disturbed child" is a catchall phrase that carries with it all the attendant dangers of any label. It implies a single, simplistic category that includes children whose emotional characteristics, social adjustment, and/or behavior patterns deviate from age and grade expectancies. It is a term that is widely used, most often without any terminological boundaries or precise definitions. It is used to describe children whose symptoms run the gamut from acute paranoia to low academic achievement, and whose behavior ranges from obnoxious to shy. The term often includes descriptors such as "handicapped," "maladjusted," "behavior disordered," or "troubled." The causes of emotional problems can be anything from total neglect to smothering overprotection. "Emotionally disturbed" is, to say the least, a broad and often- (perhaps overly) used expression.

In this chapter, the term "emotional problem(s)" refers to children whose difficulties in learning to read are linked to affective factors. In practical terms, these affective factors result in attitudes and behaviors that may be referred to as "troublesome." These are the children who seem to possess the sensory, perceptual, cognitive, and linguistic prerequisites that would allow progress with normal instruction, yet who still have difficulties learning to read because their attitudes or behavior patterns interfere with their learning. Throughout this chapter, the expressions "emotional" and "attitude and behavior" are linked.

How emotional problems and reading disabilities are related is a matter of debate. Trying to determine the relationship between the two is like trying to answer the question, "Which came first, the chicken or the egg?" The problem is typified by a first-year teacher who had in her classroom a child with both emotional and reading problems. The teacher sought the advice of both the reading specialist and the school adjustment counselor.

"Don't worry too much about the reading problems," was the school psychologist's advice. "Once the child overcomes the emotional problems, he'll learn to read fairly easily."

"Don't worry too much about the emotional problems," the reading specialist told the teacher. "Concentrate on the child's reading skills, because failure in reading is what's probably causing the emotional problems in the first place."

With conflicting advice, the young teacher was left in the original dilemma.

Emotional disturbance is linked to reading problems, to be sure. Repeated evidence[1] indicates that the incidence of emotional problems is higher among disabled readers than among more capable readers. But there are at least three ways in which the two broad problem areas can be related:

1. Some children are emotionally disturbed before they try to learn to read and fail.
2. Some children fail in reading and become emotionally disturbed as a result of reading failure.

3. Some children experience emotional problems and reading failure as a concomitant experience.[2]

To further complicate matters, there are children who are emotionally troubled but still learn to read quite well, and others who are perfectly well adjusted but fail in reading nevertheless. Also, it should be emphasized that reading per se may not be the major problem for many children with attitude and behavior problems. Rather, the problem may be the interaction with an authoritative adult that causes the difficulty in reading instruction.

That children with reading problems show maladjustments of some kind is not surprising. Failure typically causes embarrassment, doubt, frustration, anxiety, insecurity, conflict, hostility, fear, stress, aggressiveness, anger, withdrawal, or other symptoms that are marks of personality problems. Failure leaves a mark on anyone's personality. Failure in learning to read—which is such a major part of the child's school life from the earliest years—is bound to leave a mark on the child's emotional state.

There is likely a cyclic effect in the relationship between reading problems and emotional problems. That is, early reading failure causes emotional problems, which in turn bring about further difficulty in learning to read. It's a vicious circle! While arguments about the "emotional problem–reading problem" issue may continue, the teacher is faced with the practical problem of what to do in teaching reading to the child with problems in attitude and behavior. Whether reading failure is a symptom or the root cause of emotional problems, teachers need to meet both the emotional and the instructional needs of children in teaching them how to read.

For some children, emotional problems may be compounded by weaknesses in the perceptual, cognitive, and linguistic factors that are prerequisites to learning to read. This is why it is especially important for the classroom teacher and learning specialists to determine that all the child's learning systems are intact before determining that the child's learning problems are affectively based.

Even when perceptual, cognitive, and linguistic learning abilities are in order, however, psychological factors alone can interfere with instruction and learning. For all children, but especially for the child with emotional problems, the task of the teacher is to design and deliver instruction in such a way that both the basic human needs and the instructional needs of the child will be met, and that one area will reinforce the other. This involves providing a set of learning experiences that will help the child develop positive attitudes on the way to learning to read.

ATTITUDE AND BEHAVIOR

Attitudes are crucial in the education of all children. Children come to school with a set of attitudes fairly well developed: attitudes toward self, toward others, and toward learning to read. The attitudes children bring to school are reshaped and changed as a result of a school experience that brings them into contact with teachers, with other children, and with the demands of learning through a planned program of instruction. The way these attitudes are shaped as a result of the school experience (along with the child's out-of-school contacts) will influence the child's behavior in the classroom. Classroom behavior will, in turn, influence the child's learning to read.

Attitude Toward Self

"Self-concept is a person's view of himself, a self-appraisal reflecting one's good and bad points."[3] How the child sees him/herself will have an enormous influence on learning to read. Self-concept affects learning; and learning, in turn, affects the self-concept. Children who have negative feelings about themselves and their ability to learn may be convinced from the outset that they cannot accomplish the tasks demanded in learning how to read. The "deck is stacked" against these children from the start. On the other hand, a positive view of him/herself makes a child more willing to engage in a variety of new learning experiences. Children who are confident and postive about their ability will more readily attempt the new job of learning how to read, and success at the task will serve to reinforce the positive self-images they hold. Children's self-concepts have been found to correlate highly with their success in reading at all levels.[4] Improving a child's self-concept is often an important first step in improving his/her reading ability, because learning and the self-concept are inseparable.

Assessing attitude toward self

How does one determine a child's self-image? There are several formal measures available: tests, checklists, behavior inventories, character-personality scales, and other nonprojective instruments. Most of these devices, however, are designed for use beyond the elementary grades, and even those that are available for use with younger children—for example, the *Thomas Self-Concept Values Test* (ages 3–9; Combined Motivation Education Systems, Inc.); *Burk's Behavior Rating Scales* (preschool–grade 8; Arden Press); the *Tennessee Self-Concept Scale* (ages 12 and above; Counselor's Recordings and Tests)—are designed to provide a very broad picture of the child's personality. Items intended to measure aspects of the self-concept, which would be useful to the classroom teacher, are intermixed with items to determine more serious personality problems. Most tests of this nature are designed as clinical instruments. Careful interpretation of these test results can, however, give teachers some insights into the child's personality and self-concept.

Informal teacher-made scales can also be used to measure self-concept or attitude toward reading. Typically, these measures employ a bipolar model or "sliding scale" to judge children's attitudes about themselves or about reading. For example:

I like reading: a lot   not at all

or

How I feel about myself:
(or about reading)

While such instruments can give teachers information about children and their self-concepts, children often give "expected" rather than honest responses to items.

Observation of the child's ongoing classroom behavior is a more subtle (and perhaps more valid) indicator of the child's self-concept, both in general and specifically in relation to reading. Beyond the child's obvious comments like "I hate school," how children respond to a new task often indicates the status of their self-concepts. When asked to draw a picture of trees in the fall, for example, is the child hesitant about choosing colors, or is his/her self-concept strong enough to take a chance? What does the child say about his/her work that will indicate what s/he thinks about it? When the child encounters a word in reading, does s/he proceed to attack it (assuming some word attack skills have been taught), or does s/he give up with an "I don't know"? Given some free time in the classroom, will the child choose a book rather than another activity, at least once in a while? These are informal observations that will give the teacher a picture of the child's self-image and attitude toward reading. In revealing his/her self-concept, the child's actions will often speak louder than words.

The development of the self-concept

Self-concept is learned. It is acquired largely as a result of contacts with others. Children learn to perceive themselves as others perceive them. While a person's view of self continues to change on a lifelong basis, children's egos begin to develop long before they enter a classroom for the first time. The early love, attention, and support provided by the parents in the home form the basis for the way children begin to see themselves.

The home environment

It is in the home that the child begins to develop a sense of worth, a sense of acceptance, a sense of competence, and the other qualities that make up a positive self-image. Other significant people in the child's early immediate environment—older and younger siblings, relatives, playmates, babysitters—provide a further basis for the young child's developing self-image. For example, children who are incessantly reminded by older siblings that they are "dumb" or that they "can't do anything" often arrive in school convinced of their lack of ability. By contrast, children whose early achievements and success are highlighted and recognized by those around them will likely arrive in the classroom with a "can do" attitude, convinced that they are ready to continue with successful experiences.

*The school
environment*

The school is second only to the home in shaping the young child's developing self-concept. A child brings a self-concept to school, and the school acts on it. The self-image is reinforced or modified as a result of classroom contacts with teachers and classmates. Within the classroom, the teacher is the most important "significant other" that the child encounters, and how the teacher views the child will have a lot to do with how the child comes to view him/herself as a learner. Negative relationships with teachers or low teacher expectation will tend to create or compound the negative self-image a child may have. "A number of researchers and writers during the past decade have placed a growing emphasis on the relationship between teacher expectation and student performance growing from students' self-concepts. . . . Results [of this research] leave little doubt that students' self-concepts and attitudes are often adversely affected by teacher expectations and that teacher expectation can be a major factor in learning disabilities."[5] The sad and classic case is the teacher who introduced a second grader to the remedial reading teacher with, "This is Michael. He'll never learn to read."

Many children have strong images of themselves as class clowns, as good athletes, or as very capable artists, but their lack is most significant in their self-perception of their ability (or inability) to learn to read. A child may have a positive social and physical self-concept but a low academic or scholastic self-concept.

Expecting children to succeed and providing tasks well within their range of ability are important first steps in helping children develop a positive image of themselves as capable (or potentially capable) readers. The early successful reading experiences that teachers provide, with appropriate praise and reinforcement, can bolster a child's image of him/herself as a capable, achieving individual, and can go a long way in helping the child develop the "can do" attitude that is so important in learning to read. Building positive self-images is an important job for the teacher in working with all children, but it is particularly important in working with children who have problems with attitude and/or behavior.

The relationships the child maintains with classmates are also important in shaping the child's self-concept in school. Children are often brutal in reminding each other of failures and weaknesses. Teachers need to generate a classroom atmosphere in which respect, support, and pupil-pupil help are fostered. Displaying children's "best efforts" or providing opportunities for children to demonstrate areas of unique strengths and interests are means of helping children develop mutual respect that will build positive self-concepts.

Positive self-concepts are built through successful experiences. For the young child, learning to read should be success-laden. In the classroom, this may involve moving at a pace adjusted to the child's learning ability and learning rate so that s/he can build a backlog of successful experiences on the way to learning to read. It may imply making accommodations or presenting material to the child through the dominant modality so that chances for success are enhanced. At the upper levels, it involves setting achievable goals for the child. It may include adjusting the level of the material—both published

Cross-age tutoring — having an older pupil work with younger children — is an ego-building experience for the older child and provides opportunities for the purposeful use of reading. (Photo by John A. Malnati)

and teacher-made—in such a way that the child can be assured of meeting success in the demands of the task. It involves using plenty of material at the child's independent reading level. It may include providing support for tasks with which the child may have difficulty; for example, using tapes or study guides to accompany the more difficult reading material that may be required. In sum, it involves providing reading-related tasks in which the child can meet success, since a history of success has a cumulative effect on a child's self-concept.

Helping children build positive self-concepts also requires that teachers recognize and reinforce the positive, successful experiences the children have in learning to read. Recognition and reinforcement involve praise and acknowledgment for each success the child has, however modest the measure of success may be in the teacher's eye. For example, if the child gets only one of five items correct on a test, it is better to put 1 √ than 4× at the top of the page. Reinforcement involves recognition of accomplishments with comments like "Joe took excellent care of our plants today." It includes showing respect and appreciation for the child's work, even if this requires searching hard for something to highlight and praise. In short, it involves recognizing what the child *can* do instead of what s/he can't.

In helping children build more positive self-images, an effective technique is to have older disabled readers serve as reading tutors or helpers working with younger children. The older pupil's assignment might be to help a first grader with a simple reading-related task (like identifying beginning consonant sounds or vowel sounds in words), or to read a story to a group of kindergarten children. Assignments like this give the older child a sense of worth and respectability, along with justification for practicing and mastering basic reading skills. In other words, the fifth grader reading at a second-grade level has *reason* to choose a second-grade book and to practice the very basic skills required to read it to a group of younger children. Where this "cross-age tutoring" has been tried, it has proven to be an extremely effective technique, not only in building the older child's self-respect and responsibility, but also in helping improve his/her reading ability. Typically, the older child profits more than the younger one!

Change in self-concept

Because self-concept is learned, it is amenable to change. "The sense of self is learned through experience; a positive self is teachable."[6] A negative self-image can be a powerful emotional block in learning to read. Attention to the self-concept early in the child's school life is crucial. The younger the child, the more amenable the self-concept is to change. Years of failure give the older child a firmly established negative self-image that often takes more years to change. As the negative self-image is reinforced, the more powerful the emotional blocks to reading become. On the other hand, early successes are the bases for a self-concept that provides a firm emotional foundation in learning to read.

Attitude Toward Others

A person's view of self will influence his/her attitude toward others and the relationship s/he maintains with others in the learning environment of the classroom. Attitudes result in behavior, and negative attitudes tend to result in inappropriate behavior. Emotional distress often manifests itself in behavior disorders. In fact, in the educational literature, the education of children with emotional problems is often treated under the heading of topics like "Children with Behavior Disorders" or "Behavior Management Problems." This does *not* mean, however, that all children's disruptive behavior problems are emotionally based. Misbehavior does not immediately signal an emotional problem. But inappropriate behavior can become "emotionally disturbing" to others when it interferes with learning in the social setting of the classroom.

Inappropriate classroom behavior

Inappropriate behaviors in the classroom can take many forms, most of which teachers are familiar with. Behaviors typically included in the litany of classroom disorders are aggression and related forms of disruptive action: disobedience, overt refusal to engage in learning activities, temper tantrums, crying spells, swearing, and the like. These are behaviors that must be dealt with through the child's entire school experience, not only in connection with his reading instruction.

Disruptive behavior is, of course, not the only manifestation of negative attitudes that a child may have. Instead of acting out to mask perceived inabilities, many children merely withdraw from the demands of learning-related tasks and retreat into their own quiet world of introversion or daydreams. This is why the shy child has been called "a discipline problem in reverse"; i.e., one who needs as much attention as the disruptive child, yet whose behavior typically receives less attention in the classroom. In the extreme, this behavior results in running from the room, psychosomatic illness, or truancy.

A child's classroom behavior that might be described as "inappropriate" need not always be as extreme as those described above. There are often small behaviors that annoy teachers. Minor habits sometimes tend to get on our nerves, e.g., the constant tapping of a pencil or a ruler, the repeated "click-click" of the button on a ballpoint pen, or the swinging of a child's leg over the edge of a chair. With these types of annoying behaviors, it becomes necessary for the teacher to ask, "Whose problem is it, the child's or mine?" Very often, the answer will suggest the need to assume a more tolerant attitude toward the child rather than to institute extreme actions to alter the child's behavior.

Treatment   A number of treatment strategies have been suggested for helping children with emotional/behavior problems in the classroom. Kirk identifies and briefly describes Psychodynamic, Behavior Modification, Developmental, Learning Disabilities, Psychoeducational, and Ecological strategies for the educational treatment of children with behavior disorders.[7] The strategies identified and described by Hewett are these: Psychodynamic-Interpersonal, Sensory-Neurological, Behavior Modification, and Developmental.[8] Additional strategies or models have been suggested by other authors as well. Often, the emotionally upset child will be undergoing treatment or therapy outside the classroom. In such cases, the teacher's job is to reinforce the treatment model through appropriate instructional strategies in the classroom.

The techniques that the teacher uses in teaching reading to the child with attitude/behavior problems will be related to both the child's emotional/social needs and his/her instructional needs. While there are no panaceas or perfect solutions, some techniques have been found useful in teaching reading to the emotionally troubled child.

In some cases, a nondirective approach to reading instruction may be appropriate. Virginia Axline describes a second-grade classroom in which lots of opportunities were provided for the release of tensions and self-expression of feelings through art, music, play, dramatics, and other activities. Although participation in reading groups and other formal reading activities was voluntary, the results in reading achievement were dramatic.[9]

Some research suggests that establishing a rapport with a disabled reader is just as important as teaching reading skills per se.[10] This is not surprising, since interaction with an adult may be the prime emotional factor at work in causing the learning problem.

Bibliotherapy

Bibliotherapy may be another effective technique for using reading to help children with emotional problems. Bibliotherapy is the dynamic interaction between a person and a piece of literature, an interaction through which a person satisfies emotional needs or finds solutions to personal problems in the stories s/he reads. Bibliotherapy provides a means of helping children work through some of their personal, social, and affective problems through books.

Through bibliotherapy, children see book characters with problems similar to their own. By identifying with the problems of characters in a book, children may develop insights into their own problems. They may see how book characters cope with problems and relate the solutions to their own situations. The insights children develop into how characters solve problems in stories are often transferred to the reality of their own worlds. The child thus develops a heightened knowledge of self and insights into his/her own behavior.

Although bibliotherapy is an attempt to promote emotional health through literature, books don't stand alone in helping children find solutions to problems through reading. Bibliotherapy requires the careful guidance of the teacher in story selection and in interpretation through follow-up questions and discussions, retelling and role playing, writing and art projects that will highlight and reinforce the positive therapeutic effect of the book. Problem solving through books requires more than the books themselves, but research suggests[11] that books often *do* shape children's attitudes and influence their behavior. Bibliotherapy can be a successful dimension of reading instruction for children with emotional problems.

Motivation

While nondirective techniques are often appropriate, there will obviously be times when direct instruction will be necessary for the development of basic reading skills. At these times, motivation will be an especially important dimension of instruction. Motivation is, of course, important in learning for all children, but it is especially important in working with children whose attitudes may be particularly negative and resistant from the outset.

An effective starting point for skill development might be a personalized list of words that the child dictates. There's a built-in motivational factor here, since these words will have meaning to the child and s/he is the one who suggests them. These personalized dictated word lists can become vehicles for developing basic word recognition and word analysis skills, for helping the child make the transition from the speech sounds s/he knows well to the written language code s/he probably knows less well.

It's not a distant or difficult step from personalized word lists to language experience stories. The children dictate stories that are transcribed on an experience chart, and these stories become the vehicles for reading instruction. The content of the stories can be anything of interest or concern to children—maybe even their fantasies—and skill development can be extended in a way similar to that described on page 22b. The built-in motivational factor provides a particular advantage for using this approach with the poorly motivated child in the classroom.

The lyrics of popular songs may also be used as a vehicle for reading instruction. Usually, even children whose emotional and/or reading problems are severe can remember the words to popular songs. The children follow the printed words of the song as they listen to the record being played over and over. Through repetition, they learn to read the words. The "reading" occurs when children can recognize the words in print removed from the context of the song. Once the lyrics can be read independently, additional skill development—review of basic sight words, syllabication, rhyming words, long and short vowel sounds, etc.—can take place with the words of the song. Comprehension is an inherent dimension as well.

Hewett[12] details a technique that was used successfully in the case of a severely disturbed child. A flannel board with letters of the alphabet and a picture of a common object was set up in the child's work space. The letters were arranged to spell the name of each object pictured. This type of activity was expanded to copying letters, to auditory and visual discrimination practice, and to longer writing exercises that greatly facilitated the child's ability to communicate. While this activity (and other techniques that Hewett describes) were used with children who had more severe emotional problems than classroom teachers can expect to encounter, such techniques can be adapted for the use in the classroom with children whose problems fall into the mild-to-moderate range.

None of these techniques is unique or limited in use to emotionally troubled children. There are literally thousands of teaching ideas adaptable to reading instruction for the child with attitude/behavior problems in any classroom. Any technique the teacher finds effective in meeting the social/emotional needs of the child, along with his/her reading needs, ought to be used as part of the instructional program.

Behavior modification

Techniques based on principles related to behavior modification are also often recommended for children with attitude/behavior problems. Behavior modification involves a highly structured, carefully planned, and systematic program for dealing with social and instructional problems in the classroom. As a modifier of behavior, the teacher 1) identifies or stipulates acceptable behaviors; for example, to remain seated during the first five minutes of the reading period (social) or to complete ten items on a phonics worksheet (instructional); 2) defines conditions under which behaviors are to be engaged in;

for example, to work without disturbing other members of the group (social) or to work without distraction or interruption in copying and reviewing vocabulary words (instructional); 3) provides reinforcement or reward for positive behaviors; for example, allowing the child to distribute materials for the next activity (social) or to play a game related to skill development work being done (instructional). Behavior modification involves short-term goals, small steps, and immediate reinforcement.

Behavior modification techniques have been widely—and to a great extent successfully—used in special education, and particularly in the education of emotionally disturbed children. However, such techniques have not been without their share of criticism. Because of its Skinnerian orientation, critics often view behavior modification as a "rat-and-pigeon approach" to education. In terms of intrinsic motivation and broad educational goals, behavior modification techniques can be limiting in scope. The full implementation of a behavior modification program requires a person cognizant of its theory and trained in its techniques. But even without accepting its philosophy and practices lock, stock, and barrel, elements of behavior modification can be applied to reading instruction in the classroom.

The area of programmed learning, for example, is based largely on the same stimulus-response theory that is part of behavior modification. Programmed-learning devices present material to children under very controlled conditions. Material is paced in small and carefully sequenced steps. Reaction demands an overt response. Immediate feedback is provided. The child with emotional problems can work with a programmed machine like *System 80*, or one based on programming principles like *Spellbinder,* in basic reading skill development areas. Working alone with a teaching machine often saves the child emotional upset that accompanies the embarrassment resulting from failure in front of peers. Working with a programmed machine as part of a two-pupil team can give the child the controlled social contact that may be needed in developing interpersonal skills along with reading skills. With practice, the child can become the classroom "specialist" who assumes responsibility in helping classmates in the use of the programmed device; thus, social and instructional skills can be a concomitant focus.

Contracting Contracting is also suggested as an effective teaching-learning device. A contract is a joint agreement between the teacher and the child to achieve an objective or to accomplish a task. With work geared to ability, contracts can be made, for example, for the number of pages of a text to be read in a specified period of time, the number of skills exercises to be completed, or the number of activities to be finished. Contracts can be made for a single activity, for a class period, or for longer periods of time (a day or a week, for example). An "official" contract form can be made to be signed jointly by the teacher and the child; for example:

READING CONTRACT FOR___ Joe M. ___ Tuesday, October 3, 19___

Time	*Task*	*Comments*
9:00–9:05	Listen carefully to directions and assignments.	
9:00–9:10	Plan time and organize materials.	
9:10–9:20	Copy new words neatly. Make up sentences for new words.	
9:20–9:30	Free time for learning games.	
9:30–9:45	Read pp. 46–52 with reading group (or in conference with teacher).	
9:45–9:50	Answer questions about the story.	

Signed: _____   _____
                              Pupil   Teacher

When both parties agree to the contract, the child accepts a measure of responsibility for his/her own learning. In determining the learning tasks, the child should have some choice in the planning. In carrying out the contract, the child must learn to organize and use time efficiently. Part of the idea of contracting is to help the child learn to accept the consequences of work not completed. When contracted tasks have not been accomplished, the work may need to be adjusted. Classroom contracts are never carved in stone. Pupils can share in the planning of adjustments too. Comments on completed tasks should provide reinforcement and reward through positive feedback. Contracts can be made for classroom behavior as well as for instructional activities.

The idea of contracting is not new. It was used in elementary schools as early as 1920, and is still frequently used as part of individualized programs for all children. Contracts are particularly appropriate for use with children with attitude/behavior problems, however, because they help children develop a sense of responsibility for their own learning and behavior in the classroom. Contracts share with behavior modification the specification of the task, the controlled conditions for learning, and the positive reinforcement that results from accomplishments.

With emotionally troubled children, the reward for completing contract responsibilities should be clearly specified. Contingencies can be built into classroom contracts for reading. As part of the contract-making process, the reinforcement should be stated and the child can have input into the rewards s/he receives. For example, if the child would rather draw than sit in a reading group, or if the child would rather play a phonics game than work on a phonics practice exercise, then drawing can be the reinforcer contingent on participating in a reading group, or the game can be made contingent upon finishing the exercise. The preferred activities are used to reinforce successful completion of less enjoyable ones.

In behavior modification, the contingencies of schedules of reinforcements are important ingredients. The child learns that behavior has consequences, and reinforcers are presented as part of the process of modifying behaviors. Positive reinforcers aim at strengthening or maintaining positive behaviors; negative reinforcers aim at reducing or weakening negative behaviors. The purpose of reinforcement is to exercise a controlling function on the behavior.

Reinforcement   Providing feedback and reinforcement is not unique to behavior modification. Teachers have for years been using gold stars and smiley-faced stickers for motivation and as a reward for work well done. In behavior modification, however, the reinforcement takes place on a schedule and as a direct consequence of social or instructional behaviors. Direct, scheduled reinforcement can be made part of reading instruction, and positive reinforcers can be used as a direct consequence of the successful completion of reading-related tasks.

In reading instruction in the classroom, the rewards need not always be tangible "goodies" like jelly beans, M & M candies, or tokens, as they often are in more formal behavior modification programs. Calling on children who have their hands raised in response to a question is a form of positive reinforcement. So are rewards like allowing the child to water the plants, erase the chalkboard, run an errand, or help in one of the many duties that are part of the daily classroom routine. Rewards can be learning related too, like allowing the child to choose a math or reading game, or to use the typewriter to type a story, or to listen to a story with headphones on the tape recorder. Teachers can offer more subtle forms of reinforcement by standing near the child's seat, by offering a kind or congratulatory word, by a gentle pat on the shoulder, or by a smile. This type of positive feedback can be provided all day long. The type of reinforcement used will depend on the child, the teacher, and the nature of the task. What may be a reward for one child may be considered punishment for another. The idea in providing feedback is to let children know that reward will be the consequence of successful work (or at least best efforts) in attempts at learning to read.

The more immediate the reinforcement, the better will be the chances of its influencing the child's behavior. Children typically work for instantaneous rewards. A star or "good work" placed on a pupil's paper immediately after it has been completed will have a greater effect than a similar reinforcer the next day. Daily reports of progress will have a greater effect than those given at the end of the month. Simple daily report cards like this:

Name *Joe*   Date *Jan 14*

Effort   1   2   3   ④   5

Behavior   1   2   ③   4   5

Comments *Joey completed all but two assignments today, and classroom behavior continues to improve.*

---

provide an immediate vehicle for reporting progress to the child and to his/her parents.

An effective reinforcement technique that can be used in reading instruction is to allow children to chart their accomplishments or progress. The child makes a record or chart showing achievements or accomplishment over time.

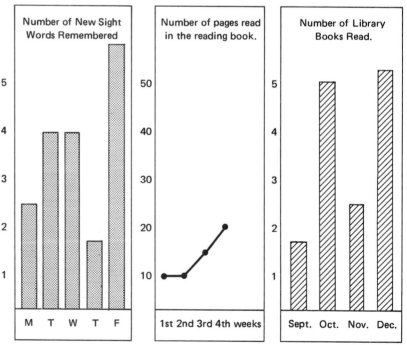

Figure 8.1   Chart to show pupil progress.

Charts like these provide positive reinforcement, since they are tangible evidence of progress. They are objective, genuine means of *showing* the child his/her progress, since when you tell a child with a poor self-image that s/he is doing good work, the child has a tendency not to believe you! Even when drop-offs occur, the child has the chart to see past accomplishments and this should instill motivation to improve future performance. Keeping the charts individual—i.e., having children keep their own records of performance over time—is important. A group or class chart containing rows of stars for Sally and only one or two for Sam can be emotionally devastating to Sam.

Techniques that are part of, or related to, behavior modification can be used effectively in teaching reading. Devices like contracting, programmed learning, positive reinforcement, or charts showing progress are not unique to behavior modification, nor are they appropriate only for children with negative attitudes or behavior problems. They have been used for a long time by skilled teachers for all children. These devices may, however, be especially effective in planning and carrying out reading instruction within the social context of the classroom for children with attitudinal or behavior problems.

Just as successful experiences are the sine qua non of helping the child build a positive self-image, so successful experiences are just as important in helping the child learn to develop positive relationships with others in the classroom. Reading instruction must always be placed in perspective with the child's broader psychoeducational needs.

> When the child enters school, he is expected to possess certain social readiness skills which will allow him to perform in a prescribed manner acceptable to school, home, and society. Failure of the child to meet certain externally imposed demands will result in internal anxiety and frustration which lead directly to maladaptive behavior. If the teacher and/or peers counter with hostile, rejecting responses, anxiety and frustration are increased. This leads eventually to a school crisis. The crisis then provides the child with another example of his inability, further lowering his self-concept, increasing his frustration, and creating a vicious cycle that will affect the child, the teacher, the parents, and his peers.
>
> The goal of intervention is to interrupt this cycle. Some of the factors that should be examined in an attempt to reach this goal would include: (1) the nature of the demands and pressures placed on the child; (2) the ability of the child to meet these demands; (3) peer group relations; (4) pupil-teacher relations; (5) the youngster's motivation for the behavior; and (6) his self-concept."[13]

Role playing

Classroom instruction should also help children discover how their own behavior affects others. A technique that has proven effective for this purpose involves role playing and role reversal. In role-playing situations, a child's activity is often reflected back with the intention of helping the child gain insight into his/her own behavior. For example, a troublesome child might be given responsibility for teaching a lesson to others in a reading group. Helping the child prepare "his/her lesson" can provide direct teaching opportunities in reading skill development areas. Letting children assume responsibility for teaching classmates may help them develop insights into why behavior disorders can be so disturbing in a group setting. The "lesson" need not always be a formal reading activity. It may be a report in an area of the child's interest or strengths: model building, how to throw a football, art, etc. Tape recording the "lesson" can be a positive incentive and provide the basis of follow-up discussion with the child.

Learning areas

The learning resource areas that the teacher sets up in the classroom—those described in Chapter 9 like the "free" reading corner, the listening station, or the skills center—can be used to give the emotionally troubled child a place to work on reading-related tasks. With positive experiences, working in these areas can be built into the schedule of reinforcement that the teacher plans. Finally, sound educational experiences are built upon close teacher-pupil contacts. This involves acceptance (not of the maladaptive behavior, but of the human being who is engaging in the behavior), understanding, and mutual respect and trust. Frequent opportunities to work with the teacher or another adult in the classroom are often important to the academic and personal growth of the child.

Systematic, successful experiences

A sound instructional program for children with attitudinal problems involves experiences that are success laden, system and structure that are planned as part of learning experiences, the appropriate use of learning materials and resource areas, and close teacher-pupil contacts. A background of reading successes that help the child build a more positive self-image will likely improve classroom behavior and reading ability at the same time. Structure is important too. These children need to know exactly what is expected of them in both learning and behavior. Structure demands systematic planning. For example, if the child refuses to read aloud in a reading group, systematic provision can be made to provide opportunities to read alone into a tape recorder and/or in safe, supportive, one-to-one conferences with the teacher. By providing systematic, successful, individual experiences, the teacher is preparing the child for the demands of reading aloud in a group.

Providing for the special needs of children with attitude or behavior problems in the regular classroom takes patience, understanding, and a lot of common sense. It is difficult for the teacher to "show the child you like him" when the child is running screaming from the room, or to "ignore the child's disruptive behavior" when that behavior is interfering with the learning of the twenty-five other children for whom the teacher has responsibility. Children with severe emotional problems usually require special treatment outside the regular classroom setting. But with an individually prescribed and carefully planned program, along with the help and support of resource personnel, the child with negative attitudes and behaviors can begin to develop the positive relationships s/he needs to maintain with others, along with mastering some basic reading skills, in the regular classroom.

While behavior problems and emotional problems are often causatively linked and treated together, it's important once again for teachers to remember that all behavior problems are not necessarily affectively based. Inappropriate behavior can sometimes be the result of physiologically based factors such as those that cause overactivity, or the behavior may be the result of a child's reaction to inappropriate instruction.

The Overactive Child

Overactivity is a genuine concern of parents and teachers alike. The popular literature currently abounds with material on the subject of hyperactivity. But hyperactivity is a misunderstood and often misused term. Before classifying a child as "hyperactive," it's important to remember that there is a wide range of normal activity levels in children, just as there is in adults. All children are normally active, but some are excessively so. Children in the upper limits of the normal activity range can cause discomfort for some teachers, and these children are often labeled "hyperactive."

Behavior patterns

The behavior patterns that result from overactivity are often similar to those associated with emotional problems, and overly active behavior can often be managed with some of the strategies suggested for working with children with emotional problems. Also, the way a child's activity is handled by teachers and peers can have emotional consequences.

The overactive child can be a disturbing influence in the classroom because of his/her excessive movement. The child may have difficulty controlling behavior. These children may have trouble sitting still for very long. They may be out of their seats, under their chairs, on their desks, fidgeting and squirming and wiggling and jiggling and moving about. Activity is usually disorganized and often random. In comparison to that of normally active agemates, the overactive child's activity is inefficient; that is, his/her activity accomplishes little. Energy is expended with nonproductive results.

The behavior of overly active children is often impulsive and thus unpredictable. Actions are taken on the spur of the moment without consideration of the consequences. "Jaunts" around the room may include impulsively bumping another child, knocking the book from the hands of a classmate, or disturbing the markers on a board game that other children are playing. This type of behavior has obvious social consequences (which may account for the fact that overactive children have more than their normal share of fights in the classroom and on the playground). The behavior is not always disturbing to others, of course. There will be times when the child wanders to the bookshelf to thumb (aimlessly) through books, or meanders to examine the bulletin board, without disturbing anyone (except, perhaps, the teacher).

Another symptom characteristic of the overactive child is that of easy distractibility or shortness of attention. Powers of concentration may be weak. The child may have trouble attending to a task and seeing a job through to the end. Though distractibility may often be a problem in reading-related activities in the classroom, the overactive child can be attentive for relatively long periods of time during activities in which s/he is interested. For example, the child may be engrossed while watching a filmstrip on volcanoes or listening to an exciting tale using a headset on a tape recorder. In these instances, it's important for the teacher to extend the activity into further reading-related tasks, to keep the child's attention once it has been captured.

Many overactive children have a low level of tolerance for failure. The child may be quickly discouraged and may tend to give up easily in the face of challenge.

While it may not be primarily an emotional problem, overactivity often has emotional consequences. Because of family friction that results from unpleasant reactions to unpredictable behavior in the preschool years, the child may develop a negative self-image that will affect his/her emotional state (and later academic performance). Because of so often being asked, "What's wrong with you?" and because the behavior may frequently be labeled "bad" by others, the overly active child may learn to perceive him/herself in a negative light. The impulsive style of behavior may alienate other children—at first brothers and sisters and later playmates and classmates—so that the child is rejected by them, with predictable emotional results. Inability to stick with and perform certain tasks may convince the child that s/he is "stupid," even though s/he may have above-average or superior intellectual ability. In sum, behavior induced by overactivity can result in negative psychological effects.

Overactivity can also be present along with other learning disabilities such as poor auditory processing, short-term and long-term visual memory problems, visual-motor difficulties, poor motor control, language disorders, and other problems that contribute to learning difficulties. But even without these specific learning disabilities, overactivity can interfere with a child's ability to achieve his/her fullest potential. Learning demands the ability to concentrate, at least for reasonable periods of time. Overactivity interferes with learning when the child can't sit still long enough to listen to a story, to understand directions that the teacher is giving, or to complete a learning-related task. Learning to read involves a certain amount of repetition and drill. The child who cannot tolerate this type of repeated practice for mastery will have difficulty mastering what the drill is designed to accomplish. Drill needs to be varied. Learning in the social environment of the classroom usually requires a certain degree of patience and a tolerance for some level of challenge. The low frustration level and impulsiveness of the overactive child can be a further source of learning difficulty.

Because the behavioral characteristics associated with high levels of activity are similar in many respects to those of children with emotional problems, many of the same instructional techniques can be used in dealing with both problem areas. These children need plenty of early successful experiences in their initial attempts at learning to read. All children, of course, need early successful experiences, but success is especially important for the very active child because of the typically low level of tolerance for failure and frustration. Tasks need to be broken down into small steps and presented with appropriate pacing. For example, instead of giving the child all four reading worksheets at the beginning of the "seatwork" period, the teacher should provide the worksheets one at a time, after each has been completed.

Environment

Overactive children need a structured learning environment, one with rules, routine, schedules, and consistency. Usually, these children do not do well in an open-classroom environment. Because of the child's often disorganized activity, establishing specific and consistent guidelines for both behavior and learning is important. The child is helped when tasks are laid out specifically and when s/he knows exactly what is expected. This provides a method of attack in doing assignments. External controls help the child organize his/her own activity. The routine planned during the reading period, for example, should be the same from one day to the next. A daily plan, similar in form to contracting, with time limits clearly established, can be useful.

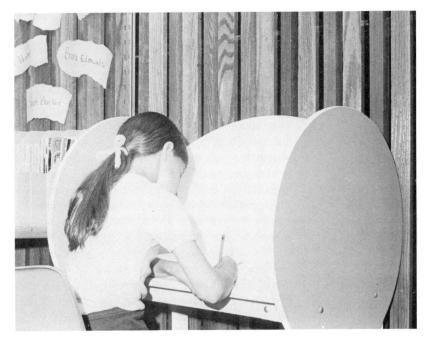

Quiet work areas provide a place for learning activities free from the distractions of the normally busy classroom. (Photo by John A. Malnati)

A schedule of immediate reinforcement can provide rewards both for behavior and for the accomplishment of learning-related tasks. Rewards should be consistent. The child should know ahead of time what s/he is working for. Reinforcement should be constant. Praise given for work well done or for improved behavior should be focused on the child's accomplishments. Rewards should be frequent, since the overactive child often forgets the last positive comment or gold star very quickly.

Distractibility can be a major problem. In giving directions, the teacher should be aware of aiming instruction at the child, so that s/he will attend to the instructions and not to the sound of traffic outside. The child's work area should be as free of distractions as possible. Two bubble gum cards on the child's desk are usually good for at least ten minutes of distractive divergence.

The overactive child may need a personal work space—a table or carrel —for seatwork activities in the classroom. This special area can be called "his / her own office" and can be surrounded by a little open space so that movement won't disturb classmates. This area should not be used as an isolation booth, however, a place where the child is sent for punishment. Letting the child use his/her "office" at his/her own discretion will build in a measure of responsibility in planning his/her own learning and determining his/her own behavior.

Reasonable time limits should be set for the completion of work. Because overactive children have a tendency to wander—mentally and sometimes physically—during quiet work times, and because they often jump from one activity to another in a helter-skelter manner, a kitchen timer can serve as an objective reminder of time limits established for the completion of work. The use of a timer establishes "speed limits" that can help a child gear his/her time to the task at hand.

The overactive child, like all children, must come to realize that behavior has consequences, positive or negative. Patterns of cause and effect may not be readily apparent to the child, so frequent direct discussion of the effects of behavior may be necessary. In the upper elementary grades, a frank discussion with the child can lead him/her to discover the conditions under which s/he learns best. This awareness is important for the pupil beyond the elementary school, where greater independence is demanded.

Finally, in dealing with children who are extremely active in the classroom, it's important for teachers to be aware of the nature of the child's difficulty. Problems of overactivity are often physiologically based. The child's activity level relates to the way his/her system works. The part of the nervous system that controls the child's ability to attend, respond, and tune out extraneous forces does not work efficiently. The child must use the system s/he has. For children who are truly hyperactive, physicians may prescribe medication. Drugs can help the child control the activity and slow the pace, providing at least some relief within the classroom. While stimulants, tranquilizers, antidepressants, and other forms of medication may have a quieting effect on the child—quieting the activity at least long enough for the child to get his/her work done—the drugs themselves have no direct effect on learning. Aware of the potential negative side effects of medication, most physicians are cautious and judicious in their .use of drugs with overly active children.

Within the classroom, the willingness of the teacher to use appropriate behavioral and instructional-management strategies can make the difference between success and failure for the overactive child in all areas of the curriculum, but especially in reading, which occupies such a large amount of time in the regular school day. Avoiding the negative consequences of the overactive behavior should be a major concern in planning and carrying out instruction.

Inappropriate Instruction

Inappropriate instruction is another potential cause of maladaptive behavior in the classroom. "The vast majority of our disability cases are brought about through faulty learning or lack of educational adjustment of one sort or another."[14] When learning tasks are not adjusted to the child's ability, behavior problems are invited. Children who destroy their worksheets, who clown around during reading groups, or who retreat into daydreaming when they should be working, may be behaving in this way not because of an emotional problem but because the work is just too difficult for them. Or assigned learning tasks may be too easy for some children. Harry is a case in point.

Two weeks after transferring to a new school, Harry, on the basis of his classroom behavior, was reported by his teacher as being "emotionally disturbed." An observer was quickly dispatched to note Harry's behavior in the classroom setting. Two minutes into a large-group phonics lesson on the long and short sounds of vowels (in which the teacher was "going over" a list of words on a worksheet), Harry was seen sliding under his chair. The observer approached him.

"What's the problem, Harry?" the adult asked.

"Nothin'," Harry replied confidently. "I don't have no problem."

"Then why aren't you sitting in your chair doing the work you're supposed to be doing?" the observer asked directly.

"I'm finished," Harry said. The observer scanned Harry's paper. Sure enough, while the teacher was talking about the vowel sound in the third word on a list of twenty, Harry had correctly marked all twenty words with the appropriate short or long vowel sound. Harry was just amusing himself while waiting for the teacher and the rest of the class to catch up. He wasn't emotionally disturbed; he was just bored. A term has been factitiously coined to describe this condition: dyspedagogia.

Appropriate instruction is crucial. "When there is a good teaching program, many of these [emotional/behavior] problems will not arise. When the material used conveys meaning, when the level of difficulty insures success and a sense of achievement, and when sufficient variety is afforded to avoid monotony, the program proceeds in a matter-of-fact manner with a minimum of upsets.''[15]

Attitude Toward Reading

In addition to attitudes toward self and others, the child's attitude toward reading itself will be a strong force in the way the child reacts to reading instruction in the classroom. Attitude is part of the affective dimension of reading that was included in Chapter 1, and early experiences will have a profound effect (positive or negative) on the attitude the child develops toward reading.

As in the case of attitude toward self and others, the child brings an attitude toward reading to school, and initial and continuing experience with reading in the classroom serves to reshape that attitude. If, for example, parents tax the young child beyond his/her capabilities with pressure to read before entering school, then the child likely comes to school with firmly rooted negative attitudes about learning to read. Even when attitudes are more positive at school entrance, early failure in the classroom may produce negative responses that very quickly turn into affective problems related to reading.

At all grade levels, attitudes and emotions continue to affect behavior. When one looks at the development of the affective dimensions of learning to read, the importance of the teacher's providing successful experiences at all levels becomes apparent. Children develop emotional responses to formal reading instruction early in their school lives. With successful early school experiences, many of the emotional problems associated with learning to read can be reduced or "cut off at the pass."

Success in mastering basic reading skills during the learning-to-read stage of a child's life produces feelings of confidence and favorable affective associations with reading. This accounts for the pride and satisfaction children often display at being able to read the "adventures" of Dick and Jane or Pam and Pat. Successful reading becomes its own emotional reward. As increasingly complex levels of reading skills are being mastered, affective rewards continue to come from the accomplishment of the learning task, but another affective dimension is added; i.e., the nature of the content that is read. Children learn to like to read because they enjoy the content of the reading material. In the mature reader, positive feelings are produced from what is read more than from the act of reading itself.

Fostering positive attitudes

Helping the child develop early positive attitudes toward reading is an important first step in avoiding later emotional problems. When teachers inherit negative attitudes in children toward reading, the challenge is to begin to turn the attitudes around by providing successful experiences, interesting materials, peer stimulation, and other devices that will promote more positive attitudes toward reading.

WORKING WITH PARENTS AND OTHERS

In dealing with the learning problems of the child with negative attitudes and behaviors, the best efforts of the most skilled teachers are often not enough. Teachers will likely need the help of parents, other school professionals, and even other children, in total treatment strategies.

Parents

Parents are key people in the education of all children, but especially in the education of the child with emotional problems. Attitudes are closely linked to home experiences, and children don't leave their attitudes toward learning in the classroom when they go home every day. There needs to be a steady two-way flow of information between the school and the home. Parents need to understand what the teacher is trying to accomplish so they can provide appropriate reinforcement and follow-up that will support the teacher's efforts. Parents also need to see reading in its proper perspective in the emotional life of the child. Learning to read often becomes an emotional issue for parents. Parental pressure for the child to achieve beyond his/her capabilities, and unfavorable comparison with other children ("Your little sister can do this; why can't you?" "Bobby Jones is in the top reading group; why aren't you?"), are home issues that carry over into the child's experiences in the classroom. Parents' expectations are bound to affect children's attitudes toward themselves, toward others, toward school, and toward learning to read.

There will be times, of course, when parents are either unwilling or unable to cope with their child's emotional disorder. While this situation can certainly be a frustrating experience for the teacher, it ought not to be a reason for giving up on the problem. Here is where help and support can come from other members of the school staff.

School staff

Other professionals in the school can be agents for treatment of the child's emotional and related learning problems. Sometimes, a child's behavior is so maladaptive that keeping him/her in the classroom is impractical or even impossible. At such times the teacher will need the direct assistance of the guidance counselor, school psychologist, or other adjustment specialist. These resource specialists provide not only "relief services" for the harried teacher, but they can also provide practical suggestions on the best way to handle the child in the classroom. The classroom teacher may be the first one to identify a potential emotional problem, so a close working relationship is important for this reason too.

Guidance personnel are not the only members of the school staff who may be called upon to help. Bringing a note to the principal's office, with arrangements for appropriate *positive* reinforcement from the principal or school secretary, can be an effective reward. The office can be a "cooling-off spot" for the child on a particularly bad day. The school custodian (who occasionally allows the child to help arrange chairs for an assembly) and the cafeteria workers (who can give an extra large portion of dessert as a reward for learning or behavior) can help too. Other teachers can provide help and support in both direct and indirect ways. Allowing an older child with emotional problems to read a story to a lower grade necessitates teacher cooperation, and an occasional informal comment from another teacher in the hallway ("I heard you had a very good morning, Tommy") may give the child a needed emotional boost.

As humans, teachers frequently sit around the teachers' room and complain about the behavior of certain children in their classrooms. When this happens, the self-fulfilling prophecy often results; i.e., because of anecdotes this year's teacher shares, other teachers are expecting the worst of Tommy when he arrives in their classes. Tommy delivers what's expected of him. Informal confabs should be kept at a professional level and should accentuate the positive in discussing children who usually have enough problems already.

Children

Other children, too, can be important in helping the learning and behavior of the child with emotional problems. The class provides an audience for the child who acts out. If children can learn to ignore or downplay the bizarre behavior of classmates, chances are that the incidence of such behavior will decrease. The help of the entire class is needed to insure that all children will be accepted as part of both instructional and social groups in the classroom.

Working closely with parents and others not only provides for effective support and treatment services; it also provides the teacher with insights into "where the child is coming from." When teachers understand some of the conditions that exist in the child's out-of-school life, they may be in a better position to understand the child and the problems s/he may be having in learning to read. Children's feelings of conflict or tension can be so strong that learning to read may be secondary in importance. For example, if the teacher knows that a child is preoccupied with worry that his mother may not be there when he gets home from school, or with fear of the beating s/he receives every day from an older brother or sister, then the teacher can better understand the cause of the child's withdrawal or inattention during reading instruction. With this type of information, the teacher will be in a better position to help solve an emotional problem that may be getting in the way of the child's learning to read. Even if the teacher's powers to solve the problem are limited, being aware of the difficulty will help the teacher see reading in relation to the broader emotional concerns the child may have.

In trying to determine how best to deal with these emotional concerns, it's important for educators to decide which ones are within the teacher's influence and which are not. The nature and demands of the classroom pressures placed upon the child are factors over which the teacher has a great deal of control. Peer group relationships are a reality that teachers have less control over. The child's problems may be related to the fact that s/he lives in a one-parent family; the teacher has no control over this situation. Thus, it becomes necessary to decide which factors can be circumvented and which compensated for in a school setting. This decision is necessary so that we don't use factors beyond our control as an avoidance strategy in facing our own responsibilities in helping children with attitude and behavior problems.

CONCLUSION

Learning is never devoid of emotion. There is an emotional component and affective dimension to the child's entire school experience. Since learning to read is such an important part of school life, the emotional effects of learning to read—or not learning to read—will be strong. For the child who acquires reading skills early, and continues to develop and improve these skills throughout the grades, learning to read will contribute to positive emotional ends. For the child who fails early and continues to falter in attempts at learning to read, the emotional effects are likely to be devastating. The child with negative attitudes will probably have more problems in learning to read than the child with more positive ones. Early school failure and the frustration it produces will start the child off with further negative attitudes that will often block further progress. It's a vicious cycle. In the sixth grader who can read only at the first- or second-grade level, the emotional effects are apparent.

Once again, the classroom teacher is a "center stage person" in the education of the child whose emotional and learning problems are closely related. All the out-of-class therapy in the world will do little good unless the child can learn to adapt his/her behavior to the demands of living and learning within a group. Whether emotional problems are the root cause or the direct result of learning problems, they must be dealt with by the teacher in the regular classroom. For children with attitude/behavior problems, the classroom is often the final proving ground.

Treating emotional problems and reading problems at the same time involves educational adaptations that take into account both the learning and the emotional needs of the child. Children with emotional problems have different learning styles and different areas of strength and weakness just as other children do. Assessment and adaptation to the child's learning abilities and disabilities are important while emotional issues are dealt with in the classroom.

The words most often used in describing the needs of a child with emotional problems are *acceptance, understanding, trust, appreciation, empathy, encouragement,* and *support.* Though all these positive human qualities are important, *instruction* is needed too, instruction that will provide for the emotional as well as the learning needs of the child.

Because attitude and behavior problems complicate the process of learning to read, children with these problems need a classroom reading program that is highly structured and individualized. Providing such a program is not easy. There are no panaceas or perfect solutions. Instruction requires time, patience, and careful planning. In addition to the cognitive demands of the task, such instruction takes into account the environmental forces that affect the accomplishment of the learning activities. And even after problems have been reduced, the child may require corrective and remedial work to make up for lost time.

This chapter has dealt largely with emotional and related problems that interfere with learning to read. But there's another side of the affective/reading issue as well. This is illustrated by Adam, a third grader. Following is the report of Adam's teacher:

> Adam is an excellent reader. His reading scores are well above grade level and his comprehension is excellent. He loves to read.
>
> Adam comes to school every day with books. He goes immediately to the reading corner and buries himself in his books. He is completely absorbed in his reading. Adam will not do math, or science, or social studies. He will not go out to recess. He has completely resisted my efforts to have him engage in group activities, even when these activities are centered around topics in the books Adam is reading. Adam just sits and reads all day.

Adam, too, had some attitude and behavior problems related to reading!

ACTIVITIES FOR PRESERVICE TEACHERS

1. The point was made in this chapter that reading per se may not be the major problem for many emotionally troubled children. Rather, the major problem may be the required interaction with an authoritative adult. Suggest alternatives to conventional classroom reading instruction for this type of child.

2. In this chapter, a number of general suggestions were made for helping build a positive self-concept through reading-related activities. Make a list of specific suggestions on how children's classroom reading experiences can be used to build their self-esteem. Plan one or two of these activities in detail, specifying provisions you would make to insure that the activity would have an image-building function for the children involved.

3. Investigate treatment strategies for helping emotionally/behaviorally dis-

ordered children (the psychodynamic model, behavior modification strategies, etc.). What specific instructional techniques for reading do these treatment strategies suggest?

4. Inappropriate instruction is often said to produce behavior problems in the classroom. If you saw a child "fooling around" during a reading lesson, what aspects of instruction might you examine in order to judge the appropriateness of the lesson for the child who is "acting up"?

5. Throughout this chapter, emotional problems and reading problems were directly related. Some children who read well may, however, still have attitude or behavior disorders. What do you think some of these problems might be? How might these difficulties influence the classroom performance of the good reader, and how might the problems be handled?

ACTIVITIES FOR IN-SERVICE TEACHERS

1. Whether reading problems are primarily the cause or the effect of emotional problems is debatable. Take a stand on the issue and state your position. Use examples from your own teaching experience to support the position you take. What implications does your position have for teaching reading in the classroom?

2. Attitude toward self, toward others, and toward reading were identified in this chapter as three important areas related to reading instruction. Identify a child in your class who has a reading and/or behavior problem and one who does not. Compare the attitudes of both children toward themselves, toward others, and toward reading. How are attitudes in each area related? What do the children say or do to indicate their attitudes? What can you do to help children begin to change some of their negative attitudes toward self, others, and learning to read?

3. Very often, "emotional problems" and "behavior problems" are treated under the same heading. What is the relationship between the two? From your experience, does a behavior problem always indicate an emotional problem? In what specific ways does inappropriate or maladaptive behavior interfere with learning to read?

4. Identify the bothersome behavior of a child whom you find particularly troublesome in your classroom. Be specific and objective in recording the behaviors that annoy you; for example, note specific comments like "S/he interrupted other children five times in the reading group this morning," rather than general sweeping statements like "S/he's always talking." Which behaviors bother you the most? Design a schedule of reinforcement

that you could institute in an attempt to change the child's behavior. How does reading fit into this schedule of reinforcement?

5. Make a list of people in the school who may serve as support or resource people to help you in teaching reading to children in your classroom with emotional problems. List the specific types of support or resource services that each person might provide.

NOTES

1. Helena H. Zolkos, "What Research Says About Emotional Factors in Retardation in Reading," *The Elementary School Journal* 52 (May 1951): 541–561.

2. Miles V. Zintz, *Corrective Reading*, 2d ed. (Dubuque, Iowa: Wm. C. Brown Publishing Co., 1972), p. 233.

3. George Kaluger and Clifford J. Koson, *Reading and Learning Disabilities* (Columbus: Charles E. Merrill Publishing Co., 1969), p. 26.

4. Janell Baker Lang, "Self-Concept and Reading Achievement—An Annotated Bibliography." *The Reading Teacher* 29 (May 1976): 787–793.

5. Eldon E. Ekwall, *Diagnosis and Remediation of the Disabled Reader* (Boston: Allyn & Bacon, 1976), p. 17.

6. Arthur W. Combs et al., *Perceiving, Behaving, Becoming: A New Focus for Education* (Washington, D.C.: Association for Supervision and Curriculum Development, 1962), p. 101.

7. Samuel A. Kirk, *Educating Exceptional Children*, 2d ed. (Boston: Houghton Mifflin, 1972), pp. 402–412.

8. Frank M. Hewett, *The Emotionally Disturbed Child in the Classroom* (Boston: Allyn & Bacon, 1968), pp. 3–43.

9. Virginia Mae Axline, "Nondirective Therapy for Poor Readers," *Journal of Counseling Psychology* 11 (March–April 1947): 61-69.

10. Ekwall, *Diagnosis and Remediation*, p. 28.

11. Viola Kantrowicz, "Bibliotherapy with Retarded Readers," *Journal of Reading* 11 (Dec. 1967): 205–211; Paul A. Whitty, "Meeting Developmental Needs Through Reading," *Education* 84 (April 1964): 451–457; Joan Hoagland, "Bibliotherapy: Aiding Children in Personality Development," *Elementary English* 49 (March 1972): 390–394; Eric Kimmel, "Can Children's Books Change Children's Values?" *Educational Leadership* 28 (Nov. 1970): 209–211.

12. Hewett, *Emotionally Disturbed Child*, pp. 219–222.

13. Kirk, *Educating Exceptional Children*, p. 409.

14. Guy L. Bond and Miles A. Tinker, *Reading Difficulties: Their Diagnosis and Correction*, 3rd ed. (Englewood Cliffs, N.J.: Prentice-Hall, 1973), p. 138.

15. Charles C. Dahlberg, Florence G. Roswell, and Jeanne Chall, "Psychotherapeutic Principles as Applied to Remedial Reading," *Elementary School Journal* 53 (Dec. 1952): 214.

REFERENCES

Alexander, J. Estill, and Filler, Ronald C. *Attitudes and Reading*. Newark, Del.: International Reading Assoc., 1976.

Ball, Samuel, ed. *Motivation in Education*. New York: Academic Press, 1977.

Dupont, Henry, ed. *Educating Emotionally Disturbed Children: Readings,* 2d ed. New York: Holt, Rinehart and Winston, 1975.

Ekwall, Eldon E., ed. *Psychological Factors in the Teaching of Reading*. Columbus: Charles E. Merrill Co., 1973.

Hewett, Frank M. *The Emotionally Disturbed Child in the Classroom*. Boston: Allyn and Bacon, 1968.

Long, Nicholas J., et al. *Conflict in the Classroom: The Education of Children with Problems,* 3rd ed. Belmont, Calif.: Wadsworth Publishing Co., 1976.

Quandt, Ivan J. *Teaching Reading: A Human Process*. Chicago: Rand McNally College Publishing Co., 1977.

Quandt, Ivan. *Self-Concept and Reading*. Newark, Del.: International Reading Association, 1972.

Robeck, Mildred C., and Wilson, John A.R. *Psychology of Reading: Foundations of Instruction*. New York: John Wiley and Sons, 1974.

9

Organizing and Managing Reading Instruction for the Special-Needs Child in the Regular Classroom

Preview

Organization refers to how children are grouped for instruction within the classroom. Various grouping patterns are appropriate for special-needs children: large groups, small groups based on different selection criteria, and individual learning situations. Management refers to the manipulation of time, space, materials, records, and other elements that directly affect reading instruction. At the heart of all organizational and management matters in the classroom are the children. While the mainstreaming of special-needs pupils into regular classrooms may extend the dimensions of organization and management, mainstreaming doesn't change the basic nature of the process that teachers have been concerned with for a long time.

The integration of the special-needs child into the regular classroom demands both instructional and organizational accommodations in the reading program. Ever since teachers have been faced with twenty-five or so children of unequal ability, they have been confronted with the task of organizing and managing instruction. The mainstreaming of special-needs children into the regular classroom, while it may add another dimension to organization and management, does not change the basic nature of the task.

There are a number of ways to organize a class for reading instruction. One obvious alternative is to have all children, row on row, follow along on the same page of the same reading book at the same time. However, this alternative violates most of what we know about sound instructional practice in reading. Another alternative is to have twenty-five children going in twenty-five different directions at twenty-five different speeds with twenty-five different pieces of reading material. Even though many teachers approach this in truly individualized reading programs, there are enormous possibilities for chaos and confusion; such an arrangement demands a skilled and highly organized teacher.

There is no single "best" approach to classroom organization and management. In any classroom, there needs to be a variety of individual, small-group and large-group (sometimes whole-class) learning activities, managed in such a way that children receive a balanced instructional program in reading.

ORGANIZATION

Organization refers to how children are grouped for instruction in reading within the classroom. Given a group of children who, apart from age, are vastly different from one another, this is a job that each teacher faces very early each school year.

Large-Group Instruction

In any classroom, the realities of school life and the nature of the curriculum are such that large-group or whole-class instruction will be appropriate at times, and the special-needs child needs to be a member of such instructional groups. These occasions arise when all the children can profit from the same instruction at the same time. Large-group or whole-class organization may be appropriate for the introduction of a new reading skill (like map reading or some aspects of dictionary use), for oral language and listening activities (like storytelling, discussion, book sharing, creative dramatics, choral speaking or choral reading, oral reporting), in shared audiovisual experiences (like viewing a film, filmstrip, or television program), for literature skills (like identifying simple plot elements in stories or determining characterization), for art activities (like making book posters), or for other reading-related instruction in areas of common need.

In planning for large groups in which special-needs children are included, there are a number of considerations for the teacher to keep in mind. The vocabulary and concepts in oral activities should be within the range of understanding of even the slowest learner. Similarly, printed material used in whole-class instruction (like material for choral reading) should be such that it can be read by all. Often, the teacher provides differentiated follow-up activities involving reading to reinforce or extend large-group instruction. For example, after a large-group discussion of current events, children of different reading abilities use different news sources, such as a daily newspaper, *My Weekly Reader,* scholastic publications, etc., to locate news items; or after seeing a filmstrip on Paul Revere, children use different materials, written at different levels, for follow-up work. These instances provide ideal opportunities for dicated stories that are part of a language experience approach to learning how to read.

Keeping the attention and involvement of all the children is often difficult. Every-pupil response techniques can be effective here. As the name indicates, these techniques involve each pupil in making a response to an instructional stimulus. In large-group situations, usually only a few children raise their hands to answer teacher questions, and only one child is called upon to give the answer. With every-pupil response techniques, each child responds to every question. For example, in activities designed to develop or reinforce auditory perceptual skills, the teacher says:

"Put up your *right* hand if the words you hear rhyme; put up your *left* hand if the words don't rhyme." (Here, the teacher may discover that some children don't know left from right, or that they don't understand the meaning of the word "rhyme.")

or

"Raise the YES card if the words I say start with the same sound; raise the NO card if they do not." (The children themselves can make their own cards for this type of activity.)

or

"Show me the letter you hear at the beginning of each word I say." (Again, the children themselves can make their own "letter cards," thus providing written reinforcement and purposeful handwriting practice.)

When every pupil in the group responds, the teacher can tell at a glance which children know the answer (or are developing the concept) and which do not. This is part of the ongoing diagnosis that characterizes effective instruction. The technique can be used to involve all children in small-group settings as well.

Large-group or whole-class instruction is appropriate for the child with special needs, because it is an essential part of the integration underlying the idea of mainstreaming. In large-group instructional situations, however, the teacher still needs to be aware of individual differences that exist within the group. A group of twenty children is not the same child twenty times; rather, it is twenty children "one time each." Thus, different parts of large-group instruction still need to be directed at individual children within the group, and differentiated follow-up is vital.

Small-Group Instruction

For a long time, teachers have divided their classes into smaller, more manageable organizational units for reading instruction. While these groups are most often formed on the basis of children's reading abilities, small groups are also formed according to children's skills needs, interests, and specific task assignments.

Ability grouping

The most common criterion for grouping children for reading instruction is the children's reading ability. Usually, three groups are formed (e.g., the Robins, the Bluebirds, and the Sparrows), with children of high, average, and low ability. The criteria used for placing children in these ability groups are usually their reading achievement test scores, their observed reading ability from an Informal Reading Inventory, and/or their reading performance in previous grades. While the teacher may divide the class into as few as two or as many as five or six ability groups, the major criterion remains the same, i.e., the child's ability to handle materials at different reading levels.

The intent of ability grouping is to gear materials and techniques as closely as possible to the reading level of the children. The teacher typically meets with each group separately every day, using materials (usually basal readers) at different levels. Instruction includes the range of skills necessary to read materials at the designated level. More often than not, all the children in any one group are instructed in basically the same way.

Although ability grouping is a means of providing manageable instruction that is more geared to children's reading levels, it is by no means a panacea. Bond and Tinker[1] present some figures on the normal range of reading ability that might be found in a typical classroom (see Figure 9.1). These figures alone indicate that even with a relatively homogeneous group, there remains a considerable range of reading abilities. At the fourth-grade level, for example, there is approximately a two-year spread in achievement scores of children in both the "high" and the "low" groups. The spread widens further along in the grades.

The effect of ability grouping on children's self-concepts is another concern. By being placed in the "low" group, less able children are constantly reminded of their reading deficiencies. This may be especially true for the special-needs child. At the other end of the spectrum, the pressure of trying to

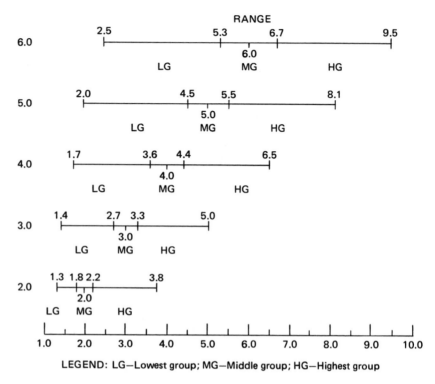

LEGEND: LG—Lowest group; MG—Middle group; HG—Highest group

(From Guy L. Bond, Miles A. Tinker, Reading Difficulties: Their Diagnosis and Correction, *3rd edition, © 1973, p. 51. Reprinted by permission of Prentice-Hall, Inc., Englewood Cliffs, New Jersey)*

Figure 9.1.   *Normal range of reading ability found in typical classrooms of grades two through six at the beginning of the school year.*

"keep up" with the rest of the Bluebirds can have a deleterious effect on the affective side of reading, even for the more capable readers in any class.

Lack of pupil mobility from group to group is a frequent critcism of this organizational pattern as well. Because criteria for grouping most often include last year's test scores and reading group placement, children are often placed in the same group year after year. The old cliché, "Once a Sparrow, always a Sparrow," too often applies. Once the groups are set, they're set in concrete. While there is usually more group-to-group mobility at the primary-grade levels than in the upper grades, pupil growth spurts or lags are too rarely taken into account. The particular danger for the special-needs child in this respect is that once diagnosed weaknesses are corrected, possibilites for placement in a higher ability group often prove to be, in practice, limited.

In a nationwide survey of reading practices, Austin and Morrison identified the three-group pattern as the most common classroom organizational arrangement, but their criticism of this pattern is strident. "Without an effort to adjust instructional techniques and without some provision for pupil mobility and flexibility . . . the organizational pattern serves as nothing more than an opiate lulling administrators and teachers into a sense of accomplishment and satisfaction which becomes, in fact, merely chimerical."[2]

Skills grouping

Another type of small-group organization in the classroom is skills grouping. Skills groups, as the name suggests, are formed on the basis of children's reading skills needs. Thus, regardless of their abilities, children may be grouped for specific instruction in skills like decoding initial consonant blends, identifying affixes, using an index, or any other subskill or reading. Once the skill has been mastered by the children, the group is usually disbanded.

Skills grouping is particularly appropriate for the comprehension aspects of learning how to read. No matter what the level of the materials or the ability of the children, comprehension is a dimension of reading instruction that cuts across levels. Children reading at the first-, third-, and fifth-grade levels, for example, still need help in determining main ideas, recalling details, seeing cause-effect relationships, and mastering other components of the comprehension process. Children can be grouped to work on these aspects of comprehension using a range of materials that correspond to their range of reading ability levels.

The concern has been expressed that slow learners and special-needs children typically need help in all areas of reading skills development, so these children would likely be found in every skills group the teacher forms. On the other hand, these are the children who need the most support and help from the teacher, and being a member of more than one skills group during the course of a week is a means of assuring this needed attention and instruction.

From a practical point of view, skills grouping requires constant, careful diagnosis to determine which pupils need help in which skills, and to ascertain when mastery of these skills has been achieved. Management systems (described later) have proven to be an enormous help in this regard. Skills grouping also requires a great deal of organization on the part of the teacher, because different children are meeting at different times to work on different skills. Nevertheless, it is a viable and workable grouping system in the classroom.

Other small-group patterns

Within the classroom, other small-group organizational arrangements are often used. Included are the following.

Interest groups

Children are grouped to work on topics of interest. For example, children may be grouped for reading and discussion on materials related to sports, hobbies, occupations, or other areas of common interest. This type of grouping is especially important for the special-needs child because, whatever the nature of his/her needs, the child often shares common interests with age-mates. Reading materials on interest-related topics can be found at different reading levels. For example, stories, poems, plays, and other reading selections on many topics can be garnered from books at different grade levels in a variety of basal programs, from magazines written for children, and from other sources of print. In addition to being a direct part of the reading instructional program in the classroom, interest groups are often effective in promoting outside reading.

Task groups Children are grouped to work on different aspects of a subject, often a curriculum-related topic. For example, if the class is studying the culture of another country, groups are formed to read and research different aspects of the culture: food, housing, transportation, recreation, and the like. This type of assignment naturally extends into oral and written reports. The special-needs child can be given a specific responsibility as a member of the group preparing and presenting the report.

Pupil teams Two or three children work together on specific reading-related tasks. For example, pupils of similar ability can be grouped for practice on sight words, for "word hunts" in the dictionary, for phonics games, or for other activities involving review and reinforcement. For the special-needs child,

Pupil team learning is an effective technique for developing learning and socialization skills in the classroom. (Photo by John A Malnati)

being a member of a pupil team provides opportunities for intensive practice and a chance to work with another child on a one-to-one basis. Cross-age tutoring (described earlier) is often an effective pupil team arrangement.

Interest groups, task groups, and pupil teams are usually ad hoc; that is, they are formed for a specific purpose and disbanded after the purpose has been accomplished. However, if group members are working well together, and if interest and motivation remain high, there is no reason why the groups can't be maintained on a long-term basis.

The various types of small-group organizational patterns described in this section are certainly not mutually exclusive. In fact, they complement one another. The teacher can set up a workable arrangement in which the initial criterion for placing special-needs children in a reading group is their level of reading achievement. Provision can be made for a strong skill development component by means of skills groups, with opportunities for pupil team practice on the skills being taught. In addition, the special-needs child can be part of interest groups and other ad hoc groups related to ongoing classroom activities. This is part of the organizational flexibility that characterizes effective grouping practices.

Apart from instructional considerations, involvement in small instructional groups is particularly important for the special-needs child in the regular classroom. True integration involves a lot more than mere physical placement. Special-needs children ought to have the social contact and interaction with peers that working in groups involves. The learning process is by no means a one-way operation. So-called "regular" children can often learn much (both academically and socially) from working in the classroom with a child with special needs.

More important than the grouping arrangements themselves is the type of instruction carried on within groups. Even after groups have been organized, instruction should be delivered with a constant awareness of children's needs. There also need to be plenty of provisions for individual work in the classroom.

Individualized Patterns

The whole purpose of grouping is to provide a greater measure of individualization in the reading instruction of children. Even as they participate in a variety of small groups, children need activities that are individual and/or individualized. There's a difference between the two terms. Individual activities are those carried out by pupils on their own, as, for example, when children do workbook exercises related to a basal story they have read in a reading group. In individual activities, children work independently on teacher-directed, group-related tasks. Individualized activities are those prescribed for the child him/herself according to the individual child's interests or needs, as, for example, when a child is working by him/herself on a taped phonics exercise designed to help him/her distinguish between long and short vowels in words. This is the type of personalized activity that is typically part of an individualized reading program.

Individualized reading

Individualized reading is an approach that has been thoroughly described,[3] and its effects have been well documented.[4] The literature of the early 1960s swelled with references on the topic, and individualized reading has been a goal of many teachers ever since. The term "individualized reading" is open to many interpretations; there are probably as many definitions as there are teachers managing individualized reading programs. In essence, the approach is characterized by three distinct features:

- *self-selection of reading material.* A large selection of reading material from different sources is made available in the classroom, and children choose their reading material according to their ability levels and interests.

- *pupil-teacher conferences.* Individual conferences are scheduled frequently, during which the teacher listens to the child read, checks on comprehension, notes progress and deficiencies in word attack skills, and guides the child in the selection of further reading material.

- *skills grouping.* While most skills teaching takes place during individual conference time and through follow-up individualized activities, there are times when groups are formed. These groups are usually formed on the basis of skills needs, however, and not on the more conventional ability basis.

A successful individualized program demands a knowledgeable and skillful teacher who has an encyclopedic knowledge of books, a thorough familiarity with his/her pupils, a sound knowledge of how to teach reading, and the ability to put all this together in an organized way. Even with these demands, the individualized approach provides a workable classroom arrangement that gives teachers a means of approaching the long-sought goal of meeting the individual needs of pupils in the classroom.

The special-needs child may (depending on the nature of his/her needs) have problems fitting into the organizational pattern of a totally individualized reading program. Special-needs children may require more direction and structure than a fully individualized approach to reading provides. Individualized reading demands a great deal of self-direction and the ability to work independently for long periods of time. For the special-needs child, adjusting instruction to his/her reading level and specific skills needs, providing a program designed to match his/her learning style, and making classroom accommodations that will facilitate learning, are important dimensions of individualization, even in classrooms where the formal criteria for an "individualized reading program" are not met. Without accepting the principles and practices of individualized reading lock, stock, and barrel, the teacher who provides for the special needs of the child is, in fact, individualizing reading instruction in the classroom.

Individual activities

Individual activities are not unique to individualized reading. In most classrooms, children are expected to work on their own much of the time in completing skill development exercises, in using supplementary materials typically found in popular reading "kits," in independent reading and research projects, and in other learning activities. All the children are working on a similar assignment, but each is doing it on his/her own.

In planning individual activities for the special-needs child, several considerations must be taken into account. It's important that learning tasks be consistent with the child's ability to complete them. Being asked to engage in activities that are consistently too difficult can have a devastating effect on pupils, especially when they are expected to complete these tasks without direct help and supervision.

Other provisions must be made to meet children's specific needs. For example, lines on dittoed worksheets should be sharp and clear for children with visual problems. The child with auditory memory deficits may need a "buddy" from whom s/he can seek direction, because teacher directions given at the beginning of an independent work period are often quickly forgotten. The child with language disorders may require a strong verbal backup for tasks that are supposed to be completed independently. Contracting or a separate work space may be needed for children who have trouble working on their own assignment while other children are working around them. For children who have difficulty in maintaining attention, a kitchen timer and/or provision for giving the child one job at a time, instead of a whole series of jobs, may be necessary to help him/her accomplish independent activities. These types of accommodations, which have been suggested throughout the preceding chapters of this book, are what make an individually oriented organizational system run smoothly in the classroom.

Two questions are important in planning individual activities for the child:

1. Is the pupil self-directed; i.e., can s/he see a task through to completion with a minimum amount of intervention? If the answer is "No," then some degree of supervision and monitoring will be necessary.
2. Can the child read; i.e., does s/he have the ability to understand directions for the task and the ability to deal with other printed material that may be involved? If the answer is "No," then alternative means of presentation will need to be used.

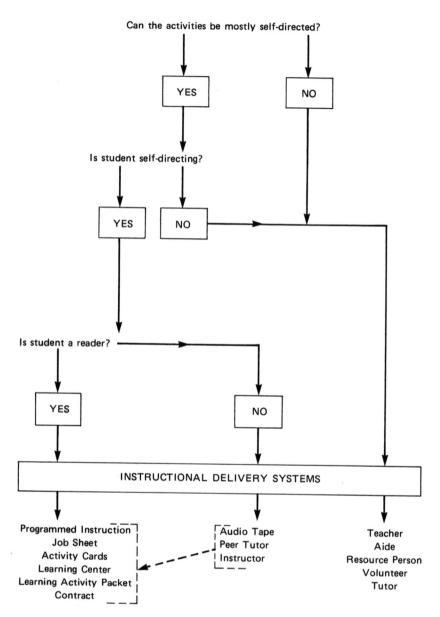

ACTIVITY OPTIONS FOR ACHIEVING OBJECTIVES

Can the activities be mostly self-directed?

YES   NO

Is student self-directing?

YES   NO

Is student a reader?

YES   NO

INSTRUCTIONAL DELIVERY SYSTEMS

Programmed Instruction   Audio Tape   Teacher
Job Sheet   Peer Tutor   Aide
Activity Cards   Instructor   Resource Person
Learning Center   Volunteer
Learning Activity Packet   Tutor
Contract

(From Bently, Glee and Smith, Pamela, Instructional Management Data Bank Guide,
*Austin, Texas: Teacher Training Program, Education Service Center, Region XIII,
1975, pp. 28–29)*

Figure 9.2   Managing and directing instruction

A useful model to follow in planning individual activities is shown in Figure 9.2. If the child is self-directed and can read, there are a number of alternative formats for presenting independent activities.

Classroom organizational patterns that provide for the uniqueness of individual children are a concern of all teachers. Providing for the special-needs child in the regular classroom may, however, require additional dimensions to the teacher's organizational planning.

Other Organizational Patterns

Other types of schoolwide organizational patterns are appropriate for consideration in planning reading instruction for the special-needs child. Included are the following.

Departmentalization

Departmentalization is a teacher-oriented organizational arrangement that is sometimes used in the upper elementary grades. In a departmentalized system, different teachers work in their academic specialty areas (science, social studies, math, language) in subject matter periods throughout the day. In the lower grades, a modified version of this arrangement is sometimes found, as when two second-grade teachers "trade" classes, so that one teaches all the math and the other teaches all the reading. Though this arrangement may offer children the benefit of teachers with particular expertise and interest in content areas of the curriculum, caution is required so that the special needs of the child do not get lost in concern for the subject matter being taught. Reading is a subject that cuts across all parts of the curriculum, and helping the special-needs child develop reading skills in content areas should be a concern of all teachers in a departmentalized pattern.

Team teaching

Teachers with different specialties work together in providing more coordinated instructional efforts with groups of children. Where such an arrangement is used, each member of the team ought to be aware of the special-needs child, to see how reading and related needs can best be met during the entire school day. Team teaching is characterized by close planning, and a focus of this planning effort should be the reinforcement and extension of learning for the special-needs child from one period of the day to another.

Interclass or intraclass grouping

Classes are combined for instruction. Interclass grouping occurs when classes at different grade levels are combined, and grade level designations are often dropped to constitute *ungraded units*. Intraclass grouping involves the combining of two or more classes at the same grade level within the school building. For the special-needs child, interclass or intraclass grouping usually affords greater opportunities for continuous progress, as long as this progress is carefully planned and monitored within the larger group.

Open education

Open education is an activity-centered environment in which children are more free to engage in interest-related learning activities. Open education achieved a large measure of popularity in the late 1960s and early 1970s when lots of schools climbed on the bandwagon to try the "open road." While many children thrive on the freedom of an open classroom, special-needs children typically need more structure and direction than an open environment usually provides. When an entire school building adopts the philosophy of "openness," important options available for special-needs children may be lost. Options for the most appropriate placement of the special-needs child need to be maintained in any school.

Each of these organizational patterns—departmentalization, team teaching, intraclass or interclass grouping, open education—represents a different philosophy or approach to education. Each has its own distinct advantages and disadvantages and, in practice, can represent the best or the worst of educational arrangements. And even in the environments in which these patterns are used, there remains a need for a balance of large-group, small-group, and individualized instruction for the special-needs child.

MANAGEMENT

Because effective classroom organization involves a combination of large-group, small-group, and individual learning activities, managing the learning environment is a crucial dimension in the instructional process. Management involves manipulating or orchestrating the variables of time, space, materials, records, and (most importantly) children. While administrative and related constraints (i.e., the number of children in the class, the size of the room, materials available, school scheduling, and the like) may place the regulation of some of these variables beyond the direct control of the classroom teacher, these are the major factors that must be considered in setting up and running a reading program for the special-needs child in the regular classroom.

Time

There's never enough of it! Yet it's a *very* important part of reading instruction for children. In reviewing research and descriptive reports on effective reading programs, Wolf[5] concluded that ". . . one of the most effective tools for teaching reading may be the simplest and most ignored: time . . . [that] the more time spent on reading (whatever the method), the better the students did," and that time consistently emerged as a crucial dimension of successful reading instruction—more crucial, perhaps, than the program or methods used.

WEEKLY SCHEDULE OF READING INSTRUCTION FOR A GROUP

	Monday	Tuesday	Wednesday	Thursday	Friday
9:00 – 9:15	Skills Group on Comprehension/Main Idea (T)	Directed Reading Lesson, Basal Reader (T)	Skills Group on Oral Reading; Reading the play "The Elves and the Shoemaker." (T)	Directed Reading Lesson, Basal Reader (T)	Skills Group on Inflectional Suffixes (T)
9:15 – 9:25	Follow-up independent work with Barnell Loft program	Follow-up independent work with basal workbook	Oral reading practice with tape recorder	Free reading activity	Pupil team practice with suffixes
9:25 – 9:45	Work with specialist	Work with specialist	Work with specialist	Work with specialist	Work with specialist
9:45 – 10:00	Free reading activity	Reading skills activity with programmed materials	Reading the play "The Elves and the Shoemaker" for the entire class (T)	Follow-up independent work with basal workbook	Booksharing or story-time with entire class (T)
10:00 – 10:15	Work in Reading Skills Center on phonics	Free reading activity		Work in Reading Skills Center on phonics	

(T) = Teacher

Figure 9.3   Suggested schedule.

Given five or six hours in a school day, the efficient use of time for reading instruction becomes a major concern. The available time must be scheduled in such a way that the instructional needs of each child will be met, and that a variety of reading experiences will provide a balanced reading program for the special-needs child.

The schedule in Figure 9.3 is suggested as a tentative model that might be used for planning reading instruction for a group of six or eight children during the course of a school week. This schedule, like any schedule the teacher plans, is certainly not inflexible. It is designed to provide for a variety of reading activities and can be adapted in a number of ways. Time blocks may need to be shortened or expanded, depending on the nature of the activity and/or the ability of the children to work on their own. Time is provided for teacher-directed instruction, independent work, and free reading activities. If the reading abilities of the children are not developed to the point where they can engage independently in free reading, other provisions can be made; for example, by using filmstrips or tapes of popular children's books, or by having an upper-grade pupil read stories to small groups. Depending on the teacher's reliance on a structured basal program, the balance of skills groups and directed reading lessons in ability groups may need to be adjusted. In short, the schedule is subject to as many changes as the teacher finds necessary or advantageous, according to his/her own teaching style and/or other conditions.

Because special resource services are often provided for special-needs children in the classroom, how the specialist fits into the schedule is an important consideration. The amount of time the specialist is available to work in the classroom will determine what kinds of in-class support services can be provided. Work with the specialist can consist of remediation of weak skills areas, or it can be an extension of work the teacher prescribes from the reading group. There may be occasions when the specialist will work with only one or two children from a group, and other occasions when s/he will work with larger numbers of children. While the teacher is working with one group, the specialist may be working with children who need extra help and support. If specialist services are not available to the classroom teacher, an aide, volunteer tutor, or other instructional assistant working under the teacher's direction, can provide a set of extra expert hands in the classroom. The use of the specialist and paraprofessional services that may be available to the classroom teacher is described in the next chapter.

In the primary grades, more time is usually devoted to reading instruction, so additional time can be spent in reading-related activities. But even in the upper grades, when time for formal reading instruction is usually reduced, reading skills development can be made a direct part of science, social studies, and other areas of the curriculum for the special-needs child. Reading is necessarily part of all areas of the curriculum at all grade levels. Also, integrating other components of the language arts—listening, spelling, handwriting, composition, literature, oral language development—is a direct way of supporting and extending reading instruction.

The schedule of the special-needs child should be planned so that maximum time is provided for reading experiences throughout the school day. This may involve setting priorities and making certain compromises. Children with learning problems typically need more time for reading instruction than their more able classmates. These children may need to miss science or social studies to receive the extra reading help they need. Here is where priorities and compromises may be necessary, and a rotating schedule should be set up so that the child does not lose preferred activities all the time. Recess, lunch, and gym should remain sacrosanct!

In the final analysis, the amount of time available for reading instruction is finite. This time should be scheduled and managed in such a way that the special-needs child receives maximum reading experiences during the school day. Economy and efficiency are the crucial qualities in the time dimension of classroom management.

Space

The arrangement of space is another practical classroom management matter. Space needs to be arranged so that a variety of reading-related learning activities can be carried out by the special-needs child.

The environment of the classroom should be lively and attractive. Displays documenting the results of pupils' learning should be everywhere. Hopefully, these displays will extend beyond lists of spelling words and copies of math worksheets done perfectly with a "happy-faced sticker" at the top, and will include art work, stories and poems the children have written, and other creative products that reflect the results of the children's learning experiences. A lively classroom environment usually includes plants, pictures, charts, pets, books, and other objects that can be used as a focus for discussion, to stimulate interest, and to promote learning. Since children spend hundreds of hours of their lives in a classroom, we owe it to them to make the environment as pleasant as possible.

Flexible grouping demands the flexible arrangement and use of space. In addition to the necessary conventional arrangement of desks and chairs, learning areas can be set up to provide for flexibility and to facilitate variety in reading instructional activities. In any classroom, these learning areas might include:

- *a reading skills center,* with games, machines, activity cards, programmed materials, supplementary skill-building materials, and other material that children can use in specific skill-related tasks.

- *a listening station*, with tape recorders, a record player, tapes, records, and appropriate backup printed materials to provide practice in listening comprehension and opportunities for children to listen to literature.

- *a writer's corner*, with story-starters and other devices that can be used as springboards to writing, commercially published writing programs, dictionaries, and other aids to writing. If available, a typewriter or two might be placed here. Writing models should be displayed, and individual files of children's writing can be housed here as well.
- *a media center*, containing a filmstrip projector, film loop projector, and other audiovisual devices for children to use.
- *interest centers,* for displays of science material (like rocks, plants, or magnets) or other material related to reading and other curricular interests.
- *individual reading-study carrels,* where children who need the separation can go for independent work.
- *a reading corner*, with a rug fragment on the floor and a couple of comfortable chairs or large pillows on which children can relax while they enjoy independent or free reading. Here is where the classroom library might be located. Bulletin boards with book jackets, children's book reports, and other interest-provoking material can be designed and arranged by the children for this area.

Obviously, the way the teacher arranges the learning environment will depend on the number of children in the class, whether the classroom walls are fixed or moveable, the amount of floor space available, the proportion of wall-to-window area in the room, the amount of material and equipment available, the type of furniture in the room, and the like. The diagram in Figure 9.4 is a suggestion of how classroom space can be used for different purposes.

Arranging this type of learning environment takes ingenuity and creativity on the teacher's part. It involves the imaginative arrangement of bookcases, file cabinets, portable dividers, and maybe a little "cardboard carpentry." One teacher, for example, joined two huge cardboard cartons (the type that refrigerators are shipped in) as the media center in her classroom. Also, rules should be established for the use of learning centers. For example, the number of children allowed in a particular center at any given time may need to be limited. Since centers are designed as independent learning areas, children will require specific instruction in the use of each area. Provision for independent work can be built in by doing such things as color-coding the buttons on the tape recorders with tape (red for *stop*, green for *go,* etc.) and by making skill-building materials self-correcting by having answer keys accessible. Here is where children learn to assume a measure of responsibility and self-direction in their own learning. Centers should be located in the room so that "quiet areas" and "noisy areas" will be far enough apart. Having the interest center next to the reading corner, for example, is bound to be distracting for children engaged in free reading. Provision should be made for rotating children through these learning centers as part of the classroom schedule.

The writer's corner—with displays to stimulate writing, space to write, and a place for files of children's writing—is an important learning area in the classroom. (Photo by John A. Malnati)

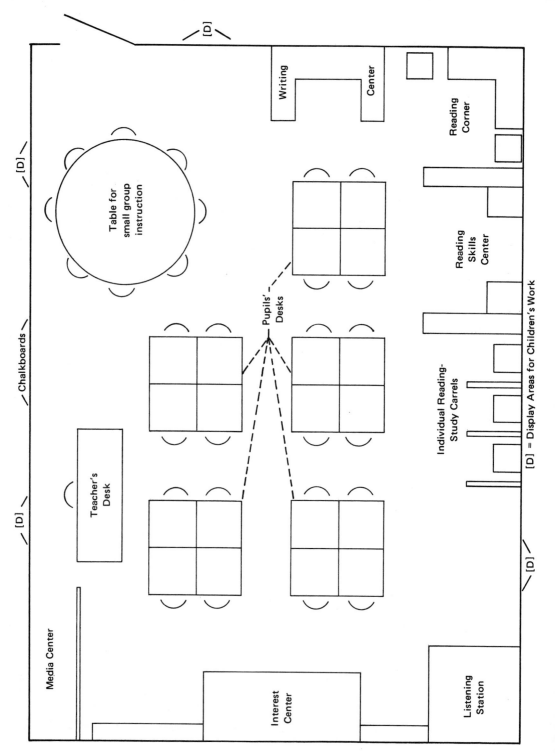

Figure 9.4   Classroom design.

The special-needs child should be given full access to all learning centers the teacher establishes. As needs become apparent, the child should be scheduled to use the appropriate learning center—either individually, as a member of a pupil team, or in a small group—according to his/her instructional needs. The learning centers could also be used for the child's work with the specialist, volunteer tutor, or instructional aide in the classroom.

Learning centers are more than storage areas for supplies and equipment. Rather, they should be *activity* areas, places where children can go for the specific purpose of developing and reinforcing reading-related skills. Work begun in reading groups and in whole-class activities can be carried over into learning centers all day long.

Materials

Ever since the days of the New England *Primer*, materials have been a dominant force in the teaching of reading. Materials are important because they provide the vehicles by which children are taught to read. Materials can even dictate the approach used in teaching reading. For example, the adoption and exclusive use of a linguistic series dictates that the child will learn to read using a linguistic approach. When children have difficulty with this approach, it promotes failure and can create special needs for the child. In some instances, there's a false expectation that the materials will do the teaching. We "plug children in" to a particular published program and expect the materials to do the teaching. Despite their unquestioned importance, materials are merely tools of the trade in reading instruction. Like any tools, they are only as good as the craftsperson who uses them. It's the teacher, not the materials, who does the teaching.

The plethora of materials available for reading instruction is mind-boggling. A balanced and flexible reading program requires balance and flexibility in the choice and use of materials. Among the types of materials used in reading instruction for the special-needs child in the classroom are basal materials, supplementary materials, audiovisual materials, games, and homemade materials.

Basal materials

Basal readers are the main staple of reading instruction in most classrooms. The basal offers a measure of coordination and security through a carefully designed scope and sequence of basic reading skills. In many classrooms, a multibasal or cobasal is used; that is, two or more basal programs are used with different groups. An alternative program is often appropriate for the special-needs child. In considering a cobasal series, however, it's important to examine the approach used within the program. To abandon one phonics or look-say or linguistic series for another of the same type is analogous to saying, "The child is allergic to roast beef, so we'll give him a steak." Alternative programs should be examined with an eye to how the child learns best.

Supplementary materials

While basal programs provide for the development of a range of basic skills, not all children develop the necessary skills by using the basal alone. Therefore, supplementary materials are essential ingredients to reading instruction in the classroom. These include materials designed to teach particular skills—e.g., the *Specific Skills Series* (Barnell Loft), which deals extensively with comprehension, or the *Phonics We Use Series* (Lyons and Carnahan), which deals with decoding skills; materials that provide additional reading matter without a specific skills focus—e.g., *The Sounds of Language Series* (Holt, Rinehart and Winston) or a series of high-interest, low-vocabulary readers; and materials that combine the two, with short reading selections followed by skill development exercises throughout—like the *Reader's Digest Skill Builders* (Reader's Digest Educational Service) or the popular reading kits published by SRA and other companies. For the special-needs child, the use of supplementary materials can be particularly important, because the child typically needs more practice than the basal provides. For special-needs children, supplementary programs like *Sound Order Sense* (Follett) or *The Frostig Program for the Development of Visual Perception* (Frostig) are important in improving essential perceptual/reading skills that are particularly weak.

Audiovisual materials

Traditionally, reading has been viewed as a book-oriented, rather than audiovisual, activity. Yet, reading is a process that combines sight and sound, and plenty of mediated materials designed to build reading skills are becoming available. Auditory media (especially tape recorders) are often effective devices for providing phonics instruction and giving children opportunities to develop and practice listening comprehension skills. Visual media (e.g., different types of projectors) provide opportunities for a variety of "screen-reading" activities in the classroom. Audiovisual media—which combine a visual image with accompanying auditory input—can be used in developing a range of skills that are part of the act of reading.[6] For example, the *Language Master* (Bell and Howell) can be used to give children extra practice in memorizing sight vocabulary words, or a sound-filmstrip presentation of a book that children might be reading can build both interest and background as an aid to comprehension. Especially important as audiovisual devices for the special-needs child are programmed instructional materials, since they present instruction in small frames and the materials can be used extensively for independent practice. Machines themselves are often motivating and, with the careful selection of software for developing specific reading skills, they can be effective means of delivering instruction for the special-needs child in the classroom.

Games

Instructional games can also be effective devices for the development and reinforcement of basic reading skills. Games add a positive motivational dimension to learning for the special-needs child, as long as the child has a

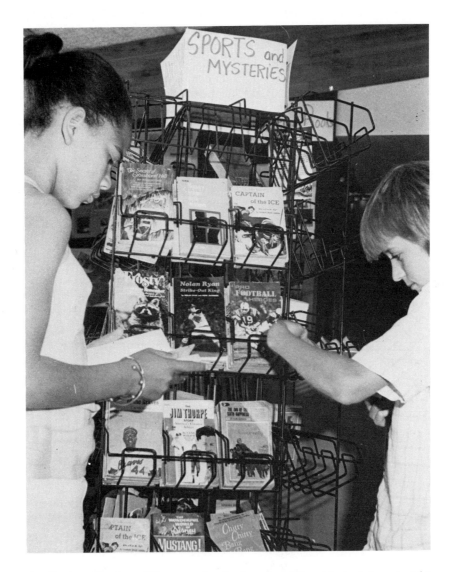

A collection of books at different reading levels and on different topics is important for a balanced reading instructional program. (Photo by John A. Malnati)

fair chance to win and the objective remains reading skills improvement and not just winning the game. Commercially produced reading games abound in the marketplace, and there is a wealth of books available to supply ideas for teacher-made games in reading; e.g., *Reading With A Smile: 90 Reading Games That Work* (Acropolis Books); *Special Kids' Stuff: High Interest, Low*

Vocabulary Reading and Language Skills Activities (Incentive Publications); and *Rescue: A Handbook of Remedial Reading Techniques for the Classroom Teacher* (Educational Services, Inc.). These games can be part of the reading skills center in any classroom.

*Homemade
materials*

There are times in every teacher's life when s/he can't find the right worksheet or filmstrip or game or other piece of instructional material at just the right time. This is when teacher-made materials are required. Homemade materials offer one overwhelming advantage over commercially produced products: they are made for the child in light of his/her individual needs. What they lack in commercial polish, they more than make up for in personalization. With time (and perhaps a little resource support), the teacher can make a variety of materials to meet every skills need of the special-needs child in the classroom. A letter to parents requesting old pieces of wood or metal, buttons, formica or styrofoam scraps, plastic containers, yarn, and other odds and ends can produce a fine supply of "recyclable junk" that can be used in making materials.

The choice of materials for reading instruction is almost limitless. Choosing the right material for the child in terms of his/her level of reading ability and skills needs, and scheduling the use of these materials, make up a major part of managing reading instruction in the classroom.

Record Keeping

Efficient classroom management requires efficient record keeping; i.e., maintaining ongoing accounts of children's learning as a continuous basis for planning reading instruction. If diagnosis is as important a part of the teaching process as it should be, then continuous records of needs and mastery should be kept. Two types of records on children are appropriate: group and individual records.

Group records

Group records can be kept on a class chart or checklist similar to the model suggested in Figure 9.5. Compiling such a record sheet not only provides an ongoing guide in forming skills groups and prescribing practice activities; it also heightens the teacher's general awareness of children's individual skills needs within a reading group. Along the top of the chart, the teacher can include whatever items are appropriate for different aspects of reading instruction: readiness factors; phonics (with specific elements identified); structural analysis (with particular prefixes and suffixes listed); word recognition (with sight words grouped on numbered lists for mastery); comprehension (with different components identified, such as main idea, sequencing, and other factors) oral reading habits (with specific aspects noted, like insertions, repetitions, and disregard for punctuation); dictionary and study skills; elements of reading maps and charts; or anything else is the focus of the

Basic Reading Skills

Children's Names	Standardized Test Scores			IRI Instr. Level	Initial Consonants	Short Vowel Sounds	Consonant Blends	Consonant Digraphs	Long Vowel Sounds	Sight Words	Inflectional Suffixes	Derivational Suffixes	Comments
	Vocabulary	Comprehension	Total										
Alan Bailey	2.3	1.9	2.2	2nd	✓	✓	X	X	X	X	X		Good progress being made. Needs help on short "u".
Cavot Davis	3.8	3.4	3.6	4th	✓	✓	✓	X	✓	✓	✓		Is in independent program.
Edward Foley	1.4	2.0	1.6	1st	✓	X	O	O	X	X	O		Uses context well. Needs basic decoding practice.
Gina Hardin	3.2	1.8	2.4	2nd	✓	✓	X	✓	✓	✓	X		Decoding skills are strong. Needs help in comprehension.
Wm. Xenkas	3.1	2.8	2.9	3rd	✓	✓	X	X	X	✓	X		Has particular trouble with blends and digraphs.
Yetta Zack	1.2	1.4	1.3	P	✓	X	O	O	O	O	O		Yetta still needs basic perceptual skill development.

O = doesn't know   X = needs practice   ✓ = has mastered

Figure 9.5   Group diagnostic chart.

teacher's instruction. The coding system should be marked in pencil, because these records are constantly subject to change as skills are mastered. Charts like these provide a running account of a group's progress in basic reading skills areas.

Individual records

Individual records are also usually maintained. These provide a cumulative account of the child's school experience. They normally contain "vital statistics" on the child (age, grade, and other biographic information), test scores (IQ, reading achievement, etc.), the results of diagnostic assessments, records of work done in previous years, and related information about the child. These records can also include informal (but useful) anecdotal observations, a list of completed contracts, samples of the child's work, and other pertinent material. Often, two sets of individual records can be kept: one in the school office with cumulative data, and one in the classroom for the teacher's ready reference.

Federal Law 94–142, legislation that is having a national impact on the education of special-needs children, makes specific provisions for an Individualized Educational Program (IEP) for each child receiving special services. The IEP requires that schools conduct a full assessment of the child's needs and develop specific instructional objectives, along with special services the child should receive. This legislation has particular implications for classroom teachers, as the law requires that the education of the special-needs child be conducted in the "least restrictive educational setting," i.e., as close as possible to the regular educational program, but with appropriate support services available. The Individualized Educational Programs (IEP's) which provide an instructional blueprint and timetable for teachers, specialists, and parents alike, will become an important part of the records of special-needs children. A sample of what an IEP might look like is contained in the instructional plan in Appendix A.

In compiling individual records on children, it's important to guard against filing prejudical information—i.e., information that will have negative short- or long-term effects on the child. Material recorded should be such that it will be helpful in planning effective instruction and in reporting progress. Recent federal legislation related to privacy and openness of records is aimed at protecting children (as well as adults) in this respect.

For the purpose of planning reading instruction, it's often helpful to include a "reading diagnostic profile" in the child's individual records. A profile such as that in Figure 9.6 presents areas of strengths and deficits at a glance. Most formal diagnostic reading batteries contain subtests that provide information to allow the teacher to make this type of profile on a child. Even when this information is gathered on the basis of different tests (which were normed on different populations) or informal measures (which lack statistical validity and reliability), this type of profile does present a rough and general picture of the child's "highs and lows" in his/her reading skills development and reading skills needs.

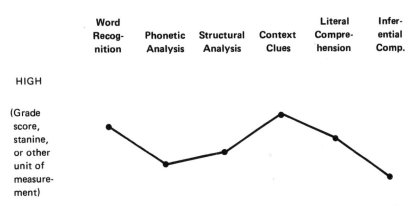

| | Word Recognition | Phonetic Analysis | Structural Analysis | Context Clues | Literal Comprehension | Inferential Comp. |

HIGH

(Grade
score,
stanine,
or other
unit of
measure-
ment)

Figure 9.6   *Reading diagnostic profile.*

Keeping group and individual records on children is an important part of classroom management, but teachers ought to exercise caution not to become so bogged down in record keeping that it takes time away from working with children. With formal and informal assessment, the alert teacher will be able to gather a mountain of information about the special-needs child. The record-keeping system established by the teacher should be efficient; that is, only useful information should be recorded, and this information should be the basis of making instructional plans for the child. It makes little sense to gather data that will then gather dust.

Management systems

Management systems facilitate the record-keeping function. A management system is a commercially prepared program that carefully monitors children's skills development in reading. Major program components of management systems are:

1. a sequentially ordered set of behavioral objectives for the various reading skills monitored by the system;
2. a set of subtests (or a set of test items) with one or more items designed to measure each objective;
3. a rule or set of rules for deciding what level of achievement constitutes mastery of each objective;
4. a resource file listing specific workbook pages, practice exercises, games or kits, and (hopefully) teaching strategies that

teachers can use to provide instruction and practice for children who have failed to attain mastery of specific objectives;

5. a method of reporting to teachers which students have or have not mastered which skills. [7]

In most management systems, lists of skills objectives number in the hundreds. The criterion-referenced tests used to measure mastery are tied directly to each objective, and a criterion of 80 or 90 percent is set for mastery. Basal and supplementary reading materials are cross-referenced to skills in the system, so that teachers have at their fingertips a list of materials that can be used in helping children strengthen weak skills areas. Some management systems provide teachers with a computer printout that identifies each child's strengths and weaknesses and indicates which children should be in which skills group. Although recent editions of some basal reading series include a management systems component, most management systems are produced independently of a particular basal program.

Management systems aim at insuring systematic and sequential instruction by very specifically measuring each child's level of skills mastery or proficiency. They are designed to help the teacher diagnose more precisely and to provide an objective instrument for assessing and reporting pupil progress.

However, management systems have not been without their share of criticisms, which include: 1) the "psycholinguistic naivete" in overfragmenting and attempting to sequence reading skills; 2) the "assembly line" approach to a process as complex as reading; 3) the elevation of skills over reading interests; 4) lack of documentation regarding the validity of the instruments; and 5) an implied overconfidence in the notion of mastery. [8] More practical concerns are the expense involved and the time-consuming demands required for formal testing.

What the teacher does with the information generated through a management system is crucial. Detailed printouts of test results and the suggested composition of skills groups do no good when they are buried in the bottom right-hand desk drawer along with the dust rags and curriculum guides. Management systems produce data on which a classroom program can be based and activated.

Putting such a program into action may require the help and support of the reading specialist. The reading specialist maintains a schoolwide perspective that extends beyond the walls of a particular classroom. S/he is often the one who should take the initiative to see that the data generated by a management system are implemented in the classroom by providing the teacher with help and suggestions on how the results can best be used. Management system data can also be a basis of instruction planned and carried out by the reading specialist and by other special-services personnel who work with the special-needs child.

A LIST OF MANAGEMENT SYSTEMS IN READING

Telar Reading/Language Program	Edits Publishing P.O. Box 7234 San Diego, Calif. 92107
Power Reading Management System	BFA Educational Media 2211 Michigan Ave. Dept. 3106 P.O. Box 1795 Santa Monica, Calif. 90406
Ransom Reading Management	Addison-Wesley 2725 San Hill Rd. Menlo Park, Calif. 94025
Diagnostic/Prescriptive Developmental Reading	Paul S. Amidon & Associates 1966 Benson Ave. St. Paul, Minn. 55116
Croft System	Croft, Inc. P.O. Box 15 Old Greenwich, Conn. 06870
Fountain Valley	Zweig Associates 20800 Beach Blvd. Huntington Beach, Calif. 92648
ICRT	Educational Progress P.O. Box 45663 Tulsa, Okla. 74145
Hoffman	Hoffman Ed. Systems 4423 Arden Drive El Monte, Calif. 91734
Individual Pupil Monitoring	Houghton Mifflin 1 Beacon Street Boston, Mass. 02107
Wisconsin Design	NCS Educational Systems Division 4401 West 76 St. Minneapolis, Minn. 55434

Despite the criticisms and concerns surrounding management systems, these devices have been a welcome innovation in reading instruction for many teachers in recent years. Management systems are by no means the be-all-and-end-all of diagnosis and instruction, but they are available to help teachers deal more effectively with the special-needs child in the regular classroom.

At Last, The Children

At the heart of all organization and management matters—the grouping and scheduling, the arrangement of furniture and selection of material, the record keeping and everything else that goes into arranging and operating a learning environment—are the children. They are the ones that arrangements are made for, and the success of what we do in schools has to be judged in terms of how well it meets the needs of the children.

Merely grouping children for reading according to their abilities or skills needs or interests is of little use unless the placement results in growth of the child. The special-needs child requires a maximum amount of time for reading-related experiences. Special provisions must be made for children unfamiliar with working in a learning center environment. While the ultimate aim of this environment is self-directed learning, self-direction cannot be the starting point. Materials for reading instruction should be chosen as much as possible according to children's abilities, needs, and interests, and children shouldn't be forced to conform in a procrustean adjustment to any reading program. Finally, records kept on children should be used for planning instruction to meet their needs.

In sum, the child is the central concern in any decision made as part of the organization and management of reading instruction in the classroom.

CONCLUSION

Not long ago, a respected older teacher was asked by a school board chairperson, "What's the best teacher-pupil ratio?"

Without hesitation, the teacher replied, "One-to-one."

Few people, however, can afford the luxury of providing one-to-one instruction for children for long periods of time. In schools, children are organized in groups of twenty or more for the purpose of learning to read. Within these larger groups, individual differences are a fact of life, so teachers reorganize these larger groups in an effort to provide more manageable clusters of children. Thus, grouping emerges as an important part of how reading is taught. In an effort to achieve effectiveness, different grouping patterns are tried within the classrooms—ability groups, skills groups, interests groups—and different organizational arrangements are made within schools—homogeneous groups and heterogeneous groups, cross-grade grouping and team teaching.

Each of these arrangements is made for the purpose of providing improved reading instruction for children. But for every action, there's a reaction; for every organizational plan advanced, there's a "Yes, but . . . ." There are pros and cons, advantages and disadvantages, to each of the possible classroom and schoolwide organizational plans. Each produces some answers, but none produces *the* answer.

Within these grouping patterns, the teacher is charged with making managerial decisions and adjustments to insure that each child receives the best reading instruction possible. Handling the reading program involves scheduling time, arranging space, choosing and assigning materials, and keeping records on children's progress (not to mention establishing a "traffic pattern" for children to work with specialists, keeping the milk money separate from the picture money, and assuming all the other administrative responsibilities that go with the job of teaching). Managing classroom instruction is indeed a many-dimensional process! .

While all these organizational and administrative factors have an effect on how reading is taught in the classroom, the teacher remains the mightiest force in the instructional program. Educators have long talked about individual differences in children, but it's also important to remember that there are individual differences in teachers. Teachers have unique teaching styles, just as children have different learning styles, and the teacher's style will determine in large measure his/her success in working in one organizational system or another. Some teachers are most comfortable working in a "freewheeling" classroom atmosphere, while others work most effectively in a more structured classroom environment. Different teachers have different ideas about how best to teach reading. A set of materials that appeals to one teacher will have no appeal at all to another. Some have a great deal of administrative ability in directing the affairs of the classroom, while others are a lot less highly organized. An organizational pattern or management technique that will work well for one teacher in one setting will not work at all for another teacher in another setting. Human diversity is, paradoxically, one of the beautiful strengths and, at the same time, one of the greatest flaws in the educational process.

In organizing and managing reading instruction in the classroom, the key is to find what will work best for the special-needs child. This may involve some experimentation, some trial and error, and some risk taking in trying a new grouping pattern or in revising a schedule. And doing something different will surely require more work! But when the right combination of organizational and management factors is found, the results will be an improved reading program for the special-needs child.

ACTIVITIES FOR PRESERVICE TEACHERS

1. Interview a teacher (or several teachers) to determine the criteria they use for forming reading groups. What seem to be the most commonly used criteria? What provision do the teachers make for variety and flexibility in their grouping practices? Based on your own experience and observations, what suggestions might you make for the consideration of these teachers?

2. Observe the reading program in an elementary school classroom with an eye to classroom organization and management. Focus your particular attention on the children who seem to need the most help. What kind of grouping patterns does the teacher use? Into what group do the "problem readers" usually fall? What other kinds of grouping might be appropriate? How much time is devoted to direct reading instruction in the classroom? What types of reading-related activities are children engaged in when they are not working directly with the teacher? How might you plan the program differently?

3. Plan a reading corner or skills center that might be set up in a primary-grade or intermediate-grade classrooms. In your plan, include a bulletin board or other display that might enliven the environment, a short inventory of materials that might be included, a list of equipment that might be used, a set of directions for using the learning area, and suggestions on how a schedule might be set up to insure maximum use of the facilities you design.

4. Examine cumulative folders or other records maintained on a child. What kind of information is included? How useful would you find this information in planning reading instruction for the child? What additional data would you find helpful? How would you acquire and use these additional data?

5. Do a little research on the topic of individualized reading. On the basis of your research, list what you consider the five most crucial elements in an individualized reading program. How do these elements apply specifically to reading instruction for the special-needs child in the regular classroom?

ACTIVITIES FOR IN-SERVICE TEACHERS

1. Identify and briefly describe the grouping patterns you currently use for reading instruction in your classroom. What criteria do you use for form-

ing reading groups? What provisions can be made for introducing more variety and flexibility in your grouping practices? Identify the practical problems you might anticipate in altering your grouping arrangements, and list one or two ways these problems might be avoided or overcome.

2. Identify two or three problem readers in your class. Review the reading program for these children in terms of the four management variables identified in this chapter (time, space, materials, record keeping). What additional provisions can be made for these children in the four management areas? List some ways in which different arrangements might be appropriate.

3. Scheduling problems are often created when children leave the room for remedial reading, the resource room, or other special services outside the classroom. What are some of the practical problems you have encountered in this respect? What adaptations might be made to reduce or eliminate this problem?

4. Examine materials from a management system currently available for use in the elementary grades. (A list of systems and publishers is presented on p.307.) What advantages and disadvantages do you perceive in these materials? How might you use a management system for the improvement of reading in your room?

5. List organizational and management modifications that would be required in your existing reading program to better accommodate special-needs children in your classroom.

NOTES

1. Guy L. Bond and Miles A. Tinker, *Reading Difficulties: Their Diagnosis and Correction* (Englewood Cliffs, N.J.: Prentice-Hall, Inc., 1973), p. 51.
2. Mary C. Austin and Coleman Morrison, *The First R: The Harvard Report on Reading in Elementary Schools* (New York: The Macmillan Co., 1963), p. 5.
3. J. Veatch, *Individualizing Your Reading Program* (New York: G. P. Putnam's Sons, 1959); H. F. Darrow and V. Howes, *Approaches to Individualized Reading* (New York: Appleton-Century-Crofts, 1960); M. Lazar, ed., *A Practical Guide to Individualized Reading* (New York: Bureau of Educational Research, Board of Education of New York, 1960).
4. W. H. Sartain, "The Roseville Experiment with Individualized Reading," *The Reading Teacher* 13 (April 1960): 277–281; I. W. Vite, "Individualized Reading—The Scorecard on Control Studies," *Education* 81 (January 1961): 285–290; P. J. Groff, "Comparison of Individualized and Ability Grouping Approaches to Reading Achievement," *Elementary English* 40 (March 1963): 258–264.
5. Alison Wolf, "Reading Instruction: Time Will Tell," *Learning* 5 (April 1977): 76–81.

6. See John F. Savage, "Teaching Reading with the Aid of Technology," *Audiovisual Instruction* 15 (Nov. 1970): 24–25, John F. Savage, "Technology in Reading Instruction," *Educational Technology* 12 (June 1972): 18–20.
7. Dale Johnson and P. David Pearson, "Skills Management Systems: A Critique," *The Reading Teacher* 28 (May 1975): 757–758.
8. Ibid., pp. 757–764.

REFERENCES

Dallman, Martha, et al. *The Teaching of Reading*, 4th ed. New York: Holt, Rinehart and Winston, 1974.

Duffy, Gerald G., and Sherman, George B. *Systematic Reading Instruction*. New York: Harper and Row, 1972.

Durkin, Dolores. *Teaching Them To Read*, 3rd ed. Boston: Allyn and Bacon, 1978.

Heilman, Arthur W. *Principles and Practices of Teaching Reading*, 4th ed. Columbus: Charles E. Merrill, 1977.

Karlin, Robert. *Teaching Elementary Reading: Principles and Strategies*, 2d ed. New York: Harcourt Brace Jovanovich, 1975.

Smith, James A., *Classroom Organization for the Language Arts*. Itasca, Ill.: F. E. Peacock, Publichers, 1977.

Spache, George D., and Spache, Evelyn B. *Reading in the Elementary School*, 4th ed. Boston: Allyn and Bacon, 1977.

Tinker, Miles A., and McCullough, Constance M. *Teaching Elementary Reading*, 4th ed. Englewood Cliffs, N.J.: Prentice-Hall, 1975.

10

HELP!

Preview

Many new and varied resources are becoming available for the support of classroom teachers as they assume responsibility for meeting the needs of children with learning and behavior problems. It is important that teachers know and understand what these resources are and how they can be used effectively. Although pupil personnel services may vary from one school district to another, there are state and national resource systems and organizations that are available to everybody. Teachers must assume the initiative to use them.

The major focus of the previous chapters has been on reading instruction for children with special needs within the regular classroom. The emphasis has been on the unique learning characteristics of children with various types of handicapping conditions and the educational implications of such conditions for the process of learning to read. Suggestions have been made for the selection and modification of reading techniques and materials as well as for the management of instruction and the learning environment.

If all this seems to imply greater flexibility and commitment on the part of classroom teachers, the implications are correct. The demands are very great indeed. However, no teacher should feel that the placement of a child with special needs into his/her classroom means that s/he must do the job alone. The acceptance invites teachers to share rather than shoulder the responsibility. There are a variety of ways of supporting the child, and the teacher and a number of professionals capable of doing it. Although each school system and school board has its own philosophy of education and set of priorities of educational services, federal legislation such as P.L. 94–142 requires that all school systems provide adequate services for special-needs children from age three to twenty-one, if these systems wish to be eligible for federal funds. The services to be guaranteed to the child must include assistance to the regular classroom teacher responsible for the child's learning experiences within the regular education program.

ORGANIZATION OF SPECIAL EDUCATION SERVICES

There are a variety of models for delivering services to children with learning and/or behavior problems. The ultimate goal for any program is to develop a continuum of services for children of varying degrees of need, from mild to severe. If such a continuum is to be effective, careful consideration must be given to entrance and exit criteria so that children do not "slip between the cracks." Progress must be carefully monitored so that children can move freely to a more integrated setting.

The following models are commonly found in the schools today: 1) itinerant program, 2) tutorial program, 3) resource or learning center, and 4) substantially separate programs.

Itinerant Program

The itinerant program is staffed by a specialist who moves from school to school or from school district to school district. Speech and hearing services are often organized on an itinerant basis, with the therapist covering two or more schools. Once the caseload has been identified within each building, services are provided once or twice a week. Services for low-vision and hearing-impaired children are often organized in this way as well.

Tutorial Program

The tutorial model is probably the least complicated method for providing services to children. An evaluation team may outline the child's remedial requirements and assign a tutor to provide the instruction. Tutors are often employed on a part-time basis and paid at an hourly rate. They tend to work with from one to three children at a time, and can be seen working in the nurse's room, a hallway, a broom closet—any place that can accommodate a small table and some chairs. Most of the early programs for learning-disabled children used a tutorial model.

Resource or Learning Center

The resource or learning center concept has become very popular in the last few years, and to some extent has replaced the tutorial model. A resource room is usually staffed by a special educator who may work alone or with aides, other specialists, or volunteers. The room itself contains a broad range of curriculum materials, particularly in reading and math, as well as a variety of audiovisual equipment designed to assist in the instruction of children with special learning needs. Children may be assigned to the resource room for anywhere from one period a week to most of the school day. Instruction is individualized to a child's identified needs and may include individual and small-group instruction.

Substantially Separate Programs

In spite of the present trend to encourage "mainstreaming" of children with special needs, there remain children who may be unable to "make it" in a regular class on anything but a very limited basis. Although many of these children may be able to move to more integrated environments eventually, the severity of a learning or behavior problem at the time of evaluation may require that the child be assigned to a substantially separate class. These classes are usually small, with approximately eight to twelve children with a teacher and possibly an aide. When a child has made sufficient progress to profit from partial integration into a regular classroom, a teacher may be asked to accept him/her into a regular education program for at least a portion of the school day.

Each of these special-service models can be used to meet the needs of children with learning and/or behavior problems. Most school systems use more than one model in providing a variety of services to children with varying degrees of special needs. Some school districts have formed cooperative programs with neighboring districts in order to combine and extend their individual resources. This collaboration allows for the broadest range of special services to children.

SPECIAL SERVICES

When a teacher decides that a child is in difficulty and requires special attention, any number of professionals from different disciplines may be called upon to determine the child's needs and provide services if necessary. In some school systems, there is a prescribed procedure for referring a child for an evaluation. This may include a written statement by the teacher and a meeting with a member of the support staff, who attempts to determine the nature of the difficulty and the extent of the evaluation that may be needed. In other school systems, the procedure is more informal and the teacher may be required to make a direct referral to the specialist s/he feels can provide the most assistance. Although services may vary from system to system, certain ones are seen most frequently.

Remedial Reading

In most schools, remedial reading services are offered for children who are underachieving. This service usually involves an evaluation and intensive individual or small-group instruction. In some systems, children are referred for remedial reading instruction when they are a year or more behind age or grade norms or below their expected capacity level. Services have usually been provided outside the classroom (which was one of the hallmarks of remedial "versus" corrective reading programs) and have conventionally been limited to children who had no apparent physical, perceptual, or emotional handicaps. In other school systems, reading teachers are working with children right in the classroom and offering direct services to teachers as well as to children. As remedial reading teachers are being called upon to provide reading instruction for children with a variety of related problems, reading specialists are assuming an increasingly important role as part of the team of resource people who provide services for the special-needs child.

Psychological Services

The school psychologist is concerned with the evaluation of cognitive functioning as well as the emotional well-being of the child. The psychologist's assessment may include an individual intelligence test, along with any formal or informal techniques used to evaluate personality development. Quite often, preliminary interviews are held with the parents and teacher in order to gain their perceptions of the child's problem and possible sources of distress. In many cases, the psychological evaluation is the first procedure completed, since the determination of intellectual capacity can give the learning specialists a better idea of the adequacy of the child's overall academic performance. When an emotional problem is identified, the school psychologist may initiate therapy or refer the child to a school adjustment counselor for individual or group therapy. When sufficient services are not available within the school, a referral may be made to an outside mental health facility. The psychologist can provide the classroom teacher with an appraisal of the child's cognitive skills and ego strengths. Although some of the family and personal history needs to remain confidential, the specialist can suggest the impact of the emotional factors on the educational process. Classroom management techniques and interpersonal issues should be identified and discussed by the teacher and psychologist, along with any other professionals who interact with the child.

Speech, Hearing, and Language Therapy

Speech therapists are responsible for the identification, evaluation, and treatment of speech and language problems. The largest percentage of the therapist's caseload is apt to be children with problems in the articulation of speech sounds. While most of these problems are not serious, they require professional attention in order to clear them up during the primary grades. Sometimes articulation problems accompany hearing loss, and/or auditory perceptual problems that contribute to academic difficulties, making the collaboration of therapist and teacher essential. Although there are many children with problems in language development, the treatment is usually more long term. The therapist can be expected to provide specific recommendations for modifications and adaptations of the language arts curriculum in order to insure the maximum opportunity for success within the regular classroom. It is very important for the teacher to know the sequence of instructional objectives prescribed as part of the therapeutic process so that s/he can reinforce these skills in the classroom. The teacher can provide important feedback by carefully observing the degree to which the child is beginning to demonstrate increased language proficiency in spontaneous verbal communication.

Special Education

Within the mild-to-moderate range of special needs, the special educator, i.e., the learning disability or resource room teacher, etc., is often the specialist responsibile for the identification and treatment of any problem areas in learning. The overall objective of this evaluation is to determine how the children learn—what they know, what they don't know, and how to teach them what they need to learn. This can be accomplished in many different ways. Some specialists prefer the very direct approach of formalized testing; others prefer more indirect, informal assessment procedures based on task analysis and diagnostic teaching. For the well-trained professional, both approaches are equally effective and lead to the kind of educational planning that can promote success. Regardless of the philosophical point of view of the special educator

Teacher aides and parent volunteers can easily supervise drill and reinforcement activities. Many children enjoy the special attention from an adult. (Photo by Edward Thomas)

involved, the classroom teacher can expect to learn what factors (if any) are interfering with the learning process, the conditions under which the child learns best, alternative strategies, classroom accommodation techniques for teaching in specific areas, and some assistance in setting realistic expectations for academic performance. This is likely to be the kind of information the teacher will find most helpful in managing the classroom experiences of children with special needs who are able to function in a regular classroom on a full- or part-time basis.

Title I Programs

Title I services are designed to provide extra academic support for children in predominantly low-income areas. In order to qualify for such services, the child must be underachieving, usually in reading and math. This population of children, whether found in urban, suburban, or rural settings, is complex indeed. There are numerous factors that may be operating against the children, e.g., nutrition, physical abuse, emotional difficulties related to family circumstances, frequent moves, foster home placements, and lack of motivation. Regulations require that children who qualify for special education services provided within a school district be excluded from Title I programs. Since primary and secondary causes of underachievement are difficult (if not impossible) to separate within this population of children, assignment to specific services on an either/or basis may be contrary to the best interests of the children the programs are designed to serve. In practice, many school districts offering a Title I program provide special education services to the most disabled learners and academic support through Title I to the less severe cases of underachievement. Classroom teachers can be of great assistance to the support personnel who must decide on the most appropriate services for a child. In return, the teacher can expect that Title I will provide individualized instruction in major academic subject areas for children considered eligible.

Bilingual Programs

In recent years, there has been an increase in programs designed to serve the needs of children whose first language is something other than English. With monies provided by Title IX, as well as those allotted by the local districts, bilingual programs are growing in terms of numbers of children and variety of languages. Many programs have substantially separate classes for these children, staffed by a teacher who is fluent in their native language. In some instances, the children learn to read in their own language first while learning English as a second language. Other programs concentrate on development of fluency in English. The bilingual resource room is beginning to emerge as an alternative to the self-contained class, on the theory that the bilingual child needs the stimulation provided by English-speaking children within a regular class, at least on a part-time basis. Teachers who have bilingual children in their classrooms should expect the bilingual teacher to point out the cultural factors that may influence the children's readiness to assimilate new learning, as well as the specific alterations in language patterns that the children may be attempting to master. Another important consideration is the planning of a "cultural exchange," allowing the mutual sharing of what is unique to the background of every class member.

Paraprofessionals

With the increased demands on classroom teachers to extend the limits of the curriculum to accommodate for children with special needs, many school systems have begun or extended the use of paraprofessionals. In some areas, community colleges are providing formal training for instructional aides to assist in regular or special educational settings. These programs usually produce aides who are exceptionally well qualified for the assignments. Although some are salaried positions, most aides are hired at an hourly rate. When funds are available, trained personnel can provide a broader range of services. When funds are not available, there is much to be said for providing a good training program for parent volunteers. While some systems have felt reluctant to commit staff time and resources to such a venture on the basis of past experience with volunteer efforts that lost momentum or "created more problems than they solved," other systems have recruited and trained volunteers quite successfully. The key to success in working with paid and volunteer aides appears to be the careful delineation of responsibilities for instruction, training to perform successfully, and an opportunity to function in a paraprofessional role. Regardless of whether an aide is paid or not, the teacher can receive invaluable assistance from such personnel. Supervision of independent exercises, direct reinforcement of specific skills, monitoring of seatwork, providing enrichment activities, etc., are just a few of the duties that can be performed by an aide (or a student teacher). The success of this team effort is probably directly related to the teacher's willingness to share her children, plan in greater detail, and remain open to differences in teaching style.

Each of these programs has the potential to provide support for children with a variety of learning and/or behavior problems. Personnel in these programs can provide direct services to children, as well as consultation and support for the classroom teacher. Some of these programs are funded in full or in part by federal or state monies and do not represent an overwhelming cost to the school district.

STATE AND NATIONAL RESOURCES

In recent years, a tremendous amount of money has been spent on the development of instructional materials. Much of the investment has come from publishers, who can make a profit from the sale of good educational media. Additional monies have been allocated by the United States Office of Education to develop national and regional resource centers. The network is very large and very complex; learning how to use it can be very helpful. At the present time, there are sixteen Regional Resource Centers (RRC) that serve specific states. These centers, as well as certain specialized offices, work closely with the National Center for Special Education Materials (NICSEM) located at the University of Southern California. This network of resources is designed to interrelate with state and local media and materials programs, and to provide supportive services to those programs so that the following general goals may be achieved:

1. Where appropriate materials do not exist to meet the needs of handicapped students, needed materials can be made available through adaptation/modification of existing materials and/or development of new materials to meet identified student needs.

2. Where users of materials are not aware of existing materials that will meet the needs of the handicapped, information about relevant and usable materials and media will be made available to the potential user.

3. Where users know about the availability of existing materials that will meet needs of handicapped students, but do not have physical access to these materials, materials will be made accessible on a convenient basis.

4. Where materials are accessible but the potential user does not know how to use them effectively, users will have access to training in the use of materials.

Most universities and colleges involved in teacher training maintain media centers that contain a variety of instructional programs, psychoeducational tests, in-service training materials, etc. Although these materials may not be available for consumption, they are often available for review. There are also information retrieval systems like the National Instructional Materials Information System (NIMIS), which is a computer-based retrieval system specifically developed for the purpose of assisting teachers, parents, and other educators in locating information about instructional materials in the field of special education. Smaller, privately financed companies provide a variety of retrieval systems, some of which are not done by computer and are lower in cost. Appendix C provides annotated references of some of these systems. Many of them place their greatest emphasis on the area of reading.

Classroom teachers should not overlook the possibility of applying on their own for state and/or federal money to obtain services and materials. Although larger school systems often have a person in charge of state and federal projects, these administrators may not have the time to apply for the small grants that would respond to a specific need within a particular school building. Local coordinators of funded programs, as well as the coordinators within state departments of education, can provide useful information as to what monies are available, who may apply, and the guidelines for writing a proposal. Unfortunately, many school boards see outside money as undesirable since it is almost always short term and the funding agency expects the services to eventually be absorbed in local budgets. School personnel may also see outside funds as undesirable, since they may require teachers and administrators to assume new roles and responsibilities. While this is sometimes true, it should not discourage any teacher from taking the initiative "to get things going." Whatever materials (hardware/software) are acquired remain as permanent acquisitions, and services that please parents and administrators are difficult for a school board to turn down.

PROFESSIONAL ORGANIZATIONS

There are a number of professional associations that have been established to provide information and services to classroom teachers and specialists within specific diciplines. The organizations most directly concerned with reading and special-needs children are The Council of Exceptional Children, The International Reading Association, The National Council for Teachers of English, The Association of Children with Learning Disabilities, and The Orton Society.

The *Council for Exceptional Children* (CEC) is the largest national organization concerned with the education and total care of children with special needs. Within the organization there are special-interest groups (divisions) that focus on specific aspects of professional services. There are groups concerned with administration of special education services, retardation, behavior disorders, learning disabilities, communication disorders, early childhood, visually handicapped, gifted, and many more. The Council plays a very active role in lobbying for the kind of legislation that will provide better education for children with special problems. It publishes the *Exceptional Children* journal, along with numerous other publications. In addition to the national conference, the Council sponsors regional conferences each year that may focus on a specific topic such as providing services to children in sparsely populated areas or early childhood programs. Many states have very active state groups that keep members alerted to changes in state legislation, sources of funding, in-service training resources and media, etc. The national headquarters will provide information on the complete scope of the Council's activities. The Council's headquarters are located at 1920 Association Drive, Reston, Virginia 22091.

The International Reading Association (IRA) is a worldwide professional organization concerned with the improvement of reading, especially as it is practiced and encouraged through instruction and supervision in schools. Through its journals and other publications, IRA makes available a wealth of materials on a range of topics related to the teaching of reading. While it has always maintained a focus on the child with special needs through committees on the blind, the retarded, and other special-needs groups, the Association is becoming increasingly involved with reading instruction for a broader range of special-needs children. IRA has joined forces with other professional organizations in lobbying for legislation that will provide for the most effective reading instruction to handicapped learners. In the United States and Canada, each state and province maintains active councils, which, in addition to regional and local affiliates, provide active forums for the exchange of ideas and information for anyone involved in the teaching of reading. The Association's international headquarters are at 800 Barksdale Road, Newark, Delaware 19711.

The National Council for Teachers of English (NCTE) is a professional organization devoted to the improvement of all facets of language arts teaching and learning. While its focus of concern is beyond the scope of reading per se, NCTE's journals, publications, task forces, and conferences reflect a strong specific commitment to reading instruction in schools. The association's central focus has traditionally been more on developmental than "remedial" instruction, but its commissions and committes deal with aspects of instruction that directly affect children with language problems. Affiliate councils give teachers the opportunity to become involved in NCTE activities in all fifty states. The Council's central offices are located at 1111 Kenyon Road, Urbana, Illinois 61801.

The Association of Children with Learning Disabilities (ACLD) is a national organization primarily concerned with children in the average and above-average range of abilities who experience difficulties in learning. It, too, has been very successful in bringing about the kind of legislation that can support better education for children with learning problems. Since it began through the initiative of both parents and professionals, it has continued to meet the needs of both groups. State affiliates and local community chapters have, for the most part, been well coordinated to achieve common goals. At the local level, the parent members have been particularly effective in advocating for the development of adequate services from preschool through high school. Individual state organizations usually maintain excellent resource libraries for parents, teachers, and specialists. Many bewildered parents have found help and moral support from the state and local organization. The national ACLD headquarters is located at 5225 Grace St., Pittsburgh, Pennsylvania 15236.

The Orton Society is a national, scientific, and educational association concerned with the study and treatment of specific language disability (termed dyslexia). The society has approximately twenty branches throughout the country. In addition to the national conference each fall, regional meetings are sponsored by the state organizations. The membership includes parents, teachers, psychologists, physicians, etc. The Society publishes the Annual Bulletin of The Orton Society as well as the periodic publication of "Perspectives on Dyslexia." The national office of The Orton Society is at 8415 Bellona Lane, Towson, Maryland 21204.

TEACHER CENTERS

In October of 1976, Congress passed legislation that would establish teacher centers throughout the country. The purpose of the centers is to provide in-service training and other services to all school personnel, paraprofessionals, student teachers, and interns. According to the legislation, the centers operated by local districts are to be governed by a teacher center policy board, with representation on the board subject to negotiation with the local teacher organization. This provision gives teachers maximum input into the determination of the content and format of staff development activities. Although there are possibilities for collaboration with colleges and universities, the control remains with the local policy board. The concept is an exciting one and worth the full exploration of every school district.

CONCLUSION

The responsibilities of a classroom teacher have changed considerably in the last few years. Added to the task of instruction in basic skills are the requirements of assessment of individual needs, curriculum modification, collaboration, and communication. This is not an easy job but it is an exciting one. No teacher need feel alone and unsupported unless s/he chooses to ignore the resources at hand and those that can be obtained through state and federal agencies.

Participation in professional organizations can be of great benefit to teachers who wish to expand their knowledge of specialized areas of education and remain current in their own areas of expertise. Attendance at state and national conferences promotes the development of a perspective broad enough to evaluate new trends and select those with the soundest theoretical base and the greatest potential for practical application. Remaining in touch with the profession at large can prevent the atrophy that comes from becoming too comfortable with the status quo.

ACTIVITIES FOR PRESERVICE TEACHERS

1. Interview the parents of a handicapped school-age child. At what age was the child's problem identified? Develop a chronological chart of parent efforts to mobilize resources on behalf of the child. Outline the steps taken by the school. What are the parents' feelings regarding the efforts of the many professionals who have been involved? What one person can they identify as providing the most help and support?

2. Write to one of your state associations that promote the welfare of children with special needs. Request any written materials that may be used with parents. Evaluate the materials from the point of view of: a) communication style (i.e., use of technical language, definition of terms, etc.), b) educational implications of handicapping conditions, c) practical suggestions for home management, d) resources available for additional help.

3. A school system has decided to employ instructional aides. Prepare a set of guidelines that define the role and responsibilities you would like to see if you were applying for this position.

4. Identify the network of Media Resource Centers that serve your state. Discover how you could gain entry into the National Center for Special Education Materials. Obtain catalogues from a variety of Media Resource Centers. Identify the instructional materials that could be of assistance in teaching reading to special-needs children.

5. Recall your own experiences in school with children with special needs. Recount your own interaction with the one you remember best. How did you and your classmates perceive him/her as a person? What was the attitude of teachers toward the child's problem? Was any effort given to helping you and the other students understand and accept him/her?

ACTIVITIES FOR IN-SERVICE TEACHERS

1. Interview a staff member from a local child advocacy group, i.e., Easter Seal Society, Association for Children with Learning Disabilities, United Cerebral Palsy. In what ways has this group lobbied for educational legislation? Does this group monitor school and community programs for handicapped children? What kinds of services does the group provide for parents? For teachers? What does this staff member see as the most pressing need in your area?

2. Review the policy statements of your school district concerning the education of children with special needs. From reading these statements, how would you describe the philosophy of education on which they were based? Does your own philosophy or approach differ?

3. The process of collaboration on a multidisciplinary team is often complex. Each specialist has his/her own expectations. In the event of conflict over priorities of therapy, scheduling, etc., how would problems be resolved? What should the role of the principal be? Of the parents? Of the teacher?

4. As a fourth-grade teacher, you have referred a child for an evaluation by the school staff. It turns out that the child has above-average intelligence, is two years below grade level in reading, and has considerable difficulty processing visual information. At the staff conference, the first question his mother asks is, "How could he reach the fourth grade without having these problems identified?" How would you respond?

5. Design a brochure for parents that describes the full range of services available within your district. Include in this an organizational chart that traces the lines of responsibility from the teacher in the classroom all the way to the school board. Briefly outline the function of the multidisciplinary team, providing a checklist for the parents of what to expect in home visit, staff conference, development of an IEP, etc.

11

The Teacher
on
the Team

Preview

The role of the classroom teacher is changing. The responsibility for educating a particular class of children can be shared with other professionals so that individual learning needs can be met. Each teacher must come to grips with the issue of collaboration and develop his/her own personal perspectives as a member of a multidisciplinary team. In the face of state and federal legislation assuring the rights of handicapped children to appropriate educational services, all professionals are confronted with the task of assuming new roles and responsibilities — the classroom teacher most of all.

Serving as an educator on a multidisciplinary team can be a very exciting and rewarding experience. It has taken a number of years for regular classroom teachers to assume an active role. In the early days of pupil personnel services, the emphasis was on direct services to children, with communication between and among disciplines a rather informal, somewhat haphazard process. As more professionals joined the group, with more disciplines represented, it became apparent that coordination and communication were central to the successful and efficient use of services. The concept of mainstreaming made the regular teacher conspicuously absent as a full participant in the decision-making process. Many states now have legislation that specifies the components of the evaluation procedure, including the role of the classroom teacher. This has meant making provisions for a class to be covered while the teacher attends team conferences. It has placed a heavy demand on the regular classroom teacher to assume some of the responsibility for referrals, record keeping, individualized planning, and curriculum modifications. The interpersonal issues are equally demanding as the teacher attempts to deal effectively with the numerous professionals involved in providing services to the child.

In making maximum use of available services, communication and coordination are crucial. The classroom teacher should be aware of programs and services the child is receiving outside the classroom. For example, the teacher should be aware of the types of skills development activities and materials being used by the remedial reading teacher and should know the sort of exercises being done by the child in the resource room. Direct, if brief, observations should be scheduled. Only through an open line of two-way communication can the teacher offer insights and suggestions to the specialists and, at the same time, gain a greater understanding of the child and how the services provided by the specialists can be reinforced and extended in the classroom.

In many instances, the classroom teacher may be the one who initiates and maintains a coordinating function. Administratively, the learning disabilities specialist may report to the Director of Pupil Personnel Services, the remedial reading teacher to the Assistant Superintendent for Instruction, and the psychologist to the system's Director of Guidance. Care should be taken so that the child does not get lost in the "administrative shuffle." Very often, it is the teacher who may need to make provisions to insure the coordination of services to the benefit of the child.

One of the most important things for a teacher to remember is that in the educational life of the child, s/he is the star performer. Everyone else is in the supporting cast. What happens in the classroom is every bit as important as what happens in any special program. It may be even more important, since it may be in a regular classroom that the child has failed in the first place. In order to "turn that around," the classroom teacher should be aware of all the goals and objectives that must be attained for the child to become a more successful learner. In order to do this effectively, the classroom teacher should keep certain points in mind.

Written Reports

Insist on written reports and recommendations. Although it is always helpful to bring team members together to discuss the findings and plan the educational program, written communication is the only secure way of making sure everyone (including the parents) is aware of the instructional objectives and the personnel responsible for the teaching. Any inconsistencies of approach can be identified immediately. In addition, carefully written documentation of the educational objectives and the child's response to the techniques should be recorded so that the individualized educational program (IEP) becomes an educational history. Without this kind of written record, a great deal of valuable information may be lost. Besides the objectives for the remedial program, the classroom teacher should be provided with written suggestions for curriculum modifications and accommodations for the child in the classroom. One of the major problems of remedial education is the change of personnel. In the absence of good written records, a new specialist attempting to follow through on a program for a child without the benefit of the original assessment information, instructional objectives, curriculum adaptations, and a record of the child's progress, must begin from the beginning. The child must be reassessed, allowing sufficient time for diagnostic teaching and the development of another educational plan. This causes unnecessary loss of time, as well as unnecessary wear and tear on the child. It is not sufficient for a classroom teacher merely to know that a child will see the learning disability or remedial reading teacher three times a week. The teacher should have a copy of the initial and all updated educational programs.

If the classroom teacher receives an educational program on a child s/he has referred that does little more than list the types of services, the names of the specialists, and a schedule of appointments, the plan should be returned with a request for more detailed information. Appendix A presents a sample of an individualized educational program that is clearly a collaborative effort by many people, including the classroom teacher. Although P.L. 94-142 requires that an IEP be developed for each child receiving services in a special education program and suggests the kind of information to be included, it does not provide an actual format. Each state or school district must develop one of its own.

Setting Priorities

Encourage the team to set priorities. One of the dangers in a multidisciplinary evaluation is that there is sometimes a tendency to provide too much help. A child who, for example, has an articulation problem, difficulty in auditory processing, and is showing the emotional strain of academic and social failures, may be scheduled for speech therapy, remedial reading, learning disability tutoring, and counseling. Intensive therapy in four areas at one time can be a bit overwhelming. Although the services are available and the specialists are genuinely committed to helping the child, it is sometimes wise to push for a reasonable remedial plan based on servicing the areas considered the most crucial, while holding others for a later time.

Realistic Goals

Be realistic about what can be done in the classroom. Since the teacher is central to the child's educational experience, the remedial staff will be making recommendations for instructional and behavior management. Depending on the regular classroom experience of the specialists involved, those recommendations may or may not be realistic. When faced with suggestions that are clearly unreasonable in the given situation, the teacher should feel secure enough to point out why the recommendations are inappropriate and to make an effort to negotiate more realistic strategies. Rather than be overwhelmed by numerous accommodation techniques, it is better for the child and the teacher to settle on those that can be managed well first, with the idea that others may be added later.

Flexibility

Be flexible in scheduling. There is never a truly convenient time for a child to miss what is happening in the classroom. However, once the teacher and the support staff have agreed on what should be done, the child's schedule should be flexible. Occasionally, a teacher can be heard to say, "He can afford to miss _____ . This may mean that the one vivid, consistent success in the classroom is removed. This practice is, indeed, unfortunate and leads many children to resent time spent away from the classroom. These feelings can interfere with the success of the special program. For this reason, a teacher can request that the specialist work with the child or group of children within the classroom. In some systems, this is done as standard procedure. The major advantage of working in the classroom rather than in a separate setting is that children become accustomed to seeing adults (teachers, aides, specialists, volunteers) working in the room. Children receiving remedial help are indistinguishable from those receiving attention for other reasons. The advantages are tremendous. Of course, not all specialists are willing nor all classroom teachers initially comfortable with such an arrangement, but children seem to adjust to it quite well.

Penalties for Problems

Don't penalize a child for having a problem. Making adjustments in scheduling, planning, and teaching is time-consuming and requires a considerable commitment on the part of the teacher. When this is done willingly and in good humor, the child will thrive and the satisfaction is far greater than that of teaching a child who learns easily and may have known it all before s/he came. At times, however, certain unrecognized negative feelings work against the child's progress. In some situations, a child is required to complete classwork during recess or at home, when time for remedial help prevented its completion in school. Another child must attend special programs during gym or other fun activities. A child cannot help but feel resentful and confused as to what is expected of him/her. In such cases, children pay a very high price for having a problem.

When the classroom teacher maintains a positive attitude toward the child, the other children often sense the teacher's commitment and affection. Most of the children will react in a similar way. Impatience and unkindness may still occur, but the effects will be far less devastating if the child experiences a greater amount of acceptance. It is definitely the adult attitude that provides the model for the peer group. The responsibility is undeniable.

Patience with Parents

Be patient with parents. Although some parents of special-needs children are often overanxious, others have been through a great deal and have developed a "sixth sense" where their child is concerned. The view of the parents is apt to be a global one. While the educational experience may be a very important component, it is not the exclusive focus as it may be with educators. Quite often, parents can provide the only comprehensive view of the child in his/her total developmental history. Parents of children whose special needs were recognized and serviced at the preschool level are usually quite knowledge-able and accepting by the time the child reaches the primary grades. Parents of children whose special needs were not recognized until the child experienced considerable academic difficulty may be confused and disappointed. Some may deny the existence of a problem and see the learning problems as related to poor teaching, class size, lack of appropriate materials, etc. Although these facors can affect learning, a good evaluation team should be able to determine the degree to which external factors have influenced the child's performance. Other parents suspect the worst and seek evaluations from hospital clinics or other agencies.

Once needs have been identified and services have been initiated, some parents become so anxious for the child to succeed that they undertake an edu-cational program at home requiring the child to read for a certain amount of time each day. When a teacher becomes concerned that such practices are exerting too much pressure on the child or are, in fact, inconsistent with the school program, s/he should attempt to suggest things the parent could do that would have more positive results. Some parents need to feel involved. When this is the case, it is better to include parents in planning sessions so they can follow the child's progress and understand what might be helpful to do at home. A parent can be the teacher's strongest ally.

FINDING A "CHAMPION"

Every child needs a "champion." For most children, their strongest advocates and fans are found within their families. Most mothers and fathers are ever-vigilant and watchful of the developmental milestones, the progress and lack of progress, the comfort and discomfort of their children. This works very well, since the parents are in the best position to observe the child's total development over the longest period of time. They are aware of the child's unique ways of interacting with the world. When a problem develops, the parents may be the first to recognize it and begin to seek solutions. They do whatever they can to restore the previous rate of progress.

Parents of a handicapped child usually assume an active role in the medical and educational management of their child. They often group together with other parents to mobilize the kinds of services that can make a difference in their child's life. To a great extent, parents, in the advocacy role, have been responsible for the state and federal legislation that promotes the welfare of children with special needs.

Unfortunately, not all children have families with the interest or resources to provide for these needs. Some families must face the more basic issues of economic survival. For them, the child's underachievement or perhaps the need for eyeglasses is not as critical as his/her daily bread. It is a reality of life that need not work against the child if a "champion" can be found somewhere else.

·Aside from parents, the teacher is an ideal person to be an advocate on a child's behalf. Within the child's educational life, the teacher sees all aspects of performance, and it is the teacher who influences so much of what happens to the child in the learning environment. For children experiencing mild problems in learning, the teacher is often the one who becomes concerned first and initiates the process that identifies and serves the child's needs. When waiting lists are long and services are limited, it is the classroom teacher who can make sure the child receives every consideration. There are a variety of approaches that teachers can use to secure services for children. Some teachers "tackle the specialist around the knees" in order to attract attention to a child's need. This method is always effective. Other teachers keep prodding quietly but forcefully. This, too, is successful. Another, somewhat smaller group of teachers insist that the specialist enter the classroom to witness the child's distress. This can be the most effective approach of all.

Today, classroom teachers have many resources at their disposal. The willingness to use these resources often depends on the teacher's self-confidence and security as a professional. Some teachers see the request for help as an admission of failure as a teacher. Actually, quite the contrary is true. The ability to "share" a child and work in consort with other professionals demands a great deal of professional skill and maturity. It requires a significant commitment of time and energy. In many instances, it means departing from the regular curriculum in order to employ a more favorable approach to the child's unique needs as a learner. This is not always an easy thing to do, especially when the reading program at any given grade level is limited to one or two choices. Sometimes reading or curriculum coordinators are unwilling to allow departures from the regular reading program. A teacher can be caught in a "curriculum bind." On the one hand, an alteration of approach may be indicated for a child and recommended by the special-services staff, yet on the other hand making the change can lead to problems with supervisors or administrators who subscribe to a different philosophy. Being caught in the middle can be a difficult position for the teacher. Playing the role of a "champion" can be risky. However, it is often less risky and more satisfying when the building principal is an advocate too. The principal's support can smooth the way for curriculum revision and modification. In some instances, this may include the development of alternative forms for report cards and exemption from group standardized testing.

Another struggle may occur as the teacher attempts to extend the lower limits of the instructional program. For some reason, "grade level" is perceived as "sacred ground." Some educators feel that if a child is in third grade, s/he should be doing third-grade work. At the end of the year, an achievement test makes the teacher accountable for teaching those third-grade skills. The fact that the teacher and support staff moved the child from a pre-primer to a 2.6 level can be overlooked. The teacher may need to insist on the child's right to develop skills in a logical, systematic fashion at his own level and his own rate of learning.

One of the most important functions of the teacher in the role of child advocate is that of monitoring. Keeping track of the child's progress in special program(s) is crucial to the integration of the regular and special instructional components. When a teacher notes that progress is not being made or has stopped, s/he should request a conference to reevaluate the objectives and methods. At the moment, there is a certain amount of role conflict for some special educators. While maintaining heavy caseloads, they are also responsible for screening and assessment. In order to assume the role of diagnostician, they must suspend direct instructional or therapeutic services to children. When a child's program is consistently disrupted, it may be time to suggest that the administration develop a better model or provide aides, paraprofessionals, or volunteers who can work under supervision. In any event, the teacher can make it clear that if s/he is to share a child with other professionals, it is with the expectation that all pledges will be fulfilled and all commitments kept.

Some teachers find themselves playing the role of advocate to the child himself. After the many failures and repeated frustrations of dealing with a physical constraint or learning problem, a child may develop a very poor self-image. It hurts to be a failure in school and a disappointment at home. The child begins to expect incompetence in himself. Having a teacher express enthusiasm for what he does well, acceptance of his limitations, and optimism that things will get better, can create hope where once there was none. It can stimulate the child's own commitment to the learning process. At the upper grade levels, motivation is the "name of the game."

In Massachusetts there is a public law enacted in 1974 that requires a complete and appropriate education for all handicapped children from ages three to twenty-one. The manual developed to assist schools in the implementation of the requirements for evaluating children's needs states:

> Chapter 766 promotes the premise that
> (a) all children are normal,
> (b) all children are different,
> (c) the differences in children are normal.[1]

It is providing for the normal differences that makes teaching a fine art and a precise science.

NOTE

1. R. Audette, "Concept Paper," in *Core Evaluation Manual* (Bedford, Mass.: The Institute for Educational Services, Inc., 1974).

Appendix A:
Evaluation Report
and Individualized
Educational Program

Name: Lori

Age: 8–8

School: Abraham Lincoln Elementary School

Grade: 3

INDIVIDUAL ASSESSMENTS

Medical History

Notes

The medical history suggests that factors relating to prematurity have contributed to developmental delay and mild brain dysfunction.

This component was prepared by the school nurse, who summarized various reports from physicians.

Following a pregnancy complicated by hemorrhaging, this 8-8 years old female was born prematurely in the sixth month and weighed 2 pounds and 9 ounces. She was hospitalized after birth for approximately 3½ months and spent the first two months in an incubator due to hyaline membrane disease and severe jaundice. Various developmental milestones lagged from three to eighteen months behind "normal." At 2½ years she had a prolonged seizure and was hospitalized. Her sleep EEG was normal. She was placed on phenobarbital for seizure control. She has had no seizures since and is not currently on medication. The neurological diagnosis was mild, nonprogressive encephalopathy with asymmetric development, paranatally acquired. Subsequent EEG results strongly suggest a mild, chronic, left-hemisphere dysfunction, with resulting mild impairment of language skills. Due to frequent episodes of otitis media, a T. & A. was done in June, 1974. Recent audiological evaluation showed hearing to be within normal limits bilaterally. Vision was normal.

Home Visit

This section is typically prepared by the school nurse and/or school social worker.

Parental anxiety related to early medical problems seems to contribute to Lori's mother's inclination to be overprotective.
This may account for Lori's preference for relating to adults rather than peers in a school setting.

The home visit was made on October 2, 1977. Both parents and the child were present. The home is located in a quiet residential section consisting of new homes. Mother reported Lori shares a bedroom with her older sister, age 12. During the initial part of the interview, Lori played quietly in an adjoining room.

Parents are in their mid-thirties and have been married for fourteen years. Lori is the youngest of three children, having a sister age 12 and a brother age 10. The father is self-employed, owning a small hardware business. He reports having to work long hours, but also states he is free to be available when and if needed at home. Both parents appear most concerned about Lori and desirous of her receiving the best care available.

Mother reports a difficult pregnancy with frequent bed rest to avoid a miscarriage. Lori was born premature (mother states at six months). She was jaundiced, weighed only 2½ lbs., and was in an incubator for two months and finally allowed home at age 3½ months. Developmental milestones were delayed, e.g., sitting at 1 year, walking at 19 months, speech at 3½ years. Mother recalls vividly her anxiety over Lori's condition, her concern that it might have been her fault for not taking care of herself better, etc. She admits to still feeling this way now. Both parents relate great shock and concern at the time of Lori's seizure when she was 2½ years old. They were told there was some "brain damage" and were overwhelmed at the thought that Lori would be a "vegetable." They admit to having been oversolicitious, doing for her, many things they later discovered she could do for herself.

When Lori's speech was delayed, they sought help from nearby hospitals and clinics and were told there was an impairment of language skills and they should obtain speech therapy. They did, privately, and have been pleased with the improvement they have seen.

At this point, Lori was invited into the room. She is a neat, well-groomed child who smiled when introduced to the interviewer. She went immediately to her parents and leaned on her mother's lap. In response to the interviewer's questions, she nodded or shook her head. She did not speak. On one occasion she pointed to a magazine on the table and the mother handed it to her. When the interviewer commented that perhaps she should ask for what she wanted, the mother replied that she had been told that often but found it easier to just give her what she wanted rather than have her agonize over saying it.

Mother states Lori gets along well with her brother and sister, although she requires much more care. The older children have accepted this and do not seem to mind. Mother adds that Lori is with her most of the time. Although there are children her age in the neighborhood, Lori does not play with them because they tease her occasionally due to her speech difficulty. Mother feels it is best to keep her in the house and avoid that painful experience.

As the interviewer was leaving, the mother picked Lori up and carried her to the door. Lori smiled over the mother's shoulder as the door closed.

School History

It is apparent that learning problems have been present throughout Lori's early educational experience.

The School History is usually written by the guidance counselor or school principal.

Lori attended the first six months of kindergarten prior to the family's move to their new home in March of 1975. General immaturity as well as a severe problem in verbal expression were cited as reasons for placement in a transitional first grade. Speech and language therapy was initiated and continued until the present. Academic progress has been slow. At the end of second grade, Lori was referred to the guidance counselor by her classroom teacher because of withdrawn behavior. At the beginning of third grade, the parents requested a full evaluation by the school.

Classroom Report

Lori has been enrolled in my third-grade classroom since the beginning of the school year. Her parents agreed to a full evaluation when I called them in for a conference in September.

Lori is an eight-year-old girl who always comes to school neatly dressed and well groomed. She likes working with adults and is very cooperative on a one-to-one basis. When she is in a group with her peers or asked to do an independent task, she does not complete her work.

Lori has a speech problem and sees the Speech and Language Specialist on a scheduled basis. It is sometimes difficult to understand what she is saying unless I listen very carefully. She rarely talks when other children are around. She will not respond in a reading group. We are presently using the Ginn 720 series, in which she is at Level 5. She does not seem to be able to learn and remember the sounds for a long period. It seems she knows the sounds for a few days and then forgets them.

When Lori reads a story silently and does a workbook page with pictures, she does quite well. If I ask her comprehension questions, she seems to know the answers but has a hard time explaining them to me. Sometimes she forgets an easy word like "tree" or "house" and then tries to describe it. She is fine if I just tell her the word.

Lori's number work is at an early first-grade level. She can count by ones to twenty and do simple addition and subtraction problems with blocks. She does not know the value of coins, cannot deal with number facts over 20, is unable to solve word problems, and refuses to take part in any math activities with a group of her classmates.

All of Lori's academic problems are compounded by the fact that her writing is practically illegible. Her printing is very small and poorly done. When we practice cursive writing, she does not seem to get the hang of it and it, too, is very cramped.

Lori saw the school counselor last year in second grade because she was so withdrawn. She responds well to me but will not play with her classmates. If I lead a game on the playground, Lori will play. She can run, skip, and hop in relay races but never seems to have a good time. If it is free play time, Lori stands near me or off by herself. She does not interact with her classmates even though some of them have tried to be friendly.

Lori often refuses to do things even though I am quite sure she is able to do them, such as open her milk carton and zipper her coat. She does not do her classroom job—erasing the boards. If I push her, she cries.

Lori is a nice little girl and, with a lot of help, might be able to work within a regular class. With twenty-two others, I cannot give her the full attention she needs at this time.

Psychological Assessment

Lori was referred to the school psychologist as part of the investigation into her learning and interpersonal problems. The teacher's concern was Lori's increasing withdrawal, isolation, and avoidance of other children. Teacher reported that Lori has always had a severe speech problem. She seems very self-conscious about this and avoids any peer interaction.

The school psychologist visited the classroom and observed Lori on two *problems in peer group relationships and overdependence on adults are apparent.*

This section of the report is prepared by the school psychologist.

It is important for the psychologist to observe a child in the classroom in order to understand the context in which problems have occurred. It is also important for the psychological examiner to establish rapport with the child prior to the actual testing.

occasions. In the classroom, Lori, although placed in center front of the class, does not interact with her peers. All activity flows around or over her. She avoids eye contact, does not respond to teacher's direct efforts to involve her in class activities, and does not volunteer answers, even those that involve a nonverbal response. In the recess yard, she remains by the teacher, does not participate.

The school psychologist was with Lori for a brief interview to introduce herself and show Lori her office and play materials. Lori left the classroom willingly, taking the psychologist's hand as they walked to the office. She seemed relaxed but was uncommunicative in response to questions. On interview, Lori was reluctant to speak, nodding or shaking her head only, until the psychologist asked for more information. When she spoke, her articulation was so poor as to be unintelligible if one did not know the context of the response. There was no verbal spontaneity. In this one-to-one contact she appeared comfortable and at ease, smiling, going toward the psychologist; she seemed to relate well with adults. In her brief play session, she chose the doll house, selecting mother and father dolls and a baby doll. She created a scene where mother doll was feeding the baby doll while the father sat close by. At the end of the session, Lori was told she would come back in two days and would do some other things such as drawing, answering questions, and putting things together. She accepted this without question.

Lori was seen two days later for testing. She was pleasant and cooperative throughout the session. She was administered the WISC-R with the following results:

On this test, the mean scaled score at each age level is 10, with a standard deviation of 3.

Verbal	Raw Score	Scaled Score
Information	7	9
Comprehension	5	7
Arithmetic	3	6
Similarities	4	8
Vocabulary	11	8
(Digit Span)	5	6
	Sum Verbal:	44

Performance	Raw Score	Scaled Score
Picture Completion	7	9
Picture Arrangement	6	8
Block Design	6	10
Object Assembly	17	12
Coding	49	7
(Mazes)	12	11
	Sum Performance:	57

Verbal Scale IQ:	84
Performance Scale IQ:	108
Full Scale IQ:	95

Test Behavior

These test scores indicate that Lori is more capable of dealing with tasks that require her to process more visual information than auditory information. The 24-point difference between the Verbal and Performance scales indicates a serious delay in the development of oral language. Further testing and observation will attempt to define the nature of the difficulty.

Lori had difficulty in understanding verbal responses but examiner felt she understood enough to score validly. She was unable to repeat any digits backwards. There was a lack of meaningful effort on verbal tests with Lori giving up quickly with "I don't know" response. When pressed, she added "I can't do it." She needed reassurance throughout, with frequent positive feedback, e.g., "That was very good." On the performance subtests, she was quick and well planned (with the exception of coding), earning some time bonuses. However, again when the items became more difficult, she quit, adding, "I can't do it."

Lori was asked to draw a person and had difficulty holding the pencil properly or securely, dropping it on two occasions. Her fine motor coordination was poor; consequently, interpretation was limited. However, the figure she drew was a small girl located in the bottom right-hand corner of the page. The head was disproportionately large with a large mouth and sightless eyes. She used the bottom of the page as a baseline for the figure. When asked to draw her family doing something, she produced a crude drawing of three figures sitting at a table. She told the story that this was she and her parents eating.

Following the test sessions, Lori was seen again for an interview. Again she approached the psychologist easily and with no manifest anxiety.

The school psychologist looks at social/emotional as well as cognitive growth. Lori's problems in fine motor skills and language have contributed to her poor self-image and subsequent reluctance to interact with other children.

She was more verbal on this occasion and spoke of her self-consciousness over her speech. She states she feels the other children laugh at her and make fun of her. She feels she cannot do things other children can because she is "stupid and clumsy," and people don't know what she is saying. She says she wishes she had some friends but is afraid to approach other children. She says she feels better when with adults.

In summary, Lori is a delightful girl of 8 years, 8 months who is functioning within the average range of intellectual ability. The spread of 24 points between the Performance and Verbal Scales of the WISC indicates the severity of her deficit in language skills. Problems in speech and language have contributed to her increasing social isolation, as well as to her academic difficulties. The amount of individual attention she receives from parents, therapists, and teachers has reinforced dependence on adults for success in completing tasks.

Although emotional issues are a recognized concern, they appear to be secondary to her difficulties in speech, language, and fine motor development. Therapeutic intervention may need to be part of her total educational program. Consideration should be given to individual or group work with Lori's mother to encourage more positive management techniques at home.

Speech and Language

This section was prepared by the speech and language therapist. Since therapy had been ongoing for some time, this section is presented as a progress report.

Lori has a history of speech and language problems. Initial evaluation at a hospital clinic at age 4½ revealed difficulties in receptive language and mild-to-moderate dyspraxia resulting in severe articulation problems. She was seen for private therapy twice a week until she moved to her new home in March 1975. In September 1975, she was scheduled for therapy in the speech and language program.

Current evaluation shows Lori's receptive language skills to be one and a half years below expectancy for a child with her mental ability. Expressively, she shows much improvement in articulation over the past two years but she continues to have difficulty with all sibilant and "th" sounds. Although she is generally intelligible, in stressful situations articulation deteriorates and she becomes more difficult to understand. Skills in sentence formulation are approximately one to one-and-a-half years below age level.

Educational Assessment

This assessment was done by the reading specialist and resource room teacher. It identifies three major

Lori is performing between one and one-and-a-half years below grade level in reading. Her test scores show a consistent pattern of performance at the high first-/low second-grade reading level. While she can recognize letter names, her slow development in word attack skills reflects her problems in auditory processing. She can work better from the visual symbols (word recognition) than recalling the auditory pattern of words (oral spelling). Due to problems in articulation, it is difficult to evaluate her ability to blend and sequence sounds.

areas of educational concern: reading, math, and handwriting.

Oral reading is also difficult for the same reason. Language deficits appear to be causing Lori problems in understanding what she read.

In math, Lori can perform simple addition and subtraction operations using concrete objects. She can recognize the correct operations for the symbols +, −, and =. She can write the correct answer to simple addition story problems if no more than two numbers are involved.

Motor problems are also apparent. Handwriting is poor in form but not in spacing. She holds her pencil awkwardly and often breaks the point. She refuses to use scissors for art activities.

Test Results (at C.A. 8-6)

Illinois Test of Psycholinguistic Abilities

ITPA results show problems in processing auditory information.

	Scaled Scores
Auditory Reception	23
Visual Reception	38
Auditory Association	28
Visual Association	34
Verbal Expression	26
Manual Expression	32
Auditory Memory	32
Visual Memory	39
Grammatic Closure	29
Visual Closure	36
Auditory Closure	Difficult to score due to articulation problems
Sound Blending	
P.L.A. 7-1	Mean Scaled Score 32
Visual-Motor Integration Test	7-0

Inability to copy geometric forms. Inability to point to picture when word presented orally

Trouble in repeating sentences	*Peabody Picture Vocabulary Test*	M.A. 6–8
	Detroit Test of Learning Aptitude	
Inadequate ability in repeating a series of words	Auditory Attention for Related Syllables	M.A. 6–6
Inadequate ability in identifying likenesses and differences in words	*Wepman Test of Auditory Discrimination*	
	Auditory Memory Span	−2
	Auditory Discrimination	−2
Reading test scores show Lori performing at the low first-/high second-grade level, approximately two years below her actual grade placement.	*Reading Tests*	
	Gray Oral Reading Test	
	performed at beginning second-grade level	
On Gates-McKillop subtests, Lori generally performs better on tasks requiring visual rather than auditory processing.	*Gates-McKillop Reading Diagnostic Test*	

I.   Oral Reading 1.9

II.   Words: Flash Presentation 1.8

III.   Words: Untimed Presentation 2.1

IV.   Phrases: Flash Presentation   1.9

V.   Knowledge of Word Parts

     V-1.   Recognizing and Blending Word Parts unable to perform

     V-2.   Giving Letter Sounds 1.7–1.9

     V-3.   Naming Capital Letters 2.2

     V-4.   Naming Lower-case Letters 2.3

VI.   Recognizing the Visual Form of Sounds

     V1-1.   Nonsense Words 1.7

     V1-2.   Initial Letters 2.0

     V1-3.   Final Letters 1.0–1.6

     V1-4.   Vowels no score

VII. Auditory Blending unable to perform

VIII. Supplementary Tests

1. Spelling 1.6

2. Oral Vocabulary 2.5

Long-Range Objectives

Lori will:

1. develop vocabulary and comprehension skills that will enable her to read independently at a second-grade level.
2. develop functional mathematical skills that will enable her to do second-grade work.
3. acquire sufficient fine motor control to allow her to reproduce simple sentences legibly in cursive writing.
4. perform basic self-help skills appropriate to children her age.
5. articulate all speech sounds correctly in spontaneous speech.
6. understand and form spoken sentences appropriate to her age/ability level.
7. develop effective skills in interacting with peers.
8. work independently on learning-related tasks.

The Individualized Educational Program (IEP) should provide a clear and concise synthesis of all assessment information. It should be written in a straightforward and nontechnical (jargon-free) style. Copies of the Educational Plan should be provided for the classroom teacher, parents, and other personnel who work with the child.

SUMMARIES OF ASSESSMENT

Areas of Strength

Lori is an attractive child of 8 years, 8 months who shows average intellectual ability on an individual measure of intelligence. Gross motor skills are adequately developed. She shows enthusiasm for gym classes, although she does not choose to join in similar activities on the playground. She interacts well with adults and is generally cooperative and responsive. The visual channel is considerably stronger than the auditory channel, and Lori makes good use of visual information.

Areas of Constraint

Cognitive

Although Lori functions within the normal range of intelligence, her profile shows a wide scatter of scores. On verbal tests her lowest scores were those involving immediate recall, storage, and retrieval, indicating a serious problem in remembering auditory information. Some of the scatter may be accounted for by her poor language skills, e.g., verbalizing solution to a practical problem. Visual skills are at or beyond normal range.

Language is significantly below development in other areas. Lori's understanding of spoken language is one to one-and-a-half years below expectancy for a child with her mental ability. This language deficit causes difficulty with instruction that relies primarily on understanding what is said. It also makes reading comprehension more difficult and accounts for difficulties encountered in peer group interaction. Expressively, Lori shows sentence formulation problems as well as poorly articulated speech sounds.

Auditory perceptual skills are not well developed, so it is difficult for her to monitor herself auditorily during remedial speech training. These deficits also contribute to problems in word attack.

Motor skills

Fine motor movements of the upper extremities are slow. Handwriting is therefore poor and characteristic of a child who can deal with spatial relationships but has trouble recalling the proper motor movements associated with letter formation.

Emotional and social

At this time, there is concern for Lori's increasing isolation, withdrawal, and avoidance of peer group contacts. She expresses fear of being mocked and made fun of, so she seems to prefer adult relationships. This is interfering with her developing social skills and personal interactions. Her feelings of competency and self-worth are poor. She refers to herself as being "stupid and clumsy." In addition, she is having secondary problems from her exclusive adult relationships by maintaining an immature level of behavior, and not having to learn to do things for herself.

Learning Style

Lori is slow and methodical in her work. She can handle only one task at a time and requires frequent feedback to keep her moving. She works well with an adult or alone. When grouped with other children, she becomes a nonparticipant and tends to rely on their initiative.

Visual cues are necessary and well used. Multisensory approaches have worked well in the past and are more motivating. Given a choice, Lori prefers activities that require manipulation of objects or art media. Although verbal expression is limited, she has excellent use of body language and frequently communicates her needs through gesture.

Placement

Lori will remain in her regular third-grade class and receive academic support services in the resource room. Speech and language therapy will be provided three times a week in thirty-minute sessions. Reading, math, and fine motor skills will be joint responsibilities of the resource teacher and the regular class teacher, with specific support and supervision by the reading specialist. Individual counseling will be deferred in favor of communication and academic priorities, but the school counselor will monitor the development of self-concept and peer relationships within the ongoing school program.

CLASSROOM ACCOMMODATION

The following is a sample of a format that can be used for providing the translation of assessment information into practical techniques for the classroom teacher. General Teaching Techniques are those that apply in any instructional activity. Subject Matter Modifications indicate appropriate alterations and commonsense approaches to those areas of the curriculum that the child will encounter during his/her participation in the regular classroom program.

General Teaching Techniques

—give directions slowly and in specific steps
—seat her close to the source of instruction so she can clearly see all visual aids
—allow her to consult a friend for clarification or repetition of directions
—limit the amount of written work until she gains more proficiency in handwriting
—allow her to tape-record responses to questions requiring lengthy written response

—use visual aids whenever possible in instruction

—prepare for a new lesson by a brief review of previous material

—encourage the use of math and phonics games to reinforce skills

—provide a daily schedule containing class assignments with space to check off completed work

—structure for twenty-minute work periods with as much feedback as possible

—avoid direct questions requiring verbal response when working with whole class

—encourage verbal response in small-group activity of two or three children

—plan group activities with friends and supportive classmates

—provide opportunities for group reporting in which Lori takes responsibility for making and presenting visual aids related to reports

—structure questions in such a way that short answers are required

Subject Matter Modifications

Language Arts/Reading:

—use a language experience or basal reader stressing meaning

—use configuration and other visual clues in introducing new words

—compile card file of sight words to be used for sentence building as well as for word recognition

—plan discussion to build language and concepts prior to reading

—provide primer- or first-level material for oral reading practice

—use games for drill and reinforcement of phonics skills taught in resource room

Math:

—reinforce basic skills through games (worksheets will be provided by the resource room teacher)

Social Studies and Science:

—introduce new vocabulary in context

—use vocabulary cards with pictures when possible

—use tapes of text

—group her with children working with art media for projects

—encourage her to photograph events of field trip for later sequencing and verbalizing of events

—alert speech therapist of new units, etc., so vocabulary can be pretaught

—provide experience with convergent and divergent thinking

—highlight cause-and-effect relationships in science

—provide supplementary materials in graphs, maps, charts, illustrations, pictures, etc.

—provide peer practice in using library and reference materials

Art:

—simplify lesson prepared for the class

—provide a model of finished product

—avoid complex directions; give one step at a time

—keep cutting to a minimum or precut her materials when working in a large group

—encourage independent cutting when working by herself

—provide clay and other manipulative materials

—give recognition for good effort

Music:

—teach songs by rote

—use rhythm instruments to provide sense of auditory patterning and sequencing

—allow child to function as part of a group rather than solo

Physical Education:

—give clear, simple directions

—allow her to watch until she understands what she is expected to do

—give her a partner who can help with rules, etc.

—be sure she takes a turn at being captain and choosing a team

—compliment good performance

Instructional Program

The following is a sample of a more detailed format for the management of the child's instructional program. Since reading, math, and fine motor skills have been designated as joint responsibilities of the regular classroom teacher and resource personnel, objectives for these curriculum areas are presented for both regular and remedial instruction. Additional objectives are presented for speech and language therapy and for social/emotional development. The objectives suggested in the area of social/emotional development are the responsibility of the classroom teacher, in consultation with the school psychologist. It's important that classroom teachers be aware of remedial instructional plans so that skills introduced and developed in remedial instruction can be reinforced as part of the classroom program.

Global or long-range objectives are suggested for each area to be addressed in the educational plan. These long-range objectives are written on an annual basis. Specific instructional objectives are written for no more than a three-month period at a time, with updating at appropriate intervals. The personnel responsible for the implementation of the plan write the initial and all subsequent objectives. It is a joint effort. The task should not be undertaken by a single member of the team.

Each person involved with the implementation of the plan records and dates mastery of objectives as they are met. The following sample educational plan includes evaluative comments on the objectives that have been met. As others are met, further evaluative notations will be made.

The long-range objectives, listed on page 347, are translated into a specific instructional plan in a format similar to the following:

Objectives	Techniques/Materials	Evaluation (Date of Mastery)*
Subject: READING		
Lori will be able to:		
1. Dictate a verbal account of a field trip or other experience as the basis for a language experience story.	Experience chart	Ten stories were collected into a booklet (Oct. 13). Lori is motivated by interest in animals. Drawings help promote recall of experience and sequencing of events.
	Photographs or drawings to promote sequencing and recall	
2. Read 175 sight words, including at least 25% of the words on the Dolch list.	Use words from basal reading and experience stories	Has acquired a mastery of sight vocabulary of 175 words, including 35% of the words on the Dolch list (Nov. 2). Picture clues helped associate with printed words. Use of words in sentences was appropriate for a word meaning, but sentence formulation problems still evident.
	Compile an individual word card file	
	Match pictures to printed words for meaning	
	Use new words in oral sentences	
	Use card reader (like the Language Master) for reinforcement of sight words	
3. State the main idea, significant details, and sequence at the literal level from passages read in basal and/or supplementary reading material.	Basal series	
	SRA Reading Lab I	
	Retell stories with details and sequence	
	Point to pictures that illustrate main ideas and details of reading selection	
	Arrange comic strip frames for sequencing	

*Mastery level set for 100% accuracy.

	Objectives	Techniques/Materials	Evaulation (Date of Mastery)
Regular Classroom Program	4. Read aloud with adequate expression from experience chart or appropriate basal story.	Experience charts Use easy reading material from basal and/or supplementary sources. Provide oral reading sessions with the teacher and/or supportive classmates Use *Plays for Echo Reading* (Harcourt Brace Jovanovich) and other easy reading level plays. Tape-record oral reading for feedback and evidence of progress Choral reading of poetry and simple stories	
Remedial Instruction	Lori will be able to: 1. Auditorily discriminate between pairs of words that differ in only one phoneme (in initial, medial, and final position) by indicating verbally whether such words are the same or different. 2. Point to the appropriate consonant letter symbol for sounds in initial position in spoken words.	Teacher and taped practice Concentrate on vowel differences Individualized and pupil team practice Taped practice *First Talking Alphabet* (Scott Foresman)	Can discriminate between words based on sound differences in initial, medial, and final position (Sept. 29).

Remedial Instruction

Objectives	Techniques/Materials	Evaulation (Date of Mastery)
3. Isolate and identify the three sounds in a phonetically regular word that conforms to the CVC pattern.	Write letters representing the sounds in words dictated by the teacher *Speech To Print Phonics* (Harcourt Brace Jovanovich)	
4. Substitute initial consonant letters to build new words with phonograms conforming to the (C)VC and (C)VCe pattern	e.g.: Use "word ladders" to build new words: fat bake cat make bat lake sat cake rat rake	
5. Identify the meaning of words generated in Objective #4 above.	Picture matching Using new words in sentences	
6. Identify the number of syllables in a list of words with one or two syllables	Use sight word lists for syllabication practice Clap out syllables	
7. Underline suffixes that mark the third-person singular of verbs (–*s*), the past tense of verbs (–*ed*), noun plurals (–*s*), and noun possessives (–'s)	Whenever possible, use words from sight vocabulary for practice and application Use newspapers and children's magazines, as well as basal and experience stories	
8. Match common contractions (*can't, don't, I'm*, etc.) with word pairs that make up these contractions	Games and "contraction board" Practice exercises from beginning basal programs	

355

Objectives	Techniques/Materials	Evaulation (Date of Mastery)
9. Identify words that tell *where* or *when* after reading sentences containing these words	Use sentences from basal, supplementary and/or experience charts Worksheets and practice exercises *Reading Comprehension worksheets* (Frank Schaffer Publications)	
10. State orally main ideas, details, and sequence implied in reading material	Teacher questions demanding inference Use short selections at beginning Use simple cartoons (*Peanuts, Family Circus*, etc.) for inference of what is happening and where humor is	

Remedial Instruction

Subject: Math

Lori will be able to:

1. Identify the value of a penny, a nickel, and a dime.	Use actual coins	Mastery (Sept. 27).
2. Make change for a dime, using different combinations of pennies and nickels.	Play "store," buying objects labeled appropriately	
3. Measure a line or an object up to 12 inches or 30 centimeters long.	Use ruler or tape to measure common objects in the classroom	Worked with group measuring oak tag designs for art project. Measured designs accurately with consistency (Nov. 7).

Regular Classroom Program

Objectives | *Techniques/Materials* | *Evaulation (Date of Mastery)*

Remedial Instruction

Objectives	Techniques/Materials	Evaulation (Date of Mastery)
Lori will be able to:		
1. Associate the spoken words *add, plus, join, take away, minus,* and *less* with the corresponding mathematical symbols and appropriate operations.	Flannel board symbols Counting and grouping objects in the room (pencils, books, etc.)	(October 3)
2. Associate the spoken word *equal(s)* with the mathematical symbol and condition of equal sets.	Use simple word problems and have Lori hold up appropriate symbol card	(October 4)
3. Write the correct equation from a verbal story problem; e.g., $4 + 3 = 7$.	Use manipulative objects (chips, blocks, etc.) for practice	Mastery using manipulative objects (October 16).
4. Add sets of 1 through 9 orally (sums less than 10).	Use flash cards for practice of number facts	
5. Add sets of 1 through 15 orally (sums less than 20).	Use games like "Addition Bingo" and "Magic Squares" for drill and reinforcement *New Ways in Numbers (D. C. Health)*	
6. Write the correct answer to simple addition story problems given orally.	Have story problems relate to common topics; i.e., add crayons, cookies, etc.	

Subject: Handwriting (Fine Motor Skills)

Objectives	Techniques/Materials	Evaulation (Date of Mastery)
Lori will be able to:		
1. Hold crayon or primary pencil in correct handwriting position.	Use rubber grip on pencil or use contoured writing implement	Can hold writing implement appropriately with consistency (Oct. 9).

357

	Objectives	Techniques/Materials	Evaluation (Date of Mastery)
Regular Classroom Program	2. Write lowercase letters *e, i, l, o, r, u, v,* and *w* in cursive.	Use primary paper with lines accentuated in black	Letters are well formed but writing is still slow and deliberate (Nov. 21).
	3. Connect three of the above letters in any random order.	Trace over models with finger, first with eyes open, then with eyes closed	
	4. Write the capital letters L, S, and G in cursive.	Use sandpaper, clay, and window screen letters first; then trace models written on paper.	
	5. Write her name in cursive.	Use vocabulary words from reading for handwriting practice whenever possible	Can write her name legibly in cursive but still needs much help on letter formation (Sept. 28).
		Limit amount of written work until more proficiency and independence in handwriting are gained	
Resource Room	Lori will be able to: 1. Use a pencil or crayon to reproduce a design or geometric forms from a model.	Use DLM materials	(Oct. 26)
	2. Cut out strips and simple geometric shapes from paper.	Make collage	
		Coordinate activities with art teacher	
		Cut out pictures from magazines and catalogues for matching in word meaning practice	
	3. Weave strips of paper in a simple "over and under" design	Make placemats for class party	
	4. Tie her shoelaces.	Practice with "Dressy Bessy" doll	

Objectives	Techniques/Materials	Evaulation (Date of Mastery)
5. Independently operate buttons, zippers, snaps, and other fasteners on her clothing	Use zipper board	
	Have Lori help kindergarten children get dressed	
	Self-help skills should be encouraged in all activities	

Subject: Speech and Language (Articulation)

Lori will be able to:

Objectives	Techniques/Materials	Evaulation (Date of Mastery)
1. Articulate /s/ correctly in isolation	Call attention to /s/ and /z/ as being "hidden" sounds. Contrast with visible sounds	Can articulate /s/ in isolation (Sept. 27).
2. Articulate /z/ correctly in isolation		Can articulate /z/ in isolation (Oct. 2).
3. Discriminate between /s/ and /z/ in isolation and in words.	Reinforce concept of voiced and un-voiced sounds Provide auditory discrimination activities for the /s/-/z/ contrast	Can discrimate the /s/-/z/ contrast (Oct. 6). Tends to subvocalize to make use of kinesthetic clues in discrimination exercises.
4. Articulate /s/ and /z/ correctly in the initial, medial, and final position in words.	Highlight tactile-kinesthetic features of sounds	
	Use placement clues	
5. Use correct articulation of /s/ and /z/ in spontaneous speech.	Incorporate words learned as sight vocabulary in reading whenever possible	
	Creative dramatics and improvised puppet shows	

Speech and Language Therapist

Objectives: Speech and Language (Receptive and Expressive Language)

Subject	Techniques/Materials	Evaulation (Date of Mastery)
Lori will be able to: 1. Name seven appropriate items in five categories: vehicles, clothing, animals, furniture, foods.	Use *Peabody Language Development Kit* for categories Early sections of *30 Lessons in Outlining* (Curriculum Associates)	Mastery (Oct. 10).
2. Correctly identify objects within the above categories based on verbal descriptions of the objects.	Teacher directions and descriptions	
3. Perform a correct motor response based on a one- or two-step direction.	Play "Simon Says" using motor movements to accompany verbal directions Play "Simon Says" using verbal directions alone Play "Giant Step"	Responds correctly to one- and two-step directions (Oct. 25).
4. Perform a correct motor response based on a three-step oral direction.	Give directions such as "Open the book, turn to page 4, and point to the door." Incorporate directions for activities suggested in Fine Motor Skills whenever possible	

Speech and Language Therapist

Objectives	Techniques/Materials	Evaulation (Date of Mastery)
5. Describe scenes and actions from pictures.	Pictures for storytelling from *Sounds of Language* series (Holt, Rinehart and Winston) and *Comprehension Instructional Center* (Steck Vaughn) Use pictures from magazines, posters, and other sources. Use dictated descriptions as basis of language experience activities in remedial reading	
6. Illustrate the present, past, and future tenses of verbs through statements accompanying an action.	Practice with statements like "I am hoppin," "Yesterday I hopped," "Tomorrow I will hop," accompanied by appropriate actions Use regular verbs that are part of reading vocabulary	

Speech and Language Therapist

*Appendix B: Finding and Helping the Special-Needs Child in the Regular Classroom**

The following charts summarize some important aspects of working with special-needs children in the regular classroom. The charts identify observable classroom behaviors for various types of learning problems, and some general teaching techniques that will allow the teacher to accommodate for the child in the regular classroom. Remedial strategies are suggested, along with suggestions for reading instruction that might be appropriate for each disability area.

In examining the observable behaviors, it should be noted that children with problems may not exhibit each and every one of the behavioral characteristics noted. Nor does one single behavior immediately indicate a learning problem for the child. For example, if a child rarely loses the place in reading, it does not mean that s/he has no problem with visual perception. And just because a child is shy and rarely talks in class, it doesn't mean that s/he has an expressive language disorder or an emotional problem. One will find the same

*The charts in this appendix are adapted from *Reading and Learning Styles,* a manual *from a videotaped program "Integration of Children With Special Needs in a Regular Class-room," by Jean Mooney and John Savage. (Lexington, Mass.: Lexington Public Schools.* Funded under Title III, ESEA, Grant #31-73-005-0 and Title IV, Education of the Handicapped Act, Grant #73-000-041, 1973), pp. 12–19. Reprinted with permission of Merrimac Educational Center.

behavior noted for different problem areas. Assessment is built upon a *pattern* of repeated behaviors, so a single behavior does not automatically signify a learning problem for the child.

Likewise, one will find similar suggestions for classroom accommodations, remedial strategies, and reading instruction. Not only does this signify the interrelatedness of many learning problems, it suggests the need for good teaching for all children, whatever their needs may be.

The observable behaviors, classroom accommodations, remedial strategies, and reading suggestions contained in these charts are tentative recommendations that the teacher might find helpful in identifying and instructing children with special needs in the regular classroom.

AUDITORY PERCEPTION
(See Chapter 4)

Observable Behavior

may have speech problems

may appear to be hard of hearing

has problems in attending to listening activities

may sequence sounds oddly

shows difficulty with auditory discrimination

may be confused by verbal directions

learns best through demonstration

may become overly active in a noisy environment

has difficulty with spelling

usually does not complete seatwork

Classroom Accommodations

face child when speaking

allow child to sit near speaker

use headphones and cassettes for reinforcement and drill

write directions and assignments on board

use "buddy" system

avoid learning activities in busy classroom environment unless quiet study space is available

Remedial Strategies

discrimination exercises

use auditory memory training, e.g., "I packed my trunk" game

sequencing exercises

practice rhythmic auditory movement training

use card reader (like Language Master) for auditory visual integration

Reading Instruction for Regular Classroom

begin with whole word approach if visual skills are intact

emphasize visual clues (configuration) in teaching new words

delay phonics until auditory perceptual skills are strong enough to support success

when ready for phonics, try a linguistic or analytic phonics approach

use phonic games for drill and reinforcement

encourage development of ability to revisualize as technique in spelling

RECALLING AUDITORY IMAGES
(See Chapter 4)

Observable Behavior	Classroom Accommodations	Reading Instruction for Regular Classroom
unable to remember verbal directions	give short, simple directions	controlled vocabulary based on sight and meaning
has difficulty remembering auditory sequences—alphabet, multiplication tables, days of the week, etc.	use visual clues to reinforce auditory learning	multisensory approach to learning sound-symbol relationship
has problem in remembering home address or phone number	keep vocabulary notebooks for science and social studies	picture clues to help child recall story sequences
has difficulty recalling new vocabulary in science and social studies	have child write material to be memorized	provide structured aids for recall; blank outlines, verbal clues ("First . . . ., then . . . , finally . . .")
unable to memorize simple poems, lines from play scripts, etc.	provide frequent review	have child locate rather than recall answer in comprehension practice
	Remedial Strategies	
	teach the use of mnemonic clues	
	work on exercises and games to develop memory in concentration sequencing games	
	use card reader to reinforce spelling	
	promote "overlearning" through drill and repetition	
	encourage revisualizing in spelling	

VISUAL PERCEPTION
(See Chapter 5)

Observable Behavior	Classroom Accommodations	Reading Instruction for Regular Classroom
may reverse letters and numbers	reduce number of examples on a worksheet, math, etc.	teach alphabet through auditory sequence first
does not enjoy pictures or books	use marker when reading	use verbal mediation to teach letter formation, i.e., Spalding
shows poor visual discrimination of similar letters	allow child to sit where s/he can see the board comfortably	begin with synthetic phonic approach if auditory skills are intact
has difficulty with different types of print	do not overload with worksheets or workbook pages	use flash cards and similar drill for extending sight vocabulary
loses place frequently in reading		
has difficulty finding word or section on a page	*Remedial Strategies*	
cannot distinguish between words with similar shapes, e.g., boy, dog	matching activities in upper- and lowercase letters	
has difficulty copying from the board	develop skill at using configurational clues	
may tilt head to "see better"	develop awareness and letter discrimination of various forms of print	
	encourage children to describe features of objects, symbols, etc.	

RECALLING VISUAL IMAGES

(See Chapter 5)

Observable Behavior	Classroom Accommodations	Reading Instruction for Regular Classroom
cannot freely recall written sequences in alphabet, math tables, etc.	encourage the use of auditory clues	emphasize decoding in beginning stages of reading instruction
may be inconsistent in remembering sight words	allow child to trace over visual patterns	use tachistoscope for work on rapid recall
has great difficulty with spelling	use color coding to make patterns more vivid	use synthetic phonics in decoding unknown words
forgets where things are left out—	encourage orderly arrangement of personal equipment	drill on sight vocabulary
misplaces his belongings		emphasize sound elements in spelling
	Remedial Strategies	
	reproducing visual sequences with blocks or beads, etc.	
	puzzles or mazes	
	dot-to-dot pictures	
	visual memory games	

UNDERSTANDING LANGUAGE
(See Chapter 6)

Observable Behavior	Classroom Accommodations	Reading Instruction for Regular Classroom
may have delayed speech development	use short, simple directions	develop "organic" vocabulary; teach words through strongest learning modality
may be slow to respond to directions or questions	give visual clue or demonstrate directions whenever possible	begin with language experience approach
has poor vocabulary due to difficulty attaching meaning to words	tape resource material in social studies and science using simpler language	when auditory perceptual skills are developed, use analytic phonics or linguistic program
has difficulty determining the main idea	keep vocabulary notebooks	check comprehension with short, direct questions
may repeat directions to him/herself until s/he understands	organize a "buddy" system	provide help with independent vocabulary practice exercises
may understand better with visual aids, gestures, or manual expression	review previous lesson before starting new ones	
may have social problem because of not understanding peer group play	*Remedial Strategies*	
experiences difficulty with idiomatic language and multiple meanings of words	train in listening skills	
	work on vocabulary development	
	write from dictation first before expecting independent writing	
	develop ability to relate story with correct sequence of ideas	
	use crossword puzzles, riddles, etc., for word building, inferential thinking, etc.	

EXPRESSING LANGUAGE
(See Chapter 6)

Observable Behavior	Classroom Accommodations	Remedial Strategies	Reading Instruction for Regular Classroom
Word-Finding Difficulty	allow sufficient time for oral responses	use picture cards for rapid naming drill	teach decoding according to strongest input modality
cannot recall words for use	do not put child "on the spot" but encourage sharing, story telling, etc.	teach meaning of idiomatic language	use language experience charts
unable to build a cohesive narrative	help child organize material to facilitate recall; use outlines, etc.	develop verbal expression	work on written language with vocabulary, sentences, etc.
uses definitions instead of words s/he cannot recall		provide specific practice in sentence formulation	use vivid and action-packed stories and pictures for stimulation and verbal expression
may use elaborate gesture system, sound effects		tape written work first, then transcribe	
appears nonfluent at times		emphasize tense forms in verbs	
Sentence Formulation Problems		use sentence completion exercises	
may be shy and seldom talks in class		use exercises in rearranging words in scrambled sentences	
uses immature syntax or "telegraphic" speech		read aloud frequently to the child	
may recognize correct sentence structure but may be unable to reproduce sentence patterns			
has problems writing sentences and stories			

PROBLEMS FORMING CONCEPTS

(See Chapter 7)

Observable Behavior	Classroom Accommodations	Reading Instruction for Regular Classroom
trouble with abstract reasoning	make generalizations for the child	develop use of appropriate picture clues
slow to respond to questions	point out similarities and differences in new material	work on context clues
inability to see similarities and differences	ask simple, direct questions	emphasize oral reading
poor reading comprehension	structure questions for logical answers	use story cards (comic strips, etc.) for getting main idea
difficulty in learning new concepts in math, science, etc.	*Remedial Strategies*	emphasize thinking skills through listening exercises prior to reading
failure to generalize	practice in categorizing and classifying	
concrete view of the world	verbal and pictorial absurdities	
unable to draw conclusions	detective game to develop inductive reasoning	
	check comprehension carefully, giving auditory and visual clues	
	riddles for inferential thinking	

EMOTIONAL PROBLEMS*
(See Chapter 8)

Observable Behavior	Classroom Accommodations	Reading Instruction for Regular Classroom
may be withdrawn or extremely shy	build on strengths in phys. ed., art, and other curriculum areas	use language experience
may refuse to engage in learning or social activities	provide opportunities for child to engage in classroom "housekeeping" chores	try to find books and stories that child can relate to
may be prone to temper tantrums or crying spells	allow child to assume leadership role in games and other group activities	provide reading experiences within child's ability
is easily frustrated at the slightest setback	provide frequent praise for jobs well done	use cross-age tutoring
may exhibit evidence of low self-concept	set aside separate work space for child	use high-interest material
may outwardly express intense dislike of school and/or school-related activities	provide time for emotional release when necessary	break longer learning activities into small segments
may have trouble getting along with classmates	*Remedial Strategies*	use contracts for reading-related tasks
	help child identify and control disturbing behavior	
may be aggressive or openly hostile to teacher and/or other children	set realistic goals	
	establish firm, consistent rules	
	reward positive behavior	

*With many children, emotional problems are a basic "overlay" on learning problems. Therefore, it is important to determine whether all learning systems are functional before coming to the conclusion that the problem is primarily emotional. This chart is useful only when that determination is made.

Appendix C:
"Information, Please":
Where to Go
for Information
on Reading and
Handicapped Learners

The knowledge explosion has created a mountain of information in the field of education as it has in other areas of learning. Getting this information to where it will do the most good—in the hands of the practicing professional educator—is no easy job.

In Chapter 10, reference was made to resource centers designed to disseminate information on materials and programs designed to help the classroom teacher in planning instruction for children with special needs. A number of agencies and organizations are available to provide this kind of supportive help and information.

For the classroom teacher, the network most immediately applicable for information on media and materials for handicapped learners is the National Information Center for Special Education Materials (NICSEM). NICSEM is a national clearing-house that provides information to answer teachers' practical questions about instructional materials that are available for use with special needs children: What materials are available? Where can I get them? How much do they cost? It is a computer based, on-line, interactive, retrieval system specifically designed for the purpose of assisting teachers and other educational professionals (as well as parents) in locating information about instructional materials in the field of special education. Information on teacher training materials (in-service as well as pre-service) is also available. In addition, NICSEM publishes two newsletters, *Frankly Speaking* and *The Program*

Tree, which review the latest information on program development and the use of various instructional materials (commercial and teacher developed) to teach disabled learners. NICSEM is located at the University of Southern California, University Park, Los Angeles, California 90007.

As part of the national network of Instructional Materials Centers, there are sixteen Regional Resource Centers providing more direct assistance to school and university personnel through activities sponsored in the individual states. The following is a list of the Regional Resource Centers and the states served.

Northwest Regional Resource Center
Clinical Service Building, Third Floor
1590 Willamette Street
University of Oregon
Eugene, Oregon   97401

States Served:
Alaska, Hawaii, Samoa,
Guam, Trust Territories
Washington, Idaho,
Oregon, Montana,
Wyoming

California Regional Resource Center
600 South Commonwealth Avenue
Suite 1304
University of Southern California
Los Angeles, California   90005

States Served:
California

Southwest Regional Resource Center
2363 Foothill Drive, Suite G
University of Utah
Salt Lake City, Utah   84109

Stat3s Served:
Nevada, Utah, Colorado,
Arizona, New Mexico,
B.I.A. Schools

Midwest Regional Resource Center
Drake University
1332–26th Street
Des Moines, Iowa   50311

States Served:
North Dakota, Oklahoma,
South Dakota, Nebraska,
Kansas, Missouri,
Arkansas

Texas Regional Resource Center
Texas Education Agency
201 East 11th Street
Austin, Texas   78701

States Served:
Texas

Mid-East Regional Resource Center
George Washington University
1901 Pennsylvania Avenue, N.W.
Suite 505
Washington, D.C.   20006

States Served:
Maryland, Delaware,
West Virginia,
North Carolina

Mid-South Regional Resource Center
University of Kentucky Research Found.
Porter Building, Room 131
Lexington, Kentucky   40506

States Served:
Kentucky, Tennessee,
Virginia

District of Columbia Regional
Resource Center
Howard University
2935 Upton Street, N.W.
Washington, D.C.   20008

States Served:
District of Columbia

Southeast Regional Resource Center
Auburn University at Montgomery
Montgomery, Alabama   36117

States Served:
Louisiana, Mississippi,
Alabama, Georgia, South
Carolina, Florida, Puerto
Rico, Virgin Islands

Pennsylvania Regional Resource Center
Pennsylvania State Department of Education
443 South Gulph Road
King of Prussia, Pennsylvania   19406

States Served:
Pennsylvania

Great Lakes Regional Resource Center
Michigan State Department of Education
Post Office Box 30008
Lansing, Michigan   48902

States Served:
Minnesota, Wisconsin,
Michigan, Indiana

Illinois Regional Resource Center
Northern Illinois University
DeKalb, Illinois   60115

States Served:
Illinois

Ohio Regional Resource Center
Ohio State Department of Education
933 High Street
Worthington, Ohio   43085

States Served:
Ohio

Northeast Regional Resource Center
New Jersey State Department of Education
168 Bank Street
Hightstown, New Jersey   08520

States Served:
Maine, Vermont, New
Hampshire, Massachusetts,
Rhode Island, Connecti-
cut, New Jersey

New York State Regional Resource Center
New York State Education Department
55 Elk Street
Albany, New York   12234

States Served:
New York

New York City Regional Resource Center
City University of New York
33 West-42nd Street
New York, New York   10036

States Served:
New York City only

While it provides information on media and materials for use with special needs children, NICSEM does not provide information on education research, journal articles, or other professionally related materials. The most complete collection of this type of information is the Educational Resources Information Center (ERIC).

ERIC is a federally funded national information network designed to gather, store, and disseminate information on education. It contains descriptions of examplary programs, research reports, bibliographies, selected journal articles and other pertinent material on a variety of educational topics. Among the 13 topic-related clearing houses that ERIC maintains are:

Clearinghouse on Reading and
Communication Skills
NCTE Headquarters
1111 Kenyon Road
Urbana, Illinois   61801

Clearinghouse on Handicapped and
Gifted Children
CEC Headquarters
1920 Association Drive
Reston, Virginia   22091

Further information about the entire ERIC system and services is available from ERIC Central, National Institute of Education, Washington, D.C. 20208.

A number of organizations and agencies—university libraries, educational service organizations, state departments of education, and private companies—offer on-line computer access to ERIC documents and other sources of published information related to education. Usually for a reasonable fee, these agencies will conduct a customized computer search for such information on specific topics. A state-by-state list of organizations and agencies that provide this type of service can be obtained from ERIC Processing and Reference Facility, 4833 Rugby Ave., Suite 303, Bethesda, Maryland 20014.

In addition to the ERIC Clearinghouses that NCTE and CEC maintains, the professional organizations identified in Chapter 10 (IRA, ACLD and the Orton Society) also offer information and services on current research and other professionally related topics.

Appendix D:
A Consumer's Guide
to Interpreting
the ITPA

There are numerous approaches to evaluating learning and language problems in children. Although its validity has been the subject of recent debate, the ITPA is an instrument that has been widely used. When properly administered, it can provide useful information about a child's development of skills that support success in reading. It can identify areas of deficit that have implications for curriculum modifications and accommodations.

Unfortunately, the test is often used by specialists who are unable to report results in terms that are meaningful to the consumers of the information (i.e., parents, teachers, administrators, counselors, etc.) When this occurs, teachers can derive some basic information from the scores reported. The following technique should by no means be considered a clinical interpretation. There is no substitute for that. However, it can provide some insight into a child's difficulties. In essence, it asks three basic questions of the data.

Question #1. *Is there a difference between the child's ability to deal with tasks at the automatic level and his/her functioning at the representational level?*

Obtain a mean scaled score for tasks at each level and compare. A difference of 7 or more points can be considered significant.

Representational	Auditory Reception	_____		
	Auditory Association	_____		
	Verbal Expression	_____		
	Visual Reception	_____		
	Visual Association	_____		
	Manual Expression	_____		
	total	_____ / 6	=	_____ mean Scaled Score

Automatic	Auditory Sequential Memory	_____		
	Grammatic Closure	_____		
	Visual Sequential Memory	_____		
	Visual Closure	_____		
	total	_____ / 4	=	_____ mean Scaled Score

Question #1 relates to the fact that some children are able to deal with the redundant and more automatic features of language, but experience difficulty when asked to deal with meaningful symbols. The reverse can also be true. Knowing the child is experiencing difficulty dealing with meaningful symbols can alert a teacher to the possibility of poor vocabulary and comprehension of pictorial as well as verbal material, weaknesses that will have serious implications for reading, which is a symbolic process using both auditory and visual input. Problems at the automatic level can be associated with problems in memory and/or auditory and visual perceptual deficits that can affect basic word attack skills.

Question #2. *Is there a difference between the child's ability to deal with auditory information and his/her ability to deal with visual information?*

Obtain a mean scaled score for all auditory and visual tasks and compare.

Auditory

Auditory Reception _____

Auditory Association _____

Verbal Expression _____

Auditory Sequential
Memory _____

Grammatic Closure _____

total _____   = _____ mean Scaled Score
5

Visual

Visual Reception _____

Visual Association _____

Verbal Expression _____

Auditory Sequential
Memory _____

Grammatic Closure _____

total _____   = _____ mean Scaled Score
5

Question #2 looks at the child's ability to deal with auditory and visual information. Some children show decided strengths or weaknesses in one modality. Identifying the area of strength can help a teacher design appropriate instructional modifications within the regular curriculum.

Question #3. *Is there a difference among the three processes of language functioning: reception, association, and expression?*

Obtain a mean scaled score for each and compare.

Question #3 looks at differences in the language processes of reception, association (mediation), and expression. When the breakdown comes in the receptive process, the child is seriously impaired in his/her ability to gain meaning from incoming information, which has implications for cognitive growth as well. For him/her, there are no significant differences among the

Reception

Auditory Reception	_____	
Visual Reception	_____	
total	_____ / 2	= _____ mean Scaled Score

Association

Auditory Association	_____	
Visual Association	_____	
total	_____ / 2	= _____ mean Scaled Score

Expression

Verbal Expression	_____	
Manual Expression	_____	
total	_____ / 2	= _____ mean Scaled Score

three processes, since a problem in reception affects the other two. A child who shows adequate receptive skills but difficulty in association (and therefore the expressive process as well) is able to comprehend the meaning of words and pictures, but cannot perform the internal manipulation with language, that is, the mediation that allows him/her to come to correct conclusions about what is said or seen. Yet another group of children can understand and associate adequately, but experience difficulty in formulating language for expression. Problems in this area may affect writing more than reading skills.

Author Index

Adams, T., 237, 239
Affleck, J.Q., 170
Alexander, J.E., 277
Anastasiow, N., 112
Audette, R., 335
Aukerman, R., 14, 39, 129, 141, 170, 189, 204
Austin, M.C., 284, 311
Axline, V.M., 256, 276

Baker, N.J., 141, 169, 204
Ball, S., 277
Barraga, N., 151, 169, 170
Barrett, T.C., 231, 245
Barsch, R., 44, 53, 61, 67, 68, 69
Bartel, N., 70, 170
Bateman, B., 45, 67, 69, 130, 141
Beery, K.E., 169
Bellugi, U., 175, 204
Bender, L., 170
Binet, A., 43
Birch, J.W., 142
Bishop, V.E., 161, 169, 170
Bloom, B.S., 32, 39, 204, 231, 244
Bloom, L., 204
Bond, G.L., 39, 79, 107, 204, 237, 238, 245, 276, 283, 311
Boyd, L., 169
Braille, L., 43
Brown, R., 175, 204
Buchananan, C.D., 170
Buckley, L., 141
Buktenica, N., 169
Burke, C.M., 108
Burns, P.C., 39
Buros, O.K., 112
Burrow, W.H., 215, 244, 245
Bush, W.J., 63, 69, 112

Carrow, E., 204
Cawley, J.F., 215, 244, 245
Chalfant, J.C., 53, 68, 169
Chall, J., 129, 141, 170, 244, 276

Charles, C.M., 70
Cicci, R., 142
Combs, A.W., 276
Corah, N.L., 169
Cruickshank, W., 44, 67
Cullum, A., 141
Cutler, R., 68

Dahlberg, C.C., 276
Darrow, H.F., 311
Deno, E., 47, 68
Dore-Boyce, K., 245
Dunn, L.M., 46, 68, 204
Dupont, H., 277
Durkin, D., 39, 312
Durrell, D.D., 142
Dyk, R.B., 68
Dykstra, R., 39, 204

Ekwall, E., 108, 112, 142, 165, 166, 170, 276, 277

Farr, R., 112
Faterson, H.F., 68
Fernald, G., 63, 69
Filler, R.C., 277
Forness, S.R., 70
Frierson, E.C., 50, 68
Fries, C., 38
Fristoe, M., 141
Frostig, M., 17, 53, 64, 68, 69, 152, 166, 169, 170

Gallaudet, 43
Gardner, W., 68
Gearheart, B.R., 70, 142, 112
Gervase, C., 245
Getman, G., 44, 62, 67, 69
Gibman, E., 169
Gibson, J., 152, 169
Gibson, J.J., 169

Giles, M., 63, 69
Gillespie, P.H., 245
Gillingham, A., 62, 69, 164, 170
Goldman, R., 141
Goldstein, H., 67
Gollin, E., 152, 169
Goodenough, D.R., 68
Goodman, K.S., 96, 108
Goodman, L., 69
Goodman, Y., 108
Goodstein, H.A., 215, 244, 245
Gray, W.S., 38
Groff, P.J., 311
Guilford, J.P., 231, 244
Guszack, F., 39

Hagen, E.P., 107
Hainsworth, P.K., 204
Hakim, C., 108
Hall, M.A., 190, 204, 205
Hallahan, D., 52, 68, 169
Hammill, D., 69, 70, 170
Hanna, J.S., 39
Hanna, P.R., 39
Hanninen, K.A., 170
Harris, Anna, 93, 108
Harris, A.J., 39, 107, 237, 238
Hay, J., 170
Hayden, D.L., 67
Heilman, A.W., 39, 312
Hewett, F.M., 53, 68, 70, 256, 258, 276, 277
Hoagland, J., 276
Hodges, R.E., 39, 205
Hoepfner, R., 244
Horne, D., 69
Horowitz, F.D., 204
Howe, S.G., 43
Howes, V., 311

Jennings, F., 38
Johnson, D.D., 39, 53, 68, 188, 201, 204, 205, 312

Johnson, L., 245
Johnson, S.W., 70
Johnson, M.S., 108
Jordan, L., 67
Junkala, J., 99, 107, 108

Kaluger, G., 276
Kantrowicz, V., 276
Karlin, R., 39, 312
Karnes, M., 63, 69
Karp, S.A., 68
Kass, C., 141
Kauffman, J., 52, 68, 169
Kagan, J., 69
Kelley, C.R., 169
Kennedy, E.C., 245
Kephart, N.C., 245
Kephart, R., 44, 53, 61, 62, 67, 68, 69
Kimmel, E., 276
Kirk, I., 67
Kirk, S.A., 44, 53, 68, 70, 141, 169, 204, 215, 219, 244, 245, 256, 276
Kirk, W., 53, 68, 141, 169, 204
Kleffner, F.R., 205
Krathwohl, D.R., 32, 39
Kress, R.A., 108

Lamport, J., 39
Lang, J.B., 276
LaPray, M., 108
Larsen, S., 69
Lazar, M., 311
Lee, L., 205
Lefiver, D., 68, 69
Lehtinan, L., 44, 67
Leland, B., 141, 169, 204
Lenneberg, E., 204
Lerner, J.W., 107, 112
Long, N.J., 277
Lord, F., 67, 70
Lowenbraum, S., 170

Lowenfeld, B., 169, 170

Marshall, J.C., 201, 205
Martin, B., 133, 141
Martuza, V.R., 112
Masia, B.B., 32, 39
Maslow, P., 152, 166, 169, 170
McCarthy, J.J., 53, 68, 141, 169,
    204
McCracken, G., 39, 170
McCracken, R.A., 108
McCullough, C.M., 312
McGuire, D., 245
McNeil, D., 204
Minskoff, E.H., 64, 69
Minskoff, J., 69
Misner, M., 245
Moffett, J., 220, 244
Monroe, M., 239, 240
Mooney, J., 141
Morasky, R.L., 70
Morency, A., 141
Morphett, 244
Morrison, C., 284, 311
Morse, W., 68
Moss, J.W., 67
Myklebust, H., 44, 52, 67, 68, 176,
    177, 188, 201, 204, 205

Newcombe, F., 201, 205
Newcomer, P., 69

Orton, S., 62, 69
Osser, H., 169

Palloway, E., 245
Payne, J., 245
Payne, R., 245
Pescosolido, J., 245
Phillips, P.P., 142
Pick, A., 169

Pittam, V.G., 159, 170
Potter, T.C., 108
Powell, B.J., 169

Quandt, T.J., 277
Quay, H.D., 68

Rae, G., 108
Randle, K., 169
Robeck, M.C., 277
Robinson, F., 195, 205
Roe, B.D., 39
Roswell, F.G., 276
Rudorf, E.H., Jr., 39, 205

Sabatino, D., 45, 67
Sanders, D.A., 141
Sanders, N.M., 231, 244
Sartain, H.W., 311
Savage, J.F., 205, 312
Scheffelin, M., 53, 68, 169
Schleichkorn, J., 68
Schmidt, H.J., 205
Schmidt, K.J., 205
Scholl, G.T., 170
Schultz, J., 141
Semel, E.M., 205
Serio, M., 68
Sherman, G.B., 312
Silvaroli, N.J., 108
Sipay, E.R., 39, 107
Siqueland, M.L., 204
Smith, F., 39
Smith, J., 245, 312
Smith, M., 175, 204
Smith, N.B., 93, 108
Smith, R., 39
Spache, E.B., 39, 69, 312
Spache, G.D., 39, 64, 69, 112, 169,
    312
Spalding, R., 164, 170
Spalding, W., 164, 170

Sperry, L., 70
Stephens, T.M., 70
Stillman, B., 62, 69, 170
Strauss, A., 44, 61, 67

Templin, M., 122, 141
Thorndike, R.L., 107
Tinker, M.A., 79, 107, 237, 238
        245, 276, 283, 311, 312
Torgenson, G., 237, 239

Van Allen, R., 205
Veatch, 311
Vite, I.W., 311

Walcutt, C., 39, 170
Washburne, C., 220, 244
Waugh, K.W., 112
Wechsler, D., 170

Wiederholt, J.L., 69
Weig, E.H., 205
Weishahn, M.W., 70, 142
Welch, E., 68
Wepman, J., 44, 67, 141
Whittlesey, J., 68, 69
Whitty, P.A., 276
Willemberg, E.P., 112
Wilson, J.A., 277
Wilson, R.M., 245
Wingo, C., 170
Wiseman, D., 45, 67, 69
Witkin, H.A., 68
Wolf, A., 311
Woodcock, R.W., 141
Wright, L., 68

Zigmond, N.K., 130, 141, 142
Zintz, M.V., 39, 276
Zolkos, H.H., 276

Subject Index

Ability grouping, 1, 283-5, 308
Accommodation, 1, 60, 104-05, 118, 126, 149, 153, 185, 200, 222, 288, 289
Achievement test, 1 (*See also* Reading achievement test(s))
Acoustic trauma, 1, 117
Activity level, 55 (*See also* Overactivity)
Acuity, 1, 24
  auditory, 84
  visual, 104
Advantageous seating, 118
Affective dimensions of reading, 32-34, 247-276
Albinism, 1-2, 147
Alphabet training, 222-3
Amplification, 2, 119
Analytic phonics, 2, 15, 136, 158, 228
Ancillary services, 2, 60
Anomia, 2
Aphasia, 1, 181
Apraxia, 2, 197
Assessment, 57, 71-105, 240, 304 (*See also* Diagnosis, Evaluation)
  auditory perceptual problems, 127
  expressive language, 197-8
  formal, 57, 83-88
  informal, 57, 82-83, 91-99
  of self-concept, 251-2
  receptive language, 183
  visual perceptual problems, 154
Association for children with learning diabilities (ACLD), 44, 324
Astigmatism, 2, 146
Attention, 55
Attitudes, 250-270 (*See also* Affective dimensions of reading)
  toward others, 255-270
  toward self, 32-34, 270
  toward self, (*See* Self-concept)
Audiometer, 2, 84

Audiovisual materials, 217, 219, 281, 296, 300
Auditory perception, 2, 121, 159, 221-2, 266
  auditory awareness, 122
  auditory discrimination, 2, 87, 122, 135, 180
  auditory figure-ground, 2, 122
  auditory localization, 122
  auditory memory, 2, 88, 104, 124, 181, 289
  auditory sequencing, 123, 137
  auditory synthesizing, 124, 136
Auditory-visual integration, 20, 102, 157, 222

Babbling, 173
Basal reader(s), 2, 215, 216, 223, 231, 234, 283, 286, 294, 299, 306
Behavior modification, 2, 258-9, 260, 263
Behavior problems, 34, 255-9
Bender Visual-Motor Gestalt Test, 87, 89, 110
Bibliotherapy, 2, 257
Bilingual education, 320
Botel Reading Inventory, 87, 110
Burk's Behavior Rating Scale, 251

California Test of Mental Maturity, 213
Carrel, 268, 296
Cataract(s), 3, 147
Choral reading, 132-3, 282
Classroom management, 281, 292-308
Classroom organization, 281-292
Classroom schedule, 292-5
Classroom teacher, 64, 105, 139, 167, 201, 273, 324
  as consumer of diagnostic information, 89-91
  as diagnostician, 82, 91-104

Classroom teacher (*Continued*)
  as implementor of educational
    plans, 104-105
  as member of interdisciplinary
    team, 105, 327-35
  role in forming child's self-
    concept, 253
Cloze, 3, 229-30 (*See also* Modified
    cloze)
Code-emphasis programs, 15, 16,
    17, 215
Comprehension, 23, 29-32, 36, 230-
    236, 241, 285, 302 (*See also*
    Critical-creative comprehen-
    sion, Inferential comprehen-
    sion, Literal comprehension)
  and auditory problems, 138
  and language disorders, 192
  and visual imagery, 166
Conceptualization, 53, 100
Conductive hearing loss, 3, 115
Configuration, 3, 15, 26 (*See also*
    Visual configuration)
Congenital, 3, 147
Content-area reading, 98, 294
Context clues, 3, 15, 23, 26, 28-9,
    36, 229-30
Contract(s), 3, 259-61, 289, 304
Controlled reader, 3, 166
Cooing, 173
Cooperative Progress Tests, 73,
    108-9
Council for Exceptional Children
    (CEC), 323
Criterion-referenced tests, 3, 74-75,
    85, 105, 306
Critical-creative comprehension, 3,
    7, 30, 233-4
Cross-age tutoring, 3, 255, 287
*Customized Objective Monitoring
    Service,* 74, 109

Decoding, 3, 235
Decoding programs (*See* Code-
    emphasis approach)

Departmentalization, 291-2
Detroit Test of Learning Aptitude,
    87-88, 89, 110, 128, 155, 185
*Developmental Test of Visual Motor
    Integration* (VMI), 87, 110,
    155
*Developmental Test of Visual Per-
    ception* (DTVP), 63, 87, 110,
    155
Diagnosis, 76-105, 241, 282, 285
    (*See also* Assessment)
*Diagnosis: An Instructional Aid
    Service,* 74, 109
Diagnostic Reading Scales, 87, 110
Diagnostic test(s), 3, 83, 86-87
Dialect, 3, 97, 179
Differential diagnosis, 3
Diagraph(s), 3-4, 27, 226
Dipthong(s), 3-4
Directionality (*See* Left-to-right
    orientation)
Discrepancy, 48
Distractability, 120, 266, 268
Doren Diagnostic Reading Test, 86,
    109
*Durrell Analysis of Reading Diffi-
    culty,* 86, 90, 109
Durrell Listening-Reading Tests,
    237
Dyslexia, 4, 201
Dysnomia, 2, 4, 197
Dyspraxia, 2, 4, 197

Eclectic approach, 18-19, 216
Educational planning, 58, 330-1
EEG (electroencephalography), 4,
    80
Emotional factors (*See* Affective
    dimensions of reading)
Emotional problems, 249-50, 273
Etilogical diagnosis, 4, 79-80, 81
Evaluation, 73-76, 79, 105
  formal, 73-75
  informal, 75-76

Every-pupil response techniques, 282
Experience, 25, 31, 224, 235
Expressive language, 175, 196
Eye-hand coordination, 24, 87, 155

Fatigue, 120
Farsightedness, 4, 84, 146
Febrile disease, 4, 117
Fixed focus stand reader, 150-1
Form perception, 151
Functional reading skills, 218

Games (*See* Instructional games)
Gates-MacGinitie Reading Readiness Tests, 85, 109
Gates-McKillop Reading Diagnostic Test, 86, 90, 109-110
Gestalt learning, 4, 61
Gilmore Oral Reading Test, 87, 110
Glaucoma, 4, 147
Goldman-Fristoe-Woodcock Test of Auditory Discrimination, 87, 110, 127
Grammatic closure, 199
Grapheme, 4 (*See also* Phoneme-grapheme relationships)
Gray Oral Reading Test, 87, 110

Handwriting, 83, 282
Hearing loss, 115
   conductive, 3, 115
   sensorineural, 8, 117
Hearing therapy, 318
High-interest, low-vocabulary materials, 4, 218-19, 300
Home made materials, 302
Hyperactivity (*See* Overactivity)

Illinois Test of Psycholinguistic Ability, (ITPA), 63, 87-8, 89, 110, 128, 156, 184, 199

Imagery, 53
Impulsivity, 266
Inappropriate instruction, 269-70
Individual activities, 281, 287, 289-91, 292
Individualized Educational Program (IEP), 4-5, 58, 304, 330
Individualized reading, 5, 281, 288-9
Inferential comprehension, 5, 7, 30, 193, 232-3
Informal reading inventory (IRI), 5, 91-99, 237, 283
Inner language, 177
Illumination, 149
Instructional games, 217, 224, 261, 295, 300-02
Integration of auditory and visual learning (*See* Auditory-visual integration)
Intelligence, 209-13, 219, 220, 231, 240
Intelligence quotient (IQ), 5, 209-10
Intelligence test(s), 5, 83, 84, 209, 211, 212-13, 214, 231, 241
Interest centers, 296
Interest grouping, 285-6, 287, 308
Interclass grouping, 291-2
International Reading Association (IRA), 323
Interpersonal relationships, 55
Inversion, 5, 162-3
Iowa Test of Basic Skills, 73, 108
Itinerant program, 315
IQ tests (*See* Intelligence tests)

Kinesthetic learning, 5, 100
Kuhlman-Anderson Tests, 213

Language, 171-205
   as a factor in reading comprehension, 234-5
   as a factor in reading readiness, 25, 220-1

Language (*Continued*)
   expressive, 178, 220, 221
   inner, 177
   receptive, 177, 212, 220
Language centers, 264
Language disorders, 84, 179, 196,
   266, 289
Language experience approach, 5,
   14, 15, 36, 189, 216, 226,
   258, 282
Language therapy, 318
Large-group instruction, 281-3, 292
Learning capacity, 210, 214, 226,
   236
Learning centers, 295, 296, 299,
   308, 316
Learning disabilities, 41, 51
Learning level, 214, 236, 241
Learning rate, 214, 217, 226, 236,
   241
Learning specialist, 78
Learning style(s), 59, 219, 273,
   288, 309
Left-right orientation, 25, 159, 222
Lee-Clark Reading Readiness Test,
   85, 109
Letter-sound relationships (*See*
   Phoneme-grapheme relation-
   ships)
Linguistic approach, 5, 14, 16, 36,
   136, 299
Lipreading, 119
Listening, 15, 221
Listening activities, 104, 221, 281
Listening comprehension, 93, 233
Listening station, 295
Literal comprehension, 5, 7, 30,
   231-2
Look-say approach, 5, 8, 14-15, 19,
   36, 63
Low vision, 145, 159
Low vision aids, 150

Mainstreaming, 5, 45-47

Management systems, 5-6, 74, 285,
   305-08
Maturity, 55
Meaning-emphasis programs, 14-15,
   17, 215
Memory, 100, 102, 201, 231 (*See
   also* Auditory perception)
Mental age, 6, 213, 219, 220, 231,
   237, 240, 244
"Mental retardation," 209-10, 219
Metropolitan Achievement Test, 73,
   109
Metropolitan Readiness Test, 85,
   109
Minimal pairs, 135
Miscue, 6, 96-97
Multidisciplinary assessment, 6, 78,
   329
Modified cloze, 195
Morpheme, 6, 28, 228
Motivation, 6, 257-8, 300, 335
Motor problems, 56
*Murphy-Durrell Reading Readiness
   Test,* 85, 109
Muscle imbalance, 6, 146
Myopia (*See* nearsightedness)

National Council of Teachers of
   English (NCTE), 323
National resources, 321
Nearsightedness, 6, 84, 146
Nonsense words, 228
Norm-referenced test(s), 6, 73-74,
   84, 105
*Northwestern Syntactic Screening
   Test,* 199
Nystagmus, 6, 147

Observation, 82-83, 105, 127, 154,
   252, 304
Open classroom, 267, 292
Oral language, 25, 187-8, 221, 233,
   234, 236, 281

Oral reading, 87, 90, 132, 201, 223, 232, 302
Orton Society, 324
Otis Quick Scoring Intelligence Scale, 213
Otitis media, 6, 116
Overactivity, 265–269
Overconvergence, 148

Paraprofessional(s), 6, 294, 320
Parents, 32, 105, 252, 270, 271–73, 332
Peabody Picture Vocabulary Test (PPVT), 88, 110, 183, 212
Perception, 20–21, 25, 53, 100 (*See also* Auditory perception, Visual perception)
Perceptual approaches to reading, 17
Perceptual-motor training, 61–2
Phoneme(s), 6 (*See also* Phoneme-grapheme relationships, Phonics)
Phoneme-grapheme relationships, 6, 15, 21–2, 222–3, 225
Phonetic analysis, 6, 23, 27–8, 36
Phonics, 7, 225–8, 302 (*See also* Phonetic analysis)
Phonics approach, 7, 14, 15, 19, 36, 63
Phonics rules, 28
Phonogram, 7, 226
Phonology, 7, 173
Physical examination(s), 83, 84
Physical factors of reading readiness, 24
PL 94-142, 5, 58, 304, 330
Prescriptive Reading Inventory, 74, 109
Prescriptive teaching, 7, 56, 104–5
Printed materials, 31, 150, 299 (*See also* Basal reader(s), Supplementary reading material)
Professional organizations, 322

Programmed learning, 7, 16, 218, 259, 300
Progress charts, 262–3
Proprioceptive feedback, 131
Psycholinguistics, 7, 13–4, 24, 36
Psychological services, 317
Psychosocial problems, 54
Pupil-team learning, 286–7

Reading, 11–37
    affective dimensions of, 32–4
    and expressive language disorders, 200
    and oral language, 176
    and receptive language disorders, 189
    and visual problems, 148
    as a cognitive process, 22–23
    as a linguistic process, 21–2
    as a perceptual process, 20–1
    as a sensory process, 20
    basic approaches to, 14–19
    definitions of, 13–14, 23, 36
    relationship to intelligence, 211–213
Reading comprehension (*See* Comprehension)
Reading achievement tests, 83, 84–6, 283
Reading corner, 296
Reading diagnostic tests, 86–87
Reading expectancy, 7, 237–40
Reading Eye Camera, 84, 112
Reading Miscue Inventory, 97, 111
Reading readiness, 7, 24–6, 33, 85, 130, 159–162, 220–3, 302
Reading readiness tests, 85–6
Reading skills center, 295
Reading specialist, 7, 249, 306
Reading-study skills, 7, 23, 32, 302
Rebus programs, 16
Record keeping, 302–05
Receptive language, 177, 180–2
Reformed alphabets, 14, 16

Regional Resource Centers, 321
Reinforcement, 7, 260, 261-3, 268
Remedial reading, 317
Remedial strategies, 59
Remediation, 7, 61, 222, 294
Resource center (*See* Resource room)
Resource room, 316
Reversal(s), 7, 152, 162-3
Role playing, 257, 263-4
Roswell-Chall Diagnostic Reading Test, 87, 110

School adjustment specialist, 249, 271, 318
School Vision Tester, 84, 111
Self-concept, 8, 251-5, 263, 283
Semantics, 8, 174
Sensation, 53
Sensorineural hearing loss, 8, 117
Sentence formulation problems, 198
Sequential Test of Educational Progress (STEP), 73, 109
Short Test of Educational Ability, 213
Sight method (*See* Look-say approach)
Sight vocabulary, 8, 26, 165, 223-4
Simultaneity, 189
Skill grouping, 8, 285, 288, 294, 308
Skills training, 134
Slosson Oral Reading Test, 90, 111
Slow learner(s), 8, 182, 207-243, 285
Small-group instruction, 281, 283-7, 292
Snellen Eye Chart, 8, 82, 84
Space in the classroom, 295-299
Special education, 318
Special services, 317-21
Speech therapy, 318
Spoken language (*See* Oral language)
SQ3R, 195

SRA Assessment Survey, 73, 108
Stanford Achievement Test, 73, 108
Stanford-Binet Intelligence Scale, 84, 109, 209, 212
Stanford Diagnostic Reading Test, 86, 109
Stress patterns, 132
Structural analysis, 6, 8, 23, 29, 36, 228-9, 302
Substantially separate programs, 47, 316
Supplementary reading materials, 217-8, 241, 300, 306
Symbolization, 8, 21, 53, 100
Syntax, 8, 175, 234
Synthetic phonics, 8, 15, 63, 158, 228

Tactual perception, 8, 159
T and A, 8
Tachistoscope, 8, 166
Tape recorder(s), 96, 261, 264, 266, 295, 296, 300
Task analysis, 8, 79, 81, 99-103, 129
Task groups, 286, 287
Taxonomy, 8, 231
Teacher centers, 324
Team teaching, 291, 292, 308
Telegraphic speech, 9, 176
Tennessee Self-Concept Scale, 251
Therapeutic diagnosis, 9, 79, 80-1
Thinking skills, (*See* Comprehension)
Thomas Self-Concept Values Test, 251
Title I programs, 319
Trade books, 9, 217
Tutorial programs, 316

Ungraded units, 291

Verbal expression (ITPA), 199
Visual imagery, 166

Visual problems, 84, 146-7

Visual perception, 9, 87, 150, 221
  position in space, 152, 163
  visual closure, 152, 164
  visual configuration, 165
  visual discrimination, 9, 101, 162
  visual figure-ground, 9, 152, 163
  visual form perception, 151
  visual memory, 9, 266
  visual sequencing, 153, 164

Visual-motor integration, 110

Visual-motor problems, 84, 266

Visual receptive language, 178 (*See also* Reading)

Visual Survey Telebinocular, 84, 111

Voice modulation, 132

Wepman Auditory Discrimination Test, 87, 110, 127

Weschler Intelligence Scale for Children (WISC), 57, 84, 89, 109, 212

Word analysis, 9, 27-28, 224-9

Word attack (*See* Word analysis)

Word banks, 9, 190, 223

Words in Color, 16

Word calling, 9, 98

Word finding problems, 197

Word recognition, 9, 23, 26-7, 36, 223-4, 302 (*See also* Sight words)

Writer's corner, 296

Writing, 179